# Learn Spanish

*The Essentials You Need to Go From an Absolute Beginner to Intermediate and Advanced*

© Copyright 2022

All Rights Reserved. No part of this book may be reproduced in any form without permission in writing from the author. Reviewers may quote brief passages in reviews.

Disclaimer: No part of this publication may be reproduced or transmitted in any form or by any means, mechanical or electronic, including photocopying or recording, or by any information storage and retrieval system, or transmitted by email without permission in writing from the publisher.

While all attempts have been made to verify the information provided in this publication, neither the author nor the publisher assumes any responsibility for errors, omissions or contrary interpretations of the subject matter herein.

This book is for entertainment purposes only. The views expressed are those of the author alone, and should not be taken as expert instruction or commands. The reader is responsible for his or her own actions.

Adherence to all applicable laws and regulations, including international, federal, state and local laws governing professional licensing, business practices, advertising and all other aspects of doing business in the US, Canada, UK or any other jurisdiction is the sole responsibility of the purchaser or reader.

Neither the author nor the publisher assumes any responsibility or liability whatsoever on the behalf of the purchaser or reader of these materials. Any perceived slight of any individual or organization is purely unintentional.

# Free Bonuses from Cecilia Melero

Hi Spanish Learners!

My name is Cecilia Melero, and first off, I want to THANK YOU for reading my book.

Now you have a chance to join my exclusive Spanish language learning email list so you can get the ebooks below for free as well as the potential to get more Spanish books for free! Simply click the link below to join.

P.S. Remember that it's 100% free to join the list.

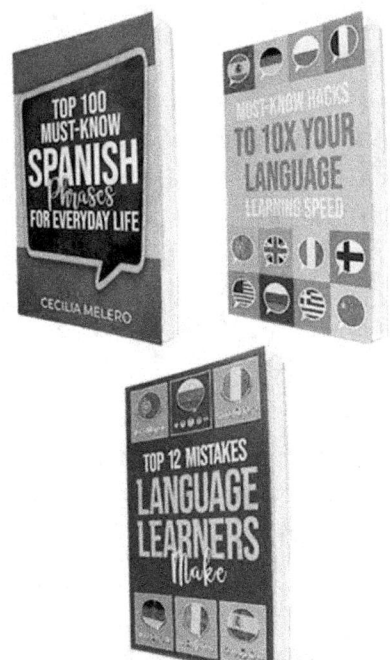

Access your free bonuses here:
*https://livetolearn.lpages.co/learn-spanish-paperback/*

# Table of Contents

PART 1: SPANISH FOR BEGINNERS ................................................... 1
   INTRODUCTION .................................................................................. 2
   CHAPTER 1: SPANISH BASICS ........................................................ 4
   CHAPTER 2: MEETING NEW PEOPLE ........................................ 15
   CHAPTER 3: CHECKING INTO YOUR ROOM ...................... 29
   CHAPTER 4: GOING SHOPPING ................................................ 44
   CHAPTER 5: GOING SIGHTSEEING ......................................... 60
   CHAPTER 6: HAVING A HOUSE PARTY .................................. 75
   CHAPTER 7: EATING OUT ............................................................. 92
   CHAPTER 8: BOOKING TICKETS ............................................. 106
   CHAPTER 9: TALKING ABOUT YOUR PAST ....................... 122
   CHAPTER 10: BASIC GRAMMAR REVISION ....................... 139
   VOCABULARY APPENDIX ............................................................ 157
   ANSWER KEY .................................................................................... 179
   EXTRA: IPA PHONEMIC CHART ............................................... 190
   EXTRA: GLOSSARY OF GRAMMATICAL TERMS ................ 195
PART 2: INTERMEDIATE SPANISH ................................................. 200
   INTRODUCTION ............................................................................. 201
   CHAPTER 1: FROM BEGINNER TO INTERMEDIATE ........ 204
   CHAPTER 2: NUMBERS, NUMBERS, NUMBERS .................. 215
   CHAPTER 3: GRAMMATICAL GENDERS ................................ 228
   CHAPTER 4: FROM PERSONAL PRONOUNS TO POSSESSIVES ....................................................................................... 239

CHAPTER 5: MASTERING ADJECTIVES AND ADVERBS ......... 255
CHAPTER 6: DEMONSTRATING HOW ARTICLES WORK .... 267
MID-BOOK QUIZ .................................................................. 276
CHAPTER 7: THE VERB I. FOCUS ON THE PRESENT ............. 280
CHAPTER 8: THE VERB II. THINKING ABOUT THE PAST ..................................................................................... 295
CHAPTER 9: THE VERB III. TOWARDS THE FUTURE ........... 309
CHAPTER 10: PREPOSITIONS AND CONJUNCTIONS ......... 322
CHAPTER 11: INTERROGATIVE, AFFIRMATIVE, AND NEGATIVE SENTENCES ....................................................... 334
CHAPTER 12: REPORTING INFORMATION (INDIRECT SPEECH) .............................................................................. 346
FINAL QUIZ ......................................................................... 356
ANSWER KEY ....................................................................... 360
PART 3: ADVANCED SPANISH .................................................. 378
INTRODUCTION .................................................................. 379
CHAPTER 1: ARE YOU A MASTER OF MAIN CONCEPTS? ..... 381
CHAPTER 2: READING STRATEGIES FOR THE ADVANCED LEARNER .......................................................... 390
CHAPTER 3: FIRST CONJUGATION (-AR) ........................ 401
CHAPTER 4: SECOND CONJUGATION (-ER) ....................... 416
CHAPTER 5: THIRD CONJUGATION (-IR) .......................... 428
CHAPTER 6: IRREGULAR CONJUGATIONS ......................... 439
MID-BOOK QUIZ .................................................................. 470
CHAPTER 7: REFLEXIVE VERBS .......................................... 473
CHAPTER 8: INFINITIVES, GERUNDS, AND PARTICIPLES ........................................................................ 482
CHAPTER 9: THE PASSIVE AND THE CONDITIONAL ........... 494
CHAPTER 10: FROM DIRECT TO INDIRECT SPEECH ........... 504
CHAPTER 11: PHRASAL VERBS AND USEFUL IDIOMS ......... 517
CHAPTER 12: FORMAL WRITING ........................................ 528
FINAL QUIZ ......................................................................... 538
ANSWER KEY ....................................................................... 541
FREE BONUSES FROM CECILIA MELERO ............................... 564

# Part 1: Spanish for Beginners

*Learn Spanish in 30 Days Without Wasting Time*

# Introduction

*¡Hola!*

It's great to have you here! We're about to embark on a 30-day Spanish-learning journey that will take us from zero to fluent, and we're thrilled to have you on board!

If your Spanish classes aren't going at your desired pace or you feel that you're not learning what you need for your trip, this book was definitely made for you. We're here to help you *really* learn Spanish in a practical way.

Spanish is an incredible language with over 560 million speakers worldwide; it is constantly enriched by the different countries and cultures in which it is spoken. You won't want to miss the opportunity of learning how to chat with its speakers.

This book will take you from the basics to different situations where you might need to speak Spanish while visiting a Spanish-speaking country. Considering that Spanish is the official language of 21 countries, after completing this course, you should be able to converse easily while visiting many Spanish-speaking destinations.

Divided into 10 chapters, this book includes some grammar-made-easy guides for you to finally understand how to use the tenses, a pronunciation guide to learn how to sound like a native, and some exercises to practice as you go along. The grammar explanations are simple and easy to understand, the pronunciation guide contains hands-on instructions to attempt a better pronunciation, and the exercises will place you in real and likely scenarios for you to practice before your actual journey.

Since the book is practically divided, it will be really easy for you to find the perfect phrase for every moment of your trip. We will go over everything you need to know to be confident enough to tackle any scenario in Spanish. And you will find some fixed expressions for you to use, but you will also learn to use your own words to say what you mean.

Unlike other books that are only devoted to grammar and vocabulary, this book will also take you on a cultural journey since we're going to travel around and talk about Spanish culture, as well as learn some phrases to use in colloquial conversations.

So, what are you waiting for? Our 30-day journey awaits, and we want you to come out the other side speaking Spanish like a pro to everyone you meet.

*¡Buen viaje!*

# Chapter 1: Spanish Basics

We told you we would build your Spanish from the ground up, so here we are! In this chapter, we will see *all* the basics so you can have a solid foundation for every situation you find yourself in. Even though this chapter will be about the basics, it might be the most important one, so pay attention!

I think it's also time to introduce ourselves. My name is Sarah. This year, for the summer holidays, I will be going on a 30-day trip to Spain with my friend Julio – who is not only Spanish but also a Spanish language teacher. Right now, all I know how to say is *hola* and *gracias*! So Julio will be teaching me everything I need to know to communicate on our trip!

Right now, we're at the airport. We bought a ticket for a plane that will take us from Hartsfield-Jackson airport in Atlanta, US, to El Prat Airport in Barcelona, Spain. We'll use the time in the airport and on the flight to get through some Spanish basics. So, I'll let Julio take over!

## Brief History of the Spanish Language

Hi! I'm Julio, your Spanish friend and teacher for the next month. How about we start with the history of the language?

Spanish is a Romance language, meaning it derives from Latin (unlike English which is a West Germanic language). First, about 5,000 years ago, some people in Spain and the Iberian Peninsula started speaking various dialects. Then, the Romans introduced

Latin to what was then called Hispania. The combination of Latin with the previous dialects resulted in what is called *Vulgar Latin*.

In the Middle Ages, Spain was conquered by the Visigoths, who continued using Vulgar Latin. But then, the Muslim Empire conquered what is - today - the province of Andalusia. As this happened, Latin started taking shape into the Romance languages we know now (French, Italian, Romanian, Portuguese, and Castilian). The Arab occupation introduced some Mozarabic words into the language, and it was spoken in some regions.

Castilian was a language with Vulgar Latin and Mozarabic influences that later became the basis for the written standard, and it also became the language for administrative tasks, the establishment of decrees, and the writing of chronicles and legal works.

The Christian Catholic Kingdoms of Castilla, Aragon, Toledo, Galicia, Zaragoza, and Leon united to expel the Arabs. With this, the Mozarabic language eventually disappeared from the region. Isabella of Castile and Ferdinand of Aragon became the King and Queen of this unified Spain and were known as the Catholic Monarchs. After this, Castilian eventually became the official language in Spain.

Nowadays, Spanish is a very diverse language and isn't spoken merely in Spain. Actually, it is spoken in 21 countries around the world, and so, of course, the vocabulary, the pronunciation, and even some aspects of Grammar change from one country to another. But do you know why it is spoken in so many countries?

In 1492, the Catholic Monarchs gave Christopher Columbus the means to seek other routes to India. In the process, as we all know, he arrived on the American continent. With the arrival of the Spanish conquerors, the American civilizations were colonized and forced to take on the Spanish language, religion, and traditions.

Between 1492 and 1989, the Spanish Empire expanded across the Caribbean Islands, half of South America, most of Central America, and part of North America. Later, these countries would fight for independence, but most kept the Spanish language.

Today, there are over 560 million Spanish speakers worldwide – many found in non-Spanish-speaking countries like the United States.

## Alphabet and Accents

Well, now that we know a bit of the eventful history of the Spanish language, let's learn about the language itself.

The alphabet in Spanish is almost the same as in English, except, of course, each letter has a different name, and there is also that thing about the mystical letter Ñ. Let's have a look at it!

| A | B | C | D | E | F | G |
|---|---|---|---|---|---|---|
| *a* | *be* | *ce* | *de* | *e* | *efe* | *ge* |
| H | I | J | K | L | M | N |
| *hache* | *i* | *jota* | *ca* | *ele* | *eme* | *ene* |
| Ñ | O | P | Q | R | S | T |
| *eñe* | *o* | *pe* | *cu* | *erre* | *ese* | *te* |
| U | V | W | X | Y | Z | |
| *u* | *uve / ve* | *uve doble / doble u / doble ve* | *equis* | *i griega* | *zeta* | |

As Sarah noticed, the V and the W have alternative names. Well, that's because depending on the Spanish speaker you are talking to, they might say it in one of these ways. Generally, in Spain, people usually say *uve* and *uve doble;* in Central America, *ve* and *doble u* are more common. In South America, *ve* and *doble ve* are the most common alternatives.

Now let's learn a bit about accents.

In Spanish, there is only one type of written accent called *tilde* which can only go on vowels and signals where the stressed syllable is (it is represented in this way: *á, é, í, ó,* and *ú*). However, not all Spanish words have *tildes*, because the rule isn't to simply graphically express every stressed syllable. Here is a table of the rules of accentuation in Spanish:

|  | Rule | Examples |
|---|---|---|
| *Agudas* | The stressed syllable of *agudas* is the last one. But they only need a *tilde* when the word ends in N, S, or a vowel. | *Agudas* with *tilde*: canción, sofá, bebé, café, menú  *Agudas* without *tilde*: amar, mujer, salud, comer, sabor |
| *Graves* | The stressed syllable of *graves* is the second to last one. But, unlike *agudas*, they need a tilde when the word *doesn't* end in N, S, or a vowel. | *Graves* with *tilde:* azúcar, móvil, ángel, lápiz, ángel  *Graves* without *tilde:* sonido, abrazo, cocina, saludo |
| *Esdrújulas* | The stressed syllable of *esdrújulas* is the third one starting from the end of the word. These are easy because they always need a *tilde*. | esdrújula, último, íntimo, política, sinónimo, sólido |

I know, this seems like a lot to take in! But for the time being, you should remember that the stressed syllable is the one with the *tilde* - and if you have any doubts about which is the stressed syllable of a word, you can always return to this table.

**Pronunciation Tips**

Before we go any further into pronunciation - and before I give you some tips - I encourage you to go to the extra chapter called "IPA Phonemic Chart" to get acquainted with every Spanish sound individually and their phonemes.

Now, about those tips... The first one, as I will probably keep on repeating throughout this book, is that practice makes perfect! So don't feel discouraged if you don't get everything right at first, it might take some time, but you'll get the hang of it in no time.

Spanish is very different from English – but also much more straightforward. Even though some pronunciations may vary from place to place, in Spanish, the vowels are always pronounced the same way (and almost all consonants, except for a few exceptions).

So, once you've mastered the basic sounds and learned to roll your Rs, you don't need to wonder if you are saying the word correctly because you probably are!

Let's see a few comparisons between Spanish and English, so you get what I mean:

In English, the Es in "essence" are different from one another and from the E in "be," and also different from the Es in "Peter." But in Spanish, *esencia, ser,* and *pedro* all use the same pronunciation for the E.

Another example is the use of As in "apple," "saber," "seat," "saw," and "wait." They all sound different! Whereas in Spanish, the As in *manzana, sable, asiento, miraba,* and *esperar* all sound the same.

The vowels are not as straightforward when you find a U and an E together after a Q or a G. In these cases, you should pronounce them as an E, which means that the U is silent. And the same happens if you find a QUI or a GUI, you should pronounce the vowels as an I. Some examples of this are *queso, panqueque, quiero, saquito, guitarra, águila, guepardo* and *albergue.*

However, there is one little exception to this rule, but it is simple, *I promise!* Whenever there is a GÜI or a GÜE with those two little dots above the U (which, by the way, are called diaereses), it means that the U should be pronounced. Though this is not that common, some examples are *pingüino* and *vergüenza.*

Now, with the consonants, you should know that there are some exceptions, but it is still quite simple. Here they are:

- If we find an R at the beginning of a word or a double R in the middle, they both sound the same and are called rolled Rs! For example, we use rolled Rs in *ratón, correr, reliquia,* and *marrón*. But, if you find a single R in the middle or at the end of a word, that's not a rolled R. This R can be found in words like *amargo, cantar, broma,* and *prado*.
- Something similar happens with the L - it has one pronunciation when it is on its own and one when it's doubled. On its own, it sounds like an English L, like in *lago, salir, mal,* and *lejos*. But when it's doubled, it may have different pronunciations depending on the region (you can find information about this in the "IPA Phonemic Chart" chapter!), and it is used in words such as *lluvia, valla, llorar,* and *allí*.
- And lastly, there's the case of the G, which sounds different depending on what vowel comes after. It is a soft G when it is followed by an A, O, or U (including when a UI or a UE follows it), like in *gato, guisante, agua,* and *amigo*. But suppose an E or an I follow it. In that case, the pronunciation is more similar to a J, like in *gelatina, gitano, ángel,* and *agitar*.
- Something similar happens to the letter C. If it is followed by A, O, or U, it is pronounced as an English K. However, if an E or an I follow it, it is pronounced more like an English S.

Regarding consonants, the last tip I can give you is to remember that the H in Spanish is silent, *so don't try to pronounce it!*

### Word order

Now we're getting closer to grammar; here's a summary of what happens with word order.

In affirmative sentences, word order in Spanish is very similar to word order in English - we usually have the subject first and then the verb with its complements, if it has any. Examples of this are: *Alejandro corre* ("Alejandro runs"), or *Sandra tiene mucho dinero* ("Sandra has a lot of money").

As a subject, we can have a person's name, but we can also have a pronoun, a word that refers to the person we are talking about (like *I, you,* or *she* in English). This is used only when we've been talking about this person, so the people in the conversation know who we are referring to.

Pronouns in Spanish are:

- First-person singular: *yo* ("I")
- Second-person singular: *tú* ("you")
- Third-person singular: *él / ella* ("he" / "she")
- First-person plural: *nosotros / nosotras* ("we")
- Second-person plural: *vosotros / vosotras / ustedes* ("you")
- *Third-person plural: ellos / ellas* ("they")

Using pronouns, the two previous examples can turn into *Él corre* ("He runs"), and *Ella tiene mucho dinero* ("She has a lot of money").

The thing about Spanish, though, is that the subject (whether a name or a pronoun) can be left out of the sentence if it is clear who we are talking about. So, if we were already talking about Sandra and then we say that she has a lot of money, we can simply say *Tiene mucho dinero* ("(She) Has a lot of money") without the need for an overt subject.

Another example of this using the first sentences could be in a conversation like this one:

- *¿Alejandro come en su tiempo libre?* ("Does Alejandro eat in his free time?")

- *No, corre.* ("No, (he) runs.")

Now, this example takes us to the word order of questions. In English, the order changes to signal a question, but in Spanish, for yes/no questions, we use the same word order, and we add an opening question mark to signal that a question has just started. For example, if we want to turn the statement *Juan quiere comer algo dulce* ("Juan wants to eat something sweet") into a question, we would simply add question marks: *¿Juan quiere comer algo dulce?* ("Does Juan want to eat something sweet?").

In the previous example, the direct object of the verb *comer* is *algo dulce*. Here, *algo* is a noun, and it is being modified by the adjective *dulce*, which describes *algo*. In Spanish, unlike in English, adjectives usually go after the noun and not before it. An example of this could be *Juan come una galleta dulce y deliciosa*, which in English would be "Juan eats a sweet and delicious cookie."

And in a sentence, there can also be adverbs, which are words that describe how the action is being made or say something about the verb. Just like adjectives come after nouns, in Spanish, adverbs usually come after verbs and even at the end of the whole sentence. So, we could say *Alejandro corre rápidamente* ("Alejandro runs fast") or *Juan come una galleta dulce y deliciosa lentamente* ("Juan slowly eats a sweet and delicious cookie").

In English, to join two clauses together in one sentence, we usually use conjunctions- words that connect the clauses. The most common ones in English are "and" and "but," whose Spanish counterparts are "y" and "pero" respectively. For example, we could join the two previous examples into one sentence in the following way: *Alejandro corre rápidamente y Juan come una galleta dulce y deliciosa lentamente* ("Alejandro runs fast and Juan slowly eats a sweet and delicious cookie").

Capitalization and Punctuation

Luckily, capitalization and punctuation in Spanish are very similar to those in English.

For starters, in Spanish, they use capital letters only at the beginning of a sentence, and with proper nouns, that is, with names. So, we will capitalize Alejandro, Sandra, and Juan, as well as other names like Barcelona, Madrid, and the Sagrada Familia. However, we do not capitalize common nouns, such as *iglesia, casa,* and *río.*

As for punctuation, it works the same way as in English, but there are a few differences. As we've seen, one of the differences is that question marks are doubled; that is, there should be one at the beginning and one at the end of a question. And the same happens to exclamation marks; they should always be doubled. For example, we can turn the statement *Ana tiene un perro* ("Ana has a dog") into a question by adding the question marks

*¿Ana tiene un perro?* ("Does Ana have a dog?") or into an exclamation by adding the exclamation marks *¡Ana tiene un perro!* ("Ana has a dog!").

Another difference is that, in Spanish, the em dash ( - ) is not as common as in English, and it is only used as parentheses and never as a colon. This means that it should always be double and that the em dashes go right next to the words they are enclosing, like parentheses. For example: *Pipo-el perro de Ana-es muy lindo* ("Pipo - Ana's dog - is very cute").

Colors

Now it's time to learn a bit of vocabulary. These are all the colors you should know

- *Rojo* means "red"
- *Naranja* means "orange"
- *Amarillo* means "yellow"
- *Verde* means "green"
- *Azul* means "blue"
- *Púrpura* and *violeta* mean "purple" (which one is used depends on the region)
- *Rosa* means "pink"
- *Gris* means "gray"
- *Negro* means "black"
- *Blanco* means "white"
- *Magenta* means "magenta"
- *Celeste* means "light blue"
- *Turquesa* means "turquoise"
- *Marrón* means "brown"

Numbers 1-10

Now let's finish this chapter with numbers 1 to 10 in Spanish!

1. *uno*
2. *dos*
3. *tres*
4. *cuatro*

5. *cinco*
6. *seis*
7. *siete*
8. *ocho*
9. *nueve*
10. *diez*

Exercises

Now it's time to review everything we've seen so far to ensure you understand everything.

1. Sarah's full name is Sarah Williams, which in Spanish is spelled "ese-a-erre-a-hache uve doble-i-ele-ele-i-a-eme-ese."

   Can you spell out loud the word *mujer*? Why doesn't it have a *tilde*?

2. What does it mean if a vowel has a *tilde*?
3. What do the words *calor, país, alimentación,* and *maril* have in common?
   a. They are all agudas
   b. They are all graves
   c. They are all esdrújulas
4. What does it mean if a word is a *grave*?
5. Regarding accents, what do the words *lápiz, mari, cálido,* and *mano* have in common?
   a. They are all *agudas*
   b. They all have a *tilde*
   c. The stressed vowel is the A
6. If there is an R at the beginning of a word (like in *receta)*, should it be a rolled R or a softer R?
7. And what if there is an R in the middle of a word (as in *fuerte)*? Should it be a rolled R or a softer R?
8. How would you pronounce *mari*? And what about *marill*?
9. In Spanish, does the verb usually come before or after the subject?

10. Can a pronoun be the subject of a sentence?
11. True or false: In Spanish, you should always have an overt subject.
12. In Spanish, does the order of a statement need to change to turn it into a question?
13. True or false: The adjectives in Spanish usually go after the noun they modify.
14. True or false: The Spanish word for the color orange is *marillo*.
15. A chessboard is usually of which two colors?
    a. Rojo y azul
    b. Gris y verde
    c. Blanco y negro
16. In Spanish, what is usually the color of strawberries?
17. What number comes after *tres*?
18. And what number comes before *ocho*?
19. How many people are there in Sarah's family if she has two brothers, a sister, a mother, and a father? (Answer in Spanish!)

# Chapter 2:
# Meeting New People

*¡Bienvenidos al capítulo 2!*

It's Sarah here, again! Julio and I have just arrived in Barcelona. For this holiday, I want to make friends with Julio's friends and meet some new people. However, there's that awful language barrier. Luckily, I have Julio.

Julio's father, Ernesto, came to pick us up at the airport. Julio taught me how to meet new people so that I can introduce myself to his father. To do so, we practiced the following conversation a few times:

| | |
|---|---|
| ○ Buenos días. ¿Cómo te llamas? | ○ Good morning. What's your name? |
| ● Hola, me llamo Sarah. ¿Y tú? | ● Hello, my name is Sarah. And yours? |
| ○ Yo soy Julio. ¿De dónde eres? | ○ I'm Julio. Where are you from? |
| ● Soy estadounidense. ¿Y tú de dónde eres? | ● I'm American. And where are you from? |

| | |
|---|---|
| ○ Soy de aquí, de Barcelona. ¿Y a qué te dedicas? | ○ I'm from here, from Barcelona. And what do you do for a living? |
| ● Soy contadora. ¿Y tú? | ● I'm an accountant. And you? |
| ○ Yo soy profesor de español. ¿Cuántos años tienes? | ○ I'm a Spanish teacher. How old are you? |
| ● Treinta y cuatro. ¿Y tú? | ● Thirty four. And you? |
| ○ Yo tengo treinta y ocho. Debo irme. Fue un placer conocerte. | ○ I'm thirty eight. I have to go. It was a pleasure to meet you. |
| ● ¡Gracias e igualmente! | ● Thank you, you too! |

Conversations like this one allowed me to learn a lot of basic phrases and expressions to meet new people. So I felt a bit more confident when Ernesto came to pick us up. The first bit of the conversation went something like this:

| | |
|---|---|
| ● ¡Hola, Ernesto! Es un placer conocerte. | ● Hello, Ernesto! |
| ○ ¡Hola! ¿Eres Sarah, verdad? | ○ Hello! You are Sarah, right? |
| ● Sí, así es. | ● Yes, that's right. |
| ○ ¿Cómo estás? | ○ How are you? |
| ● Muy bien, gracias. | ● Very well, thank you. |

Then, after we'd put our suitcases in the trunk and started on our way to Julio's home, we continued our conversation:

| | |
|---|---|
| ○ Sarah, ¿de dónde vienes? | ○ Sarah, where are you from? |
| ● De Estados Unidos. Soy estadounidense. | ● From the United States. I'm American. |
| ○ ¡Ah! ¿Es lindo donde vives? | ○ Oh! Is it nice where you live? |
| ● Sí, claro. A mí me encanta. | ● Yes, sure. I love it. |
| ○ Algún día debemos ir a visitar a Julio. ¿Cuántos años tienes? | ○ Someday we have to go visit Julio. How old are you? |
| ● Tengo treinta y dos años. ¿Y tú? | ● I'm thirty two. And you? |
| ○ Yo tengo ochenta y cuatro años. Pero luzco más joven ¿verdad? | ○ I'm eighty four. But I look younger, don't I? |

Julio is now going to teach you everything he taught me. Are you ready to meet new people? *¡Vamos!*

## Greetings and farewells

Hey! It's Julio again. To meet new people, we first need to greet them, right? Here's a list of common ways to greet someone in Spanish (with their pronunciation!)

- *Hola*: It is the standard way of saying "hello." It is pronounced /oḻä/
- *Buen día*: It is another way of saying hello that can be used throughout the day. It is pronounced /βuen̯ diä/
- *Buenos días*: This one is used to greet only during the morning, until around midday. It is pronounced /βuen̯os diäs/

- *Buenas tardes*: It is only used during the afternoon, from midday until around sundown, which is at different times depending on the season and the country. It is pronounced /βue̞na̠s ta̠ɹde̞s̠/
- *Buenas noches*: It is only used during the night and can be used to say hello or even to say goodbye when we're about to go to bed. It is pronounced /βue̞na̠s no̞tʃe̞s̠/
- *¿Cómo estás?*: It means "How are you?" but it can also be used to greet someone. It is pronounced /ko̞mo̞ e̞sta̠s̠/

Now, let's see some options to say goodbye as well:

- *Adiós*: This is the standard way of saying goodbye in most Spanish-speaking countries. It is pronounced /a̠dio̞s̠/
- *Chao*: In some countries with great Italian influence, people use *chao* or *chau* even more than *adiós*. It is pronounced /tʃa̠o̞/ or /tʃa̠u/.
- *Nos vemos*: We can also use *nos vemos* to say goodbye. It is similar to the English "see you!" and it is pronounced /no̞s̠ be̞mo̞s̠/.
- *Hasta luego*: This way of saying goodbye means "see you later!" but it is used even if you don't have plans to see that person later. You can also change the *luego* with the time or day you plan to see that person, for example, *hasta mañana* ("see you tomorrow!").

## Subject Pronouns

Now it's time to talk about subject pronouns, which we've already discussed before! So, let's refresh your memory and delve deeper into this topic.

Spanish personal pronouns can be used to replace nouns in the subject when the people in the conversation know who we're talking about. In Spanish, the personal pronouns are:

- First-person singular: *yo* ("I")
- Second-person singular: *tú / usted* ("you")

- Third-person singular: *él / ella* ("he" / "she")
- First-person plural: *nosotros / nosotras* ("we")
- Second-person plural: *vosotros / vosotras / ustedes* ("you")
- Third-person plural: *ellos / ellas* ("they")

Keep in mind that there are two options in the second-person singular. *Usted* is the formal version of *tú,* and it is used for formal situations, with elderly people, or with people you have just met for the first time.

I want to draw your attention to the second-person plural, in which you will find that there are three options. *Ustedes* is mostly used in Latin American countries, while *vosotros* and *vosotras* are used mainly in Spain. And you may be wondering what the differences are between *vosotros* and *vosotras;* I'll explain in the following section.

## Gender and Number

Gender is one of the aspects in which Spanish and English greatly differ. In Spanish, gender is not only for people, but also for *things.* Every noun has a gender that can be either feminine or masculine.

Since pronouns are used in the place of nouns, they also have a gender, which is why we saw that many of the pronouns from the table had two options. Generally speaking, the nouns (or, in this case, pronouns) that end in *A* are usually feminine, while those that end in *O* are usually masculine.

As for number, we've been indirectly talking about number in the previous section. When we talk about the number of nouns (or pronouns like in the previous section), we're referring to whether they are singular or plural.

In Spanish, we pluralize nouns in a similar way to English: by adding *-S, -ES,* or *-CES* at the end. For example, *libro* ("book") turns into *libros,* and *pez* ("fish") turns into *peces.* Here's the rule for pluralization in Spanish:

- If the singular form ends in a vowel, you must add an *-s* at the end.

- Examples: *mesa* → *mesas, casa* → *casas, mono* → *monos, pelota* → *pelotas*
- If the singular form ends in a consonant or with a stressed vowel, you must add -*es* at the end.
  - Examples: *ataúd* → *ataúdes, iglú* → *iglúes, rey* → *reyes, pared* → *paredes*
- If the singular form ends with Z, you must add -*ces* at the end.
  - Examples: *pez* → *peces, voz* → *voces, nuez* → *nueces, lápiz* → *lápices*

At this point, I should warn you that the gender and number of nouns is a bit more complicated than what we've seen so far because, in Spanish, gender and number don't only affect nouns, but also articles, verbs, and adjectives. This is what we call *concordancia* ("agreement"). Articles and adjectives should always agree in gender and number with the nouns they modify, and verbs should always agree in number with the nouns they modify. So, for instance, if we want to say "the house is pretty" in Spanish and we know that *casa* ("house") is a feminine word, we would say *la casa es linda*. However, if we want to say "the buildings are pretty" and we know that *edificio* ("building") is a masculine word, we would say *los edificios son lindos*.

The verb "to be"

As a last grammar topic in this chapter, and before we get into the vocabulary, I'd like to tell you about the conjugation of the verb "to be" in Spanish. We've just seen an example of it in use, but we should remember that, in Spanish, the verb "to be" can either mean *ser* or *estar*. Yes, another complicated Spanish thing!

To sum it up, *ser* is used for permanent or long-lasting states, for example, *Soy de París* ("I'm from Paris"). However, *estar* is for temporary states, for example, *Estoy en París* ("I'm in Paris").

These two verbs are irregular verbs in Spanish and, in the present form, are conjugated in the following way:

|  | SER | ESTAR |
|---|---|---|
| 1st person singular: *yo* | *soy* | *estoy* |
| 2nd person singular: *tú* | *eres* | *estás* |
| 3rd person singular: *él / ella / usted* | *es* | *está* |
| 1st person plural: *nosotros / nosotras* | *somos* | *estamos* |
| 2nd person plural: *vosotros / vosotras* | *sois* | *estáis* |
| 3rd person plural: *ellos / ellas / ustedes* | *son* | *están* |

You may have noticed that I told you *ustedes* was another form of the second person plural, but in the chart above, it shows up in the ***third*** person plural box.

I don't mean to confuse you (and I didn't make a mistake!) *Ustedes* is, indeed, a form of the second person plural, but its conjugation is always the same as the third person plural. Keep this in mind for future reference!

And you might also be wondering what *usted* means; it is the formal version of the second-person singular. But, you can see that it is grouped with the third person singular in the previous table because it is conjugated like the third person – exactly like with *ustedes*, but in the singular.

## Asking Simple Questions

Now it's time to get down to business. In this section, we'll see some useful phrases that you might ask or be asked when meeting people!

- *¿Cómo te llamas?* means "What's your name?"
- *¿Cuál es tu apellido?* means "What's your last name?"
- *¿De dónde eres?* means "Where are you from?"
- *¿Cuántos años tienes?* means "How old are you?"
- *¿Cuál es tu nacionalidad?* means "What's your nationality?"

And you may be wondering how to answer some of these questions, so we'll see that in the following section.

## Introducing ourselves

Let's tackle this question by question.

*¿Cómo te llamas?* can be answered in three ways. The first one is by saying *Me llamo...* followed by your name. For example: *Me llamo Julio* or *Me llamo Beatriz*.

The second way is to say *Mi nombre es...* followed by your name, which is the equivalent of "My name is..." Examples of this could be: *Mi nombre es Pedro* or *Mi nombre es Isabel*.

The third way includes a verb we've already seen, *ser*. Since how you're called is supposed to be a permanent state, we use *ser* the way we use "I am" in English. For example: *Soy Camilo* or *Soy Paula*.

If we are asked for our last name, we can simply answer with our last name or use the verb *ser* in this way: *Es Fernández* or *Es García*.

So far, so good, right?

To answer the question *¿De dónde eres?*, we could use the phrase *Soy de...* followed by your country. For example: *Soy de Alemania* ("I'm from Germany ") or *Soy de Francia* ("I'm from France").

To answer *¿Cuántos años tienes?* You say *tengo...* followed by your age and then the word *años*. But I haven't taught you numbers over 10, right? No worries; that section is right after this one! Keep in mind that while in English we use the verb "to be" when saying our age, in Spanish we can't use the verbs *ser* or *estar; instead, we* should always use *tengo*, which is the first person singular of the verb *tener*. For example: *Tengo treinta y* *cuatro años* or *Tengo quince años.*

If someone asks you what your nationality is, the only way to answer is to use the verb *ser*. For example: *Soy portugués* ("I'm Portuguese") and *Soy chilena ("I'm Chilean")*. For this answer, you should always remember that the noun should always agree in gender and number with you! So, if you're a woman and you're with your sister, you could answer *Somos venezolanas ("We are Venezuelan")*. But if I were alone, I would answer *Soy español ("I'm Spaniard")*. This response could also be used to answer the question *¿De dónde eres?* ("Where are you from?") If you want to know what your country and nationality are called in Spanish, I've made a list for you after the numbers section!

## Numbers over 20

If someone asks for your age, you probably will need to know numbers higher than 20 to be able to answer, right? Well, in this first list, you'll see what numbers 20 to 29 are called in Spanish.

| | | |
|---|---|---|
| *20.* | *veinte* | |
| *21.* | *veintiuno* | |
| *22.* | *veintidós* | |
| *23.* | *veintitrés* | |
| *24.* | *veinticuatro* | |
| *25.* | *veinticinco* | |
| *26.* | *veintiséis* | |
| *27.* | *veintisiete* | |
| *28.* | *veintiocho* | |
| *29.* | *veintinueve* | |

Now, in this second list, you can find the tens from 30 to 100:

| | | |
|---|---|---|
| *30.* | *treinta* | |
| *40.* | *cuarenta* | |
| *50.* | *cincuenta* | |
| *60.* | *sesenta* | |
| *70.* | *setenta* | |
| *80.* | *ochenta* | |
| *90.* | *noventa* | |

100.     cien

From 31 to 99, we can form the rest of the numbers that aren't on the list by adding *y* and the number we need. For example, to form the number 64, we just need to say *sesenta y cuatro*. And if we wanted to say 82, we would say *ochenta y cuatro*.

## Countries and nationalities

To answer the questions about where you come from and your nationality, you need to know some countries and nationalities, so here's a list that will come in handy. Of course, it isn't a complete list of all the countries, but you can always search for others and complete the list. We'll start with my country and Sarah's!

You should also bear in mind that, unlike in English, in Spanish, nationalities are not capitalized and should agree in gender and number with the person we are talking about (whether it is ourselves or someone else).

| Countries | Nationalities |
|---|---|
| *Estados Unidos* <br> United States | *estadounidense* |
| *España* <br> Spain | *español* |
| *México* <br> Mexico | *mexicano* |
| *Inglaterra* <br> England | *inglés* |
| *Australia* <br> Australia | *australiano* |

| | |
|---|---|
| *Francia* <br> France | *francés* |
| *Colombia* <br> Colombia | *colombiano* |
| *Perú* <br> Peru | *peruano* |
| *China* <br> China | *chino* |
| *Brasil* <br> Brazil | *brasilero* |
| *Chile* <br> Chile | *chileno* |
| *Argentina* <br> Argentina | *argentino* |
| *Guatemala* <br> Guatemala | *guatemalteco* |
| *Venezuela* <br> Venezuela | *venezolano* |
| *Cuba* <br> Cuba | *cubano* |
| *Sudáfrica* <br> South Africa | *sudafricano* |

| | |
|---|---|
| *Alemania* <br> Germany | *alemán* |
| *Italia* <br> Italy | *italiano* |
| *Egipto* <br> Egypt | *egipcio* |
| *Grecia* <br> Greece | *griego* |

# Exercises

1. Which of these expressions is not used to greet someone?
    a. Nos vemos
    b. Hola
    c. Buen día
2. If we want to say goodbye to someone and tell them that we'll see them tomorrow, how would we say it?
    a. Chao mañana
    b. Hasta luego
    c. Hasta mañana
3. Which of these is not a feminine pronoun?
    a. ellos
    b. ella
    c. vosotras
4. What is the first person masculine plural pronoun?
    a. tú
    b. nosotros
    c. ellos

5. Usually, masculine nouns end in what letter?
6. Considering the rules of pluralization in Spanish. What would be the plural forms of *mano, vaso* and *silla?*
7. What is the plural form of *luz?*
    a. lus
    b. luzes
    c. luces
8. In Spanish, many words can reflect gender. Which of these doesn't?
    a. verbs
    b. articles
    c. adjectives
9. True or false: *Estar* is used for temporary states.
10. True or false: *Ustedes* is the pronoun of the 3rd person plural, so it's conjugated in the same way as *ellos* and *ellas.*
11. What are the conjugations of *ser* and *estar* in the first person singular?
12. Which of these sentences meaning "She is happy" is correct?
    a. Ella es contentos
    b. Ella está contento
    c. Ella está contenta
13. Which one is a possible answer to the question *¿Cómo te llamas?*
    a. Soy Julio
    b. Estoy Julio
    c. Llamo me Julio
14. Which one is a possible answer to the question *¿Cuál es tu apellido?*
    a. Soy Sánchez
    b. Estoy Sánchez
    c. Es Sánchez

15. Which one is a possible answer to the question ¿*De dónde eres?*?
    a. Soy de España
    b. Estoy España
    c. Es España
16. Which one is a possible answer to the question ¿*Cuántos años tienes?*?
    a. Soy veinte años
    b. Tengo veinte años
    c. Los veinte años
17. Which one is a possible answer to the question ¿*Cuál es tu nacionalidad?*?
    a. Francia
    b. Estoy francés
    c. Soy francés
18. How do you form the number thirty-seven in Spanish?
19. How do you form the number twenty-nine in Spanish?
20. What is the feminine form of German in Spanish?

# Chapter 3:
# Checking Into Your Room

Hello – Sarah here. After visiting Julio's family in Barcelona, we took the train to Bilbao, the capital of the Basque Country. The Basque Country is an autonomous community in northwest Spain. In Spanish, the region is known as *País Vasco* or *Euskadi*. I wanted to visit it because it has its own language, a rich culinary tradition (mainly *pintxos* or small snacks of lamb, cured meats, salt cod, and cheese), and a beautiful geographic landscape (including the coast of the Atlantic Ocean and the mountains near the border with France). Besides, I wanted to take the opportunity to learn some more Spanish!

However, when we were on the train, we realized that we hadn't considered that we were going to Bilbao during the Semana Grande de Bilbao, the main city festivities. That's why we had a little trouble getting in touch with a hotel that had rooms available. When we finally got one, I asked Julio to put the phone on speaker, so I could listen to the conversation and learn some useful phrases.

| | |
|---|---|
| ○ Buenos días, se comunicó con el Hotel Conde Duque de Bilbao, mi nombre es Carlos, ¿en qué puedo ayudarle? | ○ Good morning, you are talking with the Hotel Conde Duque in Bilbao, my name is Carlos, how can I help you? |
| ● Buenos días, quería reservar una habitación para hoy. | ● Good morning, I wanted to book a room for today. |
| ○ ¿Para cuántas personas? | ○ For how many people? |
| ● Para dos personas, con dos camas y baño completo, por favor. | ● For two people, with two beds and a bathroom, please. |
| ○ Muy bien, ¿y cuántas noches van a quedarse? | ○ Very well, and how many nights are you going to stay? |
| ● Nos quedaremos tres noches. | ● We'll stay three nights. |
| ○ Vale. ¿Quieren incluir el desayuno? Se sirve en el salón comedor, con vistas a la Ría de Bilbao. | ○ Good. Do you want to include breakfast? It's served in the dining room, with a view of the Estuary of Bilbao. |
| ● Pues sí, con desayuno incluido, por favor. | ● Okay, yes, with breakfast included, please. |
| ○ ¿Podría decirme los nombres de los dos huéspedes, por favor? | ○ Could you tell me the names of the two guests, please? |
| ● Claro, yo soy Julio Sánchez y mi acompañante es Sarah Williams. | ● Sure, I'm Julio Sánchez, and my companion is Sarah Williams. |

| | |
|---|---|
| ○ De acuerdo, a partir de las 2 de la tarde estará lista la habitación, señor Sánchez. | ○ Very well, from 2 p.m. the room will be ready. |
| ● Muy amable, hasta luego. | ● Thank you, see you later. |

    We arrived at the train station and decided to walk to the hotel, which was only ten minutes away. When we crossed the Ría de Bilbao, an estuary, we caught a glimpse of the Guggenheim Museum. The state-of-the-art building is home to a museum of modern and contemporary art, and it's one of the landmarks of Bilbao. I really wanted to visit it. But first, we had to check in at our hotel; I paid attention to Julio's conversation with the receptionist.

| | |
|---|---|
| ○ Buenas tardes, tenemos una reserva. | ○ Good afternoon. We have a booking. |
| ● Buenas tardes, bienvenidos. ¿A nombre de quién está la reserva? | ● Good afternoon, wellcome. Under which name is the booking? |
| ○ La reserva está a nombre de Julio Sánchez y Sarah Williams. | ○ The booking is under the names Julio Sánchez and Sarah Williams. |
| ● Deme un momento... Aquí está. Una habitación doble, con baño completo y desayuno incluido, ¿verdad? | ● One moment, please... Here it is. A double room with bathroom, and breakfast included, right? |
| ○ Sí, es correcto. | ○ Yes, it's correct. |

| | |
|---|---|
| • Vale. El precio por las tres noches es de 250€. ¿Cómo desea abonar? ¿Con tarjeta o en efectivo? | • Very well. The price for the three nights is 250€. How would you like to pay? Card or cash? |
| ○ En efectivo, si es posible. | ○ Cash, if that's okay. |
| • Claro, por supuesto.<br>Bien, aquí tienen la llave de la habitación.<br>La habitación se encuentra en el tercer piso.<br>Es la habitación 305.<br>Pueden tomar el ascensor que está a la derecha.<br>También pueden subir por las escaleras, que se encuentran al final del pasillo.<br>¿Tienen alguna otra pregunta? | • Yes, of course.<br>Very well, here's the key to the room.<br>The room is on the third floor.<br>It's room 305.<br>You can take the elevator that's on your right.<br>You can also use the stairs, which are at the end of the corridor.<br>Do you have any other questions? |
| ○ No, por ahora no. Muchas gracias. | ○ No, not right now. Thank you very much. |

After listening to that conversation, I had a lot of questions! Luckily, Julio was able to help me with all of them.

## Definite/Indefinite Articles

The first question Sarah asked me when we got to our room in Bilbao was about something I said. She wanted to know what did *una* mean in *Tenemos una reserva ("We have a booking")*, so I took the chance to talk about definite and indefinite articles in Spanish.

Similar to English, nouns in Spanish are often preceded by a definite or indefinite article. Spanish has four variations of the definite article, whereas English uses only "the." Like many other words in Spanish, the definite article changes according to the gender and the number of single or plural nature of the noun that comes after it.

Before masculine singular nouns, we use *el*: *¿Quieren incluir el desayuno?* ("Do you want to include breakfast?")

Before feminine singular nouns, we use *la*: *La reserva está a nombre de Julio Sánchez y Sarah Williams* ("The booking is under the names Julio Sánchez and Sarah Williams.")

Before masculine plural nouns, we use *los*: *¿Podría decirme los nombres de los dos huéspedes, por favor?* ("Could you tell me the names of the two guests, please?")

Before feminine plural nouns, we use *las*: *También pueden subir por las escaleras* ("You can also use the stairs.")

Whereas English has "a," "an," and "some," Spanish also has four indefinite articles that change depending on the gender and number of the noun they are modifying.

Before singular masculine nouns, we use *un*: *Conseguimos un hotel muy bonito* ("We found a really nice hotel.")

Before singular feminine nouns, we use *una*: *Buenas tardes, tenemos una reserva* ("Good afternoon, we have a booking.")

Before plural masculine nouns, we use *unos*: *En Bilbao nos tocaron unos días espléndidos* ("In Bilbao we had some splendid days.")

Before plural feminine nouns, we use *unas*: *En el desayuno servían unas tortas deliciosas* ("For breakfast they served delicious cakes.")

And, to make things a little bit trickier, Spanish also has the neuter article *lo*. We use this gender-free article in front of adjectives to transform them into abstract nouns or talk about a quality. In English, we use "thing" or "part" when we want to do this. Let's take a look at this example: *Lo mejor del hotel es la ubicación* ("The best thing of the hotel was the location.")

|  | Masculine | | Feminine | |
| --- | --- | --- | --- | --- |
|  | Singular | Plural | Singular | Plural |
| Definite | *El* | *Los* | *La* | *Las* |
| Indefinite | *Un* | *Unos* | *Una* | *Unas* |
| Neuter | *Lo* | | | |

**Booking a Room**

I paid attention while Julio was booking the room and was able to write down these useful phrases. Then, he added some more. Next time we check into a hotel, I will do the talking!

## Asking for a room:

- *Quería reservar una habitación para esta noche*: I want to book a room for tonight.
- *¿Tiene habitaciones disponibles?*: Do you have any rooms available?
- *Quiero una habitación simple*: I want a single room
- *Me gustaría una habitación con baño privado*: I'd like a room with a private bathroom.

**Asking about the price:**

- *¿Cuál es el precio de una habitación doble?*: What's the price for a double room?
- *¿Tiene una opción más económica?*: Do you have a cheaper option?
- *¿Puedo pagar en efectivo?*: Can I pay with cash?
- *Solo tengo tarjeta de crédito*: I only have credit card

**Asking about specific features:**

- *Me gustaría una habitación con vista*: I would like a room with a view.

- *¿El desayuno está incluido?* Is breakfast included?
- *¿A qué hora se sirve el desayuno?* At what time is breakfast served?
- *¿Ofrecen servicios de traslado al aeropuerto?* Do you offer airport transfer service?
- *¿El hotel tiene Wi Fi?* Does the hotel have wifi?
- *¿Puedo ver la habitación?* Can I see the room?

## Yes/No Questions

Something that puzzled Sarah about *written* Spanish was the upside-down question mark, or, as we call it, the opening question mark, which has a very important function. We use the opening and closing question marks (and exclamation marks, as well) in writing to distinguish questions from affirmative statements (or to show exuberance or emphasis, in the case of exclamation points). In speaking, we mark the difference simply with our intonation.

Let's take a closer look at some questions from the previous section.

*¿El desayuno está incluido?* ("Is breakfast included?") has the same word order as *El desayuno está incluido* ("Breakfast is included"). The only difference is the question marks. The same happens with *¿El hotel tiene Wi-Fi?* ("Does the hotel have wifi?"), which is written in the same order as *El hotel tiene Wi Fi* ("The hotel has wifi.") So, forming yes/no questions in *written* Spanish is not such a difficult task.

## Prepositions of Place

One of the biggest challenges for non-natives are prepositions. But don't worry. We'll make it simple and, for now, we'll focus on prepositions of place. Let's use this short text Sarah wrote - describing our first day walking in Bilbao - to learn about prepositions of place.

| | |
|---|---|
| Empezamos el recorrido en el hotel. | We started the walk at the hotel. |
| Primero caminamos por las calles de alrededor. | First, we walked through the surrounding streets. |
| Después, nos dirigimos al museo. | After that, we went to the museum. |
| A la derecha del museo está la Ría. | To the right of the museum is the estuary. |
| Cerca de ahí, después de un puente, nos topamos con la Plaza Nueva Bilbao. | Near there, after a bridge, we came to Plaza Nueva Bilbao. |
| Dentro de la plaza, hay un monumento. | Inside the square, there's a monument. |
| Encima del monumento hay muchas palomas. | On top of the monument, there are many pigeons. |
| Volvimos caminando hacia el hotel. | We walked back to the hotel. |

- *en* means "in"
- *alrededor* means "about"
- *a* means "to," "by" or "at"
- *a la derecha de* means "to the right of"
- *cerca de* means "near to"
- *después de* means "after"
- *dentro de* means "in," "inside" or "within"
- *encima de* means "on top of"
- *hacia* means "toward"

# Asking for the Room Number

Something funny happened while Sarah and I were in Bilbao. When we returned to the hotel after our first day walking around the city, we had forgotten our room number! However, as the saying goes, "success is where preparation and opportunity meet," so we took the opportunity to test Sarah's preparation, and she was the one in charge of asking for our room number.

| | |
|---|---|
| ○ Hola, buenas noches. | ○ Hello, good evening. |
| ● Buenas noches, señorita, ¿en qué la puedo ayudar? | ● Good evening, miss, how can I help you? |
| ○ Perdón que lo moleste, pero mi amigo y yo olvidamos en qué habitación estamos alojados. | ○ I'm sorry to bother you, but my friend and I forgot which room we are staying in. |
| ● No se preocupe, es bastante común. ¿Podría decirme sus nombres? | ● Don't worry, it's pretty common. Could you tell me your names? |
| ○ Sí, yo me llamo Sarah Williams y él se llama Julio Sánchez. | ○ Yes, my name is Sarah Williams and his name is Julio Sánchez. |
| ● Muy bien, señorita Williams, su habitación es la 305, en el tercer piso. | ● Very well, miss Williams, your room is room 305, on the third floor. |
| ○ ¡305! Claro, ahora que lo dice me suena. Muchas gracias. | ○ ¡305! Of course, now you say it, it rings a bell. Thank you. |
| ● De nada, buenas noches. | ● You are welcome, good night. |

## Parts of a House

During my short time in Spain, I realized that Spanish houses are very similar to those in the States. For example, Ernesto's house in Barcelona had all of these parts:

- *la puerta principal*, which is the front door
- *la sala*, which is the living room
- *el comedor*, which is the dining-room
- *la cocina*, which is the kitchen
- *el trastero*, which is the storage room
- *el baño*, which is the bathroom
- *la habitación/dormitorio*, which is the bedroom
- *la chimenea*, which is the fireplace
- *la escalera*, which is the stairs
- *las ventanas*, which are the windows
- *el pasillo*, which is the hallway
- *el jardín*, which is the garden
- *el ático*, which is the attic
- *el sótano*, which is the basement

## Objects in the House

While I walked around Ernesto's house in Barcelona, I asked Julio the names of all the objects I saw. Afterward, he helped me, and together we made the following vocabulary list.

In the kitchen:

- *el fregadero* is the sink
- *el grifo* is the faucet
- *la estufa* is the stove
- *el horno* is the oven
- *el refrigerador* is the refrigerator
- *el congelador* is the freezer
- *el lavaplatos* is the dishwasher

- *los electrodomésticos* are the appliances
- *la encimera* is the counter
- *la despensa* is the pantry
- *la alacena* is the cupboard

In the living room:
- *la silla* is the chair
- *el sillón* is the armchair
- *el reloj* is the clock
- *la mesita* is coffee table
- *la lámpara* is the lamp
- *el florero* is the vase
- *la alfombra* is the carpet

In the bedroom:
- *la cama* is the bed
- *el tapete* is the rug
- *la lamparilla* is the nightlight
- *las cortinas* are the curtains
- *el armario* is the closet
- *la cómoda* is the dresser
- *el despertador* is the alarm clock

In the bathroom:
- *la toalla* is the towel
- *el espejo* is the mirror
- *la pasta de dientes* is the toothpaste
- *el cepillo de dientes* is the toothbrush
- *el jabón* is the soap
- *el peine* is the comb
- *el cepillo* is the brush
- *la maquinilla de afeitar* is the razor
- *la crema de afeitar* is the shaving cream

- *el maquillaje* is the makeup

## Describing the Room

In the hotel room, I decided to write a short text describing the room to practice the vocabulary I had learned in Barcelona:

| | |
|---|---|
| La habitación tiene dos camas individuales. | There are two single beds. |
| Las camas tienen sábanas y edredones de color blanco. | The beds have white sheets and quilts. |
| A los lados de las camas hay dos mesitas de luz y dos lamparillas. | To the sides of the beds there are two night stands with dos lamps. |
| Detrás de las camas, en el centro de la pared, hay una pintura de un tulipán. | Behind the beds, in the middle of the wall, there's a picture of a tulip. |
| Al costado de la cama que está a la derecha, hay una ventana. | To the side of the bed that's to the right, there's a window. |
| La ventana tiene cortinas oscuras con lunares claros. | The window has dark curtains with light dots. |
| Las cortinas están corridas. | The curtains are drawn. |
| Del otro lado de la ventana, al lado de la cama de la izquierda, hay una mesa redonda y un sofá. | On the other side of the window, next to the bed that's to the left, there's a round table and a sofa. |

1. Hotel room.
Source: *Can Pac Swire, CC BY-NC 2.0* <https://creativecommons.org/licenses/by-nc/2.0/?ref=openverse>, *via WordPress:* https://wordpress.org/openverse/image/cb2099c9-a51e-4463-8d79-1e01d87dab8c

## Exercises

Let's see how much you've learned during our time in Bilbao!

1. How many definite articles are there in Spanish?
    a. Just one
    b. Four
    c. Two
2. What characteristics of the noun define which definite article to use?
3. Can you name the definite articles in Spanish?
4. True or false: Spanish has six indefinite articles.
5. Can you name the Spanish indefinite articles?
6. Before *flor*, a singular, feminine noun, which of these indefinite articles would you use?
    a. Unas
    b. Un
    c. Una

7. Before *rios*, a plural masculine noun, which of these definite articles would you use?
    a. Los
    b. Las
    c. El
8. At a hotel front desk, how would you ask for a single room for the night?
9. True or false: *habitación doble* is a room for two people.
10. Can you name the means of payment mentioned in the chapter?
11. True or false: To distinguish questions from affirmative sentences in written Spanish, we use ONLY the opening question mark.
12. How do you tell the difference between questions and affirmative sentences when speaking?
13. If you want to say something is *in* or *inside* something else, which of the following prepositions of place would you use?
    a. Encima de
    b. Hacia
    c. En
14. True or false: The preposition *a* can mean "to," "by" and "at."
15. Can you name the parts of the house that you remember?
16. Cross the odd one out:
    a. La cocina
    b. El dormitorio
    c. El baño
    d. El jarrón
    e. La sala
17. Which of these objects would you NOT find in a kitchen?
    a. Un horno
    b. Una toalla

    c. Un electrodoméstico

    d. Un grifo

18. Can you name four objects normally found in a bedroom?

19. In which room do you think you can find *un espejo*? (It could be more than one room)

20. In which room do you think you can find *una cama*? (It could be more than one room)

# Chapter 4: Going Shopping

Hi! Julio here. After a few lovely days in Bilbao, I took Sarah to the amazing community of Galicia. We had a 10-hour train journey to Santiago de Compostela, Galicia's capital city, so I took advantage of that time to tell her a bit more about this autonomous community. Galicia is located in the far north western corner of Spain, just above Portugal, with the Atlantic Ocean to the west and the Cantabrian Sea to the north. Because of this, the community is famous for its coasts, which alternate between *rías* (estuaries) and beaches. Inland Galicia is full of hills and low mountains, and it's very green because the weather is humid and rainy.

    A curious thing about Galicia is that, apart from Spanish, Portuguese and Galician are also spoken in the region. The latter is a romance language closely related to Portuguese, and it's spoken daily by half the population of Galicia. The *Camino de Santiago* ("Way of St James") is also worth noting. It's a trail network that takes pilgrims to the St. James shrine, located in the cathedral of Santiago de Compostela. This brings hundreds of thousands of travelers from all over the world to the region each year.

    Besides its beautiful scenery and vibrant culture, another reason I wanted to take Sarah to Galicia is its delicious cuisine, which includes shellfish, *empanadas* (turnovers with savory filling), *pulpo a la gallega* (octopus cooked the Galician way), and *orujo* liquor (distilled from grape remains). Besides, there are also several typical *guisados* (stews) because of the link with de Celtic culture.

In Galicia, we visited Santiago, La Coruña, a port city with beaches, museums, and monuments, and Finisterre, the farthest western point in Spain.

## Demonstrative Pronouns and Articles

I was glad Julio wanted to take me to Galicia. Back home, my mom and dad are avid hikers. One of their dreams is to one day walk the *Camino de Santiago*. So, once I was in Santiago de Compostela, the ultimate mecca for hikers and pilgrims, I wanted to buy lots of presents for them. That's why I asked Julio to take me to a souvenir shop. There, I was able to buy a t-shirt for my mom, all by myself!

| | |
|---|---|
| ● ¡Buenos días! ¿En qué puedo ayudarla? | ● Good morning! How can I help you? |
| ○ Hola, me gustaría comprar una camiseta. | ○ Hello, I'd like to buy a t-shirt. |
| ● Por supuesto. ¿De niño, de hombre o de mujer? | ● Very well. For kids, men or women? |
| ○ Quiero una camiseta de mujer. | ○ I want a woman's t-shirt. |
| ● ¿De qué talla la quiere? | ● In which size do you want it? |
| ○ La quiero en talla mediana. | ○ I want it in medium size. |
| ● Muy bien, tenemos camisetas de mujer en talla mediana de color rosado, amarillo y celeste. ¿De qué | ● Great, we have women's t-shirts of medium size in pink, yellow and light blue. Which |

| | |
|---|---|
| color le gusta? | color do you like? |
| ○ Me gustaría de color rosado. Y con el logo del Camino de Santiago, como aquella camiseta que está allí. | ○ I'd like it in pink. And with the logo of the Camino de Santiago, like that t-shirt over there. |
| ● Esa no la tengo en rosado. ¿Qué le parece esta, que tiene el logo en la espalda? | ● That one I don't have in pink. What do you think about this one, with the logo on the back? |
| ○ Vale, llevo esa. ¿Cuánto cuesta? | ○ Okay, I'll take that one. How much is it? |
| ● La camiseta cuesta 10€. ¿Se la envuelvo para regalo? | ● The t-shirt is 10€. Do you want it wrapped? |
| ○ Sí, por favor. | ○ Yes, please |
| ● Aquí tiene. ¡Gracias por su compra! Adiós. | ● Here you are. Thank you for your purchase! Goodbye. |

And, as always, Julio took the chance to teach me something new about Spanish!

Demonstrative pronouns are words used instead of nouns to point at people or things, for example, **Esa** *no la tengo en rosado ("That one I don't have in pink.")* When they accompany the noun, they function as articles; for example, **aquella** *camiseta que está allí ("that t-shirt over there.")*

The demonstrative pronouns in English are "this," "that," "these," and "those." In Spanish, however, we have quite a few more. To choose from the list of 15 Spanish demonstrative pronouns, we need to consider the gender, the number, and the distance from the speaker and the addressee of the noun it's replacing.

|  | Masculine | | Feminine | | Neuter |
|---|---|---|---|---|---|
|  | Singular | Plural | Singular | Plural | Singular |
| Object close to the speaker | esto | estos | esta | estas | esto |
| Object close to the addressee | ese | eso | esa | esas | eso |
| Object far from both | aquel | aquellos | aquella | aquellas | aquello |

## Speaking about the Price of a Product

Since Sarah wanted to do some shopping in Santiago de Compostela, I taught her some useful phrases to ask for prices and, also, what to expect as an answer:

### Asking for prices
- *¿Cuánto cuesta/sale/vale esto?*: How much is this?
- *¿Cuánto cuestan/salen/valen esos?*: How much are those?
- *¿Qué precio tiene?*: What's the price?
- *¿Cuál es el precio?*: What's the price?
- *¿A qué precio está?*: What's the price?
- *¿Qué vale?*: How much?
- *¿Cuánto es?*: How much is it?

### Telling prices
- *El precio de eso son 5€*: The price of that is 5€.
- *Vale/cuesta/sale 20€*: It's 20€.
- *Es 1€*: It's 1€.

- *Son 15€:* It's 15€.

# Interrogative Pronouns/"W" questions (Why, What, Who, etc.)

I used different interrogative pronouns in the questions I taught Sarah about asking prices in stores. Let's take a look at them.

- *qué* is used in the same way as English "what": *¿Qué precio tiene este pastel?* ("What is the price of this cake?").

- *por qué* is similar to English "why": *¿Por qué están tan caros los tomates?* ("Why are tomatoes so expensive?").

- *cuál* and *cuáles* are the singular and plural equivalents of English "which": *¿Cuál prefieres, el de atún o el de pollo?* ("Which one do you want, the tuna or the chicken one?").

- *quién* and *quiénes* are the singular and plural equivalents of "who": *¿Quién quiere lechuga?* ("Who wants lettuce?").

- *cuánto* and *cuánta* are the masculine and feminine equivalents of "how much": *¿Cuánto pan compro?* ("How much bread should I buy").

- *cuántos* and *cuántas* are the masculine and feminine equivalents of "how many": *¿Cuántas piñas desea?* ("How many pineapples do you want?").

- *dónde* is used in the same way as English "where": *¿Dónde está el arroz en esta tienda?* ("Where is the rice in this store").

- *cómo* is used in the same way as "how": *¿Cómo se cocina el pulpo?* ("How is oct opus cooked?").

- *cuándo* is similar to English "when": *¿Cuándo abre el supermercado?* ("When does the supermarket open?").

Sarah noticed that all interrogative pronouns have a graphic accent and asked me about it. I explained to her that those words have more than one function in Spanish. So, to mark when they are being used as interrogative pronouns, they take an accent.

# Asking for and Finding Products in a Store

In La Coruña, instead of staying in a hotel, Julio and I rented an apartment through Airbnb. Even though we love eating out, we also wanted to cook our own meals, and I wanted to learn how to make some typical Spanish dishes. That's why we went to the supermarket, where I had a few enriching conversations. The first one was with Julio:

| | |
|---|---|
| ● Julio, ¿sabes dónde puedo encontrar el jamón serrano? | ● Julio, do you know where can I find the serrano ham? |
| ○ Mmm, la verdad que no. ¿Te has fijado al lado del sector de panadería? | ○ Mmm, actually, no. Have you looked next to the bakery sector? |
| ● Pues sí, pero solo encontré lácteos. Había queso, leche, nata, yogur, pero nada de fiambres. | ● Yes, but I only found dairy products. There's cheese, milk, cream, yogurt, but no cold cuts. |
| ○ ¿Y al final del pasillo, antes de la verdulería? | ○ And down the hall, before the greengrocers'? |
| ● También he ido hasta allí y no he visto el jamón. Pero aproveché para coger algo de fruta y bastante verdura. | ● I've also been there, but I haven't seen the ham. But I took the opportunity to grab some fruit and plenty of vegetables. |

| | |
|---|---|
| ○ ¿Qué has cogido? | ○ What have you grabbed? |
| ● Tomates, lechuga, zanahoria, pepino, patatas, calabaza, manzanas, naranjas, fresas y ciruelas. | ● Tomatoes, lettuce, carrots, cucumber, potatoes, pumpkin, apples, oranges, strawberries, and plums. |
| ○ ¿No te parece que es mucho para un par de días? | ○ Don't you think it's too much for a couple of days? |
| ● Tienes razón, es demasiado, devolveré algunas cosas. ¿Tú que has cogido? | ● You are right, it's too much, I'll put some things back. |
| ○ Yo tengo los huevos y el aceite para hacer la tortilla de patatas. También conseguí arroz para la paella, pero no he encontrado los mariscos. | ○ I have the eggs and the oil to make the potato tortilla. I also grabbed rice for the paella, but I haven't found the seafood. |

The second dialogue I had was with one of the employees of the supermarket:

| | |
|---|---|
| • Disculpe, ¿le puedo hacer una pregunta? | • Excuse me, can I ask you a question? |
| ○ Buenas tardes. Sí, por supuesto, ¿en qué puedo ayudarla? | ○ Good afternoon. Yes, of course, how can I help you? |
| • Me gustaría comprar jamón serrano. | • I'd like to buy serrano ham. |
| ○ Los fiambres están en el pasillo 8, al lado de las galletas. | ○ The cold cuts are in aisle 8, next to the cookies. |
| • Muchas gracias. ¿Hay pescadería en esta tienda? | • Thank you. Is there a fish market in this store? |
| ○ Sí, claro. Está al final del pasillo 5, en la sección de productos frescos. ¿La puedo ayudar con algo más? | ○ Yes, of course. It's at the end of aisle 5, in the fresh produce section. Is there anything else I can help you with? |
| • No, eso es todo. ¡Muchas gracias! | • No, that's all. Thank you! |

## Adverbs of Quantity

In the conversations she had in the supermarket, Sarah used a few adverbs of quantity: the words we use to answer "How much?" or "How many?" Here's a list of the most common ones:

- *mucho*: "many," "much," "a lot"
- *muy*: "very"
- *demasiado*: "too much"
- *bastante*: "enough," "quite"
- *algo*: "somewhat," "slightly," "a bit"
- *poco*: "little," "few"
- *nada*: "nothing," "at all"
- *más*: "more"
- *menos*: "less"
- *mucho más*: "a lot more"
- *tanto*: "so much"
- *tantos*: "so many"

## Present Form of Regular Verbs

We've been traveling, and I've been studying Spanish for quite a while now. So I thought it was time to face one of my fears: the Spanish tenses. Luckily, Julio said we would start with the simplest one: the present simple. Here's his explanation.

We use the present simple to talk about what is generally true, for example: *Sarah vive en Estados Unidos* ("Sarah lives in the United States"). We also use this tense to talk about what is true at the moment, for example: *Estamos en España* ("We are in Spain"). Also, we use this tense to talk about what happens regularly, for example: *De lunes a viernes, doy clases de español en un colegio* ("Mondays through Fridays, I teach Spanish in a School").

Now, let's see how the verbs change to form this tense. The first thing you need to understand is that, in the infinitive form ("**to** + **verb**" – for example, "to talk," "to find" or "to fight"), all Spanish verbs end in -AR, -ER, or -IR. The verbs ending in -AR belong to the first conjugation, the verbs ending in -ER belong to the second conjugation, and the verbs ending in -IR belong to the third conjugation. The part that comes before those letters is called the verb's *root.*

Another important thing is that, just as in English, Spanish verbs can be regular or irregular. Within the regular ones, the ones that belong to the same conjugation undergo the same changes when we conjugate them.

Let's see how the regular verbs of the first conjugation change using the verb *amar* (to love). If we separate the verb into the root and ending, we are left with AM- (root) and -AR (ending). To conjugate the verb, we leave the root and change the ending like this:

| | | | |
|---|---|---|---|
| For the present simple of the | first-person singular (yo) | we add -O | Yo amo |
| | first-person plural (nosotros / nosotras) | we add -AMOS | Nosotras / nosotros amamos |
| | second-person singular (tú) | we add -AS | Tú amas |
| | second-person singular (usted) | we add -A | Usted ama |
| | second-person plural (vosotros / vosotras) | we add -ÁIS | Vosotros / vosotras amáis |
| | second-person plural (ustedes) | we add -AN | Ustedes aman |
| | third-person singular (él / ella) | we add -A | Él / ella ama |

|  | third-person plural (ellos / ellas) | we add -AN | Ellos / ellas aman |
|---|---|---|---|

We follow the same logic with the regular verbs of the second conjugation. Let's see how we do it using *temer* (to fear).

| | | | |
|---|---|---|---|
| For the present simple of the | first-person singular (yo) | we add -O | Yo temo |
| | first-person plural (nosotros / nosotras) | we add -EMOS | Nosotras / nosotros tememos |
| | second-person singular (tú) | we add -ES | Tú temes |
| | second-person singular (usted) | we add -E | Usted teme |
| | second-person plural (vosotros / vosotras) | we add -ÉIS | Vosotros / vosotras teméis |
| | second-person plural (ustedes) | we add -EN | Ustedes temen |
| | third-person singular (él / ella) | we add -E | Él / ella teme |
| | third-person plural (ellos / ellas) | we add -EN | Ellos / ellas temen |

Lastly, let's see the same mechanism with *partir* (to leave) as an example of the third conjugation.

| | | | |
|---|---|---|---|
| For the present simple of the | first-person singular (yo) | we add -O | Yo parto |
| | first-person plural (nosotros / nosotras) | we add -IMOS | Nosotras / nosotros partimos |
| | second-person singular (tú) | we add -ES | Tú partes |
| | second-person singular (usted) | we add -E | Usted parte |
| | second-person plural (vosotros / vosotras) | we add -ÍS | Vosotros / vosotras partís |
| | second-person plural (ustedes) | we add -EN | Ustedes parten |
| | third-person singular (él / ella) | we add -E | Él / ella parte |
| | third-person plural (ellos / ellas) | we add -EN | Ellos / ellas parten |

## Vocabulary: fruits, vegetables, food

Here's a vocabulary list of the food mentioned in this chapter.

- *los mariscos* means "shellfish"
- *la empanada* is like a turnover with savory filling
- *el pulpo* means "octopus"
- *el guisado* means "stew"
- *el pastel* means "cake"
- *el tomate* means "tomato"
- *el atún* means "tuna"

- *el pollo* means "chicken"
- *la lechuga* means "lettuce"
- *el pan* means "bread"
- *la manzana* means "apple"
- *el arroz* means "rice"
- *el jamón* means "ham"
- *los lácteos* means "dairy products"
- *el queso* means "cheese"
- *la leche* means "milk"
- *la nata* means "cream"
- *el yogur* means "yogurt"
- *los fiambres* means "cold cuts"
- *la fruta* means "fruit"
- *la verdura* means "vegetables"
- *la zanahoria* means "carrot"
- *el pepino* means "cucumber"
- *la patata* means "potato"
- *la calabaza* means "pumpkin"
- *la piña* means "pineapple"
- *la naranja* means "orange"
- *la fresa* means "strawberry"
- *la ciruela* means "plum"
- *el huevo* means "egg"
- *el aceite* means "oil"
- *la galleta* means "cookie"

# Culture Section: Traditional Spanish Meals

We've already mentioned a few traditional Spanish meals, but since I wanted to learn how to cook a local dish, Julio and I went online to find a recipe that wouldn't be so hard. Finally, I decided I wanted to make *una tortilla de patatas* (an omelet made with onions, fried potatoes, and eggs), but here's some of the information I gathered during my research.

*La paella valenciana* is a rice dish cooked in a circular pan that's also called *paella*. Besides the rice, the dish has onions, peppers, mussels, chicken, shrimp, and tomatoes. As you can tell from its name, it's originally from Valencia (an eastern autonomous community), but nowadays is prepared all over Spain.

*El cocido madrileño* is a hearty stew consisting of three parts: broth, chickpeas and vegetables, and meats (chicken, pork, and cold cuts). Originally, it was a dish prepared by farmers to endure cold days working in the field. That's why it's so caloric, ideal for winter.

*El gazpacho andaluz* is a soup served cold, which makes sense since it's originally from the warm south of Spain. The soup (or juice?) is made of tomatoes, onion, garlic, and cucumber, and it's usually served with fresh bread and olive oil.

Last but not least, we have *la crema catalana*. This world-famous dessert is quite easy to make. First, you must cook the ingredients (egg yolk, milk, sugar, flour, lemon and cinnamon) together to obtain the custard. Then, you have to sprinkle lots of sugar on top of it and burn it to make a thin and hard layer.

## Exercises

1. True or false: To decide which demonstrative pronoun to use, you only need to consider the gender and number of the noun it's replacing.
2. Which are the three distances that determine which demonstrative pronoun to use?

3. If you wanted to point to a singular, feminine noun like *roca*, which is far from you but close to the person you are talking to, which of these demonstrative pronouns would you use?
   a. Estas   b. Esa   c. Aquel
4. If you wanted to point to a group of masculine nouns like *carros* which are far from you and from the person you are talking to, which of these demonstrative pronouns would you use?
   a. Esos   b. Estas   c. Aquello
5. Do you remember one of the ways to ask for the price of something?
6. If you asked for a price, which of these answers can you expect to hear?
   a. Precia
   b. Vale
   c. Los precious son
7. True or false: *quién* is the singular equivalent of English "who."
8. Which of the following interrogative pronouns are used in the same way as English "which"?
   a. Cuánto/cuánta
   b. Cuando
   c. Cuál/cuáles
9. Complete with the correct interrogative pronoun: ¿(Who).... vienen a la fiesta?
10. True or false: *poco* means "too much."
11. Cross the odd one out:
    a. Mucho   b. Demasiado   c. Nada
    d. Más     e. Muy
12. For the present simple of the first-person plural (*nosotros/nosotras*), the conjugation of the verb *temer* is *tememos*. Which is the correct conjugation of *correr*?
    a. Corremos   b. Corro   c. Corren
          d. Corremas

13. Complete with the correct form of the regular verbs of the first conjugation:
    (amar) Yo amo.
    (cantar) Yo cant...
    (bailar) Yo ...
14. Complete with the correct form of the regular verbs of the second conjugation:
    (temer) Tú temes.
    (beber) Tú beb...
    (comer) Tú ...
15. Complete with the correct form of the regular verbs of the third conjugation:
    (partir) Ella parte.
    (salir) Ella sal...
    (vivir) Ella ...
16. True or false: *zanahoria* means "cucumber."
17. What's the Spanish word for "pumpkin"?
    a. Patata            b. Calabaza            c. Naranja
18. Choose the odd one out:
    a. Atún     b. Pollo     c. Pastel
19.            d. Pulpo
20. True or false: Cheese, milk and cream are *lácteos*.
21. Choose the odd one out:
    a. Naranja   b. Piña     c. Ciruela     d. Aceite
                 e. Fresa

# Chapter 5: Going Sightseeing

Hi! It's Sarah here. After visiting Galicia, we traveled southeast from Santiago de Compostela to Salamanca. It was a short 4-hour journey, but it gave us the time to practice some Spanish and for Julio to tell me about the history of Salamanca. We arrived at around 11 a.m.

Do you remember that Julio told us that Castile is where the Castilian language first started? Well, Salamanca is one of the nine provinces that form the autonomous community of Castile and León. Here, they not only speak Spanish and Castilian but also Leonese and Galician, two varieties that are protected due to their cultural value.

Castile and Leon borders Portugal and is home to eight UNESCO World Heritage Sites – of which I visited the only one in Salamanca, the historical center or "Old City of Salamanca." Salamanca is famous for its history, its monuments, and its food. Its University is one of the oldest in the whole of Europe and has some very imposing buildings.

Julio has some friends here, so we visited them, and I put my new Spanish knowledge to the test, but he stayed with them during the afternoon, and I wanted to go sightseeing a bit on my own. It was a challenge because I could no longer have Julio translate things for me and encourage me to speak in Spanish – but we were already in the middle of our trip, so I had to start getting more confident, right?

We visited María and Rubén, Julio's friends, and after our introductions, which I'm almost an expert at already, I asked them for a few directions so that I could start my solo journey.

Luckily, their house is near the city center; they live on the corner of calle Zamora and Calle de las Isabeles. I wanted to start my journey on Plaza Mayor, the most iconic place in Salamanca. It was built in the 18th century, its design is typically baroque, and it has many bars, cafés, and restaurants where I wanted to eat a typical *hornazo*, a kind of meat pie stuffed with pork loin, chorizo, and eggs. It is a typical dish from Salamanca and Ávila only, so it was my opportunity to try it for lunch. I asked María and Rubén how to get from their house to plaza Mayor and then to la Casa de las Conchas, a historical building that is now a public library.

This is how our conversation went:

| ● ¿Cómo llego a plaza Mayor desde aquí? | ● How do I get to plaza Mayor from here? |
|---|---|
| ○ Bueno, simplemente tienes que continuar derecho por calle Zamora hasta que termina la calle. Allí está la plaza Mayor. Para entrar, tienes que doblar a la izquierda e ir hasta la esquina de plaza Mayor y calle Toro. Luego doblas a la derecha. A mitad de cuadra encontrarás una entrada a la plaza. | ○ Well, you just need to continue straight through Zamora street until the end of the street. There is plaza Mayor. To go in, you have to turn left and go to the corner of plaza Mayor and calle Toro. Then you turn right. In the middle of the block, you'll find an entrance to the square. |

| | |
|---|---|
| • Perfecto. Gracias. ¿Dónde me recomienda comer hornazo allí? | • Awesome. Thank you. Where would you recommend to eat hornazo there? |
| ○ Te recomendamos la confitería Santa Lucía. Puedes encontrarla al lado de la entrada a plaza Mayor. | ○ We recommend Santa Lucía coffee shop. You can find it next to the entrance to plaza Mayor. |
| • ¡Gracias! ¿Y cómo voy de allí a la Casa de las Conchas? | • Thank you! And how do I go from there to Casa de Conchas? |
| ○ Después de la confitería Santa Lucía, puedes salir de la plaza por la Plaza del Poeta Iglesias hasta llegar a la calle Quintana. Allí doblas a la derecha y luego a la izquierda en la primera calle. Esa es la ruta Mayor. Debes caminar por allí hasta la diagonal Rúa Antigua y encontrarás la Casa de las Conchas. | ○ After Sants Lucía coffee shop, you can exit the square through Plaza del Poeta Iglesias until reaching Quintana street. There, you turn right, and then left on the first street. That is Mayor road. You have to walk that way until reaching Rúa Antigua diagonal. There you'll find Casa de las Conchas. |
| • Perfecto. ¡Gracias! | • Awesome. Thanks! |

I ended up visiting plaza Mayor and its surroundings; I ate *hornazo* and had *tocinillo de cielo* for dessert, similar to a *flan* or pudding. Then, I went to Casa de las Conchas and La Clerecía, the building right across the street. Nowadays, it belongs to the Pontifical University of Salamanca, but it was built in the 17th century. I could actually go up one of its towers and see the whole city center. After that, I used my new phrases to ask about the way to the New and Old Cathedrals, so I walked a short distance and went there as well.

To ask for directions, I had a short interaction with someone walking nearby:

| • Disculpe, ¿dónde está la catedral? ¿Está cerca? | • Excuse me, where's the cathedral? Is it close? |
|---|---|
| ○ Sí, está a unos 200 metros. | ○ Yes, it's about 200 metres away. |
| • ¿Podría decirme cómo llegar? | • Could you tell me how to get there? |
| ○ Claro. Ve todo derecho por la ruta Mayor y lo encontrarás a tu izquierda. Son unas dos cuadras. | ○ Of course. Go straight through Mayor road and you'll see it to your left. It's about two blocks away. |
| • ¡Muchas gracias! | • Thank you very much! |

I admit that I was pretty nervous when I had to talk in Spanish for the first time without Julio to back me up, but now I feel much more confident!

As for my trip, I also wanted to visit some of Salamanca's museums, but I had run out of time for the day. So I went back to María and Rubén's house, and we went to a restaurant for dinner. Then, we stayed the night at their place.

Now, Julio will teach you a bit of vocabulary, grammar, and all the useful phrases so that you can travel on your own too.

**Transportation**

Hi! It's Julio here again. While Sarah traveled around Salamanca and visited some of its landmarks, I stayed with Rubén and María. But, of course, she didn't leave without a few lessons first.

Okay, so for a bit of vocabulary, here is the Spanish name of a few means of transportation that might come in handy for your trip:

- *El tren* means "train"
- *El autobús* means "bus"
- *El avión* means "airplane"
- *El taxi* means "taxi"
- *La bicicleta* means "bike"
- *El automóvil* means "car"
- *La motocicleta* means "motorcycle"
- *El metro* means "subway"
- *El barco* means "ship"

So as an example, we can say the following sentence: "Viajamos de Atlanta a Barcelona en avión y de Barcelona a Bilbao en tren." And let's add: "Hoy viajamos de Santiago de Compostela a Salamanca en tren."

And, you can always go places *a pie*, which means "on foot"!

# Buildings

When you're in a different city, everything might look different, but the names of the buildings stay the same, right? Well, here's a list of some buildings that can be found in almost any city:

- *La casa* means "house"
- *El apartamento* means "apartment
- *El museo* means "museum"
- *La plaza* means "square"

- *La catedral* means "cathedral"
- *La iglesia* means "church"
- *La biblioteca* means "library"
- *El cine* means "cinema"
- *El supermercado* means "supermarket"
- *El hospital* means "hospital"
- *El banco* means "bank"
- *El restaurante* means "restaurant"
- *El aeropuerto* means "airport"
- *La estación de tren* means "train station"
- *Universidad* means "university"
- *Farmacia* means "pharmacy"

For example, the buildings that Sarah visited today are: *la plaza, la biblioteca, y la catedral.*

## Asking for directions

Asking for directions can be difficult in a new language, but here's a list of phrases that will definitely help you get where you want to!

- *Disculpe* means "Excuse me." It is used to get someone's attention, and it's pronounced /dees - kool - peh/.
- *Perdone* also means "excuse me."
- *¿Dónde está...?* means "Where is...?" It should be followed by the name of the place you want to get to.
- *¿Cómo llego a...?* means "How do I get to...?" This one should also be followed by the name of the place.
- *¿Cómo voy a...?* also means "How do it get to...?" and should also be followed by the name of the place.
- *¿Podría decirme cómo llegar a...?* means "Could you tell me how to get to...?" This one should also be followed by the name of the place.

- *¿... está cerca?* means "Is ... nearby?" This one should be preceded by the name of the place you want to get to.
- *¿Sabe si hay algún/alguna... por aquí?* means "do you know if there is a ... nearby?" The ellipsis should be filled with the name of the place you want to go to, and the decision between *algún* or *alguna* depends on the gender of the following word.
- *¿... está en esta calle?* means "Is... on this street?" It should be preceded by the name of the place you want to get to.

## Adverbs of Place

Now, of course, you need to understand the directions people will give you in Spanish. So here are the most common adverbs of place in Spanish that you might hear when someone is giving direction, and you can also add them to your questions.

- *Aquí* means "here"
- *Allí* means "there"
- *Dentro de* means "inside"
- *Afuera de* means "outside"
- *Adelante* means "ahead"
- *Detrás* means "behind"
- *Abajo* means "below"
- *Arriba* means "above"
- *A la derecha* means "to/on the right"
- *A la izquierda* means "to/on the left"
- *Al lado de* means "besides" or "next to"
- *En frente de* means "in front of"
- *Al final de* means "at the end"
- *Alrededor* means "around"
- *En el medio* means "in the middle"
- *Cerca* means "near"

- *Lejos* means "far"
- *Entre* means "between"
- *En la esquina* means "on the corner"

## Giving Directions

Okay, now it's time to learn some possible answers when you ask for directions – and to learn to give them yourself!

The first thing you need to know is that we can use the verb *estar* to say where something is using some other place as a reference. For example, we can say *La confitería Santa Lucía está al lado de la entrada de la plaza Mayor* ("The coffee shop Santa Lucía is beside the entrance to plaza Mayor") *or La catedral está en frente del restaurante* ("The cathedral is in front of the restaurant"), and you can also say *La Casa de las Conchas está al final de la calle* ("La Casa de las Conchas is at the end of the street"). You can use *estar* with all of the adverbs from the previous section!

- *Tienes que seguir derecho/recto* means "you have to go straight on"
- *Dobla a la izquierda/derecha* means "turn left/right"
- *Gira a la derecha/izquierda* means "turn right/left"
- *Cruza la calle* means "cross the street"
- *Continúa por esta calle* means "continue on this street"
- *Está a ... calles* means "It's... blocks away." The ellipsis should be filled with the number of blocks.

## Asking for Tickets

Once you get to the place you want to go to, you should be able to ask for tickets. Otherwise, how will you get in? These are a few phrases that might come in handy when you are doing an activity:

- *Una entrada para..., por favor* means "A ticket for..., please." The gap should be filled with the name of a movie or play, or even the name of a museum or other type of activity. For example, *una entrada para el museo, por favor* ("one ticket for the museum, please").

If you want more than one ticket, you simply need to change the number and remember to make *entrada* a plural.

- *¿Me podría dar una entrada para...?* means "Could you give me a ticket for...?" In Spanish, we sometimes use this polite structure and don't say "please," because we consider it polite enough. However, you can add a *por favor* at the end of the question if you prefer it. Again, the gap should be filled with the name of a movie, play, museum, etc.

- *¿Tiene un mapa de...?* means "Do you have a map of the...?" Whether a map of the city center, the whole country, or a museum, you simply need to fill the gap with the place you need a map of.

- *¿A qué hora cierran?* means "When do you close?"

Present Form of Some Irregular Verbs

Well, it's time to go back to grammar now. In the previous chapter, we've seen the conjugation of some regular verbs, but now it's time to see the conjugation of some irregular ones besides *ser* and *estar*.

In this table, you will find the present form of some irregular verbs

|  | HACER | IR | HABER | TRAER | TENER |
|---|---|---|---|---|---|
| yo | hago | voy | he | traigo | tengo |
| tú | haces | vas | has | traes | tienes |
| él / ella | hace | va | ha | trae | tiene |
| nosotros / nosotras | hacemos | vamos | hemos | traemos | tenemos |
| vosotros / vosotras | hacéis | vais | habéis | traéis | tenéis |

| ellos / ellas / ustedes | hacen | van | han | traen | tienen |

As you see, the ending of these conjugations is not always different from the ending of regular verbs, but generally what changes is the root of the verb.

## Present Progressive Tense

In Spanish, the present progressive tense is conveyed through a verbal phrase that uses the conjugation of *estar* + a gerund (a "gerund" is the noun form of a verb that ends in -ing). One example of this could be *Estoy comiendo*, which means "I'm eating."

We've already seen the conjugation of *estar*, and we almost know it by heart, right? So let's talk about the gerunds.

In Spanish, gerunds are not conjugated depending on the person. Good news, right? They remain unchanged and are used for talking about things happening – that is, for the progressive tense!

The gerund is formed in the following way:

- Infinitive verbs ending in *-ar* end in *-ando* in the gerund. For example: *cantar* turns into *cantando*.
- Infinitive verbs ending in *-ir* or *-er* end in *-iendo* in the gerund. For example, *comer* and *salir* turn into *comiendo* and *saliendo*.

As we've said, the gerund is never conjugated, but to form the progressive, the verb *estar* does need to be conjugated. For this reason, we could say *él está comiendo* and *vosotras estáis comiendo*.

## Time Markers for the Present

Some time markers usually trigger the present in different sentences. For example, we would usually use the present with words like "always" in English.

As we've seen, we use the present to talk about things that are generally true, so these are a few phrases that might signal that a

present form follows:
- *Todos los días* ("Every day")
- *Los lunes* ("Every Monday"). Of course, you could use any other day of the week.
- *Siempre* ("Always")
- *En general* ("Generally")
- *Usualmente* ("Usually")
- *Casi nunca* ("Hardly ever")
- *Nunca* ("Never")

On the other hand, there are also time markers that trigger the present progressive tense, like:
- *Ahora* ("Now")
- *Ahora mismo* ("Right now")
- *En este momento* ("At this moment")

## Verb Moods

Unlike English, Spanish can have several verb moods. So far, we've only seen the indicative or *indicativo* used for real situations. But there are two more moods: the subjunctive and imperative.

The imperative mood is used to give commands or strong requests. In Spanish, the imperative is also a tense with its own conjugations. One example could be: *Come todo lo que tienes en el plato* ("Eat everything on your plate"). On the other hand, the subjunctive mood is used to express wishes, suggestions, desires, or to talk about hypotheses. In Spanish, there are three tenses with their own conjugations in the subjunctive mood: *presente de subjuntivo, futuro de subjuntivo y pretérito imperfecto de subjuntivo*. An example of the *presente de subjuntivo* could be *Es increíble que coma todo* ("It is amazing how he eats everything"); an example of the *futuro de subjuntivo* could be *Aunque él comiere todo mañana, no le daré un premio* ("Even if he eats everything tomorrow, I won't give him a reward"); and lastly, an example of the *pretérito imperfecto de subjuntivo* could be *Me dijo que comiera todo* ("She told me that I should eat everything").

# Exercises

1. How do you say "bike" in Spanish?
2. What does *autobús* mean in English?
3. How do you say "museum" in Spanish? And what about "square"?
4. What do *iglesia* and *estación de tren* mean?
5. What would you say first when you come up to someone to ask for directions?
6. How would you ask how to get to the library?
7. How would you ask whether there is a pharmacy nearby?
8. If the university is next to the library, it is...
    a. en frente
    b. b. arriba
    c. al lado
9. If there is a statue in the middle of a square, it is...
    a. en el medio
    b. afuera
    c. en la esquina
10. If someone told you *Cruza la calle y dobla a la izquierda*, what would you do?
    a. continue on this street and turn right.
    b. cross the street and turn left
    c. go straight on.
11. If you had to give directions, how would you say "turn right and walk straight on for 3 blocks"?
12. How would you ask for three tickets to the museum?
13. What is the second person singular present form of the verb *traer*?
    a. traemos
    b. traigo
    c. traes

14. What is the first person plural present form of the verb *haber*?

    a. he
    b. hemos
    c. han

15. True or false: The Spanish present progressive tense is formed with the conjugated form of the verb *estar* and a gerund.

16. True or false: if there is a verb that ends in *-ir* or *-er* in the infinitive form, the gerund form ends in *-ando*.

17. How would you say "I am singing" in Spanish?

18. Which of the following is **not** a time marker for the present progressive?

    a. todos los días
    b. ahora mismo
    c. en este momento

19. Which of the following is **not** a time marker for the present progressive?

    a. siempre
    b. casi nunca
    c. ahora

20. True or false: the subjunctive mode is used for real situations.

## Quiz

We're already halfway through our journey, so it's time to take a little quiz to review everything we've seen so far.

Unlike in the *exercises*, each right answer will be worth a point in this quiz. If you get 15-20 right answers, you're definitely great at this; keep it up! If you get 10-15 points, you're doing great, and I hope this quiz has helped with your doubts. But if your score is below 10, I encourage you to go back to the first five chapters to revise the information before moving on.

1. Regarding accents, what kind of word is *gorrión*? How would you pronounce the G and the double R?
2. Is this sentence grammatically correct? *Lucía juega al fútbol, son muy buenos.*
3. How do you ask someone how old they are in Spanish? And how do you answer?
4. Can you name the Spanish indefinite articles? When do you use each of them?
5. How would you ask if you can pay in cash?
6. How do you form yes/no questions in Spanish?
7. Which preposition would you use to say "I walk towards the museum"?
8. Which of these objects does not belong in the bathroom?
    a. *toalla*
    b. *pasta de diente*
    c. *cama*
    d. *jabón*
    e. *peine*
9. Which characteristics of the noun do you need to consider in choosing the correct demonstrative pronoun?
10. At a store, how would you ask how much is the chicken? How would the store clerk answer that it costs 20€?
11. What does *cuánto* mean? What is the difference between *cuánto* and *cuántos*?
12. How would you ask "Why are the pumpkins so expensive"?
13. At a store, how would you ask "Where are the cakes?"
14. Using adverbs of quantity, how would you say "It's too much for a few days"?
15. Can you conjugate the verb *amar* in the present with the pronouns *yo, tú, ella, nosotras, vosotras,* and *ellas*?
16. Can you conjugate the verb *temer* in the present with the pronouns *yo, tú, él, nosotros, vosotros,* and *ellos*?
17. Can you conjugate the verb *partir* in the present with the pronouns *yo, tú, ella, nosotras, vosotras,* and *ellas*?

18. How would you ask "How do I get to the supermarket?" in Spanish? And how would you answer that question if you had to turn right, walk straight on for 3 blocks and then turn left?

19. Can you conjugate the verbs *ser* and *estar* in the present with the pronouns *yo, tú, él, nosotros, vosotros,* and *ellos*?

20. What is the difference between these two sentences: *Paula come pizza y toma vino* and *Paula está comiendo pizza y tomando vino*?

Despite how you did in this quiz, keep up the good work! We're halfway there, and this journey still has a lot in store for you!

# Chapter 6:
# Having a House Party

After our lovely days in Salamanca, we took a bus to Seville, the sunniest city in Spain and the capital of the autonomous community of Andalusia. Located in the southwest of the Iberian Peninsula, the city is crossed by the River Guadalquivir. It's known for the Moorish castles, the medieval streets, the smell of orange blossoms, and the celebration of *Semana Santa* (Holy Week), one of the city's most important festivities.

## Talking About your Family

During the six-hour bus ride, Julio was very excited because a big part of his family lives in Seville. So, during the journey, he started talking about all of them. At first, I was a bit confused because I didn't know the words to talk about family members.

| | |
|---|---|
| ● Mi madrina nos va a estar esperando en la estación de autobús. | ● My godmother will be waiting for us at the bus station. |
| ○ ¿Tu madre? | ○ Your mother? |
| ● No, mi madrina es la | ● No, my godmother is my |

| | |
|---|---|
| hermana de mi madre. | mother's sister. |
| ○ Ah, madrina es "aunt." | ○ Ah, godmother is "tía." |
| ● No, "aunt" es tía. Lo que pasa es que Carola, ese es su nombre, es mi tía y mi madrina. | ● No, "tía" is an aunt. The thing is that Carola, that's her name, is my aunt and my godmother. |
| ○ Bien, creo que entiendo. Entonces su esposo es tu padrino. | ○ Okay, I think I understand. Then her husband is your godfather. |
| ● No, su esposo, José, es mi tío, pero no es mi padrino. Mi padrino es Luis, un cuñado de mi padre. | ● No, her husband, Jose, is my uncle, but he's not my godfather.<br>My godfather is Luis, my father's brother-in-law. |
| ○ ¿Cuñado? ¿Qué significa eso? | ○ ¿Brother-in-law? What does that mean? |
| ● Significa que está casado con su hermana, mi tía Cecilia. Ellos son los padres de Pancho y Josefa, mis primos. | ● It means he's married to his sister, my aunt Cecilia. They are the parents of Pancho and Josefa, my cousins. |
| ○ Ay, Julio, un poco más despacio, que me pierdo con tantas palabras nuevas. | ○ Oh, Julio, a bit slower, I get lost with so many new words. |
| ● No te preocupes que vas a conocerlos a todos el sábado, en la cena que organizó mi abuela Teresa. | ● Don't worry, you'll meet them all on Saturday at my grandmother Teresa's dinner. |

As I was going to meet his family in Seville, he took the time to explain to me his family tree, and he taught me all the words to talk about family members.

Family Members

Julio started with the words for the closest relatives:
- *La abuela* is "the grandmother"
- *El abuelo* is "the grandfather"
- *Los abuelos* are "the grandparents"
- *La madre* is "the mother"
- *El padre* is "the father"
- *Los padres* are "the parents"
- *La tía* is "the aunt"
- *El tío* is "the uncle"
- *La hermana* is "the sister"
- *El hermano* is "the brother"
- *La prima* is "the female cousin"
- *El primo* is "the male cousin"
- *La hija* is "the daughter"
- *El hijo* is "the son"
- *La nieta* is "the granddaughter"
- *El nieto* is "the grandson"
- *La sobrina* is "the niece"
- *El sobrino* is "the nephew"
- *La esposa* is "the wife"
- *El esposo* or *el marido* is "the husband"

Then, he moved on to the stepfamily:
- *La madrastra* is "the stepmother"
- *El padrastro* is "the stepfather"
- *La hermanastra* is "the stepsister," the daughter of your parent's spouse

- *El hermanastro* is "the stepbrother," the son of your parent's spouse
- *La media hermana* is "the half-sister," a female sibling by one parent
- *El medio hermano* is "the half-brother," a male sibling by one parent
- *La hijastra* is the "stepdaughter"
- *El hijastro* is "the stepson"

Finally, he delved into the extended family:

- *La madrina* is "the godmother"
- *El padrino* is "the godfather"
- *La ahijada* is "the goddaughter"
- *El ahijado* is "the godson"
- *La suegra* is "the mother-in-law"
- *El suegro* is "the father-in-law"
- *La cuñada* is "the sister-in-law"
- *El cuñado* is "the brother-in-law"
- *La nuera* is "the daughter-in-law"
- *El yerno* is "the son-in-law"

## Describing People

When we arrived, Julio's aunt and godmother, Carola, picked us up and took us around the city. She showed us the Cathedral (the third-largest church in Europe), the Plaza de España, the Torre de Oro (a watchtower in the River Guadalquivir), and Seville's Old City district.

I was a bit nervous about the dinner party that Teresa, Julio's grandmother, had organized for Saturday. I was afraid I would mix up all of Julio's relatives. To make it easier for me, Julio made me a list of everyone who was going, and he added a short description of them:

| | |
|---|---|
| Mi abuela Teresa es baja y delgada. Tiene el pelo corto y blanco. Su tez es clara. Tiene los ojos redondos y marrones. | My grandmother Teresa is short and thin. She's got short, white hair. Her complexion is pale. Her eyes are round and brown. |
| Mi tío José, el marido de Carola, es alto y fornido. Tiene la cara alargada, con una nariz aguileña. Sus ojos son oscuros, y su pelo es negro y ondulado. | My uncle Jose, Carola's husband, is tall and stout. His face is elongated, with an aquiline nose. His eyes are dark, and his hair is black and wavy. |
| Mi tía Cecilia tiene el pelo rubio, largo y lacio, aunque siempre lo lleva recogido en un rodete. Es esbelta y viste elegante. Sus ojos son claros. Está casada con Luis, mi padrino. | My aunt Cecilia has long, straight blond hair, although she always has it tucked in a bun. She's slim and she dresses elegantly. Her eyes are clear. She's married to Luis, my godfather. |
| Luis es alto y desgarbado. Su cara es cuadrada y de tez oscura. Sus ojos también son oscuros. Su pelo es negro y encrespado, y siempre lo lleva corto. | Luis is tall and ungainly. He has a square face and dark skin. His eyes are also dark. His hair is black and frizzy, and he always wears it short. |
| Mi prima Josefa es joven, tiene 20 años. Es flaca y baja de estatura. Tiene ojos celestes y un aro en la nariz. Siempre lleva el pelo teñido de colores brillantes. No sé de qué color lo tendrá ahora, pero la vas a reconocer. | My cousin Josefa is young, she's 20 years old. She's skinny and short. She's got blue eyes and a nose ring. She always dyes her hair bright colors. I don't |

| | |
|---|---|
| | know which color it is now, but you'll recognize her. |
| Mi primo Pancho es pecoso y tiene el pelo pelirrojo. Es grande y musculoso, le gusta mucho hacer deporte. | My cousin Pancho has freckles and red hair. He is big and muscular, he really likes sports. |

## Adjectives for Describing Appearances

- *Tipo de cuerpo* means "body shape"
    - *Alto/a* means "tall"
    - *Bajo/a* means "short"
    - *Corpulento/a* means "stout"
    - *Delgado/a* means "lean"
    - *Desgarbado/a* means "lanky"
    - *Esbelto/a* means "slender"
    - *Flaco/a* means "skinny"
    - *Grande* means "large"
    - *Menudo/a* means "petite"
    - *Musculoso/a* means "muscular"
- *La cara is* "the face"
    - *Barbudo/a* means "bearded"
    - *Cuadrado/a* means "square"
    - *Largo/a* means "long"
    - *Ovalado/a* means "oval"
    - *Pecoso/a* means "freckled"
    - *Redondo/a* means "round"
- *Los ojos* are "the eyes"
    - *Abierto/a* means "open"
    - *Azul* means "blue"
    - *Claro/a* means "light-colored"

- *Marrón* means "brown"
- *Negro/a* means "black"
- *Oscuro/a* means "dark"
- *Redondo/a* means "round"
- *Verde* means "green"

- *El pelo* or *el cabello* is "the hair"
  - *Abundante* means "thick"
  - *Brillante* means "shiny"
  - *Calvo/a* means "bald"
  - *Canoso/a* means "grey"
  - *Castaño/a* means "brown"
  - *Corto/a* means "short"
  - *Encrespado/a* means "frizzy"
  - *Fino/a* means "thin"
  - *Lacio/a* means "straight"
  - *Largo/a* means "long"
  - *Negro/a* means "black"
  - *Ondulado/a* means "wavy"
  - *Pelirrojo/a* means "red"
  - *Rizado/a* means "curly"
  - *Rubio/a* means "blonde"
  - *Teñido/a* means "dyed"

- *La nariz* is "the nose"
  - *Aguileño/a* means "hooked"
  - *Ancho/a* means "wide"
  - *Angosto/a* means "narrow"
  - *Recto/a* means "straight"
  - *Respingado/a* means "turned-up"
  - *Torcido/a* means "crooked"

- *La edad* is "the age"
    - *Viejo/a* means "old"
    - *Joven* means "young"
    - *Arrugado/a* means "wrinkly"
    - *De mediana edad* means "middle-aged"
    - *Juvenil* means "youthful"
    - *Entrado/a en años* means "elderly"

## Gender of Adjectives

When I gave Sarah this list of adjectives to describe people's appearance, she noticed that many had two endings, so I explained the gender of adjectives.

Adjectives are used to describe nouns, so they have to agree in gender (and number) with the noun they describe. Many nouns that end in -A are feminine, and many nouns that end in -O are masculine, and the same happens with the adjectives. For example, I said *Mi abuela Teresa es baja*, but if I was referring to a man, I would have said *Su hermano es bajo*.

Maybe you've noticed that, on the list, some adjectives have only one ending. These adjectives are invariable: they don't change depending on the gender of the noun they describe. For example, we say *Su cabello* (masculine noun) *es oscuro y abundante*, but *Su cabellera* (feminine noun) *es oscura y abundante*. As you can see, the adjective *abundante* stays invariable, while *oscura/oscuro* change depending on the gender of the noun.

Adjectives also vary depending on the number of the noun. To make an adjective plural, you just need to add -S or -ES at the end. For example: *Sus ojos son claros*.

And finally, don't forget that adjectives normally go after the noun in Spanish.

# The Human Body

To describe my family, I mentioned some parts of the body. Here we have some more:

- *El cuerpo* is "the body"
- *Los labios* are "the lips"
- *La espalda* is "the back"
- *El pie* is "the foot"
- *El dedo* is "the finger"
- *El dedo del pie* is "the toe"
- *La cabeza* is "the head"
- *El cuello* is "the neck"
- *La mano* is "the hand"
- *La pierna* is "the leg"
- *El tobillo* is "the ankle"
- *La boca* is "the mouth"
- *El diente* is "the tooth"
- *La uña* is "the nail"
- *El hombro* is the "the shoulder"
- *El brazo* is "the arm"
- *El estómago* is the "the stomach"
- *La rodilla* is "the knee"
- *El codo* is "the elbow"
- *La oreja* is "the ear"

# Possessive Adjectives and Pronouns

Possessive adjectives and pronouns are the words we use to show that something belongs to someone. Possessive adjectives go together with the noun, for example: *Esa es **mi** casa* ("That's my house"). Possessive pronouns replace the noun, for example: *La **mía** no se ve desde aquí* ("Mine is not visible from here"). Note that in Spanish, possessive pronouns and adjectives agree with what they describe (not with the person who owns the thing). And, as you can see, possessive pronouns go together with a definite article (*la*, in the example), which also needs to agree with the gender of the thing owned.

- Possessive adjectives

|  | Singular | | Plural | |
|---|---|---|---|---|
|  | *Masculine* | *Feminine* | *Masculine* | *Feminine* |
| "My" (belonging to me) | *Mi* | *Mi* | *Mis* | *Mis* |
| "Your" (belonging to someone you address as *tú*) | *Tu* | *Tu* | *Tus* | *Tus* |
| "His," "her," "its," "your" (belonging to someone you address as *usted*) | *Su* | *Su* | *Sus* | *Sus* |
| "Our" (belonging to us) | *Nuestro* | *Nuestra* | *Nuestros* | *Nuestras* |

| "Your" (belonging to people you address as *vosotros/vosotras*) | *Vuestro* | *Vuestra* | *Vuestros* | *Vuestras* |
|---|---|---|---|---|
| "Their," "your" (belonging to people you address as *ustedes*) | *Su* | *Su* | *Sus* | *Sus* |

- Possessive pronouns (together with the article)

|  | Singular | | Plural | |
|---|---|---|---|---|
|  | *Masculine* | *Feminine* | *Masculine* | *Feminine* |
| "Mine" (belonging to me) | *El mío* | *La mía* | *Los míos* | *Las mías* |
| "Yours" (belonging to someone you address as *tú*) | *El tuyo* | *La tuya* | *Los tuyos* | *Las tuyas* |

| | | | | |
|---|---|---|---|---|
| "His," "hers," "its," "yours" (belonging to someone you address as *usted*) | *El suyo* | *La suya* | *Los suyos* | *Las suyas* |
| "Ours" (belonging to us) | *El nuestro* | *La nuestra* | *Los nuestros* | *Las nuestras* |
| "Yours" (belonging to people you address as *vosotros/vosotras*) | *El vuestro* | *La vuestra* | *Los vuestros* | *Las vuestras* |
| "Theirs," "yours" (belonging to people you address as *ustedes*) | *El suyo* | *La suya* | *Los suyos* | *Las suyas* |

Some examples:

- -***Mi*** *padre vive en Barcelona, ¿****el tuyo****?* -***El mío*** *vive en Washington DC.*
- ***Sus*** *hermanas son mellizas.*
- *¿****Tus*** *padres están divorciados?* ***Los suyos*** *están casados.*
- -***Nuestras*** *familias no se conocen. ¿****Las vuestras****?* -***Las nuestras*** *se conocieron el año pasado.*

### Objective Pronouns
- Direct Object

The direct object (DO) is the person or thing that receives the action of the verb. Both in Spanish and in English, we can replace the DO with a pronoun once we've already mentioned it, for example: *Su pelo es largo, aunque siempre lo lleva recogido* ("She has long hair, but she always wears it up"). As you can see in the example, *lo* is replacing *su pelo*. Have you noticed the change in the word order? When we replace the DO for a pronoun, we put it before the verb. Also, note that the objective pronoun has to agree in gender and number with the noun that's being replaced. Take a look at this list of all the different direct object pronouns.

|  | **Masculine** | **Feminine** |
|---|---|---|
| "Me" (first person singular) | *Me* | *Me* |
| "You" (second person singular *tú*) | *Te* | *Te* |
| "Him," "her," "it" (third person singular); "you" (second person singular *usted*) | *Lo* | *La* |
| "Us" (first person plural) | *Nos* | *Nos* |
| "You" (second person plural *vosotros/vosotras*) | *Os* | *Os* |
| "Them" (third person plural); "you" (second person plural *ustedes*) | *Los* | *Las* |

Some examples:

- *Mi madre adoptó un perro. **Lo** encontró abandonado en la calle* ("My mother adopted a dog. She found it abandoned on the street").
- *La abuela de Julio **me** invitó a la cena* ("Julio's grandmother invited me for dinner").
- *Compré unas flores y se **las** llevé de regalo* ("I bought flowers and gave them to her as a present").
- Indirect Object

The indirect object (IO) is the person or thing the action is intended to benefit or harm. To distinguish it from the DO, you can ask yourself to whom the direct object is given to. Take a look at this example: *La abuela le compró a Julio un regalo* ("His grandmother bought Julio a present"), where *a present* is the DO, and *a Julio*, to whom the DO is given to, is the IO.

The IO sometimes is duplicated, like in the example above: *le* (an indirect object pronoun) also means *a Julio*. When the person or thing that receives the DO is understood from context, you can leave out the construction *a* + noun and have only the pronoun, for example. *Como era el cumpleaños de Julio, la abuela le compró un regalo*. Take a look at the list of the indirect object pronouns:

| "Me," "to me," "for me" (first person singular) | *Me* |
|---|---|
| "You," "to you," "for you" (second person singular *tú*) | *Te* |
| "Him/Her/It," "to him/her/it," "for him/her/it" (third person singular); "You," "to you," "for you" (second person singular *usted*) | *Le* |
| "Us," "for us," "to us" (first person plural) | *Nos* |

| "You," "to you," "for you" (second person plural *vosotros/vosotras*) | *Os* |
|---|---|
| "Them," to them," "for them" (third person plural); "you," "to you," "for you" (second person plural *ustedes*) | *Les* |

Some examples:

- *La abuela de Julio nos invitó a cenar, y nosotros **le** respondimos la invitación* ("Julio's grandmother invited us for dinner, and we answered the invitation").
- *La abuela de Julio **me** agradeció el regalo* ("Julio's grandmother thanked me for the present").
- *Luego de comer, todos **le** ofrecimos ayuda para levantar la mesa* ("After dinner, we all offered her our help clearing the table").

The last thing we did before the dinner party was buy a gift for the hostess. In Spain, it's common to get invited to dine at someone's house, even if you don't know them very well. A gift is not expected, but I didn't want to arrive empty-handed. Julio said that his grandmother probably had already thought of the wine and dessert that matched the dinner, so I settled for a nice flower bouquet. In the end, the dinner party was a total success.

## Exercises

1. True or false: *Abuela* means grandfather.
2. Cross the odd one out.
   a. Hermanastra   b. Prima   c. Media hermana
   d. Tío
3. True or false: *Marido* and *esposo* both mean "husband."
4. What is the Spanish word to talk about your children's female partner?
5. What is the Spanish word to talk about your partner's father?

6. True or false: *Esbelto/a*, *bajo/a* and *rizado/a* are used to describe the body shapes.
7. True or false: *Canoso/a*, *arrugado/a* and *entrado/a en años* are things you would say to describe an elder person.
8. Which of the following adjectives can be used to describe a feminine noun?
    a. Alta
    b. Celeste
    c. Abundante
    d. Respingada
9. What's the Spanish word for "mouth"?
10. Choose the odd one out.
    a. Mano
    b. Brazo
    c. Cabello
    d. Dedos.
11. True or false: Possessive articles replace the noun and are used together with a definite article.
12. With which noun do possessive pronouns and adjectives agree? With what they refer to or with the person who owns the thing?
13. Can you name the possessive adjectives equivalent to English "my"?
14. Can you name the definite article that comes before the possessive pronoun *suyos*?
15. Which definite article comes before vuestra?
    a. Los
    b. La
    c. Las
16. True or false: The direct object is the person or thing that receives the action of the verb.
17. With which characteristics of the noun does the direct object pronoun need to agree?

18. Correct the word order in the second sentence: *Tiene un coche nuevo. Compró lo hace poco.*
19. True or false: The indirect object is the person or thing the action is intended to benefit or harm.
20. Which of the following is not an indirect object pronoun?
    a. Le
    b. Les
    c. Os
    d. Las

# Chapter 7: Eating Out

Hey, there! It's Sarah. After we visited Seville and spent some days with Julio's family, we stayed in the autonomous community of Andalusia, but this time we went to Malaga, which is a coastal province on the shores of the Mediterranean. We took a train that took us from Seville to Malaga in about two hours.

Malaga is in the Costa del Sol, a region in the south of Spain with coastal towns and one of the most important tourist areas in the whole of Spain. The sun shines more than 320 days a year in this region. Amazing, right?

Here, we wanted to take advantage of the beautiful beaches to simply rest, get in the water and... eat, since Malaga has a great variety of restaurants and bars to visit.

## Eating Habits

Did you know that in Spain and Latin American countries, they have four meals a day instead of three? Well, I didn't either, and it blew my mind because we're definitely missing the best one of them all!

Just like in the United States, they have breakfast, lunch, and dinner, which are called *desayuno, almuerzo* (o simplemente, *comida*), and *cena,* respectively. And then, they have the amazing *merienda* – like a big snack in the afternoon. For this meal, you can eat cake, muffins, toast, cookies, waffles, and other snacks, and drink tea, coffee or juice, but in some places, you might also eat a sandwich.

But why do they have an extra meal? Well, in Spain, they have breakfast early in the morning and lunch at about midday, but their dinner is at around 9 p.m. or even later, which means that they are probably hungry at around 5 p.m. – and that's when they decide to have a *merienda*.

## Talking about your Favorite Food

Well, as you might have already noticed, I love food. When Julio and I were traveling from Fuengirola to Marbella (two cities in Malaga), we started talking about our favorite foods and what we wanted to eat once we had arrived. The conversation went something like this:

| • Mi comida preferida es la paella. ¿Y la tuya, Sarah? | • My favorite food is paella. And yours, Sarah? |
|---|---|
| ○ Uf, es difícil elegir. Mi comida preferida de Estados Unidos son los macarrones con queso. | ○ Ugh, it's hard to choose. My favorite food in America is macaroni and cheese. |
| • ¿Cuál es tu comida española favorita? | • What's your favorite Spanish food? |
| ○ Pues, a mí no me gustó mucho la paella. Lo que más me gustó fue la tortilla de patatas que preparamos. | ○ Well, I didn't like paella that much. What I liked the most was the potato tortilla we made. |
| • ¡Sí! Estaba muy buena. | • Yes! It was very good. |

| | |
|---|---|
| ○ ¿Y cuál es tu comida favorita de<br><br>Estados Unidos? | ○ And what's your favorite American food? |
| ● La comida que más me gusta de<br><br>Estados Unidos son las costillas con<br><br>salsa barbacoa. | ● The food I like the most in the United<br><br>States is ribs with barbecue sauce. |
| ○ Sí, ¡qué rico! Tanto hablar de comida<br><br>me dio hambre. | ○ Yeah, yummy! So much talk of food<br><br>made me hungry. |
| ● ¿Qué quieres comer hoy en Marbella? | ● What do you want to eat today in Marbella? |
| ○ No sé qué hay, ¿tú qué me recomiendas? | ○ I don't know the options, what do you recommend? |
| ● Podríamos ir a comer al restaurante<br><br>La Milla Marbella que está sobre la playa. | ● We could go and eat at La Milla<br><br>Marbella, a restaurant on the beach. |
| ○ ¿Qué hay allí? | ○ What do they serve there? |
| ● Un poco de todo, pero tienen las mejores<br><br>ostras. También tienen un gazpacho<br><br>buenísimo. | ● A little bit of everything, but they have<br><br>the best oysters. They also have an<br><br>amazing gazpacho. |

| | |
|---|---|
| ○ Ahora no puedo esperar para llegar. ¡Vayamos! | ○ Now I can't wait to get there. Let's go! |

Now, I'm going to leave you with Julio so that he can teach you everything he taught me in order to be able to have this conversation!

Hey! It's Julio again! Let's learn how to talk about food - clearly, one of our favorite topics.

To talk about your favorite food, you can use the phrase *Mi comida preferida/favorita es...* ("My favorite food is...") and then add the name of your favorite food. Simple as that!

## Expressing Likes/Dislikes

Now, let's move on to talking about our likes and dislikes. To do this, we can use different verbs depending on how much we like or dislike something. We use the verbs *encantar* or *gustar*.

*Encantar* means "to love" and can be used with people, things, and activities. *Gustar* is the one that is used the most because it is the most "neutral" option. It means "to like" and can also be used with people, things, and activities.

We use *encanta* and *gusta* with singular nouns and verbs, but *encantan* and *gustan* with plural nouns. For example, we can say *Me gusta la paella* and *Me gusta comer paella*, but *Me gustan las ostras*.

You may be wondering what the *me* at the beginning of the example sentences means. Well, unlike other verbs, these verbs need some personal pronouns that are different from the ones we've seen so far. These pronouns are called *pronombres átonos* and, just like with the personal pronouns we already know, their use depends on the person and number of the person we are talking about in the following way:

- 1st person singular: *Me encanta/gusta la paella*
- 2nd person singular: *Te encanta/gusta la paella*
- 3rd person singular: *Le encanta/gusta la paella*
- 1st person plural: *Nos encanta/gusta la paella*

- 2nd person plural: *Os encanta/gusta la paella*
- 3rd person plural: *Les encanta/gusta la paella*

Furthermore, before these personal pronouns, we can add the ones we've seen – before but preceded by *a*. This, however, is only optional.

- 1st person singular: *(A mí) me encanta/gusta la paella*
- 2nd person singular: *(A ti) te encanta/gusta la paella*
- 3rd person singular: *(A él/ella) le encanta/gusta la paella*
- 1st person plural: *(A nosotros/nosotras) nos encanta/gusta la paella*
- 2nd person plural: *(A vosotros/vosotras) os encanta/gusta la paella*
- 3rd person plural: *(A ellos/ellas) les encanta/gusta la paella*

Now, what about dislikes? Well, to say that we don't love or like something, we simply add a *no* before the *pronombre átono*. Let's see how that would look like:

- 1st person singular: *(A mí)* **no** *me encanta/gusta la paella*
- 2nd person singular: *(A ti)* **no** *te encanta/gusta la paella*
- 3rd person singular: *(A él/ella)* **no** *le encanta/gusta la paella*
- 1st person plural: *(A nosotros/nosotras)* **no** *nos encanta/gusta la paella*
- 2nd person plural: *(A vosotros/vosotras)* **no** *os encanta/gusta la paella*
- 3rd person plural: *(A ellos/ellas)* **no** *les encanta/gusta la paella*

## Comparatives and Superlatives

Well, you're already almost a pro at talking about your likes and dislikes now. But it's time to talk about comparatives and superlatives to talk about the things we like or dislike more, less, or the most.

In Spanish, we compare adjectives, nouns, and adverbs using the following formulas depending on the relationship between

the things we are comparing:
- Superiority: *más* + adjective/noun/adverb + *que*
- Inferiority: *menos* + adjective/noun/adverb + *que*
- Equality: *tan* + adjective/adverb + *como*

Of course, you should always remember that when we compare adjectives, they should always agree in gender and number with the element we are comparing.

For example, we can say *La paella es más sabrosa que la tortilla* ("*Paella* is tastier than *tortilla*"), *La paella es menos sabrosa que la tortilla* ("*Paella* is less tasty than *tortilla*"), and *La paella es tan sabrosa como la tortilla* ("*Paella* is as tasty as *tortilla*").

The only exception to the use of *más* and *menos* are the adjectives *bueno, malo, grande* (when it refers to age), and *pequeño* (when it refers to age), which in the comparative form turn into *mejor, peor, mayor,* and *menor* respectively, instead of *más bueno, más malo, más grande* and *más pequeño*.

If we want to compare nouns with a relationship of equality, we don't use *tan*, but *tanto, tanta, tantos,* or *tantas,* depending on the gender and number of the nouns we are comparing. For example: *No como tantas ostras* como *patatas fritas.*

We can also compare verbs using the following formula:
- verb + *más que*
- verb + *menos* que
- verb + *tanto* como

For example: *Yo como más que Sarah ("I eat more than Sarah"), Yo como menos que Sarah ("I eat less than Sarah"),* and *Yo como tanto como Sarah ("I eat the same as Sarah").*

Now let's move on to the superlatives. To say that something is at the top or bottom of its class, we use the following formula:
- *el/la/los/las* + *más* + adjective (+ *de* + group)
- *el/la/los/las* + *menos* + adjective (+ *de* + group)

For example: *Esta es la paella más rica del mundo* ("This is the tastiest paella in the world"), or *La paella de este lugar es la menos rica de todas* ("The paella of the place is the one I liked *the least")*.

For this formula, remember that the article choice depends on the gender and the number of the thing we are talking about.

Here's an example sentence to sum up everything we've seen on likes, dislikes, comparatives, and superlatives:

- Me gusta más la paella que la tortilla, pero lo más rico de todo son las ostras ("I like paella more than tortilla, but oysters are what I like the most ").

## Types of Meals

Sarah has already told you about the four meals we eat in Spain, but now it's time to see what we might eat at a restaurant for lunch and dinner.

In Spain, the appetizer eaten before the main course is generally called *primeros*, the main course is called *segundos*, and the dessert is called *postre*.

*De primero* we can have things like *gazpacho, lentejas,* and *tortilla de patatas*. *De segundo* we can have things like *paella, merluza,* and *lomo*. And *de postre* we can have things like *arroz con leche, fruta,* and *helado*.

## Ordering Food

Now it's time to learn how to order some food. Here is a list of phrases that would be useful at a restaurant:

- *Una mesa para dos, por favor* ("A table for two, please")
- *¿Cuál es el menú del día?* ("What's today's special?")
- *¿Qué plato me recomienda?* ("What dish do you recommend?")
- *¿Qué trae este plato?* ("What does this dish have?")
- *Soy alérgico a las nueces* ("I'm allergic to nuts")
- *Yo quiero un gazpacho* ("I'd like a *gazpacho*")
- *¿Me podría traer la cuenta, por favor?* ("Could you bring the bill, please?")

We finally went to La Milla Marbella. It was a great sunny day, and the lounge chairs of the restaurant were excellent for enjoying the sun and the view. Here's the conversation we had with the waiter:

| | |
|---|---|
| ■ ¡Buenos días! ¿Serán ustedes dos? | ■ Good morning! Is it the two of you? |
| ● Hola, sí, una mesa para dos, por favor. | ● Hello, yes, table for two, please. |
| ■ Claro, por aquí. | ■ Sure, over here. |
| (...) | (...) |
| ■ Aquí les dejo el menú. | ■ Here's the menu. |
| ○ Muchas gracias. | ○ Thank you very much. |
| (...) | (...) |
| ■ ¿Ya saben qué van a pedir? | ■ Do you know what are you going to have? |
| ● Sí. De primero, yo quiero un gazpacho y de segundo el solomillo. | ● Yes. As a starter, I want a gazpacho, and as a main, the sirloin. |
| ■ Genial, ¿y usted? | ■ Great, and for you? |
| ○ Yo de primero quiero unas ostras y de segundo el lomo. | ○ As a starter I want some oysters, and as a main, the loin. |
| ■ Muy bien. ¿Qué desean | ■ Very good. What would you |

| | |
|---|---|
| para beber? | like to drink? |
| ● Yo, un agua mineral. | ● For me, a mineral water. |
| ○ Y yo una cerveza. | ○ And I'll have a beer. |
| ■ Perfecto, en un momento lo traigo. | ■ Perfect, I'll get it in a minute. |
| ● Gracias. | ● Thank you. |
| (...) | (...) |
| ○ Disculpe, ¿podemos ver el menú de postres? | ○ Excuse me, can we see the dessert menu? |
| ■ Sí, claro. Aquí tienen. | ■ Yes, of course. Here you are. |
| ● Gracias. | ● Thank you. |
| (...) | (...) |
| ■ ¿Les apetece algún postre? | ■ Would you like something for dessert? |
| ○ Sí. Queremos un arroz con leche para compartir. | ○ Yes. We want milk with rice to share. |
| ● ¿Tiene nueces? Yo soy alérgica. | ● Does it have any nuts? I'm allergic. |
| ■ No, no tiene nueces. | ■ No, it doesn't have nuts. |

| | |
|---|---|
| ● Perfecto. Gracias | ● Perfect. Thanks. |
| ■ Claro, ya os lo pongo. | ■ Sure, I'll be right back. |
| ○ Gracias. | ○ Thank you. |
| (...) | (...) |
| ● Disculpe, ¿podría traer la cuenta, por favor? | ● Excuse, could you bring the bill, please? |
| ■ Claro. ¿Qué tal ha estado la comida? | ■ Of course. How was your meal? |
| ● Todo ha estado riquísimo. | ● Everything has been delicious. |
| ■ Me alegro. Ya os traigo la cuenta. | ■ Happy to hear. I'll bring you the check. |

## Adverbs of Mode

When we talked about comparatives and superlatives, we also discussed how to compare adverbs. We've already defined them, talked about adverbs of place and quantity, and now it's time to get to some adverbs of mode so that you can use them to compare. Here are some adverbs:

- *Bien* means "well"
- *Mal* means "bad"
- *Mejor* means "better" (remember that it is one of the exceptions of the comparative form with *más*)
- *Peor* means "worse" (remember that it is one of the exceptions of the comparative form with *más*)
- *despacio* means "slowly"

- *rápido* means "fast"
- *deprisa* means "fast"

And there are also other adverbs of mode in Spanish, which are formed with the ending *-mente* and are similar to the English adverbs ending in "-ly." These adverbs are formed with the feminine singular form of adjectives plus the ending *-mente*. Furthermore, these adverbs are an exception to the accent rules because if the adjective has a *tilde*, then the adverb formed with that adjective will maintain that *tilde*.

Here are a few examples of these adverbs:
- *rápidamente* means "fastly"
- *solamente* means "only"
- *difícilmente* means "hardly"
- *claramente* means "clearly"
- *comúnmente* means "commonly"
- *últimamente* means "lately"
- *felizmente* means "happily"
- *tímidamente* means "timidly"
- *simplemente* means "simply"

## Conjunctions

Since we're starting to get into more complex sentences, I believe it's high time we see some conjunctions to connect sentences. Conjunctions are words used to join two or more elements or sentences. We've already talked a bit about *y* and *pero*, which mean *and* or *but*, respectively. Now, let's see some other conjunctions:

- *O*: it means "or"
- *Ni*: it means "neither" or "nor" and is used when we want to add something negative
- *Porque*: it means "because"
- *Aunque*: it means "although"
- *Sin embargo*: it means "however"
- *Como*: it means "as," "since" or "like"

- *Aún*: it means "yet"
- *A pesar de que*: it means "In spite of"
- *Mientras*: it means "while"
- *Cuando*: it means "when"
- *Si*: it means "if"

# Exercises

1. True or False: Desayuno and Merienda are the same in Spanish
2. How do you say "My favorite food is spaghetti" in Spanish?
3. True or False: the verbs *encantar* and *gustar* mean exactly the same.
4. To talk about our likes and dislikes, which of these two options do we use with verbs?
    a. encanta
    b. encantan
5. Which of these is the correct form of saying "I like oysters" in Spanish?
    a. Gusta me las ostras
    b. Me gustan las ostras
    c. A mí gustan las ostras
6. And which of these is the correct form of saying "They like paella" in Spanish?
    a. Ellos gustan paella
    b. A ellos gustan paella
    c. A ellos les gusta la paella
7. Which of these is the correct form of saying "He doesn't like eating pasta" in Spanish?
    a. No te gustan comer pasta
    b. No le gusta comer pasta
    c. No gustan comer pasta

8. How do we say "This shirt is smaller than that one" in Spanish?
    a. Esta camisa es más pequeña que aquella
    b. Esta camisa es pequeña que aquella
    c. Está camisa es pequeña como aquella
9. How do we say "I like the table less than the chair" in Spanish?
    a. Me gusta menos la mesa que la silla
    b. Me gusta mejor la mesa que la silla
    c. Me gusta menos la silla que la mesa
10. How do we say "Érica is older than Carlos" in Spanish?
    a. Érica es más grande que Carlos
    b. Érica es más mayor que Carlos
    c. Érica es mayor que Carlos
11. How do we say "This book is worse than the previous one" in Spanish?
    a. Este libro es más malo que el anterior
    b. Este libro es más mejor que el anterior
    c. Este libro es peor que el anterior
12. True or False: In Spain, they call *primeros* to the main course.
13. How do you ask what is in a dish in Spanish?
    a. ¿Cuál es el menú del día?
    b. ¿Qué trae este plato?
    c. ¿Qué plato me recomienda?
14. How would you order a pizza?
15. How would you ask for the bill?
16. What is the Spanish adverb to say "well"?
17. How are adverbs ending in *-mente* formed?
    a. the feminine form of the adjective + *-mente*
    b. the masculine form of the adjective + *-mente*
    c. the plural form of the adjective + *-mente*

18. What does the conjunction *o* mean?
19. To give a reason, which of these conjunctions would we use?
    - *a.* y
    - *b.* como
    - *c.* aún
    - *d.* porque
20. What does the conjunction *si* mean? Is it the same as *sí*?

# Chapter 8: Booking Tickets

For one of our last destinations before returning to the US, I wanted to take Sarah to the city with the most Muslim heritage in Spain. Granada was under a Muslim government for 781 years (from 711 to 1492), more than any other Spanish territory. The Alhambra, an Islamic citadel and palace, is one of the most visited monuments in Spain and one of the best-preserved examples of Islamic architecture in the world. It's an amazing place, with many sites worth visiting, like the Nasrid Palaces, the Generalife, the Alcazaba, the Palace of Carlos V, and the Bath of the Mosque.

Besides its amazing architecture and heritage, Granada is famous for having the Mediterranean Sea and the Sierra Nevada mountain range, only 45 minutes away. This means that, on some days, you can go skiing or snowboarding in the morning and you can swim in the ocean in the afternoon. This also means that Granada can get cold in the winter, with temperatures dropping to around 1 °C (34 °F) during the night, and it's warm in the summer months, with temperatures reaching over 40 °C (104 °F).

# Booking a Ticket

Julio and I took a bus from Málaga to Granada. It was a two-hour bus ride, and we used that time to book the tickets to visit Alhambra. Since it's a historical site, they limit the number of people that can visit it at the same time. As always, Julio used it as an excuse to teach me some more Spanish.

First of all, we entered the official Alhambra website, and checked the opening and closing times. This is what we found:

| 16 de marzo a 15 de octubre | March 16th to October 15th |
|---|---|
| Mañana: de 8:30 a 12:00 | Morning: from 8:30 to 12:00 a.m. |
| Tarde: de 2:00 a 8:00 | Afternoon: from 2:00 to 8:00 p.m. |
| Noche: de 10:00 a 11:30 (de martes a sábado) | Night: from 10:00 to 11:30 p.m. (Tuesday to Saturday) |
| 16 de octubre a 15 de marzo | October 16th to March 15th |
| Mañana: de 8:30 a 12:00 | Morning: from 8:30 to 12:00 a.m. |
| Tarde: de 2:00 a 6:00 | Afternoon: from 2:00 to 6:00 p.m |
| Noche: de 8:00 a 9:30 (viernes y sábados) | Night: from 8:00 to 9:30 p.m. (Fridays and Saturdays) |

With this information, we went to the booking section to see what was available. This is the conversation that we had:

| | |
|---|---|
| ○ Como estamos en verano, la Alhambra está abierta desde las ocho y media de la mañana hasta las ocho de la noche. Y después abre de nuevo a la noche, de diez a once y media. ¿Te gustaría hacer una visita nocturna? | ○ As it's the summer, the Alhambra is open from eight thirty in the morning until eight in the evening. And then it opens again at night, from ten to eleven thirty. Would you like to make an evening visit? |
| ● No, prefiero hacer la visita de día, para poder ver mejor. | ● No, I prefer to visit it during the day, so I can see better. |
| ○ Sí, estoy de acuerdo. Y creo que lo mejor es ir temprano a la mañana, para evitar el calor, ¿no? | ○ Yes, I agree. And I think it's best to go early in the morning, to avoid the heat, right? |
| ● Vale, temprano a la mañana o a última hora de la tarde, cuando baja el sol. | ● Okay, early in the morning or late in the afternoon, when the sun goes down. |
| ○ Lo bueno de ir a la tarde es que no tenemos que madrugar. | ○ The good thing about going in the afternoon is that we don't have to get up early. |
| ● Sí, después de tanto tiempo viajando ya estoy algo cansada. | ● Yeah, after all this time traveling, I'm a little tired. |
| ○ Bien, déjame fijarme si hay entradas disponibles para mañana a la tarde. ¿A qué hora quieres ir, más o menos? | ○ Okay, let me see if there are any tickets available for tomorrow afternoon. Around what time do you want to go? |

| | |
|---|---|
| ● ¿Qué te parece alrededor de las cinco de la tarde? Así tendremos tiempo de ver todo antes de que cierre. | ● What do you think about five o'clock in the afternoon? Then we'll have time to see everything before it closes. |
| ○ Perfecto. | ○ Perfect. |

Once we decided when we wanted to go, Julio tried to book the tickets online, but the web page wasn't working. So he had this great idea: I was going to call the booking office to buy the tickets over the phone. I wasn't thrilled, but I did it anyways, and this is the dialogue I had with the phone operator:

| | |
|---|---|
| ○ Buenas tardes, se comunicó con la boletería de la Alhambra, ¿en qué puedo ayudarle? | ○ Good afternoon, you've reached the Alhambra ticket office, how can I help you? |
| ● Buenas tardes, quería comprar entradas para visitar el complejo. | ● Good afternoon, I wanted to buy tickets to visit the complex. |
| ○ Para comprar entradas deberá ingresar a nuestra página web. | ○ To buy tickets you will need to access our website. |
| ● Lo sé, pero la página web no anda en este momento. ¿Podrá venderme las entradas por teléfono? | ● I know, but the website isn't up and running right now. Can you sell me the tickets over the phone? |
| ○ Bien, como la página no anda, podemos hacer una excepción. ¿Cuántas personas visitarán el complejo? | ○ Okay, since the page isn't working, we can make an exception. How many people will visit the complex? |
| ● Seremos dos personas. | ● We'll be two people. |

| | |
|---|---|
| ○ ¿Dos adultos? | ○ Two adults? |
| • Sí. | • Yes. |
| ○ ¿Cuándo os gustaría venir? | ○ When would you like to come? |
| • Vamos mañana, si quedan entradas. Idealmente, a eso de las cinco de la tarde. | • We'll go tomorrow, if there are tickets available. Ideally, around five in the afternoon. |
| ○ Muy bien, hoy es vuestro día de suerte, porque justo quedan dos entradas de adultos para mañana, martes 15, a las 17:00 hs. | ○ Very good, today is your lucky day, because there are just two adult tickets left for tomorrow, Tuesday 15, at 17:00 hs. |
| • ¡Qué bien! | • Wonderful! |

After that, I gave her my credit card details, and she emailed me the tickets.

## Telling the Time/Date

Sarah did a great job booking the tickets over the phone. After that, we talked a bit more about telling the time and date in Spanish.

To tell the time, we use the verb *ser* conjugated in the third person plural of the present tense (that is, *son*). Next, we add the feminine definite article *las*, and finally, we say the part of the day:

- *De la mañana* means "in the morning" or "a.m."
- *De la tarde* means "in the afternoon" or "p.m." We use this after midday.
- *De la noche* means "at night" or "p.m." We use this when it's dark outside.
- *Son las cinco de la tarde* means "It's five p.m."

- *Son las dos de la mañana* means "It's two a.m."
- *Son las nueve de la noche* means "It's nine p.m."

For 1 a.m. and 1 p.m., we use the singular conjugation of the third person in the present tense of the verb *ser* (that is, *es*) followed by the feminine definite article *la* and the part of the day:

- *Es la una de la mañana* means "It's one a.m." We can also say *madrugada* instead of *mañana* for the early hours of the morning: *Es la una de la madrugada*.
- *Es la una de la tarde* means "It's one p.m." Around noon, you can also say *mediodía*. *Son las doce del mediodía* means "It's 12 a.m." or "It's midday."

These are some useful phrases to ask for the time:

- *¿Qué hora es?*, which means "What time is it?"
- *¿Tienes hora?*, which means "Do you have the time?"
- *¿Puedes decirme la hora?*, which means "Can you tell me what's the time?"

Telling the date is quite simple. As a rule of thumb, you can use this formula: Day of the week + number + *de* + month of the year + *de* + year. For example:

*Martes tres de marzo de 2020* means "Tuesday, March 3rd, 2020."

To say the date in English, we normally use ordinals ("third," "fifth"). However, in Spanish, we use the cardinals (*tres, cinco*), that is, just the number, except for the first day of the month, in which case we use *primero* ("first"):

*Hoy es primero de enero* ("Today is January, 1st.")

To be able to say the date correctly, let's go over the days of the week and the months of the year:

*Los días de la semana*

- *Lunes* means "Monday"
- *Martes* means "Tuesday"
- *Miércoles* means "Wednesday"
- *Jueves* means "Thursday"
- *Viernes* means "Friday"

- *Sábado* means "Saturday"
- *Domingo* means "Sunday"

*Los meses del año*
- *Enero* means "January"
- *Febrero* means "February"
- *Marzo* means "March"
- *Abril* means "April"
- *Mayo* means "May"
- *Junio* means "June"
- *Julio* means "July"
- *Agosto* means "August"
- *Septiembre* means "September"
- *Octubre* means "October"
- *Noviembre* means "November"
- *Diciembre* means "December"

Another thing worth noting is that, in Spanish, the names of days and months are not capitalized as in English:

- *Hoy es viernes 27 de mayo* ("Today is Friday, May 27th.")
- *Ayer fue jueves 26 de mayo* ("Yesterday was Thursday, May 26th.")
- *Mañana será sábado 28 de mayo* ("Tomorrow will be Saturday, May 28th.")

**Ordinal Numbers**

In the previous section, we mentioned cardinal and ordinal numbers. Cardinal numbers are the ones we saw in the first chapter: *uno, dos, tres,* and so on and so forth. You already know them. So now we'll focus on ordinal numbers or ordinals, for example, *primero*, which means "first." We can think of them as adjectives made from numbers; like many other Spanish adjectives, they change according to the gender and number of the noun they are modifying. Let's see some examples:

- *Mi cuarta hija irá a la universidad el año que viene* ("My fourth daughter will go to college next year")
- *Los primos segundos de Julio vendrá de visita desde Valencia* ("Julio's second cousins will come to visit from Valencia")

Here's a list of the most common ordinal numbers:

- *Primero, primera, primeros, primeras* mean "first"
- *Segundo* and its variants mean "second"
- *Tercero* and its variants mean "third"
- *Cuarto* and its variants mean "fourth"
- *Quinto* and its variants mean "fifth"
- *Sexto* and its variants mean "sixth"
- *Séptimo* and its variants mean "seventh"
- *Octavo* and its variants mean "eighth"
- *Noveno* and its variants mean "nineth"
- *Décimo* and its variants mean "tenth"

Another difference between English and Spanish regarding ordinals is that in Spanish, they are less common than in English. We tend to use just the number, especially in oral speech. So, it's common to modify a sentence so that the ordinal is not used (this is especially true for numbers above ten). For example, while in English we talk about "the 21st century," in Spanish, we call it *el siglo XXI* (centuries are normally written in Roman numerals) and not *el siglo vigésimo primero*.

The last thing you need to know about Spanish ordinals is that when *primero* ("first") and *tercero* ("third") are placed before a singular masculine noun, they are shortened to *primer* and *tercer*, respectively. Take a look at these examples:

- *El primer día de clases, los alumnos ingresarán una hora más tarde* ("On the first day of school, students will start an hour later")
- *Guardo los cubiertos en el tercer cajón de la cocina* ("I keep the cutlery in the kitchen third drawer")

## Unisex Nouns

By now, you already know that Spanish nouns have gender. Some are always masculine, like *el árbol* ("the tree"), others are always feminine, like *la luz* ("the light"), and there's a third group, normally those referring to people, which change their ending according to whom we are talking about. For example, we say *el enfermero* ("the male nurse") and *la enfermera* ("the female nurse"). However, as always, there are exceptions. Here's a list of nouns that stay the same regardless of who we are talking about. In these cases, we express the gender of the person through the article preceding it:

| Masculine | Feminine | Translation |
|---|---|---|
| el artista | la artista | the artist |
| el astronauta | la astronauta | the astronaut |
| el atleta | la atleta | the athlete |
| el comentarista | la comentarista | the commentator |
| el dentista | la dentista | the dentist |
| el estudiante | la estudiante | the student |
| el modelo | la modelo | the model |
| el oficinista | la oficinista | the office worker |
| el periodista | la periodista | the journalist |
| el policía | la policía | the police officer |

## Talking About Future Plans

In this chapter, we spoke about the future. Like in English, we have several ways to refer to the future in Spanish.

We can use the present:

- ***Vamos** mañana, si quedan entradas* ("We are going tomorrow, if there are tickets left")
- *La semana que viene **volvemos** a Estados Unidos* ("Next week we get back to the States")

Another option is using the present tense of the verb *ir* followed by the preposition *a* and an infinitive. This is similar to the English "going to" followed by an infinitive:

- *Mañana a las cinco **vamos a visitar** la Alhambra* ("Tomorrow at 5 we are going to visit the Alhambra")
- *Después de unas semanas de vacaciones, pronto **van a volver** a casa* ("After some weeks on holidays, they are going to return home")

A third way of talking about the future is using the future tense.

## Future Tenses for Regular / Irregular Verbs

This is the tense we use to talk about things that will happen or that will be true in the future:

- ***Tendremos** tiempo de ver todo antes de que cierre* ("We'll have time to see everything before it's closed")
- *Para comprar entras **deberá** ingresar a nuestra página web* ("To buy tickets you'll need to go to our web page")
- *¿Cuántas personas **visitarán** el complejo?* ("How many people will be visiting the complex?")

As with the other tenses, for regular verbs, we form the future tense by changing the ending. Let's take a look at the conjugation of the three model verbs: *amar*, *temer*, and *partir*.

|  | AMAR | TEMER | PARTIR |
|---|---|---|---|
| yo | amaré | temeré | partiré |
| tú | amarás | temerás | partirás |
| él / ella | amará | temerá | partirá |
| nosotros / nosotras | amaremos | temeremos | partiremos |
| vosotros / vosotras | amaréis | temeréis | partiréis |
| ellos / ellas / ustedes | amarán | temerán | partirán |

Finally, let's also take a look at the future form of some irregular verbs:

|  | DECIR | HACER | HABER | PONER | TENER | QUERER |
|---|---|---|---|---|---|---|
| yo | diré | haré | habré | pondré | tendré | querré |
| tú | dirás | harás | habrás | pondrás | tendrás | querrás |
| él / ella | dirá | hará | habrá | pondrá | tendrá | querrá |
| nosotros / nosotras | diremos | haremos | habremos | pondremos | tendremos | querremos |
| vosotros / vosotras | diréis | haréis | habréis | pondréis | tendréis | querréis |
| ellos / ellas / ustedes | dirán | harán | habrán | pondrán | tendrán | querrán |

# Choosing a Movie

After visiting the Alhambra, we had some *tapas*: small plates of food served as a snack alongside beer or wine. Luckily, Granada is one of the places in Spain where they still serve them for free with each drink you order. We were exhausted after walking all day, so we decided to watch a movie in our hotel room. Choosing the right one wasn't easy! This is the conversation I had with Julio:

| | |
|---|---|
| ○ Quizás deberíamos ver una película española, ¿o no? Así practicas. | ○ Maybe we should watch a Spanish movie, right? So you can practice. |
| ● Sí, es una buena idea. Pero voy a tener que prestar mucha atención y estoy demasiado cansada. | ● Yes, that's a good idea. But I'm going to have to pay attention and I'm too tired. |
| ○ Tienes razón, yo también estoy cansado. ¿Qué te parece si vemos una película española con subtítulos? | ○ You're right, I'm tired too. What do you say we watch a Spanish movie with subtitles? |
| ● ¡Buena idea! Me gustaría ver la última de Almodóvar, que todavía no la he visto. | ● Good idea! I'd like to see Almodóvar's last one, which I haven't seen yet. |
| ○ Yo tampoco la he visto. ¿Esa es la película en la que Penélope Cruz hace de una madre bondadosa y trabajadora, con un marido miserable y borracho? | ○ I haven't seen her either. Is that the movie in which Penelope Cruz plays a kind and hardworking mother, with a miserable and drunk husband? |
| ● ¡No, Julio! Esa es Volver, es del 2006. | ● No, Julio! That's "Volver," it's from 2006. In this one, Penelope Cruz plays as a |

| | |
|---|---|
| En esta Penélope Cruz hace de madre soltera. Es una mujer determinada que se hace amiga de una joven un poco abandonada por sus propios padres. | single mother. She's a determined woman who befriends a young woman abandoned by her own parents. |
| ○ Parece interesante. Vale, veámosla. | ○ Sounds interesting. Okay, let's watch it. |

## Adverbs of Affirmation/Negation/Doubt

In the previous dialogue, Sarah and I used some adverbs to express affirmation, negation, and doubt. Here's a list of the ones we used and some others:

Affirmation:
- *Sí* means "yes"
- *Claro* and *por supuesto* mean "of course"
- *En efecto* means "indeed"
- *Verdaderamente* means "truly"
- *Cierto* means "true"
- *También* means "too"

Negation:
- *En absoluto* means "not at all"
- *Jamás* and *nunca* mean "never"
- *Tampoco* means "neither"
- *Ni* means "nor"

Doubt:
- *Quizá(s)*, *a lo mejor*, and *tal vez* mean "perhaps," "maybe"
- *Posiblemente* means "possibly"
- *Probablemente* means "probably"
- *Seguramente* means "surely"

## Adjectives for Describing People's Personality

Trying to decide which movie to watch, we used some adjectives to describe the character's personalities. Here you have a list of some other Spanish personality adjectives to describe people:

- *Afectivo* means "affectionate"
- *Bondadoso* means "good-natured"
- *Caprichoso* means "whimsical"
- *Cobarde* means "cowardly"
- *Crédulo* means "gullible"
- *Culto* means "cultured"
- *Desgraciado* means "miserable"
- *Despistado* means "absent-minded"
- *Digno* means "dignified"
- *Egoísta* means "selfish"
- *Encantador* means "charming"
- *Engañoso* means "deceitful"
- *Exigente* means "demanding"
- *Fiel* means "loyal"
- *Gracioso* means "funny"
- *Hablador* means "talkative"
- *Humilde* means "humble"
- *Listo* means "clever"
- *Mimado* means "spoiled"
- *Orgulloso* means "prideful"
- *Presumido* means "smug"
- *Reservado* means "reserved"
- *Seguro* means "confident"
- *Sensato* means "sensible"
- *Sensible* means "sensitive"
- *Sincero* means "sincere"
- *Torpe* means "clumsy"

- *Trabajador* means "hard-working"
- *Tranquilo* means "calm"
- *Valiente* means "courageous"

**Exercises**

1. True or False: *¿Qué hora es?*, *¿Tienes hora?*, and *¿Puedes decirme la hora?* are three ways of asking what's the time.
2. Which of the following means "in the morning"?
    a. *de la noche*
    b. *de la tarde*
    c. *de la mañana*
3. Which of the following mean "in the afternoon"?
    a. *de la noche*
    b. *de la tarde*
    c. *de la mañana*
4. Which of the following mean "at night"?
    a. *de la noche*
    b. *de la tarde*
    c. *de la mañana*
5. How would you say "It's eight a.m."?
6. Choose the right option for saying "It's one a.m."
    a. *Son la una de la mañana*
    b. *Es la una de la mañana*
7. ¿What's the word for "noon"?
8. Can you list the days of the week in Spanish?
9. And now, can you list the month of the year in Spanish?
10. *Hoy es viernes 27 de mayo* means "Today is Friday, May 27th." Can you say the date on which you are reading this in Spanish?
11. Choose the correct ordinal for the cardinal number *cinco*.
    a. *Segundo*

b. *Quinto*

c. *Décimo*

12. True or false: In Spanish, ordinal numbers above ten are very frequent.
13. True or false: Unisex nouns are the ones that stay the same regardless of the gender of the person we are referring to.
14. Which of the following is used to talk about the future in Spanish?
    a. The present tense
    b. *ir* + *a* + infinitive
    c. The future
    d. All of the above
15. Can you conjugate the regular verb *gustar* in the future with the pronouns *yo, tú, él, nosotros, vosotros,* and *ellos*?
16. Can you conjugate the regular verb *leer* in the future with the pronouns *yo, tú, ella, nosotras, vosotras,* and *ellas*?
17. Choose the odd one out:
    a. *Tal vez*   b. *Quizá*
    c. *En efecto*
    d. *A lo mejor*
18. True or false: *Sensible* means "sensible."
19. How would you describe someone who is very selfish?
20. Choose a movie that you like and watch. Afterward, complete this chart with the information about the main character:

    Nombre:

    Edad:

    Características positivas:

    Características negativas:

# Chapter 9:
# Talking About Your Past

Hi! It's Sarah here again. We've come to our last stop on this trip: the beautiful city of Madrid.

Julio and his family used to live here when he was young. He still has some friends from school here, and they organized a meet-up to see him. I was lucky enough to go along with him. They spent a lot of time reminiscing about their past, and they got up to date with their current lives and careers.

Everybody was friendly, and I had a great time. Plus, I got to listen to many conversations using the past and talking about jobs. Here is one of the conversations Julio had with his friend Fernanda.

| • ¿Recuerdas cuando caminábamos hasta el lago de la Casa de Campo? | • Remember when we walked to the l ake at Casa de Campo? |
|---|---|
| ○ Claro que lo recuerdo. Nos caímos al lago en pleno invierno. Pasamos mucho frío. | ○ Of course I remember. We fell into the lake in the middle of winter. We were so cold. |

| | |
|---|---|
| ● ¡Sí! ¿Cómo olvidarlo? Fuimos corriendo a nuestras casas a cambiarnos y abrigarnos. | ● Yes! How could I forget? We ran to our houses to change and warm up. |
| ○ Pero después nos reunimos en tu casa para comer una pizza. | ○ But then we met at your house for pizza. |
| ● Cierto, ¡Alguien comió casi una pizza entera! | ● Right, someone ate almost a whole pizza! |
| ○ ¡Cierto! Ese fue Juan. Ahora es doctor y vive en Valencia ¿sabías? | ○ True! That was Juan. Now he's a doctor and lives in Valencia, did you know? |
| ● No lo sabía. Oí que se casó, ¿verdad? | ● I didn't know. I heard he got married, didn't he? |
| ○ Sí, con Sandra. Tienen dos hijas preciosas. | ○ Yeah, with Sandra. They have two beautiful daughters. |
| ● Guau... ¿Y tú? ¿A qué te dedicas estos días? | ● Wow... What about you? What do you do these days? |
| ○ Bueno, este año renuncié a mi trabajo y comencé una empresa de arquitectura. ¿Y tú? | ○ Well, this year I quit my job and started an architecture firm. And you? |
| ● Como sabes, ahora vivo en Estados Unidos. Allí doy clases de español en escuelas. | ● As you know, I live in the United States now. There, I teach Spanish in schools. |
| ○ ¿Y te gusta la vida allí? | ○ And do you like your life there? |

| | |
|---|---|
| • Sí, me encanta. Por suerte, el clima de Atlanta es muy parecido al clima de aquí, así que no tuve que acostumbrarme a temperaturas más bajas o más altas. | • Yeah, I love it. Fortunately, Atlanta's weather is very similar to the weather here, so I didn't have to get used to lower or higher temperatures. |
| ○ ¡Qué bueno! ¿Hace cuánto que vives allí? | ○ That's good! How long have you been living there? |
| • En septiembre serán cuatro años. | • In September it will be four years. |

## Seasons

Hey! It's Julio here. Let's talk a bit about seasons since it came up in my conversation with Fernanda, and I realized that you probably don't know them.

The *estaciones* ("seasons") are:

- *verano,* which means "summer," the season we're now.
- *otoño,* which means "fall."
- *invierno,* which means "winter," the season in which my friends and I fall into the lake.
- *primavera,* which means "spring."

You should remember that in Spain, the seasons are simultaneous with the United States or England. However, in many Latin American countries, the opposite happens.

What do I mean? Well, in countries like Argentina, Bolivia, Chile, and Perú, which are in the southern hemisphere, the seasons are opposite of the ones in Spain, England, and the United States. There, it is summer, when in the northern hemisphere, it's winter. Conversely, it's winter in the southern hemisphere when it's summer in the northern hemisphere.

# Talking about Past Events: the *Pretérito Perfecto Simple*

Let's see one of the tenses we use to talk about past events. In Spanish, we use the *pretérito perfecto simple* to talk about events that started and finished in the past and have no connection with the present. For example, once we get back to Atlanta, we will be able to say: *Sarah y yo fuimos a España* ("Sarah and I went to Spain").

An example of the *pretérito perfecto simple* in the conversation I had with Fernanda would be the part where we talk about the one time we all fell in the lake. This is because it was a single event that happened in the past and had no relation to the time of our conversation.

Now, let's see the conjugation of this tense.

Here is the conjugation of *amar, temer,* and *partir,* three regular verbs that you can use as models to conjugate other regular verbs ending in *-ar, -er,* and *-ir.*

|  | **AMAR** | **TEMER** | **PARTIR** |
|---|---|---|---|
| yo | amé | temí | partí |
| tú | amaste | temiste | partiste |
| él / ella | amó | temió | partió |
| nosotros / nosotras | amamos | temimos | partimos |
| vosotros / vosotras | amasteis | temisteis | partisteis |
| ellos / ellas / ustedes | amaron | temieron | partieron |

Note that the conjugation of regular verbs ending in *-er* and *-ir* is the same, making it easier to remember!

Now is a good time to mention that the *pretérito perfecto simple* is the Spanish tense with more irregular verbs. Here are some of the most used irregular verbs:

|  | SER/IR | ESTAR | HABER | TRAER | TENER |
|---|---|---|---|---|---|
| yo | fui | estuve | hube | traje | tuve |
| tú | fuiste | estuviste | hubiste | trajiste | tuviste |
| él / ella | fue | estuvo | hubo | trajo | tuvo |
| nosotros / nosotras | fuimos | estuvimos | hubimos | trajimos | tuvimos |
| vosotros / vosotras | fuisteis | estuvisteis | hubisteis | trajisteis | tuvisteis |
| ellos / ellas / ustedes | fueron | estuvieron | hubieron | trajeron | tuvieron |

The verbs *ser* and *ir* are in the same column because their *pretérito perfecto simple* conjugation is the same. Weird right? But also true. We know which one we're talking about, depending on the context.

## Talking about childhood habits: *the préterito imperfecto*

The English simple past can be translated into Spanish as two tenses, the *pretérito perfecto simple*, which we've talked about in the previous section, and the *pretérito imperfecto*, which is the one we're going to talk about now. Why two tenses? Well, as we've mentioned, the *pretérito perfecto simple* is used to talk about single events in the past, which is something for which we'd use the present simple. While the *pretérito imperfecto* is used to talk about habits or actions that used to happen in the past and have no temporal limits, which is something for which we'd also use the present simple in English.

For example, in my conversation with Fernanda, she mentioned *¿Recuerdas cuando caminábamos hasta el lago?* In this sentence, *caminábamos hasta el lago* is in the *pretérito imperfecto* tense because it's something that we used to do a lot when we were kids.

Let's see the regular conjugations of this tense:

|  | **AMAR** | **TEMER** | **PARTIR** |
| --- | --- | --- | --- |
| yo | amaba | temía | partía |
| tú | amabas | temías | partías |
| él / ella / usted | amaba | temía | partía |
| nosotros / nosotras | amábamos | temíamos | partíamos |
| vosotros / vosotras | amabais | temíais | partíais |
| ellos / ellas / ustedes | amaban | temían | partían |

In this tense, the conjugations of the regular verbs ending in *-er* and *-ir* are also the same. Moreover, the conjugations of the first- and third-person singular are also the same for every verb!

Now, let's see the conjugations of some irregular verbs:

|  | **SER** | **VER** | **IR** |
| --- | --- | --- | --- |
| yo | era | veía | iba |
| tú | eras | veías | ibas |

| él / ella / usted | era | veía | iba |
|---|---|---|---|
| nosotros / nosotras | éramos | veíamos | íbamos |
| vosotros / vosotras | erais | veías | ibais |
| ellos / ellas / ustedes | eran | veían | iban |

As you can see, even in the conjugation of the irregular verbs, the first- and third-person singular are the same for every verb.

## Time Expressions for Past Events

Now it's time to see some time expressions we use with these verbs. When you see one of these time expressions, you will most generally find that there is a past tense following it.

For the *pretérito perfecto simple*, we can use time expressions such as:

- *Ayer,* which means "yesterday"
- *Anoche,* which means "last night"
- *El año pasado,* which means "last year"
- *La semana pasada,* which means "last week"
- *El mes pasado,* which means "last month"
- *Hace días,* which means "days ago"
- *El otro día,* which means "the other day"

We can also use the *pretérito perfecto simple with specific dates, months, or years.*

For the *pretérito imperfecto*, we can use time expressions such as:

- *A los* + age, which means "when I was..." + age
- *Cuando tenía* + age, which means "When I was..." + age

- *Antes,* which means "before"
- *En aquella época,* which means "at that time"
- *Entonces,* which means "back then"
- *Cuando era niño/joven,* which means "when I was a kid/young"

Now I will transcribe another piece of my conversation with Fernanda in which we used some of these expressions and the two different past tenses we've seen so that you can see it all in use!

| | |
|---|---|
| • En aquella época andábamos mucho en bicicleta. Nos encontrábamos en plaza Mayor y luego íbamos hasta el lago. | • At that time we rode bikes a lot. We used to meet in Plaza Mayor and then we went to the lake. |
| ○ Sí, lo recuerdo. A los 15 años estábamos muy en forma. Ahora no puedo ni andar en bicicleta ni correr. | ○ Yes, I remember. When we were 15, we were in great shape. Now I can't ride a bike nor run. |
| • Pues yo estoy igual. El año pasado comencé a ir al gimnasio, pero no me gustó nada. Cuando era joven disfrutaba de hacer ejercicio. | • Yeah, me neither. Last year I started going to the gym, but I didn't like it at all. When I was young I enjoyed exercising. |
| ○ Sí, yo también. Jugaba mucho al fútbol... Oye, ¿fuiste a la reunión del año pasado? Me contó Joaquín que jugaron al fútbol. | ○ Yes, me too. I used to play soccer a lot... Hey, did you go to last year's reunion? Joaquin told me they played soccer. |
| • Ah, ¡sí! Jugué fatal, pero participé. | • Oh, yes! I played awful, but I took part. |

| | |
|---|---|
| ○ Nadie juega bien a esta edad. Ya no es como era antes. | ○ Nobody plays well at this age. It's not like it used to be. |
| • Eso es cierto. | • That's true. |

## Indefinite Pronouns

Indefinite pronouns are words used to talk about people or things or express some quantity in a vague or general way. Examples of indefinite pronouns in English are "all," "none," "any," etc. For example, in the previous piece of conversation I transcribed for you, I told Fernanda, "Nadie juega bien a esta edad." In this example, "nadie" is an indefinite pronoun that means "nobody" or "no one" and refers vaguely to people in general.

These pronouns are useful in almost any conversation when trying to refer to someone or something that has already been mentioned or can be understood in context. Some of them need to agree on gender, some need to agree in number, and some need to agree in gender and number with the referred person or object.

There are two types of indefinite pronouns in Spanish. The first group is made up of pronouns that are always indefinite, and the second group is made of words that only function as indefinite pronouns when a noun does not follow them.

The ones that are always indefinite pronouns are:

- *nadie,* which means "nobody" and doesn't need to agree in gender nor number.
- *alguien,* which means "someone" and doesn't need to agree in gender nor number.
- *nada,* which means "nothing" and doesn't need to agree in gender nor number.
- *algo,* which means "something" and doesn't need to agree in gender nor number.
- *quienquiera,* which means "whoever" and needs to

agree in number. When it is plural, it becomes *quienesquiera*.

The ones that sometimes function as indefinite pronouns are:

- *todo*, which means "everything," "everybody" or "all" and needs to agree in gender and number by changing its ending: *toda, todos, todas.*
- *Mucho*, which means "a lot" or "many" and needs to agree in gender and number by changing its ending: *mucha, muchos, muchas.*
- *Poco*, which means "a little," "few" and needs to agree in gender and number by changing its ending: *poca, pocos, pocas.*
- *Má,s* which means "more" and doesn't need to agree in gender nor number.
- *Meno,s* which means "less" and doesn't need to agree in gender nor number.
- *Alguno*, which means "some" or "a," and needs to agree in gender and number by changing its ending: *alguna, algunos, algunas.*
- *Otro*, which means "another" and needs to agree in gender and number by changing its ending: *otra, otros, otras.*
- *Ninguno*, which means "none"
- *Cualquiera*, which means "any" and doesn't need to agree in gender nor number.
- *Bastante*, which means "some," "quite"
- *Demasiado*, which means "too" and needs to agree in gender and number by changing its ending: *demasiada, demasiados, demasiadas.*
- *Uno*, which means "one" and needs to agree in gender and number by changing its ending: *una, unos, unas.*
- *Demás*, which means "the rest" and doesn't need to agree in gender nor number.
- *Cada*, which means "every" and doesn't need to agree in gender nor number.

# Relative Pronouns

Now that we've seen the indefinite pronouns, we should see the relative pronouns as well. Relative pronouns are used to introduce relative clauses, that is, clauses that add information about an element of the principal clause. For example, we could say *La taza que rompí era de vidrio* ("The cup I broke was made of glass"). In this sentence, the clause *"que rompí"* is a relative clause that adds information about the cup, and the relative pronoun, in this case, is *que*.

*Que* isn't the only relative pronoun in Spanish. There are actually many and which one we use depends on what we are talking about:

- If we want to talk about a person or thing, we can use the relative pronouns:
    - *Que,* which means "that." For example: *La silla que compré ayer es rosa* ("The chair I bought yesterday is pink")
    - *el que, la que, los que,* or *las que,* which mean "who" or "that" and need to agree in gender and number with the person or thing we are talking about. For example: *La silla en la que estoy sentada es rosa* ("The chair that I'm sitting in is pink").
    - *el cual, la cual, los cuales* or *las cuales* which mean "which" and need to agree in gender and number with the person or thing we are talking about. For example: *La silla en la cual estoy sentada es rosa* ("The chair in which I'm sitting is pink")
- If we want to talk about a person, we can also use the relative pronouns *quien* and *quienes* which mean "who" or "whom" and need to agree in number with the person or persons we're talking about. For example: *Mis amigos, a quienes conocí en el colegio, son españoles* ("My friends, whom I met at school, are Spanish")

- If we want to talk about possession, in English, we use "whose," but in Spanish, we use *cuyo, cuya, cuyos,* or *cuyas,* depending on the gender and number of the thing we are talking about. For example: *La silla, cuyas patas están rotas, es rosa* ("The chair, whose legs are broken, is pink")
- If we want to talk about an amount, we can use the pronouns *cuanto, cuanta, cuantos,* or *cuantas* which mean "those," "all those" or "everything." For example: *Hace todo cuanto le pido* ("He does everything I ask him to do")

Remember that though some of these pronouns are similar to the interrogative pronouns, these are never written with a graphic accent, while the interrogative pronouns always do.

## Jobs/Professions

Now it's time to talk about jobs. When I met my friends from school, we had a lot of catching up to do, so many of us talked about our current and old jobs and other people's jobs (as you already saw in my conversation with Fernanda).

Before we get into how to describe jobs and professions, we need to know some jobs and occupations in Spanish, right? Here's a list with a few examples:

- *estudiante* means "student"
- *arquitecto/arquitecta* means "architect"
- *ingeniero/ingeniera* means "engineer"
- *abogado/abogada* means "lawyer"
- *enfermero/enfermera* means "nurse"
- *doctor/doctora* means "doctor"
- *mecánico/mecánica* means "mechanic"
- *cocinero/cocinera* means "cook"
- *mesero/mesera* means "waiter"
- *bombero/bombera* means "firefighter"
- *profesor/profesora* means "teacher"
- *pintor/pintora* means "painter"

- *actor/actriz* means "actor/actress"
- *cantante* means "singer"
- *empresario/empresaria* means "business person"
- *secretario/secretaria* means "secretary"
- *artista* means "artist"
- *contador/contadora* means "accountant"
- *policía* means "police officer"
- *dentista* means "dentist"
- *periodista* means "journalist"
- *traductor/traductora* means "translator"
- *veterinario/veterinaria* means "vet"

**Describe Someone's Job**

Now it's time to learn how to describe a job. To do so, we can talk about where we work, who we work with, how many hours we work, what we usually do, and our opinion of the job.

For example, I could say: *Por las mañanas trabajo en un colegio secundario enseñando español a niños y por la tarde doy clases de español para adultos en un centro comunitario. A veces el trabajo es difícil, pero nunca es aburrido ni repetitivo.* ("In the morning, I work at a secondary school teaching Spanish to kids, and in the afternoon, I teach Spanish for adults at a community center. Sometimes it's a difficult job, but it's never boring nor repetitive").

We've already learned the exact words to say all of this in Spanish; we just have to put them together:

- To talk about where we work, we use the preposition *en;* for example: *Trabajo en un banco* ("I work in a bank").
- To talk about who we work with, we use the preposition *con;* for example: *Trabajo con clientes* ("I work with clients").
- To talk about our working hours, we can use phrases such as *Trabajo a la mañana, trabajo a la tarde,* or *trabajo de noche* ("I work in the morning/afternoon/evening"). We can also specify the

hours in which we work, for example: *Trabajo de 9 de la mañana a 7 de la tarde* ("I work from 9 a.m. to 7 p.m.").

- To say what we usually do, we use the present form. Some verbs that we can use are:
    - *vender*: "to sell"
    - *llamar*: "to call"
    - *comprar*: "to buy"
    - *supervisar*: "to supervise"
    - *conducir*: "to drive"
    - *escribir*: "to write"
    - *escuchar*: "to listen"
- Finally, to give our opinion on our job, we might use different adjectives, such as:
    - *entretenido*: "entertaining"
    - *divertido*: "fun"
    - *bien pagado*: "well-paid"
    - *mal pagado*: "badly paid"
    - *estresante*: "stressful"
    - *difícil*: "difficult"
    - *demandante*: "demanding"
    - *enriquecedor*: "enriching"
    - *repetitivo*: "repetitive"
    - *aburrido*: "boring"

Sarah has written the following text about her job to practice:

| | |
|---|---|
| Soy contadora en una empresa internacional de tecnología. | I'm an accountant at an international tech company. |
| Trabajo todos los días de 8 de la mañana a 5 de la tarde. | I work every day from 8 a.m. to 5 p.m. |

| En la oficina, trabajo con mucha gente divertida. | At the office, I work with a lot of fun people. |
|---|---|
| Mi trabajo es difícil, pero también es bien pagado. | My job is hard, but it's also well paid. |
| Para algunos es aburrido, pero en mi opinión es muy divertido. | For some it's boring, but in my opinion it's a lot of fun. |
| A veces puede ser estresante. | Sometimes it can be stressful. |

**Exercises**

Now it's time to practice everything we've seen in this chapter, which covers a lot of information.

1. Which season comes before *primavera*? And which one before *otoño*?
2. What do we use the *pretérito perfecto simple* for?
    a. to talk about past habits
    b. to talk about past events
3. True or false: the first person singular and the third person singular conjugations of the *pretérito perfecto simple* are the same.
4. True or false: the *pretérito perfecto simple* conjugations of *ser* and *ir* are the same.
5. What do we use the *pretérito imperfecto* for?
    a. to talk about past habits
    b. to talk about past events
6. True or false: the ending of the conjugations for regular verbs ending in -*er* and -*ir* are the same in the *pretérito perfecto simple* and in the *pretérito imperfecto*.
7. What is the *pretérito imperfecto* conjugation of the second person singular of the verb *amar*?
    a. amabas
    b. amaban

    c. amaron
    d. amaste
8. If I want to talk about one time I got sunburnt at the beach, should I use the *pretérito perfecto simple* or the *pretérito imperfecto?*
9. If I want to talk about how I used to travel around the country with my parents when I was young, should I use the *pretérito perfecto simple* or the *pretérito imperfecto?*
10. What is the *pretérito perfecto simple* conjugation of *estar* in the first person plural?
    a. fuimos
    b. estuvimos
    c. estuvieron
    d. estábamos
11. With which tense do we usually use the time expression *el año pasado?*
12. With which tense do we usually use the time expression *antes?*
13. Which tense do we usually use these time expressions with? There is one that doesn't belong to this group. Which is it?
    a. Entonces
    b. cuando era joven
    c. hace días
    d. a los 14 años
14. What does the indefinite pronoun *nada* mean?
    a. nobody
    b. somebody
    c. everything
    d. nothing
15. What does the indefinite pronoun *ninguno* mean?
    a. many
    b. everybody
    c. none

d. nobody

16. Does the relative pronoun *el cual* need to agree in gender and number with the thing or person it refers to?

17. Which relative pronouns do we use to talk about possession?

18. How would you say "the places that I visited in Spain are beautiful" in Spanish?

    a. Los lugares que visité en España son hermosos.

    b. Los lugares cuyo visité en España son hermosos.

    c. Los lugares el cual visité en España son hermosos.

    d. Los lugares quienes visité en España son hermosos.

19. How do you say "business person" in Spanish?

    a. cantante

    b. actriz/actor

    c. periodista

    d. empresario/a

20. Which preposition do we use to talk about the place we work at?

    a. *por*

    b. *con*

    c. *en*

    d. *de*

# Chapter 10:
# Basic Grammar Revision

Hey! It's Julio here again and for the last time. Our journey through my beautiful country has ended, and Sarah and I will be arriving home soon; we're on our plane right now. So we thought we'd go over every grammar topic we've seen throughout this journey over our flight. We encourage you to revise with us! Plus, at the end of this chapter, you will find another quiz to see how you've done this last half of the book.

Let's start our revision!

## Word Order

- The most common word order for affirmative sentences is:
  - Noun/Pronoun + Adjective + Verb + Complement + Adverb
- The most common word order for negative sentences is:
  - Noun/Pronoun + Adjective + *no* + Verb + Complement + Adverb
- The most common word order for yes/no questions is:
  - ¿ + Noun/Pronoun + Adjective + Verb + Complement + Adverb + ?

You should remember that in Spanish, the subject can be dropped from the sentence, so it isn't always necessary to mention the noun/pronoun or the adjective that describes the thing/person we're talking about.

Subject Pronouns

- First-person singular: *yo* ("I")
- Second-person singular: *tú* / usted ("you")
- Third-person singular: *él* / *ella* ("he" / "she")
- First-person plural: *nosotros* / *nosotras* ("we")
- Second-person plural: *vosotros* / *vosotras* / *ustedes* ("you")
- *Third-person plural: ellos* / *ellas* ("they")

Keep in mind that the pronouns need to agree with the gender of the person we're talking about

Remember that *usted* is the formal version of *tú*, and that *ustedes* is mostly used in Latin American countries, while *vosotros* and *vosotras* are used mostly in Spain.

## Gender of Nouns and Adjectives

In Spanish, every noun has one of two genders: masculine or feminine. Some words are inherently feminine, and some words are inherently masculine. Generally speaking (and especially when we're talking about people), we distinguish feminine from masculine nouns because of their endings:

- Feminine words usually end in *-a*
- Masculine words usually end in *-o*

Usually, with people, we can choose between ending a word with *-a* to talk about a woman or *-o* to talk about a man. For example: *la mexicana* and *el mexicano.* However, there are also some nouns (referring to people) that remain unchanged, for example *la artista* and *el artista.* In these cases, we can tell whether we are talking about a man or a woman if we pay attention to the words surrounding the noun, like the articles and adjectives, which, as you may remember, need to agree in gender with the noun they are referring to.

To make adjectives agree with the noun we're talking about, we usually need to decide whether to end the adjective with an *-a* if the noun is feminine (e.g., *linda)* and *-o* if the noun is masculine (e.g., *lindo)*, but we can also find some invariable adjectives as well (e.g., inteligente).

## Number of Nouns and Adjectives

The rules for the pluralization of nouns and adjectives in Spanish are:

- If the singular form ends in a vowel, you need to add an *-s* at the end.
  - Examples: *mesa → mesas, casa → casas, mono → monos, pelota → pelotas*
- If the singular form ends in a consonant or with a stressed vowel, you need to add *-es* at the end.
  - Examples: *ataúd → ataúdes, iglú → iglúes, rey → reyes, pared → paredes*
- If the singular form ends with Z, you need to add *-ces* at the end.
  - Examples: *pez → peces, voz → voces, nuez → nueces, lápiz → lápices*

Remember that in Spanish, adjectives, articles, and verbs need to agree in number with the noun we're talking about.

Definite and Indefinite Articles

Spanish has four variations for the definite articles and four variations for the indefinite articles. They vary according to the gender and number of the noun we're talking about, just like we said before.

The definite and indefinite articles in Spanish are:

|            | Masculine |       | Feminine |       |
|------------|-----------|-------|----------|-------|
|            | Singular  | Plural| Singular | Plural|
| Definite   | *El*      | *Los* | *La*     | *Las* |
| Indefinite | *Un*      | *Unos*| *Una*    | *Unas*|
| Neuter     | *Lo*      |       |          |       |

## Demonstrative Pronouns and Articles

Demonstrative pronouns are words used instead of nouns to point at people or things. There are 15 Spanish demonstrative pronouns in Spanish, while in English, there are only four. This difference is because, in Spanish, we need to consider the gender, number, and distance from the speaker and addressee of the noun it's replacing.

These are the 15 Spanish demonstrative pronouns:

|                                | Masculine |        | Feminine |       | Neuter   |
|--------------------------------|-----------|--------|----------|-------|----------|
|                                | Singular  | Plural | Singular | Plural| Singular |
| Object close to the speaker    | esto      | estos  | esta     | estas | esto     |
| Object close to the addressee  | ese       | eso    | esa      | esas  | eso      |

| Object far from both | aquel | aquellos | aquella | aquellas | aquello |

## Interrogative Pronouns

Remember that, in Spanish, all interrogative pronouns take a graphic accent. They are:

- *qué* is used in the same way as English "what?"
- *por qué* is similar to English "why?"
- *cuál* and *cuáles* are the singular and plural equivalents of the English "which?"
- *quién* and *quiénes* are the singular and plural equivalents of "who?"
- *cuánto* and *cuánta* are the masculine and feminine equivalents of "how much?"
- *cuántos* and *cuántas* are the masculine and feminine equivalents of "how many?"
- *dónde* is used in the same way as English "where?"
- *cómo* is used in the same way as "how?"
- *cuándo* is similar to English "when?"

## Possessive Adjectives and Pronouns

Possessive adjectives and pronouns are the words we use to show that something belongs to someone. While possessive adjectives go together with the noun, possessive pronouns replace the noun. In Spanish, possessive pronouns and adjectives agree with what they describe (not with the person who owns the thing). And, as you can see, possessive pronouns go together with a definite article, which also needs to agree with the gender of the thing owned.

The Spanish possessive adjectives are:

|  | Singular | | Plural | |
| --- | --- | --- | --- | --- |
|  | Masculine | Feminine | Masculine | Feminine |
| "My" (belonging to me) | *Mi* | *Mi* | *Mis* | *Mis* |
| "Your" (belonging to someone you address as *tú*) | *Tu* | *Tu* | *Tus* | *Tus* |
| "His," "her," "its," "your" (belonging to someone you address as *usted*) | *Su* | *Su* | *Sus* | *Sus* |
| "Our" (belonging to us) | *Nuestro* | *Nuestra* | *Nuestros* | *Nuestras* |
| "Your" (belonging to people you address as | *Vuestro* | *Vuestra* | *Vuestros* | *Vuestras* |

| | | | | |
|---|---|---|---|---|
| vosotros/ vosotras) | | | | |
| "Their," "your" (belonging to people you address as *ustedes*) | *Su* | *Su* | *Sus* | *Sus* |

The Spanish possessive pronouns (with their articles) are:

| | Singular | | Plural | |
|---|---|---|---|---|
| | Masculine | Feminine | Masculine | Feminine |
| "Mine" (belonging to me) | *El mío* | *La mía* | *Los míos* | *Las mías* |
| "Yours" (belonging to someone you address as *tú*) | *El tuyo* | *La tuya* | *Los tuyos* | *Las tuyas* |

| | | | | |
|---|---|---|---|---|
| "His," "hers," "its," "yours" (belonging to someone you address as *usted*) | *El suyo* | *La suya* | *Los suyos* | *Las suyas* |
| "Ours" (belonging to us) | *El nuestro* | *La nuestra* | *Los nuestros* | *Las nuestras* |
| "Yours" (belonging to people you address as *vosotros/vosotras*) | *El vuestro* | *La vuestra* | *Los vuestros* | *Las vuestras* |
| "Theirs," "yours" (belonging to people you address as *ustedes*) | *El suyo* | *La suya* | *Los suyos* | *Las suyas* |

# Objective Pronouns

The direct object can be replaced by a pronoun, in which case we put it before the verb. In Spanish, that pronoun needs to agree in gender and number with the noun that's being replaced in the following way:

|  | Masculine | Feminine |
|---|---|---|
| "Me" (first person singular) | *Me* | *Me* |
| "You" (second person singular *tú*) | *Te* | *Te* |
| "Him," "her," "it" (third person singular); "you" (second person singular *usted*) | *Lo* | *La* |
| "Us" (first person plural) | *Nos* | *Nos* |
| "You" (second person plural *vosotros/vosotras*) | *Os* | *Os* |
| "Them" (third person plural); "you" (second person plural *ustedes*) | *Los* | *Las* |

The indirect object can also be replaced by a pronoun when the person or thing that the action is intended to benefit or harm is understood from the context. In these cases, we use one of the following indirect object pronouns depending on the person and number:

| "Me," "to me," "for me" (first person singular) | *Me* |
|---|---|
| "You," "to you," "for you" | *Te* |

| | |
|---|---|
| (second person singular *tú*) | |
| "Him/Her/It," "to him/her/it," "for him/her/it" (third person singular); "You," "to you," "for you" (second person singular *usted*) | *Le* |
| "Us," "for us," "to us" (first person plural) | *Nos* |
| "You," "to you," "for you" (second person plural *vosotros/vosotras*) | *Os* |
| "Them," to them," "for them" (third person plural); "you," "to you," "for you" (second person plural *ustedes*) | *Les* |

## Expressing Likes and Dislikes

To express likes, we can use the following phrases:
- 1st person singular: *(A mí) me encanta/gusta la paella*
- 2nd person singular: *(A ti) te encanta/gusta la paella*
- 3rd person singular: *(A él/ella) le encanta/gusta la paella*
- 1st person plural: *(A nosotros/nosotras) nos encanta/gusta la paella*
- 2nd person plural: *(A vosotros/vosotras) os encanta/gusta la paella*
- 3rd person plural: *(A ellos/ellas) les encanta/gusta la paella*

And to express dislikes, we can use the following phrases:
- 1st person singular: *(A mí)* **no** *me encanta/gusta la paella*
- 2nd person singular: *(A ti)* **no** *te encanta/gusta la paella*

- 3rd person singular: *(A él/ella)* **no** *le encanta/gusta la paella*
- 1st person plural: *(A nosotros/nosotras)* **no** *nos encanta/gusta la paella*
- 2nd person plural: *(A vosotros/vosotras)* **no** *os encanta/gusta la paella*
- 3rd person plural: *(A ellos/ellas)* **no** *les encanta/gusta la paella*

Remember that we use *encanta* and *gusta* with singular nouns and verbs, but *encantan* and *gustan* with plural nouns.

## Comparatives and Superlatives of Adjectives

In Spanish, we compare adjectives, nouns, and adverbs using the following formulas depending on the relationship between the things we are comparing:

- Superiority: *más* + adjective/noun/adverb + *que*
- Inferiority: *menos* + adjective/noun/adverb + *que*
- Equality: *tan* + adjective/adverb + *como*

We can also compare verbs using the following formula:

- verb + *más que*
- verb + *menos* que
- verb + *tanto* como

To say that something is at the top or bottom of its class, i.e. that it is a superlative, we use the following formula:

- *el/la/los/las* + *más* + adjective (+ *de* + group)
- *el/la/los/las* + *menos* + adjective (+ *de* + group)

For this formula, remember that the article choice depends on the gender and number of the thing we are talking about.

## Indefinite Pronouns

Indefinite pronouns are words used to talk about people or things or to express some quantity in a vague or general way.

Here's a list of indefinite pronouns:

- *nadie* means "nobody" and doesn't need to agree in gender nor number.
- *alguien* means "someone" and doesn't need to agree in gender nor number.
- *nada* means "nothing" and doesn't need to agree in gender nor number.
- *algo* means "something" and doesn't need to agree in gender nor number.
- *quienquiera* means "whoever" and needs to agree in number. When it is plural, it becomes *quienesquiera*.
- *todo* means "everything," "everybody" or "all" and needs to agree in gender and number by changing its ending: *toda, todos, todas*.
- *mucho* means "a lot" or "many" and needs to agree in gender and number by changing its ending: *mucha, muchos, muchas*.
- *poco* means "a little," "few" and needs to agree in gender and number by changing its ending: *poca, pocos, pocas*.
- *más* means "more" and doesn't need to agree in gender nor number.
- *menos* means "less" and doesn't need to agree in gender nor number.
- *alguno* means "some" or "a," and needs to agree in gender and number by changing its ending: *alguna, algunos, algunas*.
- *otro* means "another" and needs to agree in gender and number by changing its ending: *otra, otros, otras*.
- *ninguno* means "none."
- *cualquiera* which means "any" and doesn't need to agree in gender nor number.
- *bastante* means "some," "quite"

- *demasiado* means "too" and needs to agree in gender and number by changing its ending: *demasiada, demasiados, demasiadas.*
- *uno* means "one" and needs to agree in gender and number by changing its ending: *una, unos, unas.*
- *demás* means "the rest" and doesn't need to agree in gender nor number.
- *cada* means "every" and doesn't need to agree in gender nor number.

**Relative pronouns**

Relative pronouns are used to introduce relative clauses, that is, clauses that add information about an element of the principal clause.

- If we want to talk about a person or thing, we can use the relative pronouns:
    - *que* means "that."
    - *el que, la que, los que,* or *las que* which mean "who" or "that" and need to agree in gender and number with the person or thing we are talking about.
    - *el cual, la cual, los cuales* or *las cuales* which mean "which" and need to agree in gender and number with the person or thing we are talking about.
- If we want to talk about a person, we can also use the relative pronouns *quien* and *quienes* which mean "who" or "whom" and need to agree in number with the person or persons we're talking about.
- If we want to talk about possession, in English, we use "whose," but in Spanish, we use *cuyo, cuya, cuyos,* or *cuyas*, depending on the gender and number of the thing we are talking about.
- If we want to talk about an amount, we can use the pronouns *cuanto, cuanta, cuantos,* or *cuantas* which mean "those," "all those" or "everything."

# Present, Future, and Past Forms of Regular Verbs

Let's go over the different ways in which we can talk about the present, the future, and the past.

- Present: we use the present tense to talk about things that are generally true. We can also talk about the present progressive with the verbal phrase *estar* + gerund.
- Future: we use the future tense to talk about things that will happen in the future. And we can also talk about the future with the present tense and the verbal phrase *ir* + infinitive
- Past: We use the *pretérito perfecto simple* to talk about single events that happened in the past. And we use the *pretérito imperfecto* to talk about habits in the past or things that used to be a certain way in the past.

Here's a chart with the regular conjugations of the different tenses we've seen so far:

|  | Infinitivo | Presente | Futuro | Pretérito perfecto simple | Pretérito imperfecto |
|---|---|---|---|---|---|
| yo | -ar | -o | -aré | -é | -aba |
| | -er | | -eré | -í | -ía |
| | -ir | | -iré | | |
| tú | -ar | -as | -arás | -aste | -abas |
| | -er | -es | -erás | -iste | -ías |
| | -ir | | -irás | | |

|  | -ar | -a | -ará | -ó | -aba |
|---|---|---|---|---|---|
| él / ella / usted | -er | -e | -erá | -ió | -ía |
|  | -ir |  | -irá |  |  |
| nosotros / nosotras | -ar | -amos | -aremos | -amos | -ábamos |
|  | -er | -emos | -eremos | -imos | -íamos |
|  | -ir | -imos | -iremos |  |  |
| vosotros / vosotras | -ar | -áis | -aréis | -asteis | -abais |
|  | -er | -éis | -eréis | -isteis | -ían |
|  | -ir | -ís | -iréis |  |  |
| ellos / ellas / ustedes | -ar | -an | -arán | -aron | -aban |
|  | -er | -en | -erán | -ieron | -ían |
|  | -ir |  | -irán |  |  |

## Present progressive

Remember that we've also seen the present progressive tense, which is conveyed by the verbal phrase formed by the conjugation of *estar* + gerund.

In Spanish, gerunds are never conjugated and are formed in the following way:

- Infinitive verbs ending in *-ar* end in *-ando* in the gerund.
- Infinitive verbs ending in *-ir* or *-er* end in *-iendo* in the gerund.

*Estar* is an irregular verb in almost every tense, so this is its conjugation:

|  | Presente | Futuro | Pretérito perfecto simple | Pretérito imperfecto |
|---|---|---|---|---|
| yo | estoy | estaré | estuve | estaba |
| tú | estás | estarás | estuviste | estabas |
| él / ella / usted | está | estará | estuvo | estaba |
| nosotros / nosotras | estamos | estaremos | estuvimos | estábamos |
| vosotros / vosotras | estáis | estaréis | estuvisteis | estabais |
| ellos / ellas / ustedes | están | estarán | estuvieron | estaban |

*Ir* + infinitive

We use this verbal phrase to talk about the future much the same as we do in the English "going to." To do so, we must conjugate the verb *ir* in the present. Since *ir* is an irregular verb, here's its conjugation in the present:

|  | IR |
|---|---|
| yo | voy |
| tú | vas |
| él / ella / usted | va |

| nosotros / nosotras | vamos |
|---|---|
| vosotros / vosotas | vais |
| ellos / ellas / ustedes | van |

# Quiz

Now that we're done revising, it's time for a quiz on the last five chapters so that you test your knowledge. Like in the previous quiz, each right answer is worth one point.

Ready? Let's do it!

1. If I say *Julia es la hermana de mi mamá, la madre de mi prima y la esposa de mi tío*, then who is Julia to me in Spanish?
2. How would you describe your face?
3. What would be the Spanish equivalents to the parts of the body mentioned in the song "head and shoulders, knees and toes"?
4. What are the four possessive pronouns of the first-person with their articles?
5. What is the direct object pronoun for the first person singular masculine and feminine?
6. What is the indirect object pronoun for the third person plural?
7. How would you say "I like *lentejas*, but I don't love *gazpacho*" in Spanish?
8. How would you say "This is the best *paella* in the world" in Spanish?
9. How do you ask for a table for four in Spanish?
10. Which adverb can be formed with the adjective *difícil*?
11. How would you say "Today is Sunday, July 18th, 2021" in Spanish?

12. Can you conjugate the regular verb *cantar* in the future tense with the pronouns *yo, tú, ella, nosotras, vosotras,* and *ellas*?
13. How would you say "Tomorrow we are going to sing all night" in Spanish using the verbal phrase *ir +* infinitive?
14. Is *en absoluto* an adverb of affirmation, negation, or doubt? What does it mean?
15. If a man is *torpe*, what is he?
16. What is the difference between the *pretérito perfecto simple* and the *pretérito imperfecto*? What are each of them used for?
17. Can you conjugate the regular verb *salir* in the *pretérito perfecto simple* with the pronouns *yo, tú, él, nosotros, vosotros,* and *ellos*?
18. Now can you conjugate with the same pronouns in the *pretérito imperfecto*?
19. What does *algo* mean? What type of word is it?
20. What is the relative pronoun *quien* used for? What does it mean?

Now you can go over to the answer key to check how you did!

- If you got 15-20 right answers: Congratulations! You've finished this book, and you have made some great strides in learning Spanish. Keep up the good work, and keep on practicing!

- If you got 10-15 right answers: you're doing great, but maybe you should review the book again (especially any parts you struggled with) to help clear up any doubts or confusion.

- If you got a score below 10: don't get discouraged! You're doing fine, but maybe you need to practice a bit more. I encourage you to go back to the last five chapters and then Chapter 10's revision and take the quiz again!

# Vocabulary Appendix

Welcome to the vocabulary appendix! Here, you will find all the vocabulary seen in this book classified by topic. However, you will find the words written in English so you can complete the Spanish part independently.

You can do this once you're done with the book to check your knowledge, or you can complete it as you go!

I recommend you read each chapter while taking notes, then take another day trying to remember everything you've seen in the chapter. Then, on the third day, try to check your knowledge in this section. But it's entirely up to you!

Let's get into the vocabulary and remember that sometimes there is more than one word in Spanish with the same meaning in English!

## Colors

- Red:
- Orange
- Yellow:
- Green
- Blue
- Purple
- Pink

- Gray
- Black
- White
- Magenta:
- Light Blue:
- Turquoise:
- Brown

# Numbers

- One:
- Two:
- Three
- Four:
- Five:
- Six:
- Seven:
- Eight:
- Nine:
- Ten
- Eleven
- Twelve:
- Thirteen:
- Fourteen:
- Fifteen:
- Sixteen:
- Seventeen:
- Eighteen:
- Nineteen:
- Twenty:
- Twenty-one:
- Twenty-two:

- Twenty-three:
- Twenty-four:
- Twenty-five:
- Twenty-six:
- Twenty-seven:
- Twenty-eight:
- Twenty-nine:
- Thirty:
- Forty:
- Fifty:
- Sixty:
- Eighty:
- Ninety:
- One hundred:

## Greetings and Farewells

- Hello:
- Good day:
- Good morning:
- Good evening:
- Good night:
- How are you?:
- Goodbye:
- See you!:
- See you later!:

## Introducing ourselves and asking questions

- What's your name?:
- What's your last name?:
- Where are you from?:

- How old are you?:
- What's your nationality?:
- My name is...:
- I'm from...:
- I'm... years old:

## Countries and nationalities

- United States:
    - American:
- Spain:
    - Spanish:
- Mexico:
    - Mexican:
- England:
    - English:
- Australia:
    - Australian:
- France:
    - French:
- Colombia:
    - Colombian:
- Peru:
    - Peruvian:
- China:
    - Chinese:
- Brazil:
    - Brazilian:
- Chile:
    - Chilean:
- Argentina:
    - Argentinian:

- Guatemala:
    - Guatemalan:
- Venezuela:
    - Venezuelan:
- Cuba:
    - Cuban:
- South Africa:
    - South African:
- Germany:
    - German:
- Italy:
    - Italian:
- Egypt:
    - Egyptian:
- Greece:
    - Greek:

## Booking a Room

- I want to book a room for tonight:
- Do you have any rooms available?:
- I want a single room:
- I'd like a room with a private bathroom:
- What's the price for a double room?:
- Do you have a cheaper option?:
- Can I pay with cash?:
- I only have credit card:
- I would like a room with a view:
- Is breakfast included?:
- At what time is breakfast served?:
- Do you offer airport transfer service?:
- Does the hotel have wifi?:

- Can I see the room?:

## Prepositions of Place

- in:
- about:
- to, by, at:
- to the right of:
- near to:
- after:
- in, inside, within:
- on top of:
- toward:

## Parts of a House

- front door:
- living room:
- dining-room:
- kitchen:
- storage room:
- fireplace:
- stairs:
- windows:
- hallway:
- garden:
- attic:
- basement:

## Objects in the House

- sink:
- faucet:
- stove:
- oven:

- refrigerator:
- freezer:
- dishwasher:
- appliances:
- counter:
- pantry:
- cupboard:
- chair:
- armchair:
- clock:
- coffee table:
- lamp:
- vase:
- carpet:
- bed:
- rug:
- nightlight:
- curtains:
- closet:
- dresser:
- alarm clock:
- towel:
- mirror:
- toothpaste:
- toothbrush:
- soap:
- comb:
- brush:
- razor:
- shaving cream:
- makeup:

## Going shopping

- How much is this?:
- How much are those?:
- What's the price?:
- How much?:
- How much is it?:
- The price of that is...:
- It's ...:

## Adverbs of Quantity

- many, much, a lot:
- very:
- too much:
- enough, quite:
- somewhat, slightly, a bit:
- little, few:
- more:
- less:
- a lot more:
- so much:
- so many:

Fruits, vegetables, and food

- shellfish:
- octopus:
- stew:
- cake:
- tomato:
- tuna:
- chucken:
- lettuce:
- bread:

- apple:
- rice:
- ham:
- dairy products:
- cheese:
- milk:
- cream:
- yogurt:
- cold cuts:
- fruit:
- vegetable:
- carrot:
- cucumber:
- potato:
- pumpkin:
- pineapple:
- orange:
- strawberry:
- plum:
- egg:
- oil:
- cookie:

## Means of Transportation

- train:
- bus:
- airplane:
- taxi:
- bike:
- car:
- motorcycle:

- subway:
- ship:

## Buildings

- house:
- apartment:
- museum:
- square:
- cathedral:
- church:
- library:
- cinema:
- supermarket:
- hospital:
- bank:
- restaurant:
- airport:
- train station:
- university:
- pharmacy:

## Asking for and giving directions

- Excuse me:
- Where is...?:
- How do I get to...?:
- Could you tell me how to get to...?:
- Is... nearby?:
- Do you know if there is a... nearby?:
- Is... on this street?:
- You have to go straight on:
- Turn left/right:
- Cross the street:

- Continue on this street:
- It's... blocks away:

## Adverbs of Place

- here:
- there:
- inside:
- outside:
- ahead:
- behind:
- below:
- above:
- to/on the right:
- to/on the left:
- besides, next to:
- in front of:
- at the end:
- around:
- in the middle:
- near:
- far:
- between:
- on the corner:

## Asking for Tickets

- A ticket for..., please:
- Could you give me a ticket for...?:
- Do you have a map of the...?:
- When do you close?:

# Time Markers for the Present

- Every day:
- Every Monday:
- Always:
- En general:
- Usualmente:
- Casi nunca:
- Nunca:
- Ahora:
- Ahora mismo:
- En este momento:

# Family Members

- grandmother:
- grandfather:
- grandparents:
- mother:
- father:
- parents:
- aunt:
- uncles:
- sister:
- brother:
- female cousin:
- male cousin:
- daughter:
- son:
- granddaughter:
- grandson:
- niece:
- nephew:

- wife:
- husband:
- stepmother:
- stepfather:
- stepsister:
- stepbrother:
- half-sister:
- half-brother:
- stepdaughter:
- stepson:
- godmother:
- godfather:
- goddaughter:
- godson:
- mother-in-law:
- father-in-law:
- sister-in-law:
- brother-in-law:
- daughter-in-law:
- son-in-law:

## Adjectives for Describing Appearances

- body shape:
- tall:
- short:
- stout:
- lean:
- lanky:
- slender:
- skinny:
- large:

- petite:
- muscular:
- face:
- bearded:
- square:
- long:
- oval:
- freckled:
- round:
- eyes:
- open:
- blue:
- light-colored:
- brown:
- black:
- dark:
- round:
- green:
- hair:
- thick:
- shiny:
- bald:
- grey:
- brown:
- short:
- frizzy:
- thin:
- straight:
- long:
- black:
- wavy:

- red:
- curly:
- blonde:
- dyed:
- nose:
- hooked:
- wide:
- narrow:
- straight:
- turned-up:
- crooked:
- age:
- old:
- young:
- wrinkly:
- middle-aged:
- youthful:
- elderly:

## The Human Body

- body:
- lips:
- back:
- foot:
- finger:
- toe:
- head:
- neck:
- hand:
- leg:
- ankle:

- mouth:
- tooth:
- nail:
- shoulder:
- arm:
- stomach:
- knee:
- lbow:
- ear:

## Ordering Food

- A table for two, please:
- What's today's special?:
- What dish do you recommend?:
- What does this dish have?:
- I'm allergic to nuts:
- I'd like a...:
- Could you bring the bill, please?:

## Polite Interjections

- sure:
- perfect:
- great:
- right:

## Adverbs of Mode

- well:
- bad:
- better:
- worse:
- slowly:
- fast:

- fastly:
- only:
- hardly:
- clearly:
- commonly:
- lately:
- happily:
- timidly:
- simply:

## Conjunctions

- or:
- neither, nor:
- because:
- although:
- however:
- as, since, like:
- yet:
- in spite of:
- while:
- when:
- if:

## Telling the Time and Date

- in the morning:
- in the afternoon:
- at night:
- it's ... p.m.:
- it's... a.m.:
- What time is it?:
- Do you have the time?:
- Can you tell me what the time is?:

- Monday:
- Tuesday:
- Wednesday:
- Thursday:
- Friday:
- Saturday:
- Sunday:
- January:
- February:
- March:
- April:
- May:
- June:
- July:
- August:
- September:
- October:
- November:
- December:

## Ordinal Numbers

- first:
- second:
- third:
- fourth:
- fifth:
- sixth:
- seventh:
- eighth:
- nineth:
- tenth:

# Adverbs of Affirmation/Negation/Doubt

- yes:
- of course:
- indeed:
- truly:
- true:
- too:
- not at all:
- never:
- neither:
- nor:
- perhaps, maybe:
- possibly:
- probably:
- surely:

# Adjectives for Describing People's Personality

- affectionate:
- good-natured:
- whimsical:
- cowardly:
- gullible:
- cultured:
- miserable:
- absent-minded:
- dignified:
- selfish:
- charming:
- deceitful:

- demanding:
- loyal:
- funny:
- talkative:
- humble:
- clever:
- spoiled:
- prideful:
- smug:
- reserved:
- confident:
- sensible:
- sensitive:
- sincere:
- clumsy:
- hard-working:
- calm:
- courageous:

## Seasons

- summer:
- fall:
- winter:
- spring:

# Time Expressions for Past Events

- yesterday:
- last night:
- last year:
- last week:
- last month:
- days ago:

- the other day:
- when I was... + age:
- before:
- at that time:
- back then:
- when I was a kid/young:

## Jobs/Professions

- student:
- architect:
- engineer:
- lawyer:
- nurse:
- doctor:
- mechanic:
- cook:
- waiter:
- firefighter:
- teacher:
- painter:
- actor/actress:
- singer:
- business person:
- secretary:
- accountant:
- police officer:
- dentist:
- journalist:
- translator:
- vet:

# Verbs and Adjectives to Describe a Job

- to sell:
- to call:
- to buy:
- to supervise:
- to drive:
- to write:
- to listen:
- entertaining:
- fun:
- well-paid:
- badly paid:
- stressful:
- difficult:
- demanding:
- enriching:
- repetitive:
- boring:

# Answer Key

## Spanish Basics

1. jota-u-ele-i-o ese-a-ene-ce-hache-e-zeta.
2. eme-u-jota-e-erre. It doesn't have a *tilde* because it's a *grave* that ends in R.
3. It means that that is the stressed syllable.
4. a. They are all *agudas*.
5. It means that the stressed syllable is the second to last.
6. c. The stressed vowel is the A.
7. It should be a rolled R because all Rs are rolled at the beginning of words.
8. If should be a softer R because a single R in the middle of a word is soft, whereas a double R is a rolled R.
9. /geṟä/ and /goṟilä/. Both are pronounced with a soft G. The U in *guerra* shouldn't be pronounced, and the double R is rolled. The R in *gorila*, however, is softer.
10. It generally comes after.
11. Yes, a pronoun can be the subject of a sentence.
12. False. In Spanish, the subject can be tacit; that is, it can be absent from the sentence because it is already implied in the verb conjugation.

13. No, it doesn't need to change. Unlike English, the order of words can remain the same but we should always include opening and closing question marks.
14. True. Unlike English, in Spanish, the adjectives usually go after the noun.
15. False. The Spanish word for orange is *naranja*. *Amarillo* is the word for yellow.
16. c. Blanco y negro (black and white)
17. Rojo
18. Cuatro
19. Siete
20. Seis (including her)

## Meeting New People

1. a. Nos vemos
2. c. Hasta mañana
3. a. ellos is the third person masculine plural pronoun.
4. b. nosotros
5. Masculine nouns usually end in *-O*.
6. To form these plurals, you just need to add an *-S*: *manos, vasos* and *sillas*.
7. c. luces, because the singular form ends in *-Z*.
8. a. verbs don't need to agree in gender with the noun, but they do need to agree in number
9. True. *Estar* is used for temporary states while *ser* is used for permanent ones.
10. False. *Ustedes* is the second person plural pronoun, but it is conjugated in the same way as *ellos* and *ellas*.
11. *Soy* and *estoy*
12. c. *Ella está contenta*. *Ella* is feminine, so *contenta* should agree in gender and number with her and *contenta* is a temporary state, so we should use *estar* and not *ser*.
13. a. Soy Julio
14. c. Es Sánchez

15. a. Soy de España
16. b. Tengo veinte años
17. c. Soy francés
18. Treinta y siete
19. Veintinueve
20. alemana

## Checking Into Your Room

1. b. Four
2. The gender and number of the noun define which definite article to use.
3. The Spanish definite articles are *el, los, la* and *las*.
4. False. Spanish has four indefinite articles.
5. The Spanish indefinite articles are *un, unos, una,* and *unas*.
6. c. Una
7. a. Los
8. *Quiero una habitación simple para esta noche, por favor.*
9. True. *Habitación doble* is a room for two people.
10. *Efectivo* and *tarjeta de crédito*.
11. False. To distinguish questions from affirmative sentences, we use the opening and the closing question marks when WRITING Spanish.
12. When speaking, the difference between questions and affirmative sentences is marked through intonation.
13. c. En
14. True. The preposition *a* can mean "to," "by" and "at."
15.
16. Cross the odd one out: d. El jarrón
17. b. Una toalla
18.
19. *Podemos encontrar un espejo* (a mirror) *en el baño, en la sala o en la habitación.*
20. *Podemos encontrar una cama* (a bed) *en la habitación.*

# Going Shopping

1. False. To decide which demonstrative pronoun to use, you need to take into account the gender, the number, and the distance from the speaker and the addressee of the noun it's replacing
2. Object close to the speaker, object close to the addressee, object far from both.
3. b. Esa
4. c. Aquellos
5. 
6. b. Vale 5€
7. True
8. c. Cuál/cuáles
9. ¿Quiénes vienen a la fiesta?
10. False. *Poco* means "little," "few"
11. c. Nada
12. a. Corremos.
13. Yo canto. Yo bailo
14. Tú bebes. Tú comes
15. Ella sale. Ella vive
16. False. *Zanahoria* meand "carrot"
17. b. Calabaza
18. c. Pastel
19. True
20. c. Aceite

# Going Sightseeing

1. *bicicleta*
2. "bus"
3. *museo* and *plaza*
4. "church" and "train station"
5. *Perdone* or *disculpe*

6. *¿Podría decirme cómo llegar a la biblioteca?* or *¿Cómo llego a la biblioteca?*
7. *¿Sabe si hay alguna farmacia por aquí?*
8. c. al lado
9. a. en el medio
10. b. cross the street and turn left.
11. *Gira a la derecha y sigue derecho por tres cuadras.*
12. *Tres entradas para el museo, por favor* or *¿Me podría dar tres entradas para el museo?*
13. c. traes
14. b. hemos
15. True.
16. False. if there is a verb that ends in *-ir* or *-er* in the infinitive form, the gerund form ends in *-iendo*. The gerund form ends in *-ando* when there is a verb whose infinitive form ends in *-ar*.
17. *Estoy cantando*
18. a. todos los días
19. c. ahora
20. False. The indicative mode is used for real situations, while the subjunctive mood is used for desires, wishes, suggestions or hypotheses.

## Quiz

1. Gorrión is an *aguda*. It should be pronounced with a soft G and a strong/rolled R.
2. The sentence is grammatically incorrect because the verbs should agree in number with Lucía (third-person singular) and the adjective should agree in gender and number with Lucía (feminine third-person singular). A grammatically correct sentence would be: *Lucía juega al fútbol, es muy buena.*
3. You can ask using the phrase *¿Cuántos años tienes?* and answer with *Tengo...* and the number of years

4. The Spanish indefinite articles are *un, unos, una* and *unas*. We use *un* with masculine singular nouns, *unos* with masculine plural nouns, *una* with feminine singular nouns, and *unas* with feminine plural nouns.
5. *¿Puedo pagar en efectivo?*
6. You use the same sentence as in the affirmative but add opening and closing question marks.
7. We would use the preposition *hacia*: *Camino hacia el museo.*
8. c. cama. The bed does not belong in the bathroom.
9. You should take into account the gender, number and the distance from the speaker.
10. We could ask *¿Cuánto cuesta/vale/sale el pollo?*, *¿Qué precio tiene el pollo?*, *¿Cuál es el precio del pollo?* or even *¿A qué precio está el pollo?* The store clerk could answer *Vale/cuesta/sale 20€, son 20€* or *El precio del pollo es 20€.*
11. *Cuánto* means "how much." However, *cuántos* means "how many." It is not the plural equivalent of *cuánto.*
12. *¿Por qué están tan caras las calabazas?*
13. *¿Dónde están los pasteles?*
14. We would use the adverbs *demasiado* and *poco*: *Es demasiado para unos pocos días.*
15. *Yo amo, tú amas, ella ama, nosotras amamos, vosotras amáis,* and *ellas aman.*
16. *Yo temo, tú temes, él teme, nosotros tememos, vosotros teméis,* and *ellos temen.*
17. *Yo parto, tú partes, ella parte, nosotras partimos, vosotras partís,* and *ellas parten.*
18. We could ask *¿Cómo llego al supermercado?* or *¿Podría decirme cómo llegar al supermercado?* And we could answer *Tienes que doblar/girar a la derecha, seguir derecho por tres cuadras y luego doblar/girar a la izquierda.*
19. he conjugation of the verb *ser* is: *Yo soy, tú eres, él es, nosotros somos, vosotros sois,* and *ellos son.* And the

conjugation of the verb *estar* is: *yo estoy, tú estás, él está, nosotros estamos, vosotros estáis, and ellos están.*
20. The first one is in the present form and the second one is in the present progressive form. The present progressive is formed by the conjugation of the verb *estar* and a gerund.

## Having a House Party

1. False. *Abuela* means grandmother, and *abuelo* means grandfather.
2. d. Tío
3. True. *Marido* and *esposo* both mean "husband."
4. The Spanish word to talk about your children's female partner is *nuera*.
5. The Spanish word to talk about your partner's father is *suegro*.
6. False. *Esbelto/a* and *bajo/a* are used to describe the body shapes. *Rizado/a* is used to describe hair.
7. True. *Canoso/a, arrugado/a* and *entrado/a en años* are things you would say to describe an elder person.
8. All of the adjectives mentioned can be used to describe a feminine noun.
9. The Spanish word for "mouth" is *boca*.
10. c. Cabello
11. False. Possessive pronouns replace the noun and are used together with a definite article.
12. Possessive pronouns and adjectives agree with the noun they refer to.
13. The possessive adjectives equivalent to English "my" are *mi* and *mis*.
14. The definite article that comes before the possessive pronoun *suyos* is *los*.
15. b. La
16. True. The direct object is the person or thing that receives the action of the verb.

17. The direct object pronoun needs to agree in gender and number with the noun it's replacing.
18. *Lo compró hace poco.*
19. True. The indirect object is the person or thing the action is intended to benefit or harm.
20. d. Las

# Eating Out

1. False. *Desayuno* is in the morning and *Merienda* is in the afternoon
2. *Mi comida preferida es el espagueti* or *Mi comida favorita es el espagueti*
3. False. *Encantar* means "to love" and *gustar* means "to like"
4. a. encanta
5. b. Me gustan las ostras
6. c. A ellos les gusta la paella
7. b. No le gusta comer pasta
8. a. Esta camisa es más pequeña que aquella
9. a. Me gusta menos la mesa que la silla
10. c. Érica es mayor que Carlos
11. c. Este libro es peor que el anterior
12. False. *Primeros* is the starter and *segundos* is the main course
13. b. ¿Qué trae este plato?
14. *Yo quiero una pizza*
15. *¿Podría traer la cuenta, por favor?*
16. *Bien*
17. a. the feminine form of the adjective + *-mente*
18. It means "or"
19. d. *porque*
20. It means "if" and it is different from *sí*, which means "yes"

# Booking Tickets

1. True
2. c. *de la mañana*
3. b. *de la tarde*
4. a. *de la noche*
5. *Son las ocho de la mañana*
6. b. *Es la una de la mañana*
7. *Mediodía*
8. *Lunes, martes, miércoles, jueves, viernes, sábado, domingo.*
9. *Enero, febrero, marzo, abril, mayo, junio, julio, agosto, septiembre, octubre, noviembre, diciembre.*
10. b. *Quinto*
11. False.
12. True.
13. d. All of the previous
14. *Gustaré, gustarás, gustará, gustaremos, gustaréis, gustarán.*
15. *Leeré, leerás, leerá, leeremos, leeréis, leerán.*
16. c. *En efecto*
17. False.
18. Egoísta
19.

# Talking About Your Past

1. *Invierno* comes before *primavera*, and *verano* comes before *otoño*.
2. b. to talk about past events
3. False. That is the case for the *pretérito imperfecto*
4. True.
5. a. to talk about past habits
6. True.
7. a. amabas

8. The *pretérito perfecto simple* because it is an isolated event.
9. The *pretérito imperfecto* because it is something that used to happen often in the past.
10. b. estuvimos
11. The *pretérito perfecto simple*
12. The *pretérito imperfecto*
13. c. hace días
14. d. nothing
15. c. none
16. Yes, it does
17. *cuyo, cuya, cuyos,* or *cuyas*
18. a. Los lugares que visité en España son hermosos
19. d. empresario/a
20. c. en

# Quiz

1. *Julia es mi tía*
2. You can use the phrase "*mi cara es*" with the adjectives: *barbuda, cuadrada, redonda, larga, ovala, pecosa* or *redonda*.
3. *cabeza, hombros, rodillas y dedos del pie*
4. *el mío, la mía, los míos, las mías*
5. *nos*
6. *les*
7. *Me gustan las lentejas, pero no me encanta el gazpacho*
8. *Esta es la mejor paella del mundo*
9. *Una mesa para cuatro, por favor*
10. *difícilmente*
11. *Hoy es domingo 18 de julio de 2021*
12. *cantaré, cantarás, cantará, cantaremos, cantaréis, cantarán*
13. *Mañana vamos a cantar toda la noche*

14. *En absoluto* is an adverb of negation and means "not at all"
15. "clumsy"
16. The *pretérito perfecto simple* is used to talk about single events in the past, while the *pretérito imperfecto* is used to talk about past habits.
17. *salí, saliste, salió, salimos, salisteis, salieron*
18. *salía, salías, salía, salíamos, salíais, salían*
19. *algo* means "something" and it is an indefinite pronoun.
20. It is used to talk about a person and it means "who."

# Extra: IPA Phonemic Chart

Hi! It's Julio here again. I've come to teach you the Spanish phonemes. The IPA (International Phonetic Alphabet) is made up of symbols used to describe language sounds. The sounds used in Spanish are very different from those used in English. The symbols may appear a bit difficult to understand, but I've got you covered! I'll make it clear and simple for you to understand so you can go back to this page anytime you need to.

This is a simplified Spanish IPA chart:

| Vowels | ä (sala) | e̞ (querer) | i (iris) | o̞ (oso) | u (luz) |
|---|---|---|---|---|---|
| Consonants | b (futbol) | β (bebé) | d (cuando) | ð (dado) | f (foco) |
| | g (gota) | j (ayuda) | k (caja) | l (leer) | ʎ (llave) |
| | m (mala) | n (nene) | ɲ (ñandú) | ŋ (tengo) | p (papel) |
| | r (barro) | ɾ (caro) | s (seco) | θ (zorro) | t (torta) |

|  | tʃ (charco) | v (afgano) | x (mojar) | ʃ (show) |  |
|---|---|---|---|---|---|

I know, it looks like a lot! But do not fret! Let's break it down so you can understand it and make the most of it.

Let's start with the vowels. To be honest, none of the Spanish vowels sounds exactly like any English vowel. But here's a trick to attempting a better pronunciation that worked for Sarah:

- /ä/: It sounds like the A in "father," only Spanish A is a bit shorter.
- /e̞/: It sounds like the E in "men," only your tongue should be a bit forward.
- /i/: It sounds like the EE in "see," only shorter.
- /o̞/: It sounds like the O in "pot," only the sound isn't made from the very back of the throat but from the middle of the mouth.
- /u/: It sounds like the OO in "soothe," only shorter.

Consonants are a bit more complicated because, depending on the region, their pronunciation may vary greatly. But let's try to make the chart above a bit simpler:

- /b/: This phoneme is the same as the English B in "but" and is generally used when there's a V or a B at the beginning of a word or after a consonant. Did you notice that I said a V or a B? Well, that's because there isn't a phonetic difference between the two in Spanish. They sound the same! Consider that in Spanish, we shouldn't blow that much air when pronouncing this consonant.
- /β/: This phoneme is also used for Bs and is used in many instances in Spanish, but it doesn't sound like the English B. It is between an English B and a V, but your lips shouldn't touch, and your teeth shouldn't touch your lower lip either.
- /d/: This sound does have an English counterpart; it is the D sound in "dog." However, many Spanish learners tend to use it everywhere they see a D when, most often than not, they should use the /ð/ sound. The /d/ sound

is generally used only after some consonants.

- **/ð/**: This sound also exists in English; it is the TH sound in "this." When we see a D, we should probably pronounce it like a TH. To remember how to pronounce this consonant, remember that *madre* and "mother" use the same sound!
- **/f/**: This sound is pronounced the same as the English F in "follow," and you can use it almost every time you see an F in Spanish. There's finally one that gives us a break, right?
- **/g/**: For this consonant, there is also an English equivalent; it sounds just like the G in "goat." However, like in English, not all Gs sound the same in Spanish. When G is followed by E or I, it is pronounced with this phoneme: /x/
- **/j/**: This is a sound that isn't used by all Spanish speakers, and it doesn't have an English equivalent, but it is between the "j" sound in "jeep" and the "y" sound in "yet." Those who use this sound use it whenever a vowel follows a Y.
- **/k/**: This sound is the same as the English C in "cat." It is used when the letter C is followed by A, O, or U and whenever there's a letter K.
- **/l/**: This is the same sound as the English L in "light." The letter L always has this sound, except when it is doubled.
- **/ʎ/**: This sound is very similar to the sound of the Y in "yet," only it is a bit more open. It is used in some places whenever there is a double L. However, in some other places, the double L may be pronounced with a /j/ sound or a /ʃ/ sound.
- **/m/**: This is another straightforward sound, thankfully. This is the same as the M sound in "mole" and is used whenever there is an M in Spanish.
- **/n/**: The N sound in "nice" is the same as this! And it is used whenever there is an N in Spanish.

- **/ɲ/**: This may be a tricky sound because neither the letter Ñ nor the /ɲ/ sound exist in English. This phoneme sounds a bit like an N followed by a Y, like in the last name of actress Lupita Nyong'o, or the name of the artist Kanye West. It is used whenever there is an Ñ.
- **/ŋ/**: Like in Spanish, this sound is used whenever there is an N and a G together, like in any "-ing" ending, or an N and a K together.
- **/p/**: This sound is also the same in English as it is in Spanish, but, like the /b/, in Spanish, we shouldn't blow as much air when we pronounce it. It is used whenever there is a P, and it sounds like the P in "point."
- **/r/**: For English speakers, this is a tough one. This sound is used whenever a word starts with R, or when there is a double R. To pronounce it, your tongue should be in the same position as when you pronounce the English R, but you have to make a trill between your tongue and ridge of bone behind your teeth. It may take practice to master it, but I know you can learn to roll your Rs.
- **/ɾ/**: In English, this is called a voiced alveolar tap, and it is the TT sound used by some English speakers, like Americans, when they say "better." In Spanish, it is used whenever there is a single R in the middle of a word.
- **/s/**: Another sound that is the same in English as in Spanish! This one is the S sound in "see" and, in Spanish, is used whenever there is an S at the beginning of a word (unless it is followed by an H).
- **/θ/**: This is the sound that Spanish people use when a word starts with a C followed by I or E, or when there is an S or a Z after a vowel. And it sounds like the TH sound in "thing."
- **/t/**: This is the T sound used in "stay." And in Spanish, it is used for all Ts.
- **/tʃ/**: Whenever there is a CH in Spanish, this phoneme is used, and it sounds like the CH in "choose."
- **/v/**: This is not a common sound in Spanish; it is used only when a G follows the F.

- /x/: This sound does not exist in English, but it is similar to the H sound in "hall," only it is a bit stronger. It is used when an E or an I follow a J or a G. Sometimes, although it is an exception, it can be the sound of the X in words like "México."
- /ʃ/: This is the sound of the SH in "show," and, in Spanish, it is used whenever there is an SH. As we've mentioned, it is also used in some places when there is an LL.

I hope this has made Spanish pronunciation a bit easier for you. Remember that practice makes perfect, so once you get acquainted with the phonemes and with the language, you'll definitely be a pro!

# Extra: Glossary of Grammatical Terms

Before saying goodbye, I wanted to share the glossary of grammatical terms I have been compiling with the words Julio used during the trip. I hope you find it helpful!

adjective (adjetivo): a word that modifies a noun or its referent.

adverb (adverbio): a word that modifies a verb, an adjective or another adverb.

affirmative sentence (oración afirmativa): a sentence that states something; it expresses validity of truth.

agreement (concordancia): the correspondence in some grammatical feature (number, gender or person) between words.

article (artículo): the words used together with nouns to limit them, such as "a," "an," and "the."

cardinal number (número cardinal): a number used in simple counting, and to indicate how many elements there are in a group.

clause (cláusula): a group of words that have a subject and a predicate, and are part of a larger sentence.

common noun (sustantivo común): a noun that refers to a class of entities and is used to designate instances of a class of beings or things.

comparative (comparativo): related to or constituting the intermediate degree of comparison of adjectives.

complement of the verb (complemento del verbo): a word, phrase, or clause that is necessary to complete the meaning of the verb.

conjugation (conjgación): the way in which we change the form of a verb to reflect tense, aspect, mood, voice, and person.

conjunction (conjunción): the words we use to join two or more elements, clauses, or sentences, such as "and," "but," "because," and "however."

definite article (artículo definido): an article put before a noun when the identity of the noun is known to the addressee.

demonstrative article (artículo demostrativo): a word that modifies a noun while it points out the one referred to, and distinguishes it from others.

demonstrative pronoun (pronombre demostrativo): the words we use to point out the one referred to, and to distinguish it from others.

diaeresis (diéresis): an orthographic mark (¨) used on top of vowels to indicate a change in pronunciation.

dialect (dialecto): a regional variety of language.

direct object (objeto directo): the noun or noun group which is directly affected by or involved in the action of the verb.

gender (género): a grammatical subclass, partly arbitrary and partly based on distinguishable characteristics, such as biological sex, which determines agreement with and selection of other words (such as nouns, pronouns, articles, adjectives, etc.)

gerund (gerundio): a nonpersonal form of the verb, which in English ends in -ing and, in Spanish, in -ndo, used in verbal periphrasis or as a modifier with adverbial nature.

graphic accent (tilde): Spanish orthographic mark (´) used to show the accented syllable or as a diacritic.

imperative (imperativo): the grammatical mood that expresses the will to influence the behavior of the addressee.

indefinite article (artículo indefinido): an article used before a noun when the identity of the noun is unknown to the addressee.

indefinite pronoun (pronombre indefinido): a word that doesn't have a specific familiar referent, and that's used to talk about people or things, or to express some quantity in a vague or general way.

indicative (indicativo): the grammatical mood which expresses that what's said by the predicate is believed to be factual information.

indirect object (objeto indirecto): is the person or thing that the action of the verb is intended to benefit or harm.

infinitive (infinitivo): a nonpersonal form of the verb, which in Spanish, ends in -ar, -er, or -ir, used in verbal periphrasis or as a modifier with noun nature.

interrogative pronoun (pronombre interrogativo): a pronoun used to ask questions; they are used for reference to people or to things.

intonation (entonación): the fall and rise in pitch of the voice when talking.

irregular verb (verbo irregular): a verb that doesn't conform to the usual pattern of inflection.

mood (modo): a grammatical feature of verbs that signals modality, that is, the attitude of the speaker toward what they are saying (for example, is it a fact, a desire, a command?)

noun (sustantivo): a type of word that works as the name of an object or set of objects, such as: living creatures, actions, qualities, places, or concepts.

number (número): a grammatical category of different types of words (nouns, pronouns, adjectives, and verbs) that expresses count distinctions; in English and Spanish, number can be singular or plural.

object pronoun (pronombre de objeto): a personal pronoun normally used as the direct or indirect object of a verb, or as the object of a preposition.

ordinal number (número ordinal): a number used to represent the position or rank of a noun.

person (persona): the grammatical distinction between those speaking (first person), those being addressed (second person), and those who are neither speaking nor being addressed (third person).

phoneme (fonema): in a given language, a unit of sound that can distinguish two words.

possessive adjective (adjetivo posesivo): a type of adjective that modifies a noun by identifying who has ownership or possession over it.

possessive pronoun (pronombre posesivo): a type of pronoun that shows a noun's ownership or possession.

predicate (predicado): a part of a sentence or clause that contains a verb, and states something about the subject.

pronoun (pronombre): a word used as a substitute for a noun or a noun phrase; it's used to refer to people, animals or things without naming them, when the referent has been named or is understood from context.

proper noun (nombre propio): a word or group of words that designate a particular person, place, or thing, and is usually capitalized in English.

regular verb (verbo regular): a verb that follows the usual pattern of inflection when it's conjugated, without modifying its root.

relative clause (oración de relativo): a type of clause that compliments a noun or a noun phrase.

relative pronoun (pronombre relativo): a grammatical device used to introduce a relative clause.

root (raíz): the element from which a word is derived by phonetic change or by extension.

sentence (oración): a grammatical structure formed by the union of a subject and a predicate; in writing, it usually begins with a capital letter and concludes with end punctuation.

stressed syllable (sílaba tónica): the syllable of a word that carries the phonetic emphasis or prominence.

subject (sujeto): a noun, pronoun, or noun phrase that designates the entity of which something is predicated.

subject pronoun (pronombres de sujeto): a personal pronoun normally used as the subject of a clause.

superlative (superlativo): related to or constituting the degree of comparison that denotes an extreme or unsurpassed level or extent of adjectives.

tense (tiempo): a category of the verb that expresses a distinction of time or duration of the action or state denoted by that verb.

time marker (marcador temporal): a word or expression used in discourse to indicate time.

verb (verbo): a word that is the center of a predicate and that's inflected for agreement, tense, voice, mood, or aspect.

# Part 2: Intermediate Spanish

*The Fast-Track Guide to Mastering Spanish in 30 Days*

# Introduction

*¡Hola! ¿Cómo estás?*

Are you a beginner-to-intermediate speaker of Spanish? Do you want to continue studying this fascinating language but don't have the time to take lessons? Do you get bored in a classroom? Do you think studying grammar in the abstract is hard? Do you like reading short stories? If any of this resonates with you, you've come to the right place.

*Intermediate Spanish: The Fast-Track Guide to Mastering Spanish in 30 Days* is a Spanish-learning book, but it's not just any book. Here, you will learn the language in a practical way thanks to our 11 Spanish short stories that will make the grammar fun and easy to understand and the exercises fun to solve.

Starting from the second one, each chapter in this book begins with a fun short story in Spanish — don't worry, we will also provide a vocabulary list for you to check the words you don't know! — that will give context to grammar topics you need to learn to advance from beginner to intermediate student. Besides, the book has plenty of quizzes and exercises for you to test how much you've learned.

To start this 30-day intermediate Spanish-learning journey, we will quickly review and quiz you on all the basic topics that you already know: the Spanish alphabet and its accents; word order in Spanish; numbers up to a hundred; the verbs *ser* and *estar*;

talking about the family; regular conjugation in the present tenses; vocabulary on food, parts of the house, and parts of the city; reading comprehension of simple texts; and writing simple descriptions.

In the second chapter, we'll study how to use numbers in Spanish in a wide range of situations, like telling the time and the date, talking about big numbers, using the cardinal and ordinal numbers, and using collective numbers.

The third chapter is dedicated to a tough topic of Spanish: gender. But don't worry; you'll learn what is the grammatical gender, the rules to determine the gender of nouns, the feminine and masculine forms of nouns and adjectives, gender agreement, and the generic masculine in Spanish. The fourth chapter is all about pronouns: personal, subject, object, demonstrative, relative, interrogative, reflexive, and possessive pronouns, among others.

We'll focus on other types of words in chapters five and six. First, we'll deepen your knowledge of adjectives and adverbs by studying adjectives used as nouns, adjectives used as adverbs, and the position of adjectives and adverbs, among other topics. Then, we'll delve into the definite and indefinite articles to tackle everything there is to know about them.

When you reach this part of the book, you'll be halfway through! So, it will be time for a Mid-Book Quiz, where you'll be tested on everything you will have learned.

Moving on, we'll have three chapters dedicated to the Spanish tenses. In chapter 7, we'll focus on the present; in chapter 8, we'll think about the past; and in chapter 9, we'll look towards the future. Chapter 10 will tackle short but important words: conjunctions and prepositions.

In chapter 11, you'll put everything learned into practice to create and organize interrogative, affirmative, and negative sentences. You'll be able to ask and answer yes/no questions, wh-questions, rhetorical questions, tag questions, polite questions, and negative statements. To finish the book, just before the final quiz, we'll talk about what other people said: we'll learn how to report information through indirect speech.

What are you waiting for? Let's embark on this 30-day journey. In this book, you'll find everything you need to continue learning Spanish and become an intermediate speaker. Let's get to it!

# Chapter 1:
# From Beginner to Intermediate

This chapter intends to work as a bridge for you to advance from being a basic user of Spanish to an intermediate language student. With that in mind, first, we'll start with a historical and cultural overview of the Spanish language. Then, we'll move on to a basic-Spanish quiz. Afterward, we'll present a helpful tool for students of any language: the IPA chart. We'll finish off with some tips on how to best use this book.

## The History of the Spanish Language

The Royal Academy of the Spanish Language tells us that the word *español* comes from the Provencal *espaignol*, which in turn comes from the Medieval Latin *hispaniolus*, meaning "of Hispania." That was the name the Romans had given to the Iberian Peninsula. This means that Spanish comes from Latin, like Portuguese, Catalan, Galician, Provencal, French, Italian, and other Romance languages. This is because most of the Iberian Peninsula was conquered by Rome and lived under its reign, like many other European territories.

In the 5th century, the fall of the Roman Empire brought a decrease in the influence of Cultured Latin among the people. Vulgar Latin was already widely spoken, a similar language but with different phonetics, syntax, and lexicon. In this context in which Latin was losing its pure shape, the Castilian dialect was born in the Spanish region nowadays known as the Autonomous Community of Castile and León. Apart from Vulgar Latin, this first version of Spanish or Castilian had Greek, Celtic, and Germanic influences. Later, in the 7th Century, the Muslim invasion also brought its influence.

In the year 1200, under the reign of Alfonso X of Castile, the creation of a standard Spanish language based on the Castilian dialect began. The King and his court of scholars adopted the city of Toledo as the base for their activities. There, they wrote original works in Castilian, translated stories and chronicles, and scientific, legal, and literary works from other languages (mainly Latin, Greek, and Arabic). This enormous translation effort was a significant vehicle for disseminating knowledge through Ancient Western Europe. Alfonso X also adopted Castilian as the language of all administrative and official documents and decrees.

During the reign of Queen Isabella I of Castile and King Ferdinand II of Aragon, the Catholic Monarchs, the Castilian dialect was widely spread. The Monarchs completed the reconquest of Spain in 1492, after which they made Castilian the official language in their kingdom. In that same year, a very important book appeared: *Gramática de la lengua castellana* ("Grammar of the Castilian language"), by Antonio de Nebrija. It was the first treatise to study and try to define the grammar of a European language.

Just as Latin arrived in the Iberian Peninsula through conquest, the same happened with the Spanish language in the Americas. The Spanish conquerors imposed their language on the different native peoples. Through the Hispanization of the continent, Spanish was rooted as the primary language in the entire region. However, the indigenous languages greatly influenced Spanish, adding several words such as *aguacate* ("avocado"), *chocolate*, and *tiza* ("chalk") from the Aztecs; *cóndor* and *vicuña* from the Incas; and *hamaca* ("hammock") and *huracán* ("hurricane") from the Arawakan language.

All this trajectory made the resulting dialect a hybrid language that, like all languages, continues evolving, influenced by migration, mass media, science, technology, and many other factors.

Nowadays, the Spanish language is spread throughout the planet, and more than 560 million people speak it as a native, second, or foreign language. Spanish is the second language of a number of native speakers in the world, it's also second in international communications, and it's the official language of 20 countries. Being able to communicate fluently in such a universal and multicultural language is going to open lots of doors for you.

## Are You an Intermediate Speaker?

This quiz is designed to test your grasp of some basic Spanish topics. Let's see how much you remember about:

- the Spanish alphabet and its accents;
- word order in Spanish;
- numbers up to a hundred;
- basic vocabulary (words for food, parts of the house, parts of the city, colors);
- talking about the family;
- the verbs *ser* and *estar*;
- common verbs conjugated in the present tenses;
- reading comprehension of a simple text;
- writing a simple description.

Are you ready? Here we go!

1. Can you write down the corresponding Spanish words for these English words? Then, spell them out loud following the example:
    a. Woman: (Mujer: eme-u-jota-e-erre)
    b. Man:
    c. Girl:
    d. Dog:
    e. House:

2. Should these words have a *tilde* (graphic accent)? Justify your answer following the example.

a. *Cancion:* It should have a tilde in the O because it's an *aguda* word that ends in N: *canción*.
   b. *Papel:*
   c. *Tragico:*
   d. *Esposa:*
   e. *Lapiz:*
3. What are *tildes* for?
4. What do the following words have in common? Choose the correct option: *azúcar, nunca, maleta, útil,* and *trébol.*
   a. They are all *agudas*
   b. They are all *graves*
   c. They are all *esdrújulas*
5. Is the R in *fuerza* a rolled R or soft R? What about the R in *rápido*? And the double R in *perro*?
6. Can you write down the rule for the uses of the rolled R and the soft R?
7. Choose the odd one out and justify your answer:
   a. *Agua*
   b. *Guitarra*
   c. *Merengue*
   d. *Águila*
8. All of these sentences are grammatically correct. However, there's one in each pair that is more commonly used. Can you point out which one?
   a. El libro lo escribió María.
   b. María escribió el libro.
      Los alumnos se portan mal.
   c. Se portan mal los alumnos.
   d. José preparó la cena.
   e. La cena fue preparada por José.
9. Are these sentences grammatically correct? Correct the ones that are not.
   a. Mi hermana juegan muy bien al fútbol.
   b. Tu casa nueva es muy lindo.

- c. Los niños tiene hambre.
- d. No preparé la cena.
- e. Siempre desayuno algo dulces.
- f. Mañana viene mi novia a almorzar. Le voy a cocinar pastas.
- g. Hice las compras, pero me lo olvidé en el mercado.
- h. Estoy llevando al perro al parque. Las llevo todas las mañanas.

10. True or false: In Spanish, the verb usually comes after the subject.
11. True or false: In Spanish, the subject is always explicit.
12. True or false: In Spanish, a statement's order must change to turn it into a question.
13. True or false: In Spanish, the adjectives usually go after the noun they are modifying.
14. Complete the sentence with the correct color. Remember that when colors are adjectives, they have to agree in gender and number with the noun they are modifying:
    - a. El cielo es ......
    - b. Las bananas son ......
    - c. Las hojas de los árboles son ......
    - d. La sangre es ......
    - e. Las nubes son ......
    - f. Si mezclas blanco y negro, obtienes ......
    - g. Por fuera, el kiwi es ......
    - h. Las naranjas son ......
15. Solve these calculations and write down the answers in Spanish:
    - a. Dos más dos:
    - b. Tres más cinco:
    - c. Siete por dos:
    - d. Diez más tres:
    - e. Veinte menos uno:

f. Veinticinco por dos:
  g. Treinta por dos:
  h. Ochenta más quince:
16. Complete the sentences with the correct word for family members.
    a. El esposo de mi abuela es mi ......
    b. El hijo de mi tía es mi ......
    c. La hija de mi madre es mi ......
    d. El hermano de mi padre es mi ......
    e. Mi mamá y mi papá son mis ......
    f. La pareja de mi padre es mi ......
17. Cross the odd one out and justify your answer like in the example:
    a. *Cocina, baño, árbol, dormitorio.* Árbol, porque no es una parte de la casa.
    b. *Alfombra, sofá, cama, banana.*
    c. *Fresa, cerdo, ciruela, melón.*
    d. *Pasto, arroz, azúcar, harina.*
    e. *Sopa, habitación, cocido, pizza.*
    f. *Al horno, grillado, al vapor, blanco.*
    g. *Estrella, ayuntamiento, escuela, hospital.*
    h. *Acera, calle, semáforo, río.*
    i. *Martes, domingo, marzo, jueves.*
    j. *Viernes, octubre, abril, agosto.*
18. Match the questions on the left with what they are inquiring about on the right:

| | | |
|---|---|---|
| a. ¿Cómo te llamas? | - | el nombre |
| b. ¿Cuántos años tienes? | - | la nacionalidad/el lugar de origen |
| c. ¿A qué te dedicas? | - | la edad |
| d. ¿Tienes correo electrónico? | - | la profesión |
| | - | el número de teléfono |

e. ¿Cuál es tu número de teléfono?  - el correo electrónico
f. ¿Cuál es tu nombre?
g. ¿En qué trabajas?
h. ¿De dónde eres?
i. ¿Tienes móvil?

19. Complete the following card with your information:
    Me llamo ......... y soy (de) ......... . Vivo en ......... . Tengo ......... años y soy/trabajo en ......... . Mi número de teléfono es ......... y mi (dirección de) correo electrónico es ......... .

20. Complete the following sentences with *ser* or *estar*.
    a. El verbo ...... se utiliza para hablar de estados que duran mucho tiempo o son permanentes.
    b. El verbo ...... se utiliza para hablar de estados temporales.

21. Now, complete the following sentences with the present simple of *ser* or *estar*.
    a. Mi nombre ...... Alejandra.
    b. ...... de Argentina.
    c. En este momento, ...... en Venezuela.
    d. Mi novia ...... de aquí.
    e. Su nombre ...... María.
    f. ...... de vacaciones juntas.

22. Complete the following chart with the conjugation of these regular verbs in the present simple:

|  | **AMAR** | **TEMER** | **PARTIR** |
|---|---|---|---|
| yo | amo | ...... | ...... |
| tú | ...... | ...... | partes |
| él / ella | ...... | teme | ...... |

| nosotros / nosotras | ...... | ...... | partimos |
|---|---|---|---|
| vosotros / vosotras | amáis | ...... | ...... |
| ellos / ellas / ustedes | ...... | temen | ...... |

23. Read this short text about a Chilean-Spanish film director and answer the questions below.

    *Alejandro Amenábar nace en Santiago de Chile en 1972. Al año siguiente, su familia se muda a vivir a España, a Madrid.*
    *En 1990 empieza a estudiar la carrera de Imagen y Sonido, pero no termina los estudios. En 1996 estrena su primer largometraje,* Tesis.
    *Poco después, llegan sus películas más famosas.* Abre los ojos, *de 1997, fue un gran éxito. En 2001 se estrena* Los Otros, *una película de terror y suspenso con Nicole Kidman como protagonista.*
    *En los últimos años ha filmado más películas, pero también video clips de música y series de televisión.*

    a. ¿En qué año nace Alejandro Amenábar?
    b. ¿Qué edad tiene cuando sus padres se mudan a España?
    c. ¿Qué estudió en la universidad? ¿Terminó la carrera?
    d. La película que tiene como protagonista a Nicole Kidman, ¿de qué género es?
    e. ¿Qué ha hecho en los últimos años?

24. Write a short description about how you feel studying Spanish. You can use the one below as a model:
    *Soy un poco tímida y me siento insegura cuando tengo que hablar en español con otras personas. En cambio, hacer los ejercicios de gramática me divierte. Soy una persona estudiosa y me gusta leer, por lo que los*

*ejercicios de lectura y comprensión me resultan fáciles. Sin embargo, no soy buena escribiendo: todavía no aprendo las reglas de acentuación.*

## IPA phonemic chart

Since you already have some experience with Spanish, you probably know that Spanish pronunciation is quite different from English. However, you may also know that it's more straightforward. Once you learn how to say each letter aloud, you are pretty much set.

The IPA phonemic chart is a useful tool that can help you pronounce each letter of the Spanish alphabet. Instead of using letters, this chart uses symbols to represent the exact sound we need to make to pronounce a word. We've created one for you where you'll find the IPA symbol, then a Spanish word with that sound, and finally an English word with a similar sound. Remember that the pronunciation of the two languages is different, so the English example *is just an approximation.* When there's an X, it means there is no similar English sound.

Let's delve into this chart so that you can refer back to it in case you need help pronouncing any of this book's words.

| | | | | | |
|---|---|---|---|---|---|
| Vocales | ä *mal* "bad" | e̞ *tren* "Ben" | i *mina* "dean" | o̞ *oro* "lot" | u *tu* "moon" |
| Consonantes | b *bar* "bar" | β *prueba* X | d *caldo* "dad" | ð *dato* "this" | f *fuego* "fire" |
| | g *gato* "game" | j *ayuda*\* X | k *coche* "car" | l *luz* "light" | ʎ *lluvia* "young" |
| | m *mamá* "mother" | n *normal* "normal" | ɲ *ñoqui* "Kanye" | ŋ *conga* "going" | p *punto* "point" |

| | r | ɾ | s | θ | t |
|---|---|---|---|---|---|
| | *r*opa<br>X | pa*r*o<br>"butter"** | *s*ur<br>"south" | *z*apato*<br>"thought" | *t*ipo<br>"type" |
| | tʃ<br>*ch*ocolate<br>"chocolate" | v<br>A*f*ganistán<br>"vocal" | x<br>*h*oja<br>"hall" | ʃ<br>*sh*erpa<br>"show" | |

* This sound is not present in all Spanish dialects.
** In American pronunciation.

Hopefully, this chart will help you master Spanish pronunciation. Remember to come back to it when you have doubts about the pronunciation of any word in this book.

**Tips**

To finish this first chapter, we'll leave with some tips on using this book so that you can make the most of it.

As we said in the introduction, starting from chapter 2, at the beginning of each chapter, you'll find a short story. These stories are written in a level of Spanish that you'll be able to understand. However, if you have difficulty getting the gist of the text, try re-reading it a couple of times. Also, the words that can be a bit harder are **bolded** and listed below the story with their English translation. For other words you might not know, it's a good idea to try to guess their meaning from context and then check it in a dictionary. After that, we encourage you to make your own vocabulary lists or flashcards.

After each short story, there's a grammar section. There, you'll find a deep yet simple explanation for a number of topics needed to become an intermediate speaker of Spanish. We know it can be a bit overwhelming, but we've done our best to make it entertaining! So don't be afraid, and read these sections as often as you need. Sometimes, taking your own notes as you read can help the new concepts settle.

The last section in each chapter is a quiz and will cover everything in that chapter. If you don't do so well on the first attempt, we encourage you to go back to the beginning of the chapter and revise the information. Then, you can retake the quiz. Remember, practice makes perfect!

# Chapter 2:
# Numbers, Numbers, Numbers

## Short Story: Piso trece

Antes de entrar al edificio, Helena mira la **hora** en su **reloj**. Son las **nueve y veinticinco**. Llegó a su entrevista **cinco** minutos **antes**. Eso la relaja. Helena siente que esos cinco minutos le dan un **margen** de maniobra. Los necesita, porque es su primera entrevista **en mucho tiempo**. Quiere tener todo bajo control.

El lobby es un lugar elegante. El edificio es antiguo y está muy bien mantenido. Fue uno de los primeros rascacielos de la ciudad, construidos durante **la década del treinta**. Tiene **casi cien años**.

Helena se acerca al recepcionista.

—Disculpe, soy Helena Gamboa. Estoy aquí para una entrevista en el **piso trece**. Es **a las nueve y media**.

—¡Shh! —responde el recepcionista.

—¿Cómo? —pregunta Helena.

—Aquí no decimos piso tre...**Treceavo**. Es de mala suerte —aclara el recepcionista—. Pase, tome el ascensor **número dos**.

Helena decide ignorar el comentario. "Hay gente muy supersticiosa", piensa. Entonces entra en el **segundo** ascensor. Allí descubre que el edificio todavía tiene ascensorista. Es una mujer pequeña, aún más baja que Helena, con el cabello corto y blanco.

"Debe tener **por lo menos ochenta años**", piensa Helena. "Es **casi tan** vieja como el edificio". Por su expresión, la ascensorista parece estar dormida. Sin embargo, su trabajo es necesario. El ascensor no tiene botones, sino una especie de palanca ancha de bronce. No parece fácil de manipular.

—¿A qué piso? —pregunta la ascensorista.

—Al piso trece, por favor —responde Helena.

La ascensorista abre los ojos con una expresión de horror. Ya no parece estar dormida. Ahora parece aterrada.

—¡¿Qué dijo?! —pregunta la ascensorista.

—Piso trec... —responde Helena.

—Por favor, no lo repita —dice la ascensorista, mientras cubre la boca de Helena con su mano. Helena siente el olor penetrante del guante de cuero sobre su nariz—. No... Lo siento —se disculpa la ascensorista, mientras suelta a Helena—. La costumbre. Usted no sabe... Pero no tiene por qué saber. Es mejor así —se interrumpe.

Helena la mira extrañada. Sigue asustada por su reacción.

—Al **piso doce y medio**, entonces —dice la ascensorista.

Helena no responde, pero ve cómo la ascensorista maneja la palanca. En **pocos minutos** llegan a destino.

—Piso doce y medio —dice la ascensorista—. ¡Mucha suerte, señorita!

## Vocabulary List

| Spanish | English |
|---|---|
| la hora | time |
| el reloj | watch |
| nueve y veinticinco | twenty five past nine |

| | |
|---|---|
| cinco | five |
| antes | before |
| el margen | margin |
| en mucho tiempo | in a long time |
| la década del treinta | the 30s |
| casi cien años | almost a hundred years |
| el piso trece | thirteenth floor |
| a las nueve y media | at half past nine |
| treceavo, treceava | thirteenth |
| el número dos | number two |
| segundo, segunda | second |
| por lo menos | at least |
| ochenta años | eighty years |
| casi tan | almost as |
| el piso doce y medio | twelve and a half floor |
| pocos, pocas | few |

# Grammar Section

As we can tell from this chapter's short story, numbers are all around us! By the end of this chapter, you will be able to:

- talk about big numbers
- ask and tell the time and date
- use collective numbers
- use cardinal and ordinal numbers

Are you ready?

**From cien to mil**

To become an intermediate Spanish speaker, we need to be able to do more than counting to one hundred! Let's start by learning how to form big numbers. In the short story, Helena goes into a building that's almost a hundred years old (*Tiene casi cien años*). Do you know how to form numbers above *cien* ("a hundred")? For instance, "a hundred and one" is said *ciento uno*. Let's break that number down to learn how to form it. You have to add the *-to* ending after *cien*, followed by the corresponding number, in this case, *uno*.

Let's take a look at some examples:

- *Ciento tres* means "a hundred and three."
- *Ciento cinco* means "a hundred and five."
- *Ciento treinta* means "a hundred and thirty."
- *Ciento ochenta y cuatro* means "a hundred and eighty four."

After *ciento noventa y nueve* ("one hundred and ninety nine") comes *doscientos* ("two hundred"). From this number on, we add two components to the word *ciento*: a previous *dos-*, *tres-*, *cuatro-*, which indicates that we are talking about two, three, four hundred, and a final *-s* to make it plural because we are talking about more than one hundred.

Let's take a look:

- *Doscientos* means "two hundred."
- *Trescientos* means "three hundred."
- *Cuatrocientos* means "four hundred."

- *Seiscientos* means "six hundred."
- *Ochocientos* means "eight hundred."

But there are some numbers missing, right? That's because, as always, there are some exceptions.

- *Quinientos* means "five hundred."
- *Setecientos* means "six hundred."
- *Novecientos* means "nine hundred."

These last numbers don't follow the rule above, but since it's only three, I'm sure you'll remember them.

Don't forget that gender also affects numbers when we talk about hundreds. We say *cientos* when we refer to masculine things and *cientas* when we talk about feminine things. Look at the examples:

- *Helena viajó trescientos kilómetros para llegar* ("Helena traveled three hundred kilometers to get there.")
- *Había doscientas treinta y cuatro oficinas en el edificio* ("There were two hundred and thirty four offices in the building.")

Let's continue forming three-digit numbers in Spanish. After the hundred (for example, *doscientas*) comes the decimal (for example, *treinta*), followed by the word *y* plus the unit (for example, *cuatro*): *doscientas treinta y cuatro* ("two hundred and four.")

### *Mil* and above

Do you think you can go a little further? Don't worry; the thousands and millions are quite easy in Spanish. We just need to follow the same structure as in English:

- *Tres mil* means "three thousand."
- *Cinco millones* means "five million."

And just like in English, knowing all this, you can just add as many numbers as you need. Let's see some examples:

- *Ocho mil* means "eight thousand."
- *Cuatro mil uno* means "four thousand and one."
- *Seis mil quinientos noventa y dos* means "six thousand five hundred and ninety two."

- *Cuarenta mil* means "forty thousand."
- *Ciento setenta mil* means "one hundred seventy thousand."
- *Seis millones* means "six million."
- *Once millones trescientos dos mil cuatrocientos ochenta* means "eleven million three hundred two thousand four hundred and eighty."

Let me finish the big numbers section with two differences between English and Spanish that can be quite confusing.

While English uses the comma to divide big numbers, Spanish uses a point:

- 10.900 (Spanish)
- 10,900 (English)

Knowing this, can you guess how Spanish expresses decimals? Yes, they use commas instead of points:

- 3,14 (Spanish)
- 3.14 (English)

Saying decimal numbers out loud is just like in English, but instead of saying "point", we say *coma*. So, 3,14 would be *tres coma catorce*. It can be a little confusing at first, but in the end, you just need to remember: in writing numbers, commas and points are used the other way around.

The second difference has to do with false friends, i.e., words in a language that look and sound like words in another language but that have different meanings. The Spanish *billones* does not mean the same as the English "billions". The Spanish equivalent to "billions" is *mil millones*. And *un billón* is equivalent to "trillion". So, if we wanted to talk in Spanish about the most populated country on earth, we would say:

- *China tiene **mil cuatrocientos millones** de habitantes.*

Whereas in English, we would say:

- "In China, there are **one billion four hundred million** inhabitants".

### Talking about the time and the date

The most common ways to ask for the time in Spanish are the following:

- *¿Qué hora es?*, which means "What time is it?"
- *¿Tienes hora?*, which means "Do you have the time?"
- *¿Puedes decirme la hora?*, which means "Can you tell me what's the time?"

If someone asks you what's the time, or if you need to say at what time something is happening, just follow this structure:

**The conjugation of the verb *ser* (*es* or *son*) + *la* or *las* + a number from 1 to 12 + *y* + the number of minutes + *de* + the part of the day**

Let's see some examples:

- *Son las diez y cuarenta de la mañana* ("It's ten forty in the morning.")
- *La reunión es a la una en punto de la tarde* ("The meeting is at one o'clock in the afternoon.")

Note that for 1 a.m. and 1 p.m., we conjugate the verb *ser* in the third person singular (*es*). We do it in the plural (son) for all the other times of the day.

### In a minute!

Just like in English, in Spanish, we divide the hours into ten-, fifteen- or twenty-minute intervals:

- *Son las doce en punto* means "It's twelve o'clock."
- *Son las tres y diez* means "It's ten past three."
- *Son las ocho y cuarto* means "It's a quarter past eight."
- *Es la una y veinte* means "It's twenty past one."
- *Son las seis y media* means "It's half past six."
- *Son las diez menos veinte* means "It's twenty to ten."
- *Son las doce menos cuarto* means "It's a quarter to twelve."
- *Son las siete menos diez* means "It's ten to seven."

**What's the date?**

Saying the date in Spanish is easy. Just use this structure:

*Hoy es* + the day of the week + the date + *de* + the month + *de* + the year

Let's see the formula applied to an example:

- *Hoy es viernes quince de julio de 2022* means "Today is Friday, July 15th, 2022."

Now, there are two differences with English worth noting. On the one hand, in English, we use ordinals, like "15th", to say the date, whereas, in Spanish, we use the cardinals, like *quince*. We only use the ordinal for *primero* ("first"). We'll talk more about cardinal and ordinal numbers in a minute. And on the other hand, as you probably already know, in Spanish, we don't use capital letters for the days of the week and the months of the year.

**One or more than one?**

The type of words we'll study in this section exist in English and Spanish, and "both" belong to the group! Collective numbers are used to name several persons or things as a unit, just like we did with "both" in the previous sentence. Let's see a vocabulary list with some *números colectivos*.

| Spanish | English |
|---|---|
| solo | alone |
| el dúo, el par, la pareja | duet, pair, couple |
| el trío | threesome |
| el cuarteto | quartet |
| el quinteto | quintet |
| el sexteto | sextet |

| | |
|---|---|
| la decena | group of ten |
| la docena | dozen |
| la quincena | fortnight |
| la veintena | group of twenty |
| la cuarentena | group of forty |
| el centenar | hundred |
| el millar | thousand |

The following group of collective numbers is dedicated to time periods:

| Spanish | English |
|---|---|
| el trimestre | trimester |
| el semestre | semester |
| el bienio | two-year period |
| el trienio | triennium |
| el cuatrienio | four-year period |
| el lustro | five-year period |
| el sexenio | six-year period |
| la década | decade |

| | |
|---|---|
| el siglo | century |
| el milenio | millenium |

**Primero, el uno; segundo, el dos**

We've already mentioned cardinal and ordinal numbers, and you are probably already familiar with them, even if you don't know what they are called. So, let's define them and see when we use them.

Cardinal numbers are the ones we use in counting. They indicate the number of elements in a given group. Have you guessed what we are talking about? Yes! They are just regular numbers, like *uno*, *veintidós*, and *diez*.

Ordinal numbers, as their name indicates, designate the place or order of an item in a sequence. For example, *primero*, *vigésimo segundo*, and *décimo*. Ordinals are adjectives derived from numbers, but they can sometimes work as nouns ().

The Spanish ordinals corresponding to numbers one to ten are pretty common, but Spanish speakers tend to avoid the ones above ten. For example, instead of saying *la doceava semana* ("the 12th week"), they would say *la semana doce* ("week twelve"). That's why we'll only list the most used ordinal numbers:

| Spanish | English |
|---|---|
| primero, primera, primeros, primeras | first |
| segundo, segunda, segundos, segundas | second |
| tercero, tercera, terceros, terceras | third |
| cuarto, cuarta, cuartos, cuartas | fourth |

| | |
|---|---|
| quinto, quinta, quintos, quintas | fifth |
| sexto, sexta, sextos, sextas | sixth |
| séptimo, séptima, séptimos, séptimas | seventh |
| octavo, octava, octavos, octavas | eighth |
| noveno, novena, novenos, novenas | nineth |
| décimo, décima, décimos, décimas | tenth |

As you can see from the table above, each Spanish ordinal has four variants. That's because ordinals are adjectives, so they vary in gender and number to match the noun they are modifying. One last thing worth noting about ordinals is that when *primero* and *tercero* are placed before a singular masculine noun, they become *primer* and *tercer*, like in the following example:

- *Mañana es mi primer día de trabajo en el nuevo puesto* ("Tomorrow is my first day of work in the new position.")

**Exercises**

1. Answer the following calculations by writing the numbers in Spanish – as shown in the example. These are the names of the basic operation you'll need: *más* ("plus"), *menos* ("minus"), *por* ("times"), and *dividido* ("divided").

    a. 100 + 35: *Cien más treinta y cinco es ciento treinta y cinco.*
    b. 560 - 20:
    c. 10.100 + 4.700:
    d. 225 x 6:
    e. 1.000.000 % 2,5:

2. The following chart shows the annual sales of three items in three given years. Look at it and complete the sentences, as shown in the example.

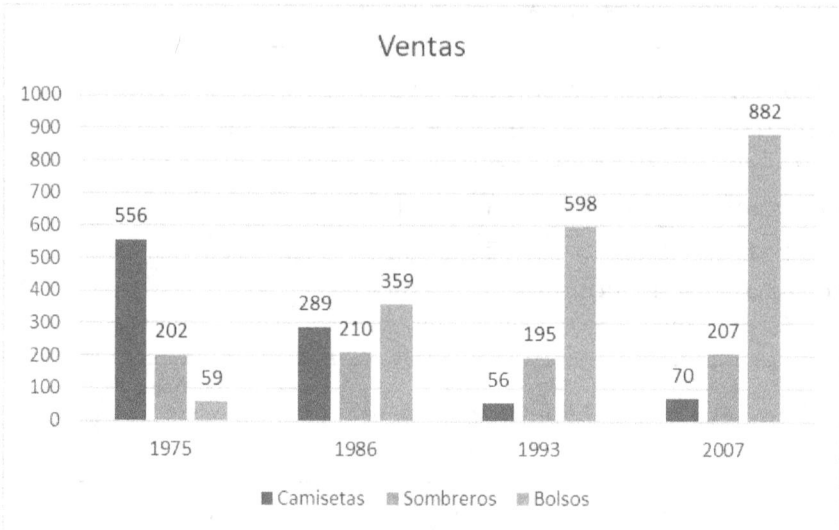

a. *En el año mil novecientos setenta y cinco, se vendieron quinientos cincuenta y seis camisetas, doscientos dos sombreros y cincuenta y nueve bolsos.*

b. En el año ......... (1986), se vendieron ......... (289) camisetas, ......... (210) sombreros y ......... (359) bolsos.

c. En el año ......... (1993), se vendieron ......... (56) camisetas, ......... (195) sombreros y ......... (598) bolsos.

d. En el año ......... (2007), se vendieron ......... (70) camisetas, ......... (207) sombreros y ......... (882) bolsos.

3. Looking at the chart above, decide whether the following statements are true or false. Correct the false ones.

a. En el año 1975 se vendieron más bolsos que sombreros.

b. Se vendieron más bolsos en 2007 que en 1993.

c. En 1986 y 2007 se vendió casi la misma cantidad de sombreros.

        d. El año en el que más bolsos se vendieron fue 1993.
4. Go back to the short story and read it again. Pay special attention to any references to time. Then, answer these questions in Spanish.
    a. What time is it when the narration starts?
    b. How early is Helena?
    c. At what time is the interview?
5. Read the following text in which someone is talking about their routine:
    a. *De lunes a viernes, me levanto a las siete y media de la mañana. Comienzo a trabajar a las nueve. Entre las doce y cuarto y la una del mediodía, me tomo un descanso para almorzar. Termino de trabajar a las cinco de la tarde. A las ocho y media, ceno. Me acuesta sobre las diez y media u once de la noche.*
    b. Now, write a similar text describing your routine. Make sure you include when you wake up, start work, have lunch, finish work, have dinner, and go to bed.

Congratulations on the good work! Now that you've finished the chapter, you can go back to the beginning of the grammar section and tick the topics you think you've learned.

# Chapter 3: Grammatical Genders

## Short Story: Alicia y la coneja

**De pronto**, Alberto deja de caminar. Silvia **avanza** un paso más, hasta que él le hace un gesto con la mano. Entonces ella también **se detiene**.

—Mira —dice Alberto **en voz baja. Señala** hacia adelante.

Silvia sigue la indicación de Alberto. Es de noche, y no hay nadie más en esa zona de la ciudad. Es un barrio comercial. De noche, las tiendas cierran y casi no hay tránsito.

—¿Qué pasa? —pregunta Silvia, intrigada.

—Un conejo —responde Alberto.

Entonces Silvia lo ve. Delante de un **cubo de basura, en plena calle**, hay un conejo blanco. Es grande. Parece suave y muy limpio.

—No lo puedo creer —dice Silvia.

—¿Un **conejo**, en la ciudad? —contesta Alberto.

—Bueno, quizás es una **coneja** —dice Silvia.

—No sé si eso es lo realmente importante —responde Alberto. Está sorprendido por la situación.

—Es muy grande —continúa Silvia—. Tiene el tamaño de un perro. ¿Los conejos son **más grandes** que las conejas? ¿O es **al revés**?

—No tengo ni idea —dice Alberto.

—¿Qué hace aquí? —pregunta Silvia—. En este barrio, esperaba ver palomas. Esas **palomas** feas que andan por la ciudad. O **ratas**.

—¿Cómo sabes que no son **palomos**? —contesta Alberto, **juguetón**—. O **ratones**.

—Creo que las ratas y los ratones son animales distintos —dice Silvia.

—Mira, se mueve —contesta Alberto.

El conejo (o la coneja) da unos saltos hacia el frente. Es bastante rápido (o rápida).

—¡Sigámosla! —dice Silvia.

Ambos avanzan detrás del conejo (o la coneja). Mantienen una **distancia segura** para no asustarlo (o asustarla). Sin embargo, la aventura no dura mucho tiempo. A los pocos metros, una niña **recoge** al animal. Ella está delante de la puerta de una casa vieja. Detrás, la espera su madre.

—¡Terminó el paseo! —dice la niña cuando recoge a su **mascota**.

—¿El conejo es tuyo? —pregunta Alberto.

—Es una coneja —responde la niña.

—¡Te lo dije! —dice Silvia.

—¿Cómo se llama? —pregunta Alberto, sin darle importancia a lo que dice su amiga.

—Blanquita —dice la niña.

—Es un nombre muy apropiado —responde Alberto—. Ella es en verdad muy blanca.

—¡Alicia, entra ya! —grita la madre, desde el interior de la casa—. ¿Qué te dije de hablar con **desconocidos**?

# Vocabulary List

| Spanish | English |
|---|---|
| de pronto | suddenly |
| avanzar | move forward |
| detenerse | stop |
| en voz baja | in a low voice, whispering |
| señalar | point at |
| el cubo de basura | trash can |
| en plena calle | in the middle of the street |
| el conejo | rabbit |
| la coneja | doe |
| más grande | bigger |
| al revés | the other way around |
| la paloma | pigeon |
| la rata | rat |
| el palomo | cock pigeon |
| juguetón, juguetona | playful |

| | |
|---|---|
| el ratón | mouse |
| distancia segura | safe distance |
| recoger | pick up |
| la mascota | pet |
| el desconocido, la desconocida | stranger |

## Grammar Section

By now, you probably know that Spanish is a gendered language. While English only shows gender in personal pronouns, in Spanish, everything has gender. Even animals, as we can tell from the story above! But, what *is* gender? Well, in this chapter, we'll tackle that question, together with the following subjects:

- what is the grammatical gender
- the rules for determining the gender of words
- the feminine and masculine forms of nouns and adjectives
- gender agreement
- referring collectively to masculine and feminine nouns

Are you ready? Let's get to it!

### Grammatical gender

Grammatical gender is a property of languages. It's used to divide nouns, pronouns, and adjectives (i.e., nominal elements) into classes. In Spanish, there are two grammatical genders: masculine and feminine. Some languages have more, like German, which has three (masculine, feminine, and neuter), and other languages don't have this distinction. In English, for example, there's no gender agreement between nominal elements, and gender is only reflected in pronouns referring to people.

So, Spanish is a gendered language. But, what does it mean? It means that all nouns have gender and that the pronouns, articles, and adjectives around nouns have to reflect that gender. This is what we call agreement or concord: the need to change a word to make it match a grammatical feature of another word to which it's syntactically connected.

It sounds confusing, doesn't it? But let's take an example of agreement from English so that you can get the gist of it. In English, there is agreement between demonstratives and nouns: the number of a noun determines which demonstrative we are going to use. So, with a singular noun such as "car," we need a singular demonstrative. We say "this car" or "that car." If we take that same noun in its plural form, we must use a plural demonstrative. We say "these cars" or "those cars." See? It wasn't so hard.

Now that we understand the concept of agreement, we need to take it to Spanish, where every word related to a noun has to agree in gender and number with that noun, and where all nouns have gender. Even though it might sound weird to you, *mesa* ("table") is feminine, and *coche* ("car") is masculine. Furthermore, if we used those nouns with an article, we would say *la mesa* ("the table") and *el coche* ("the car"). So, *la* is the definite article (equivalent to English "the") that comes before feminine nouns, and *el* is the one for masculine ones. This is important to remember. Throughout this book, we always put an article together with a noun in the vocabulary lists so that you can know the gender of the word if it's not that clear.

Now let's talk about why some nouns are feminine and others masculine. It has to do with the word's etymology, the language's evolution, and other more complicated causes. However, in order to be fluent in Spanish, you don't need to go back in history. All you need to know is whether the noun is masculine or feminine; we'll help you with that in the next section.

**Feminine or masculine?**

Establishing the gender of a noun is not easy, but some concepts will help you. The first rule is that nouns referring to women tend to be feminine, and nouns referring to men tend to be masculine. Let's see some examples:

- *La mujer* is "the woman."
- *La niña* is "the girl."
- *La hija* is "the daughter."
- *La hermana* is "the sister."
- *La prima* is "the female cousin."
- *La tía* is "the aunt."
- *El hombre* is "the man."
- *El niño* is "the boy."
- *El hijo* is "the son."
- *El hermano* is "the brother."
- *El primo* is "the male cousin."
- *El tío* is "the uncle."

You can probably infer the second rule from going back to the examples above and paying attention to the last letter of all the words. Can you draw any conclusions?

In the nouns we listed, all the feminine ones end in -A, and almost all the masculine ones end in- O. Although the sample is not representative of the language, we can say that most nouns ending in -A are feminine and that most nouns ending in -O are masculine. However, as with any rule, there are many exceptions. For example, *la foto* ("the photo") is feminine, and *el programa* ("the program") is masculine. Besides, there're plenty of nouns that end in other letters, like *el hombre*, above.

Other typically masculine endings are -MA, like in *el pijama* ("the pajama"), and -OR, like in *el olor* ("the smell"). On the other hand, there are some other feminine endings besides -A. Nouns ending in -SIÓN, -CIÓN, -DAD, -TAD, -TUD, or -UMBRE are always feminine. Some examples are *la confusión* ("the confusion"), *la acción* ("the action"), *la soledad* ("the loneliness"), *la libertad* ("the freedom"), *la juventud* ("the youth"), and *la costumbre* ("the habit").

As you can see, there are some rules, but there are also many exceptions. Our recommendation: try to learn each new noun together with its article so that you can be sure of its gender.

### How to form feminine and masculine words

It's time to talk about morphemes! Morphemes are the minimum unit carrying meaning within a word. To form words, we take the root (for example *herman-*) and add morphemes: -O and -A to indicate gender, and -S to indicate number.

So, to indicate gender, we follow this process:

- herman + o = hermano ("brother").
- herman + a = hermana ("sister").

And, to indicate number:

- *herman + o + s = hermanos* ("brothers" or "siblings," because of the generic masculine, a concept we will see in a following section).
- *herman + a + s = hermanas* ("sisters").

These changes, called nominal flexions, apply to nouns and also adjectives. Let's see what happens with *lindo/linda* ("cute"):

- *lind + o: lindo* ("cute" used to describe masculine nouns).
- *lind + a: linda* ("cute" used to describe feminine nouns).

And let's see gender combined with number:

- *lindo + s: lindos* ("cute" used to describe plural, masculine nouns).
- *linda + s: lindas* ("cute" used to describe plural, feminine nouns).

Let's see some examples:

- *Mi hermano es lindo* ("My brother is cute.")
- *Mis hermanas son lindas* ("My sisters are cute.")

### Gender agreement: How does it work?

We have explained how gender works at the lexical level, that is, what happens with words. Now it's time to talk about what happens with gender throughout the sentence: we need to talk about agreement. We'll use some examples to show you how concord works:

- *La <u>casa</u> **amarilla** estaba **alta*** ("The yellow house was high.")
- *El <u>barco</u> **amarillo** estaba **hundido*** ("The yellow boat was sunk.")

As we already established, in Spanish, everything regarding gender is determined by nouns. In the examples above, all the bolded words express gender in agreement with the nouns, which are underlined.

When we talk about *casa*, a feminine noun, the article (*la*) and the adjectives that modify it (*amarilla* and *alta*) must also be feminine. The same would happen if we used a pronoun to replace the feminine noun *casa*, like in the following examples:

- *La <u>casa</u> **amarilla** estaba **alta**. Nos costó llegar a **ella*** ("The yellow house was high. It was hard to get to it.")

The same applies when we talk about *barco*, a masculine noun. We can see how the article (*el*), and the adjectives (*amarillo* and *hundido*) are also in the masculine. And what would happen if we used a pronoun to replace de masculine noun *barco*? Let's see:

- *El <u>barco</u> **amarillo** estaba **hundido**. Debieron descender mucho para dar con **él*** ("The yellow boat was sunk. They had to descend a lot to reach it.")

The examples above show us graphically how gender is spread throughout the sentence, affecting all the articles, adjectives, and pronouns connected to a noun. It may look a little overwhelming, but don't worry! You'll get the hang of it in no time.

### Generic masculine

As we said, Spanish has two genders that determine much of what happens in speech. On the one hand, masculine nouns take masculine articles and adjectives and are replaced by masculine pronouns. On the other hand, feminine nouns take feminine articles and adjectives and are replaced by feminine pronouns. But, what happens when we have a group that includes masculine and feminine nouns? We'll talk about that in this section.

- *Juan tiene tres hijas: Sofía, Clara y María* ("Juan has three daughters: Sofía, Clara and María.")
- *Carlos tiene dos hijos: Manuel y Pedro* ("Carlos has two sons: Manuel and Pedro.")
- *Mario tiene dos hijos: Joaquín y Mónica* ("Mario has two children: Joaquín and Mónica.")

Let's take a closer look at these examples. In the first case, Sofía, Clara, and María are three girls; that's why we say that Juan has three *hijas* ("daughters"). In the second case, Manuel and Pedro are two boys, so it makes sense to say that Carlos has two *hijos* ("sons"). But what happens in the last case? Joaquín is a boy's name, and Mónica is a girl's name, so we can assume that Mario has a son and a daughter. However, we say he has two *hijos*, in the masculine.

What we've just described is called *masculino genérico* ("generic masculine"). This means that whenever we refer to mixed groups of people, animals, or things (i.e., groups that include feminine and masculine nouns), we use the masculine as generic. This is true both for the nouns and the adjectives. Let's check out some examples:

- *Mi madre tiene cuatro nietos: un niño y tres niñas* ("My mother has four grandchildren: one boy and three girls.")

We can see how *nietos* includes both the three granddaughters and the grandson.

- *Las casas y los edificios de esta ciudad son muy bellos* ("The houses and the buildings in this city are very beautiful.")

Here, *bellos* (masculine) is describing both *las casas* (feminine) and *los edificios* (masculine).

With that, we've covered everything you need to know about gender to be an intermediate student. Now, let's put it into practice through some exercises!

# Exercises

1. Go back to the short story at the beginning of the chapter and answer the following questions in Spanish.

    c. ¿Por dónde están caminando Silvia y Alberto?

    d. ¿En qué momento del día transcurre la historia?

    e. ¿Qué animales se mencionan en la historia?

    f. ¿Por qué la aventura de seguir a la coneja no dura mucho?

2. Decide whether the following statements are true or false. Correct the false ones.

    a. Grammatical gender has to do with the gender of people.

    b. There are languages that have no grammatical gender.

    c. In Spanish, there are no grammatical genders.

    d. Agreement is the need to change a word to make it match a grammatical feature of another word.

3. Complete the sentences with these endings: -TUD; -OR; -SIÓN; -A; -MA; -O. Provide an example of each.

    a. Most nouns ending in ... are feminine, for example ......

    b. Most nouns ending in ... are masculine, for example ......

    c. Other typically feminine endings are ... (for example: ......), and ... (for example: ......)

    d. Other typically masculine endings are ... (for example: ......), and ... (for example: ......)

4. Choose the correct article, adjective, or pronoun to match the gender of the main noun: *Mi nombre es Soledad. Mi lugar ...... (favorito/a) de ...... (el/la) casa es mi habitación. Allí paso ...... (el/la) tiempo libre. Me gusta escuchar música, leer ...... (muchos/as) libros y dibujar. Me siento muy ...... (cómodo/cómoda) en mi habitación. Al entrar por ...... (el/la) puerta se ve al fondo ...... (el/la) ventana, que deja entrar ...... (un/una)*

*luz ...... (claro/clara). Las paredes están ...... (pintados/pintadas) en un tono ...... (oscuro/oscura). La cama es muy ...... (cómodo/cómoda). Encima de ...... (él/ella), hay un poster de mi banda ...... (preferido/preferida). Al lado de ...... (el/la) cama hay ...... (un/una) armario. En ...... (él/ella), guardo mi ropa bien ...... (doblado/doblada).*

5. Write a short description of your favorite room following the model above (around 100 words).

# Chapter 4: From Personal Pronouns to Possessives

## Short Story: Una familia tradicional

Casandra **estaciona** el coche y apaga el motor. Desde su asiento, mira primero a la casa de sus padres, y después a Guadalupe. Ella sonríe desde el **asiento del acompañante**.

—Mira, Lupe —dice Casandra, **titubeando**—. Mi familia es... ¿cómo decirlo? Especial.

—Todas las familias son especiales —contesta Guadalupe con una sonrisa.

—Sí, eso es cierto, pero... —dice Casandra—. Tú solo tienes que **seguirles la corriente**, ¿sabes? Yo los quiero, pero son... difíciles.

—No creo que haya problema —responde Guadalupe.

—¿Recuerdas quiénes estarán en el almuerzo de hoy? —pregunta Casandra.

—Creo que sí —dice Guadalupe—. Tus padres, por supuesto. Tu hermano, Héctor. Tus tíos, Aquiles y Alejandro. Y tu abuela... ¿Cómo se llamaba?

—Mi abuela se llama Circe —dice Casandra.

—¡Eso, Circe! —contesta Guadalupe—. Es un nombre extraño. Por eso no lo recordaba.

—Ya sabes, es nuestra tradición —dice Casandra—. Todos tenemos nombres salidos de la *Ilíada* y la *Odisea*. Mi **bisabuelo** era griego, y estaba muy orgulloso de serlo.

—¿Ese es el que hizo un viaje de doscientos kilómetros **a pie**? —pregunta Guadalupe.

—No, esos fueron mis padres —responde Casandra—. Fue su **luna de miel**. Mi bisabuelo es el que hablaba **en verso**.

—¿En verso? —pregunta Guadalupe.

—**Rimando** —responde Casandra, **encogiéndose de hombros**—. Ya te dije, son todos muy originales.

—Me parece que exageras —dice Guadalupe.

Casandra **suspira**, gira sobre su asiento y mira a Guadalupe a los ojos.

—¿Qué hace tu familia en Navidad? —pregunta Casandra.

—**Pues**... Nos juntamos en casa de mi abuela —responde Guadalupe—. Cocinamos, comemos. Nos peleamos, por supuesto. Esta última vez, el primo de mi madre, Sebastián, hizo unos comentarios horrorosos sobre la **herencia** de su tía Gladys.

—Me contaste, lo recuerdo —dice Casandra—. Estuvo **fuera de lugar**. Pero suena bastante normal. Nosotros, en cambio, hacemos un torneo de **tiro con arco**.

—¿Sabes tirar con arco y flecha? —pregunta Guadalupe, entusiasmada.

Casandra mira a Guadalupe y ve la emoción en sus ojos. Cualquiera diría que está lista para empezar sus lecciones de tiro. Eso le **arranca una sonrisa**. Entonces mira su reloj y ve que ya es hora de entrar.

—Sí, y de hecho soy la campeona **vigente** —contesta Casandra—. Cuando quieras, te enseño.

—Encantada —dice Guadalupe.

—¿Estás lista, entonces? —pregunta Casandra.

—Por supuesto —responde Guadalupe.

—Vamos —dice Casandra, y abre la puerta del coche.

# Vocabulary List

| Spanish | English |
|---|---|
| estacionar | park |
| el asiento del acompañante | passenger seat |
| titubear | hesitate |
| seguir la corriente | go along with |
| el bisabuelo | great-grandfather |
| a pie | on foot |
| la luna de miel | honeymoon |
| en verso | in verse |
| rimar | rhyme |
| encogerse de hombros | shrug one's shoulders |
| suspirar | sigh |
| pues | well |
| la herencia | inheritance |
| fuera de lugar | inappropriate |
| el tiro con arco | archery |

| | |
|---|---|
| arrancar una sonrisa | make somebody smile |
| vigente | current |

## Grammar Section

As a basic student of Spanish on your way to becoming an intermediate user of the language, you have undoubtedly encountered pronouns before, so these words are probably not new to you. However, in this chapter, we'll review the basic types of pronouns and add some more complex ones. So, by the end, you'll master:

- personal pronouns;
- subject and object pronouns;
- pronouns used with prepositions;
- reflexive pronouns and reciprocal;
- demonstrative pronouns;
- numeral pronouns;
- quantitative pronouns;
- indefinite pronouns;
- interrogative and exclamatory pronouns; and
- relative pronouns.

The list of Spanish pronouns is long, so let's get to it!

**Pronouns: What are they?**

The word "pronoun" comes from the Latin word *pronōmen*, meaning "instead of the name." Pronouns are the words we use to replace names or nouns in a sentence. Their function is to stand for any grammatical person mentioned—including people, animals, or things. Also, they reflect the gender (feminine, masculine or neutral) and number (singular or plural) of such person. Let's see how they work with a few examples:

- ***Sara*** *está enojada. Habla con **ella*** ("Sara is mad. Talk to her.")

In the example, the pronoun *ella* ("her") is replacing the name, Sara. As you can see, it reflects the third person singular feminine.

Pronouns also serve to refer to elements that function as antecedents of a topic. For example:

- ***María es muy amable con todo el mundo. Eso** hace que todos la quieran* ("María is very nice to everybody. That makes everyone love her.")

In this case, *eso* ("that") is standing for the whole previous sentence.

### Personal pronouns

Personal pronouns designate the participants of speech. The first person refers to the speaker, the second person refers to the listener, and the third person refers to someone outside the conversation. Spanish personal pronouns have different functions in the sentence, showing the relationship that participants have between them, i.e., who is the doer of the action, who is the receiver, etc. And depending on their function, they take different forms, as you can see in the table below.

|  |  | Subject | Direct Object | Indirect Object | Prepositional |
|---|---|---|---|---|---|
| Singular | 1ra persona | yo | me | | mí |
| | 2da persona | tú, vos | te | | ti |
| | 2da persona | usted | la, lo | le, se | usted |
| | 3ra persona | ella, él | | | ella, él |

|  |  |  |  |  |
|---|---|---|---|---|
| Plural | 1ra persona | nosotras, nosotros | nos | nosotras, nosotros |
|  | 2da persona | vosotras, vosotros | os | vosotras, vosotros |
|  | 2da persona | ustedes | las, los / les, se | ustedes |
|  | 3ra persona | ellas, ellos |  | ellas, ellos |

Have you noticed the *tilde* on *tú* ("you"), *él* ("he"), and *mí* ("me")? That's a diacritical accent so that they don't get mixed up with *tu* ("your"), *el* ("the"), and *mi* ("my").

Another thing worth mentioning when talking about personal pronouns is the difference between *tú*, *vos*, and *usted* ("you"), which you probably already know: *usted* is used to express respect when speaking to someone older or in a higher position. *Tú* and *vos* are both informal: the first one is used in almost every Spanish-speaking country, and *vos* is used in some Latin American countries, such as Argentina, Uruguay, Paraguay, and in regions of Chile, Bolivia, Venezuela, Costa Rica, etc.

Let's see the different forms of personal pronouns in more detail.

**Subject pronouns**

Personal pronouns often have the function of the subject of a sentence, that is, the author of the action of the verb. Subject personal pronouns always match the person and number of the verb. This concord between the subject and the verb is what makes possible the tacit subject in Spanish since we can infer the doer of the action from the inflection of the verb. Let's see some examples:

- *Yo tengo novia* ("I have a girlfriend." *Tengo novia* is also possible.)
- *Ella se llama Lucrecia* ("She's called Lucrecia." *Se llama Lucrecia* is also possible.)

### Direct object pronouns

The direct object completes the meaning of transitive verbs; it refers to a thing or person, and a direct object pronoun can replace it.

- *Estoy comiendo una manzana* → *La estoy comiendo* ("I'm eating an apple → I'm eating it.")
- *Estoy esperando a mis padres* → *Los estoy esperando* ("I'm waiting for my parents → I'm waiting for them.")

### Indirect object pronouns

The indirect object designates the recipient of the action described by the verb, which is always an animated being. Like the direct object, it can be replaced by a pronoun. When a sentence has both a direct object pronoun (*lo, la, los, las*) and an indirect object pronoun (*le, les*), the latter is replaced by *se* to avoid the cacophony.

- *María compró un regalo **a sus padres*** → *María **les** compró un regalo* → *María **se** los compró* ("María bought a present **for her parents** → María bought **them** a present → María bought it **for them**.")

### Placement of direct and indirect object pronouns

Regardless of the tense, direct and indirect object pronouns go before the verb:

- *Susana **la** conoce desde hace años* ("Susana has known her for years.")
- ***Me** encanta cantar canciones* ("I love singing songs.")

If a sentence has both pronouns, the indirect object always precedes the direct object:

- *-¿Dónde compraste esa silla? -**Me la** regaló mi mamá* ("-Where did you get that chair? -My mom gave it to me.")

In sentences containing a gerund or an infinitive, the pronoun may precede or follow the entire verbal group:

- *Quiero tocar otra canción* → ***La** quiero tocar/Quiero tocarla* ("I want to play another song → I want to play it.")

In affirmative imperative sentences, the personal pronoun goes after the verb. In negative imperative sentences, it goes before the verb.

- *¡Lava los platos!* → *¡Lávalos!* ("Wash the dishes! → Wash them!")
- *¡No hagas eso!* → *¡No lo hagas!* ("Don't do that! → Don't do it!")

**Prepositional pronouns**

Prepositional personal pronouns go after prepositions (*a, con, hacia, para, por, sobre, sin,* etc.)

- *Escribo canciones para **ella*** ("I write songs for her.")

The singular first and second person pronouns *mí* and *tú* have incorporated the proposition *con*: *conmigo* ("with me") and *contigo* ("with you").

- *Me encanta escuchar música **contigo*** ("I love listening to music with you.")

**Reflexive pronouns**

We use reflexive personal pronouns to indicate that the action falls on the subject.

|  |  | Subject Pronoun | Reflexive Pronoun |
|---|---|---|---|
| **Singular** | 1ra persona | yo | me |
|  | 2da persona | tú, vos | te |
|  | 2da persona | usted | se |
|  | 3ra persona | ella, él | se |

| Plural | 1ra persona | nosotras, nosotros | nos |
|---|---|---|---|
| | 2da persona | vosotras, vosotros | os |
| | 2da persona | ustedes | se |
| | 3ra persona | ellas, ellos | se |

For example:

- *Cuando Marta sale, **se** pone su mejor vestido* ("When Marta goes out, she wears her nicest dress.")
- *José **se** baña por las mañana* ("José takes a shower in the mornings.")

**Reciprocal pronouns**

Reciprocal pronouns (*os, nos, se*) show the reciprocity of actions between two or more subjects, that is, that the action concerns several individuals. One way of testing if a pronoun is reciprocal is adding the adverb *mutuamente* ("mutually"). For example:

- *Ramón y yo **nos** juramos lealtad eterna (mutuamente)* ("Ramón and I swore eternal loyalty to each other.")
- *Mis primos **se** llevan muy mal (mutuamente)* ("My cousins don't get along with each other.")

**Possessive pronouns**

They are used to express the possession of a thing by a noun. They have gender, number and person inflection (inflection is the change of form in words to mark grammatical cases). Unlike the ones in English, in Spanish, they agree with the thing that's possessed, not with the person who owns it. Let's check them out:

|  | Feminine | | Masculine | |
| :---: | :---: | :---: | :---: | :---: |
| Owner | Singular | Plural | Singular | Plural |
| yo | mía | mías | mío | míos |
| tú, vos | tuya | tuyas | tuyo | tuyos |
| usted | suya | suyas | suyo | suyos |
| ella, él | suya | suyas | suyo | suyos |
| nosotras, nosotros | nuestra | nuestras | nuestro | nuestros |
| vosotras, vosotros | vuestra | vuestras | vuestro | vuestros |
| ustedes | suya | suyas | suyo | suyos |
| ellas, ellos | suya | suyas | suyo | suyos |

If we take the first row, we can say that *mía* is the pronoun the speaker uses to talk about something that belongs to them that is feminine and singular. *Mío* is used when the thing possessed is masculine and singular; *mías*, when it's feminine and plural; and lastly, *míos*, when it's masculine and plural.

For example:

- *Estas camisetas son **tuyas** y este pantalón también es **tuyo*** ("These t-shirts are yours, and these trousers are also yours." The owner is the same person, and regardless of their gender, we use first *tuyas*, because *camisetas* is a feminine plural noun; and then *tuyo*, because *pantalón* is a masculine singular noun.

- *La decisión es **nuestra*** ("The decision is ours.")

If we want to emphasize that the possessors are different, we use the definite article.

- *Estas medias son **tuyas**. **Las mías** ya las guardé* ("These socks are yours, I've already put away mine.")

### Demonstrative pronouns

Demonstrative pronouns indicate a relationship of proximity between the designated person and the other participants of the conversation.

| | Femenine | | Masculine | | Neuter |
|---|---|---|---|---|---|
| Distance | Singular | Plural | Singular | Plural | Singular |
| Cerca del hablante | esta | estas | esto | estos | esto |
| Cerca del destinatario | esa | esas | ese | esos | eso |
| Lejos de ambos | aquella | aquellas | aquel | aquellos | aquello |

For example:

- *¿Cuál es el precio de **aquel**?* ("What's the price of that one?")
- ***Eso** no estuvo bien* ("That was not okay.")
- *¿Encontraste tu taza? **Esta** es la mía* ("Have you found your glass? This one's mine")

### Numeral pronouns

We've already talked about numbers in chapter 2. Now, we'll see how they can also function as pronouns to indicate the number of objects represented in a sentence.

| Cardinals | Ordinals | Fractions | Multiples |
|---|---|---|---|
| uno, dos, tres, etc. | primero, segundo, tercero, etc. | tercio, mitad, cuarto, etc. | doble, triple, cuádruple |

For example:

- *Me gustan estas rosas. Deme **doce**, por favor.* ("I like these roses. Give me twelve, please.")
- *Que pase el **primero**.* ("The first one can come in.")
- *Iba a comprar un kilo de harina, pero solo había **medio**.* ("I wanted to buy one kilo of flour, but there was only half.")
- *Hoy hicimos 500 kilómetros. Mañana deberíamos hacer el **doble**.* ("Today we did 500 kilometers. Tomorrow we should do twice as many.")

**Quantitative pronouns**

They represent indeterminate quantities of elements. They all vary in number, and most also vary in gender, with a couple of exceptions. Let's take a look at them:

|  | Singular | Plural |
|---|---|---|
| **Neuter** | bastante, suficiente | bastantes, suficientes |
| **Femenine** | poca, mucha, toda | pocas, muchas, todas |
| **Masculine** | poco, mucho, todo | pocos, muchos, todos |

For example:

- *No te olvides de comprar agua. No tenemos **suficiente*** ("Don't forget to buy water. We don't have enough.")

- *A Victoria la agarró la lluvia en la calle. Está **toda** mojada* ("Victoria was caught in the rain in the street. She's all wet.")
- *Hace tiempo que espero, pero ya falta **poco*** ("I've been waiting for a long time, but I won't have to wait much longer.")

**Indefinite pronouns**

They point to an imprecise or unknown person.

|  | **Singular** | **Plural** |
|---|---|---|
| **Neuter** | cualquiera, quienquiera | cualesquiera, quienesquiera |
| **Femenine** | alguna, ninguna, otra, una | algunas, ningunas, otras, unas |
| **Masculine** | alguno, ninguno, otro, uno | algunos, ningunos, otros, unos |

For example:
- *No puedes confiar en **cualquiera*** ("You can't trust anyone.")
- *Siempre usas el mismo sombrero. ¿No tienes **otro**?* ("You always wear the same hat. Don't you have another one?")
- *Les avisé a mis amigas del cambio de horario, pero **algunas** no leyeron el mensaje y llegaron tarde* ("I told my friends about the change in the schedule, but some didn't read the message and arrived late.")

**Interrogative and exclamatory pronouns**

They are the same words with different functions. Interrogative pronouns are used to ask questions related to identity or quantity. Exclamatory pronouns are used to emphasize the expressiveness of the statement. They are all written with a *tilde*.

|           | Singular              | Plural           |
|-----------|-----------------------|------------------|
| Neuter    | qué, quién, cuál      | quiénes, cuáles  |
| Femenine  | cuánta                | cuántas          |
| Masculine | cuánto                | cuántos          |

For example:

- *¿**Quién** era la persona que te saludó?* ("Who was the person who said hi?")
- *¿**Cuánto** vas a tardar en llegar?* ("How long are you going to be?")
- *Mira la vista desde aquí. ¡**Qué** maravilla!* ("Look at the view from here. How wonderful!")

**Relative pronouns**

They have more than one function: they point out other people who have been mentioned before, and they introduce subordinate sentences. Let's see them in the following chart.

|           | Singular                                      | Plural                                |
|-----------|-----------------------------------------------|---------------------------------------|
| Neuter    | que, quien                                    | quienes                               |
| Femenine  | la que, la cual, cuanta, cuya                 | las que, las cuales, cuantas, cuyas   |
| Masculine | el que, lo que, el cual, lo cual, cuanto, cuyo | los que, los cuales, cuantos, cuyos   |

For example:

- *Mara, **que** siempre anda a las corridas, salió sin desayunar.* ("Mary, who is always rushing, left without having breakfast.")
- *José, **quien** era el médico de turno, me atendió muy bien* ("José, who was the doctor in charge, took good

care of me.")

- *El sillón tenía varias manchas, **las cuales** pudimos limpiar* ("The sofa had several stains, which we were able to remove.")

**Exercises**

1. Go back to the short story at the beginning of the chapter and write down all the pronouns you find.
2. Decide whether the following statements are true or false. Correct the false ones.
    a. Pronouns are the words we use to replace adjectives or adverbs in a sentence.
    b. Pronouns reflect gender and number.
    c. Pronouns are not used as antecedents.
3. In each sentence, you have the information you need to choose the correct personal pronoun:
    a. ...... vamos a partir temprano porque estamos cansadas. (1ra persona, plural, femenino, en posición sujeto)
    b. Mi hermano ganó un premio. Se ...... dieron en una ceremonia de entrega de diplomas. (3ra persona, singular, masculino, en posición objeto directo)
    c. A ...... no se los conté, pero he cambiado de trabajo. (2da persona, plural, femenino, en posición preposicional)
    d. Organizó esta fiesta para ...... (1ra persona, singular, masculino, en posición preposicional)
4. Choose the correct possessive pronoun:
    a. ¿Estas manzanas son suyas/tuyo?
    b. Tenemos que decidir si vamos en vuestro auto o en el nuestra/nuestro.
    c. Mi esposa se compró lentes porque se olvidó la suya/los suyos en casa.
    d. Encontré una lapicera en casa que estoy segura de que no es mía/tuya.

5. Write one sentence using each of the following pronouns:
    a. cuanta
    b. ninguno
    c. bastante
    d. tercio

Now that we've finished covering all the types of pronouns, you can go back to the start of the chapter and cross out everything you've learned from the list!

# Chapter 5: Mastering Adjectives and Adverbs

## Short Story: El pretendiente

El día está **soleado**. Hace calor. Por eso, Rebeca y Miriam buscan la **sombra** de los árboles para su **caminata**. Es el único lugar del club donde pueden **pasear** cómodamente. El único sin aire acondicionado, por lo menos.

—¿Qué me dices del hijo de Susana? —pregunta Rebeca.

—¿Daniel? —dice Miriam—. Me pareció un hombre **encantador**. Es médico, ¿sabías?

—Kinesiólogo, Miriam —dice Rebeca, **con tono aleccionador**—. Es kinesiólogo. No es lo mismo. Pero sí, un hombre encantador... aunque un poco **charlatán**, ¿no lo crees?

—No lo sé, Rebeca —contesta Miriam—. Es cierto que hablaba muy rápido... O muy bajo. Digamos que yo no le entendía bien. Pero eso me pasa con todas las personas jóvenes.

—Quizás deberías hacerte un **estudio de audición** —dice Rebeca—. Ya estamos en edad...

—Es cierto —contesta Miriam—. De hecho, quizás Daniel conoce a alguien. Le preguntaré. Además, es una buena excusa para conseguir su teléfono. Quiero **presentárselo** a mi hija.

—¿A Elisa? —pregunta Rebeca—. ¿Por qué? Ella es una muchacha tan hermosa, tan vital. ¿Tú crees que es un buen **pretendiente**?

—Es mejor candidato que **el anterior** —dice Miriam—. Ese hombre era increíblemente aburrido. Y me lo habías recomendado tú.

—Yo no sabía que Samuel era así —contesta Rebeca—. Parecía muy amable.

—Era muy amable, y **más aburrido que chupar un clavo** —dice Miriam **contundentemente**—. En cambio, Daniel es gracioso.

—Es cierto, no lo puedo negar —responde Rebeca—. Pero, ¿no crees que es un poco bajo?

—¿Bajo? —pregunta Miriam—. ¡Pero si mide más de un metro ochenta!

—¿En serio? —responde Rebeca—. A mí me pareció **bajito**. Quizás es por la forma de su cabeza. Tiene la cabeza muy grande. Eso lo hace parecer más pequeño.

—No sé si tiene la cabeza grande —contesta Miriam—. Pero la tiene bien ordenada. Es muy **buen mozo**. Yo creo que a Elisa le gustará.

—Si tú lo crees... —dice Rebeca, **derrotada**.

—Eso sí: es una lástima que Daniel esté casado —contesta Miriam—. Pero bueno, nadie es perfecto.

## Vocabulary List

| Spanish | English |
|---|---|
| soleado, soleada | sunny |
| la sombra | shade |
| la caminata | stroll |
| pasear | go for a walk |

| | |
|---|---|
| encantador, encantadora | charming |
| con tono aleccionador | like teaching a lesson |
| charlatán, charlatana | chatterbox |
| el estudio de audición | hearing test |
| presentar | introduce |
| pretendiente | suitor |
| el, la anterior | the previous one |
| más aburrido que chupar un clavo | like watching paint dry |
| contundentemente | bluntly |
| bajito, bajita | a little short |
| buen mozo | handsome |
| derrotada, derrotado | defeated |

## Grammar Section

As an intermediate student, you probably know that adjectives are the words we use to describe nouns and, in turn, that adverbs are the words we use to describe adjectives and adverbs. So, in this chapter, we'll go a bit deeper into these two important types of words, and we'll cover the following topics:

- adjectives used as nouns and adverbs
- the position of adjectives and adverbs
- comparison of adjectives and adverbs

- irregular comparatives
- idioms and sayings that use adjectives

**Adjectives used as nouns and adverbs**

Typically, adjectives are used to describe nouns. However, they have other functions. For example, adjectives can be used as nouns to refer to a person or thing that has the characteristic of the adjective. This characteristic identifies the noun and distinguishes it from the rest. As a general rule, we put an article before the adjective to make it a noun. It sounds a bit complicated, but it's really simple. Let's check some examples:

- *De todos los coches,* ***el rojo*** *es el que más me gusta* ("Out of all the cars, the red one is my favorite.")
- ***El alto*** *es el mejor jugador del equipo* ("The tall one is the best player on the team.")

Some adjectives can also work as adverbs. To do so, they have to be in their masculine singular form. Their function is to complement the verb, to tell us how the action is done. Let's see some examples:

- *Los equipos rivales jugaron* ***sucio*** ("The opposing teams played dirty.")
- *La comida olía* ***feo*** ("The food smelled bad.")

Let's look at those same word functioning as adjectives to see the difference:

- *Los* ***sucios*** *rivales ganaron con trampa* ("The dirty opponents won by cheating.")
- *La comida de ese lugar es* ***fea*** ("The food in that place is bad.")

**The position of the adjective**

Syntax is how a language arranges words to create sentences. If we are talking about adjectives and nouns, we can say that English and Spanish have a syntactical difference. In Spanish, as a general rule, the adjective should always be placed after the noun it's modifying. And as we can see in the example below, English does the opposite thing:

- *Siéntate en la silla **roja*** ("Sit in the red chair.")

However, as with any rule, there are some exceptions, some cases in which the adjective is placed before the noun. Let's take a look at them:

Demonstrative (*ese, este, aquel*) and possessive (*tu, mi, su, nuestro*) adjectives come before the nouns they describe. For example:

- ***Ese*** *coche no anda* ("That car doesn't work.")
- ***Mi*** *hermana vive lejos* ("My sister lives far away.")

Limiting adjectives, the ones that define number, quantity or amount, always come before the noun:

- *Vimos **diez** cóndores* ("We saw ten condors.")
- *Pasó **mucho** tiempo* ("A lot of time has passed.")

Adjectives that don't describe nor give new information, but put emphasis in an essential quality of the noun, tend to go before it:

- *La **fría** nieve caía sin parar* ("The cold snow came down nonstop.")
- *Probó la **dulce** miel* ("She tried the sweet honey.")

If we take the first example, we can say that being cold is an essential quality of snow, so the adjective does not add any new information; it just emphasizes this characteristic.

In the last exception, we can group the adjectives that present a change in meaning when we change their position:

- *El **pobre** hombre perdió a su familia en un accidente* ("The unfortunate man lost his family in an accident.")
- *El hombre **pobre** mendigaba en la calle* ("The indigent man begged in the street.")
- *Llegaron el **mismo** día que nosotros* ("They arrived on the same day as us.")
- *Quiere todo para ella **misma*** ("She wants everything for herself.")

It is common to see that these adjectives, which vary in meaning depending on their position in relation to the noun, usually have a valuative, subjective meaning when they are placed before the noun, and a determinative, objective meaning when they are placed after it. Some illustrative examples of such cases are the following:

- *Es una profesional, pero tiene* **verdaderos** *problemas para controlar su genio* ("She is a professional, but has serious problems controlling her temper.")
- *Esta película está basada en una historia* **verdadera** ("This film is based on a true story.")
- *Bastó un* **simple** *trámite para poner en marcha la obra municipal* ("A single paperwork was enough to get the municipal work underway.")
- *Era un examen muy* **simple***, no voy a suspender* ("It was a very easy exam, I am not going to fail.")

### The position of the adverb

The adverb moves more freely in the sentence. Its position will depend on what you want to emphasize. However, there are certain guidelines that we must know and follow, so let's check them out.

For the most part, adverbs are placed after the verb. This rule applies especially to adverbs of quantity and manner. Let's look at an example:

- *Me divierto* **mucho** *con mis amigas* ("I have a lot of fun with my friends.")

In compound tenses, the adverb cannot be placed between the auxiliary and the main verbs, as it happens in English. Let's see it below:

- **Siempre** te he escuchado; or
- Te he escuchado **siempre**; but not
- ✗ Te he **siempre** escuchado ("I've always listened to you.")

When adverbs modify an adjective or another adverb, they are placed before that adjective or adverb. For example:

- *No sabía **muy** bien qué quería, así que pidió una recomendación* (She didn't know exactly what she wanted, so she asked for a recommendation.)

Many adverbs of mode, place, or time can be placed at the beginning of a sentence or after the verb, like in these examples:

- ***Realmente** habían hecho un buen trabajo,* or
- *Habían hecho **realmente** un buen trabajo* ("They had done a really good job.")

Time adverbs are very versatile: they can be at the beginning of the sentence, after the verb, or at the end of the sentence:

- ***Mañana** llega tu hermano,* or
- *Llega **mañana** tu hermano,* or
- *Tu hermano llega **mañana*** ("Your brother arrives tomorrow.")

### Comparison of adjectives and adverbs

To indicate that something is superior to something else, we use the following formula:

- *más + adjetivo/adverbio + que* (more + adjective/adverb + than or adjective/adverb + -er + than)

We have an example of this in the short story; have you noticed it?

- ***más aburrido que** chupar un clavo* (the literal translation would be "more boring than sucking on a nail")

Another example:

- *Luis está **más dormido que** yo* ("Luis is sleeper than me.")

If we want to indicate inferiority, we use a similar formula:

- *menos + adjetivo/adverbio + que* (less + adjective/adverb + than)

For example:

- *El libro me pareció **menos entretenido que** la película* ("I found the book less entertaining than the movie.")

Lastly, to indicate that two things are equal using adjectives or adverbs, we use this construction:

- *tan + adjetivo/adverbio + como* or *igual de adjetivo/adverbio que* (as adjective/adverb + as)

For example:

- *Mi hijo es **tan lindo como** su padre* ("My son is as handsome as his father.")

**Superlatives**

Superlatives are used to say which noun (in a group of three or more) is "the most" or "the least." To do so, we use a very similar construction to the one used for comparatives. The only difference is that we add a definite article:

- *el/la/los/las + más + adjetivo* (the + most + adjective)
- *el/la/los/las + menos + adjetivo* (the + least + adjective)

For example:

- *Mi hija es **la más perfecta** de todos* ("My daughter is the most perfect girl of all.")
- *Estas son **las menos dulces*** ("These are the least sweet.")

**Irregular comparatives**

There are a few adjectives in Spanish that don't follow the rules we've just mentioned. We are talking about the irregular comparatives. I know the word "irregular" might frighten you, but don't worry, the list of irregular comparatives is short. Let's check it out:

| Adjective | Comparative | Superlative |
|---|---|---|
| bueno | mejor | la/el mejor |
| malo | peor | la/el peor |
| grande | mayor | la/el mayor |
| pequeño | menor | la/el menor |

One last thing worth noting about irregular comparatives is that *menor* and *mayor* are used for age. When we are talking about size, *grande* and *pequeño* follow the normal rules:

- *Esta es la casa más grande del vecindario* ("This is the biggest house in the neighborhood.")

**Idioms and sayings with adjectives**

To finish off this chapter, let's have some fun! Do you know any Spanish sayings? Do you want to learn some? We've made a list of the most common Spanish idioms that have adjectives in them for you to read and learn! Let's check it out:

| Spanish | English |
| --- | --- |
| Estar más fresco que una lechuga. | Being as fresh as a daisy. |
| Ser más aburrido que una ostra. | Being as boring as watching paint dry. |
| Ser más viejo que Matusalén. | Being older than dirt. |
| Estar más contento que un perro con dos colas. | Being as happy as a clam. |
| Quedarse frito. | To fall asleep. |
| A caballo regalado no se le miran los dientes. | Don't look a gift horse in the mouth. |
| A ojo de buen cubero. | At a guess. |
| Andar de capa caída. | Being in low spirits. |
| Año nuevo, vida nueva. | New year, new life. |

| | |
|---|---|
| Blanco y en botella, leche. | If it looks like a duck and walks like a duck, it is a duck. |
| Quedarse con la boca abierta. | Be left with one's mouth open. |
| Pasar la noche en blanco. | To not sleep a wink. |
| Sacar los trapos sucios. | Don't wash your dirty linen in public. |
| Pagar los platos rotos. | To pay the piper. |
| Más vale tarde que nunca. | Better late than never. |
| Quien mucho abarca, poco aprieta. | Jack of all trades, master of none. |
| En menos de lo que canta un gallo. | In a jiffy. |
| Echar más leña al fuego. | To add fuel to the flames. |
| Al mal tiempo, buena cara. | If life gives you lemons, make lemonade. |

Now that you have deepened your knowledge of the uses of adjectives and adverbs, let's test you!

## Exercises

1. Use the definition between brackets to complete the following sentences with an adjective. What type of word is the adjective replacing?

    e. Mis perros están comiendo ...... (cantidad o intensidad escasos respecto de lo regular), lo que me tiene preocupada.

    f. Había tres mozos trabajando en el restaurante. A

nosotros nos atendió el ....... (de gran estatura).

g. Las palomas son aves de ciudad que suelen volar ...... (de poca altura).

h. María se compró un auto nuevo. Había de muchos colores, pero se decidió por

2. Decide whether the following statements are true or false. Correct the false ones.

   a. Syntax is the way in which languages put in order the different types of words to create sentences that make sense.

   b. In Spanish, the adjective is always placed after the noun it's modifying.

   c. Demonstrative and possessive adjectives are placed after the noun.

   d. *Nuevo* belongs to the group of adjectives that present a change in meaning depending on their position.

3. Decide whether the adjective in brackets should go before or after the noun:

   a. Mi ...... problema ...... es que no me gusta mi trabajo. (único)

   b. Le hicimos un ...... regalo ......: una primera edición de su libro preferido. (único)

   c. Mi hermano y yo somos ...... personas ......, pero igual nos llevamos muy bien. (diferentes)

   d. Antes de entrar a la universidad, deben rendir ...... exámenes ...... para corroborar el nivel. (diferentes)

4. Follow the example to provide the formula and an example to indicate:

   a. Superiority: *"más + adjetivo/adverbio + que"*: *Corro más rápido que mis rivales.*

   b. Inferiority:

   c. Equality:

   d. Positive superlative:

e. Negative superlative:

5. Match the common saying on the left with their meanings on the right:

| | |
|---|---|
| a. Andar de capa caída. | • Significa lo mismo que "pagar las consecuencias". |
| b. Quedarse frito. | |
| c. Pagar los platos rotos. | • Se usa para decir que una persona está triste. |
| d. Sacar los trapos sucios | • Se usa para decir que se está hablando de cosas privadas en público. |
| | • Significa lo mismo que quedarse dormido. |

# Chapter 6: Demonstrating How Articles Work

## Short Story: El viaje

La **maleta** es más pequeña de lo que recordaba. No hay forma de que allí entre todo lo que quiere llevar.

"Una vida no **cabe** en una maleta como esta", piensa María. "Aunque, en realidad, una vida no cabe en ninguna maleta".

**A pesar de todo**, intenta otra vez guardar su ropa allí. Toma las **playeras** y las vuelve a doblar. Forma una bola con los **calcetines**. **Pliega** los **pantalones** hasta darles forma de cuadrado.

"Un **abrigo**", piensa María. "En Canadá hará frío".

María revisa su closet. Ve una **chaqueta de invierno**, un **sobretodo** y un **saco grueso**. Decide llevar la chaqueta, más **cálida**. Ya tendrá tiempo de comprar las demás prendas en Vancouver.

En ese momento, Jorge entra a la habitación.

—¿Cómo va eso? —pregunta Jorge.

María muestra sus manos llenas de ropa como respuesta. Jorge ríe y se acerca a ella. Comienza a doblar ropa. Es muy bueno en eso. Él siempre fue la persona más ordenada de la relación. Es meticuloso. Cuando salían de vacaciones, sus maletas siempre pesaban cinco kilos menos que las de María, pero jamás **echaba nada en falta**. Llevaba exactamente lo necesario.

—Pon unos **zapatos** extra —dice Jorge, mientras acomoda la ropa en la maleta—. **Por si se mojan** los que **llevas puestos**.

—No **entran** —responde María—. Ya lo intenté.

—Déjame a mí —dice Jorge.

Jorge saca la ropa de la maleta y la deja cuidadosamente sobre la cama. Después la vuelve a meter, pero en otro orden. Pone primero las playeras, los suéteres y los pantalones, más geométricos. Cuando está seguro de que todo el espacio está ocupado, empieza a colocar las prendas con forma más irregular: los calcetines, la ropa interior y la chaqueta de invierno. De pronto, la maleta parece más **espaciosa**. Antes de meter los zapatos, Jorge los rellena de calcetines, para no dejar ese espacio desocupado.

—Gracias —dice María finalmente—. Jorge, estoy **asustada**.

—¿Por qué? —pregunta Jorge—. Vancouver es una gran oportunidad. Es el trabajo que siempre soñaste.

—Sí, lo sé, pero... —contesta María—. Cuando soñaba con ese trabajo, no esperaba estar sola en una ciudad **helada**.

—Te las **arreglarás** —dice Jorge.

—Te voy a extrañar —responde María.

Jorge no responde. En cambio, busca en los cajones de la habitación compartida y saca una bufanda azul.

—Toma, no quiero que **pases frío** —dice Jorge, mientras se la pasa por el cuello a María.

## Vocabulary List

| Spanish | English |
|---|---|
| la maleta | suitcase |
| caber | fit |

| | |
|---|---|
| a pesar de todo | despite everything |
| la playera | t-shirt |
| los calcetines | socks |
| plegar | fold |
| los pantalones | trousers |
| el abrigo | coat |
| la chaqueta de invierno | winter jacket |
| el sobretodo | overcoat |
| el saco | jacket |
| grueso, gruesa | thick |
| cálido, cálida | warm |
| echar en falta | miss |
| los zapatos | shoes |
| por si | in case |
| mojarse | get wet |
| llevar puesto, puesta | be wearing |
| entrar | fit |

| | |
|---|---|
| espacioso, espaciosa | spacious |
| asustado, asustada | scared |
| helado, helada | freezing |
| arreglárselas | manage |
| pasar frío | be cold |

## Grammar Section

This is going to be a short chapter in which we'll deal with only two types of words:

- definite articles, and
- indefinite articles.

However, despite being short, functional words, they are critical. So, let's get to them!

In English and Spanish, nouns are often preceded by a definite or indefinite article. But, while English uses only "the," in Spanish, we choose from the four variations of the definite article, depending on the gender and number of the noun that comes after it.

The same happens with the indefinite article. English has "a," "an," and "some," whereas Spanish has four indefinite articles that change according to the gender and number of the noun.

And that's not all, because Spanish also has neuter article *lo*. This article, which doesn't carry gender, is used before adjectives to transform them into abstract nouns. For example, *Lo ideal sería que llegaras temprano* ("The ideal thing would be for you to arrive early.")

Take a look at this table with definite, indefinite, and neuter articles:

|  | Masculine ||  Feminine ||
|---|---|---|---|---|
|  | Singular | Plural | Singular | Plural |
| Definite | el | los | la | las |
| Indefinite | un | unos | una | unas |
| Neuter | lo ||||

Definite and indefinite articles are some of the most used words in the Spanish language, so it's essential to learn to use them correctly. Definite articles are used to talk about concrete things that are known to the people involved in the conversation. Indefinite articles are used when one of the people involved in the conversation doesn't know precisely the noun being discussed. Let's take a more detailed look at the different uses of these articles.

**Uses of the definite article:**

1. To talk about people or things that are unique, of which there is not more than one.

- *El padre de Rita* ("Rita's father.")

Most people have only one father, so we are talking of a specific person.

2. To refer to a specific thing or person that we know.

- *La médica de mi familia atiende los martes* ("My family's doctor works on Tuesdays.")

We are talking about a specific doctor we know, not just any doctor.

3. To talk about things or people in general.

- *Los caribeños son alegres* ("Caribbeans are lively people.")

We are talking generally about all Caribbeans.

4. To talk about the time.

- *Son las cinco de la tarde* ("It's five o'clock in the afternoon.")
- *Quedamos a las dos* ("Let's meet at two.")

5. To talk about dates. Remember that, like in English, months don't take an article.

- *El 24 de mayo es mi cumpleaños* ("May 24th is my birthday.")
- *En agosto, empieza un trabajo nuevo* ("In August, she starts a new job.")

6. For parts of the day (morning, afternoon and evening).

- *Por la tarde iré a la farmacia* ("In the afternoon, I'll go to the chemist.")

7. To discuss quantities or frequencies with days, weeks, or months.

- *Me ducho una vez al día* ("I shower once a day.")
- *Trabajo veinte días al mes* ("I work twenty days a month.")

**Uses of the indefinite article:**

1. To talk about something or someone that is not concrete, that we don't know or that is part of a larger group.

- *Estoy buscando una médica de cabecera nueva* ("I'm looking for a new family doctor.")

We are talking about any doctor, one we don't know yet.

2. To talk about quantities in the singular and the plural.

- *Compré unos zapatos nuevos* ("I bought some new shoes.")
- *Tengo un auto* ("I have a car.")

**Common mistakes**

Now, let's talk about the most common mistakes Spanish students make with definite and indefinite articles.

- Using the definite article when you have to use the indefinite one, and vice versa
- Not using the articles when it's needed

- Using the article where it's not needed
- Using the definite or indefinite articles instead of the possessive

Let's pay attention to these two sentences to see how important it is to use them correctly:

- *Pregúntale a la maestra* ("Ask the teacher.")
- *Pregúntale a una maestra* ("Ask a teacher.")

Is there a difference between the two sentences? All we've done is change the definite article for an indefinite one. If we say *Pregúntale a una maestra*, we are telling you to go ask any teacher, the one you like the most. But if we say *Pregúntale a la maestra*, we are talking about a teacher that we both know - someone we've mentioned before.

Let's look at one last example.

- *Voy a comprar un ordenador* ("I am buying a computer.")
- *Voy a comprar el ordenador* ("I am buying the computer.")

What's the difference here? Again, the only difference between these two sentences is the articles, but those little words completely change the meaning. When we say *Voy a comprar un ordenador*, it means that we haven't yet chosen which computer we want; we just know that we are getting one. If we say *Voy a comprar el ordenador*, it means that we have already seen several computers and chosen one. We've already talked about which computer I liked, and we both know about it.

So, in sum, we can say that we use the definite article when the person who speaks and the person who listens know exactly the object being spoken about. And we use the indefinite article when the person speaking or the person listening doesn't exactly know the object being spoken about.

## Exercises

1. Go back to the short story at the beginning of the chapter and underline all the articles you can find. Remember that these words can have other functions, like pronouns

or adjectives. So, pay attention and only select the ones that are working as articles.

2. Decide whether the following statements are true or false. Correct the false ones.

   a. To choose the correct article, we have to consider the gender and number of the noun that comes after it.
   b. *Lo* is a masculine article.
   c. *Lo* is used in front of adjectives to transform them into abstract nouns.
   d. Definite articles are used to talk about things that are not known to the people involved in the conversation.

3. Rewrite the following sentences changing the nouns into abstract nouns made of adjectives like in the example

   a. La belleza de la vida es compartirla con los seres queridos: *Lo bello de la vida es compartirla con los seres queridos.*
   b. María se desesperó ante la dificultad del problema.
   c. Debieron cancelar la excursión por la frialdad del día.
   d. La simpleza de la vida en el campo resulta muy atractiva.

4. Complete the following short story with the corresponding articles.

   *José y Luz están de vacaciones en Francia con ... pareja amiga, Miguel y Ana. A Miguel le encanta visitar edificios históricos, y José accede a acompañarlo a visitar algunos. Mientras, Luz y Ana deciden ir a conocer ... bar famoso. Caminando por ... pueblo, José y Miguel ven ... hermosa iglesia antigua. Sin embargo, cuando entran, hay ... servicio en marcha.*

   *—¡Shh! Quedémonos sentados en silencio para no llamar ... atención. Actuemos como ... demás —susurra Miguel. Como no saben francés, José y Miguel se sientan en silencio y observan ... iglesia. Durante ... servicio, se*

*ponen de pie, se arrodillan y se sientan imitando lo que hace ... resto de ... asistentes.*

*—¡Espero que no estemos llamando ... atención! —le dice Miguel a José.*

*En un momento, ... cura dice algo, y ... hombre sentado delante de ellos se pone de pie.*

*Siguiendo su ejemplo, Miguel y José también se ponen de pie. De pronto, todos ... asistentes comienzan a reír.*

*Al finalizar ... servicio, ... cura se acerca a ... dos hombres y los saluda en español.*

*—¿Por qué todos se rieron? —pregunta José.*

*—Bueno, muchachos, ayer hubo ... nacimiento, y le pedí al padre que se pusiera de pie para felicitarlo.*

5. Now, write a short story or narrate an anecdote in 150 words.

Awesome! After finishing the quiz, you can go back to the beginning and cross off everything you've learned from the list!

# Mid-Book Quiz

*¡Felicitaciones!* You've reached the middle of the book. It's been quite a journey, hasn't it? But we are sure you have been learning a lot of Spanish while having a bit of fun. Now, it's time to test you on everything we've seen so far.

In this quiz, each correct answer is worth 2 points. If you get between 15 and 20 points, you're doing great! If you score between 10 and 15 points, you too are doing very well, but you are still in the middle of the learning process; we encourage you to go back and reread the sections on the questions you got wrong. If you get less than 10 points, don't worry! There's no rush. Take your time to go back to the beginning of the book and review everything. Once you've done that, you can retake the quiz. We are sure you'll do great the second time!

1. Resolve the following sums and write down the numbers in Spanish:
    a. 1.500 + 235:
    b. 10.000 + 9.583:
       And if we were talking about cows? How would you write those same numbers?
2. Can you write down two ways of asking for the time in Spanish?
   And now, answer the question with the following times:
    a. 11:45 am

b. 4:10 pm
3. Are the following nouns masculine or feminine? Decide by choosing the correct article
   a. ... solución
   b. ... problema
   c. ... foto
   d. ... tortuga
   e. ... lumbre
   f. ... mano
   g. ... pie
4. What do we mean when we say that Spanish is a gendered language? What does "grammatical agreement" or "concord" mean?
5. What is the bolded pronoun replacing in each case?
   a. María llegó ayer a la noche. Todavía no **la** he visto.
   b. **Le** regalamos un rompecabezas a tu hermano. Hoy comenzó a armar**lo**.
   c. Estás enojado. **Eso** no te deja pensar con claridad.
   d. Mi madre nació en 1961 y mi padre en 1965, por lo que **ella** es mayor.
6. Complete with the corresponding demonstrative pronoun.
   a. ¿Me alcanzas ... cacerola? (object far from speaker and recipient)
   b. ¿Qué tal está ... tomate? (object close to recipient)
   c. Me gusta ... . ¿Sabes quién lo pintó? (object far from speaker and recipient)
   d. ... uvas que trajiste están buenísimas. (object close to speaker and recipient)
7. Where is the adjective typically placed in Spanish? Which types of adjectives are placed elsewhere?
8. Match the formula with the meaning:

Superiority: "menos + adjetivo/adverbio + que"
Inferiority:
Equality: "más + adjetivo/adverbio + que"
Positive superlative "el/la/los/las + más + adjetivo"
"tan + adjetivo/adverbio + como"

9. Complete the following sentences with *definido* or *indefinido*:
   a. Para hablar de cantidades, usamos el artículo ......
   b. Usamos el artículo ...... para referirnos a cosas únicas, de las que no existe más de una.
   c. Para hablar de fechas y horas, usamos el artículo ......
   d. Cuando todas las personas involucradas en la conversación conocen de lo que se está hablando, usamos el artículo ....... Por otro lado, usamos el artículo ...... cuando una de las personas de la conversación no conoce de lo que se está hablando.

10. Match the common saying in the left with their meanings in the right:

| | |
|---|---|
| a. Blanco y en botella, leche. | • Se usa para decir que una persona que hace muchas cosas, no puede hacerlas todas bien. |
| b. Echar más leña al fuego. | • Significa medir algo de una forma imprecisa, sin ningún elemento de medición. |
| c. Quien mucho abarca, poco aprieta. | • Se usa cuando alguien está haciendo crecer un tema problemático. |

d. A ojo de buen cubero.  • Se usa para decir que, si algo se parece a algo, probablemente lo sea.

# Chapter 7: The Verb I. Focus on the Present

## Short Story: ¿Quién es el más famoso?

Julio y Federico están sentados en una mesa del café de Paco. Ese es su lugar favorito. Paco siempre les **guarda** esa mesa. A partir de las tres de la tarde, nadie más que ellos puede sentarse allí. Y, desde hace veinte años, Julio y Federico la ocupan religiosamente.

En general, cuando se sientan en su mesa, Julio y Federico hacen dos cosas: beber café y discutir. El café siempre es el mismo, pero la discusión varía. A veces aprovechan los temas de actualidad. En esas ocasiones, uno de los dos **suele** tener un **periódico** en la mano, al que, al calor de la discusión, golpea y **agita sin piedad**.

Ese día, el tema de la discusión es otro. Julio y Federico debaten sobre cuál es el español más famoso del mundo. Han estado discutiendo ya por una hora. El **ambiente está caldeado**.

—¡Rafael Nadal! —exclama Federico—. ¿Lo dices en serio? ¿Quién será el próximo, Fernando Alonso?

—Nadal ha tenido una mejor carrera que Alonso —responde Julio.

—Si es por carreras, mejor ha sido la de Antonio Banderas —dice Federico.

—¡Antonio Banderas! —exclama Julio, indignado—. ¡Si la mitad del mundo cree que es mexicano! **Ni que fuera** Penélope Cruz. O Pedro Almodóvar.

—Nadie recuerda los nombres de los **directores de cine** —contesta Federico.

En ese momento, Paco, el **mozo** y dueño del café, interrumpe la discusión.

—Muchachos, bajen la voz —pide Paco—. Están **ahuyentando** a los clientes.

Julio y Federico miran a su alrededor. El café de Paco está casi vacío. Solo una de las mesas está ocupada por Herman, un hombre **rubio** de cara ancha.

—Aquí solo quedó Herman —dice Paco—. Quizás porque no habla muy bien español. Le resulta más fácil ignorarlos.

—Lo sentimos —agrega Julio.

—No se **preocupen**, no hay problema —responde Paco—. En realidad, sí hay problema. ¿Por qué ninguno habla de Picasso, o de Dalí?

—¡Dalí! —contesta Federico, otra vez **a los gritos**—. ¡No me hagas hablar de Dalí!

—Basta —dice Julio—. Terminemos con esto. Preguntémosle a Herman. Él es alemán. El primer español que nombre, es el más famoso. Y allí termina la discusión. Es casi como tirar una **moneda**. ¿Estamos de acuerdo?

—Vale —contesta Federico.

Entonces, Paco se **acerca** a la mesa de Herman, quien está mirando el móvil frente a su taza de café.

—Herman, disculpa —interrumpe Paco—. Quería hacerte una pregunta. ¿Quién es el español más famoso? El más famoso de todos.

Herman levanta la mirada del móvil. Responde sin dudar:

—Cervantes.

# Vocabulary List

| Spanish | English |
| --- | --- |
| guardar | keep |
| soler | usually do |
| el periódico | newspaper |
| agitar | shake |
| sin piedad | mercilessly |
| el ambiente caldeado | tense atmosphere |
| ni que fuera | not even if |
| el director de cine, la directora de cine | movie director |
| el mozo, la moza | waiter, waitress |
| ahuyentar | drive away |
| rubio, rubia | blond |
| preocuparse | worry |
| a los gritos | yelling, out loud |
| la moneda | coin |
| acercarse | get closer |

## Grammar Section

Verbs are often considered the most difficult part of a language to learn. But you don't need to worry. There is nothing to fear about a few conjugations. In this chapter, you will see that present tense verbs are not really difficult, and you will soon master:

- the present indicative
- the progressive or continuous present
- the present subjunctive

### The present indicative

Since you are not new to the language, you probably already know that the present indicative tense in Spanish is similar to how it is used in English. The difficult part is that, in Spanish, the conjugations vary greatly depending on whether the verbs are regular or irregular.

In this section, we will start reviewing the regular verbs ending in -AR, -ER, and -IR and their conjugations. To conjugate a verb in the present indicative, you must drop the ending and then add the specific ending according to each pronoun.

Let's see three examples: *cantar* ("to sing"), *comer* ("to eat"), and *vivir* ("to live").

|  | cantar | comer | vivir |
|---|---|---|---|
| yo | canto | como | vivo |
| tú | cantas | comes | vives |
| él/ella | canta | come | vive |
| nosotros/nosotras | cantamos | comemos | vivimos |
| vosotros/vosotras | cantáis | coméis | vivís |

| | | | |
|---|---|---|---|
| ellos/ellas | cantan | comen | viven |

When it comes to irregular verbs, things get a bit more difficult. Languages are often whimsical and follow particular rules. Therefore, don't worry if you can't correctly conjugate all the verbs below on the first try. Remember that practice makes perfect!

It's time to see some of the most used irregular verbs in Spanish and their conjugations in the present indicative. We will divide them into categories according to how the stem is modified.

**Irregular verbs with vowel irregularities:**

| | **contar** ("to tell") | **perder** ("to lose") | **pensar** ("to think") |
|---|---|---|---|
| yo | cuento | pierdo | pienso |
| tú | cuentas | pierdes | piensas |
| él/ella | cuenta | pierde | piensa |
| nosotros/nosotras | contamos | perdemos | pensamos |
| vosotros/vosotras | contáis | perdéis | pensáis |
| ellos/ellas | cuentan | pierden | piensan |

**Irregular verbs with consonant irregularities:**

| | **decir** ("to say") | **hacer** ("to do") | **caer** ("to fall") |
|---|---|---|---|
| yo | digo | hago | caigo |

| tú | dices | haces | caes |
|---|---|---|---|
| él/ella | dice | hace | cae |
| nosotros/nosotras | decimos | hacemos | caemos |
| vosotros/vosotras | decís | hacéis | caéis |
| ellos/ellas | dicen | hacen | caen |

**Irregular verbs that completely change their stems:**

|  | **ser** ("to be") | **ir** ("to go") |
|---|---|---|
| yo | soy | voy |
| tú | eres | vas |
| él/ella | es | va |
| nosotros/nosotras | somos | vamos |
| vosotros/vosotras | sois | vais |
| ellos/ellas | son | van |

### Uses of the present indicative

Now that we have reviewed the conjugations of the present indicative, let's refresh its uses. We use the present indicative to:

1. Talk about something specific that's happening at this very moment:

- *Quiero comer una hamburguesa* ("I want to eat a hamburger.")

2. Talk about frequent actions:
- *Héctor **va** a la escuela en autobús* ("Héctor goes to school by bus.")

3. Mention present desires:
- *Martín **piensa** en mudarse* ("Martín thinks about moving.")

4. Talk about situations that are going to happen in the near future:
- ***Tengo** una entrevista de trabajo el viernes* ("I have a job interview on Friday.")

5. Talk about things that are always true:
- *Los perros **ladran** y los gatos **maúllan*** ("Dogs bark and cats meow.")

6. Narrate events from the past:
- *La Primera Guerra Mundial **empieza** en 1914* ("World War I begins in 1914.")

**The progressive present**

The present progressive in Spanish, also known as "present continuous," is the tense we use to talk about something happening at the moment of speaking. It is also used to talk about actions that you are doing continuously for a certain period of time. Sounds familiar to you, right? You probably already studied this tense. And besides, English also has a present continuous: it's the tense formed by the verb "to be" plus a second verb followed by -ING, forming a gerund. "I sing" is in the simple present, and "I'm singing" is in the present continuous.

Now, let's review how to form the present continuous in Spanish. The formula is as follows:

**The subject** (it can be implicit) + **a reflexive pronoun** (*me, te, lo, nos*; if applicable) + **the verb *estar* conjugated** + **the stem of the main verb** + **the suffix -ANDO or -IENDO**

Take a look at three simple example sentences. Below them, you can see a table in which we will break down each sentence, so you can see the formula in detail:

- *Estoy comiendo* ("I am eating.")
- *El perro está ladrando* ("The dog is barking.")
- *Mis hermanas se están peinando* ("My sisters are combing their hair.")

| Subject | Reflexive Pronoun | Conjugated Verb "estar" | Verb Stem | Suffix -ANDO or -IENDO |
|---|---|---|---|---|
| (Yo) | | Estoy | com | iendo |
| El perro | | está | ladr | ando |
| Mis hermanas | se | están | pein | ando |

You might be wondering how to know when to use the suffix -ANDO and when to use the suffix -IENDO:

- Verbs ending in -AR: -ANDO. For example, *caminar* becomes *caminando* ("walking"), *mirar* becomes *mirando* ("looking"), and *cantar* becomes *cantando* ("singing").
- Verbs ending in -ER and -IR: -IENDO. For example: *escribir* becomes *escribiendo* ("writing"), *comer* becomes *comiendo* ("eating"), and *leer* becomes *leyendo* ("reading".)
  - Let's stop for a moment on the verb *leer*. As you have no doubt noticed, its gerund is not ✗ *leiendo*, but *leyendo*, with a Y. This happens with a few verbs, such as *ir* (*yendo*, "going"), *huir* (*huyendo*, "fleeing"), *caer* (*cayendo*, "falling"), and *creer* (*creyendo*, "believing").

Now, let's see a few example sentences with the present progressive:

- *Estoy escribiendo una novela* ("I am writing a novel.")
- *Parece que estás disfrutando de ese viaje* ("You seem to be enjoying that trip.")

- *Mariana está viniendo a mi casa* ("Mariana is coming to my house.")
- **Estamos teniendo** *algunos problemas con la conexión* ("We're having some problems with the connection.")
- *Os* **lo estáis pasando** *bien, ¿no?* ("You're having a great time, aren't you?")
- *Carlos y Walter* **se están convirtiendo** *en grandes amigos* ("Carlos and Walter are becoming great friends.")

**The present subjunctive**

The subjunctive is a verbal mood used to talk about hypothetical, possible or desired actions or situations. Verbs in the subjunctive mood are subordinate to another verb (which is in the indicative mood) within a sentence.

Forming present subjunctive in Spanish with regular verbs, the first step is to get their *root*. For example, the stem of *cantar* ("to sing") is *cant*, and the stem of *comer* ("to eat") is *com*. Then, you have to add the proper termination, depending on the case:

|  | Verbs ending in -AR | Verbs ending in -ER and in -IR |
|---|---|---|
| yo | -e | -a |
| tú | -es | -as |
| él/ella | -e | -a |
| nosotros/nosotras | -emos | -amos |
| vosotros/vosotras | -éis | -áis |
| ellos/ellas | -en | -an |

Now, let's see the regular verbs *amar* ("to love"), *temer* ("to fear") and *partir* ("to leave") in the present subjunctive.

|  | **amar** | **temer** | **partir** |
|---|---|---|---|
| yo | ame | tema | parta |
| tú | ames | temas | partas |
| él/ella | ame | tema | parta |
| nosotros/nosotras | amemos | temamos | partamos |
| vosotros/vosotras | améis | temáis | partáis |
| ellos/ellas | amen | teman | partan |

But what happens with irregular verbs? Once again, irregular verbs typically follow their own rules. Next, we will see the conjugation of the present subjunctive of some of the most used irregular verbs in Spanish.

|  | **ser** ("to be") | **decir** ("to say") | **ir** ("to go") |
|---|---|---|---|
| yo | sea | diga | vaya |
| tú | seas | digas | vayas |
| él/ella | sea | diga | vaya |
| nosotros/nosotras | seamos | digamos | vayamos |
| vosotros/vosotras | seáis | digáis | vayáis |
| ellos/ellas | sean | digan | vayan |

**Uses of the present subjunctive**

We've already mentioned that the present subjunctive expresses hypothetical, possible, or desired actions or situations. However, there are some other uses, so let's see an example of each:

1. Expressing desire

    - *Me gustaría que **llegaras** temprano* ("I would like for you to arrive early.")

2. Expressing necessity

    - *Necesitamos que **repares** el coche para seguir el viaje* ("We need you to repair the car to continue with the trip.")

3. Expressing interests or feelings

    - *Le encanta que le **regalen** flores* ("He loves to get flowers.")

4. Stating opinions or perceptions with a negative statement (check the difference between the two sentences below)

    - *Creo que mañana **ceno** con mis padres* ("I think I'm having dinner with my parents tomorrow," *ceno* is in the indicative mood)
    - *No creo que mañana **cene** con mis padres* ("I don't think I'm having dinner with my parents tomorrow," *cene* is in the subjunctive mood)

5. Expressing doubt and probability

    - *Quizás **pueda** pasar mañana, pero no te lo prometo* ("I might be able to go tomorrow, but I'm not sure.")

6. Giving advice

    - *Les recomiendo que **lleguen** temprano* ("I would advise you to arrive early.")

7. Giving orders

    - *Mis padres me prohíben que **me acueste** muy tarde* ("My parents won't let me go to bed too late.")

8. Asking people to do something

    - *Mi madre me pidió que **pase** por el supermercado* ("My mother asked me to go to the supermarket.")

9. Expressing purpose
- *Te regalamos la computadora para que **trabajes*** ("We gave you the computer so that you would work.")

10. Besides the uses listed above, there are some words and expressions that trigger the subjunctive:

| Spanish | English |
|---|---|
| a no ser que | unless |
| a pesar de que | even though |
| antes de que | before |
| aunque | even if |
| con tal de que | as long as |
| cuando | when |
| después de que | after |
| en el caso de que | in case of |
| hasta que | until |
| sin que | without |
| tan pronto como | as soon as |

Let's see some example sentences of present subjunctive in action:
- *Verónica siempre me pide que **sea** optimista* ("Verónica always asks me to be optimistic.")
- *Ojalá **apruebes** ese examen* ("I hope you pass that exam.")

- *Me alegra que **tengas** muchos amigos* ("I'm glad you have many friends.")
- *No creo que **llueva** mañana* ("I don't think it will rain tomorrow.")
- *¿Crees que Francisco **deba** estudiar mucho para ese examen?* ("Do you think Francisco should study hard for that exam?")
- *Mi vecino Pedro no siente que **esté** preparado para ese trabajo* ("My neighbor Pedro doesn't feel he is prepared for that job.")
- *Mi mamá dice que **vayamos** a comer* ("My mom says we should go eat.")
- *Espero que **tengáis** ganas de ir al parque* ("I hope you feel like going to the park.")
- *Quiero que mis hijos **lean** más* ("I want my children to read more.")

Are you ready to see how much you've learned in this chapter? Take the quiz and, afterward, go back and see if you can tick all the boxes!

### Exercises

1. Miguel de Cervantes Saavedra is the most famous Spanish person, according to the German client in the bar in the short story at the beginning of this chapter. Complete the following text with the present indicative conjugations of the verbs, *llevar, pensar, haber, situar,* and, *ser* and *estar.*

   *Cervantes ......... considerado uno de los hombres más famosos de España. Muchos ......... que su obra más importante, El Quijote, es una de las mejores de la literatura universal. El Museo Cervantes ......... en Madrid, España, en la casa en la que se cree que nació el autor. Sin embargo, algunos ......... su casa de nacimiento a unos minutos a pie, donde hoy ......... un teatro que ......... su nombre.*

2. In the first column, you have some verbs, accompanied by their roots. In the right column, you have the endings of those verbs in the present indicative. Match the items

on the left with the items on the right to form the correct conjugations.

| | |
|---|---|
| tener (ten-) | -emos |
| estar (est-) | -omos |
| decir (dec-) | -amos |
| hacer (hac-) | -imos |
| ser (s-) | -emos |

3. In the next dialogue, complete the empty spaces with the present progressive. You have to use the verbs *construir*, *tener*, *ir* and *hacer*.
   A. ¿Cómo te ......... ......... en tu nuevo emprendimiento? Me dijo Julieta que ......... ......... muchos clientes.
   B. Sí. Mudarnos al centro de la ciudad fue una gran decisión. El único problema es que ......... ......... un edificio al lado de la tienda. ¡El ruido de las máquinas se nos ......... ......... insoportable!

4. Here you have some verbs. Below them, there are four possible options to form their gerund. Underline the correct one.

   | Ser | Comer | Hacer | Bailar |
   |---|---|---|---|
   | *siendo* | *comando* | *haciando* | *bailendo* |
   | *siando* | *comiando* | *haciendo* | *balando* |
   | *sendo* | *comiendo* | *hiciendo* | *bailondo* |
   | *siondo* | *comiondo* | *haciondo* | *bailando* |

5. Decide whether the following statements are true or false. Correct the false ones.
   a. The present indicative is used to talk about frequent actions.
   b. The present indicative can't be used to talk about the near future.

c. The present progressive is used to talk about something that is happening at this very moment.
d. The present subjunctive is used to talk about hypothetical, possible or desired actions or situations.

# Chapter 8: The Verb II. Thinking About the Past

## Short Story: La ciudad antigua

—Muy bien, aquí termina el tour por la Catedral de Sevilla —dijo Laura—. Si queréis, ahora podéis subir a la Giralda, que es esta torre de aquí. —Laura señaló la entrada a un edificio de **ladrillo** de unos noventa metros—. Como ya sabéis, originalmente no era parte de la Catedral. En realidad, la Giralda era parte de la mezquita de la ciudad, construida durante el siglo XII. Sigue siendo uno de los puntos más altos de Sevilla, así que os recomiendo subir. El único problema es que no tiene elevadores. Ahora sí: ¡adiós!

Los turistas aplaudieron para despedir a Laura. Ella les agradeció y después recogió los **auriculares** que les había entregado al principio del tour. Laura siempre estaba muy atenta a los auriculares. Una vez, hacía dos años, había perdido uno y había tenido que pagarlo con su propio dinero. No eran **baratos**.

Laura decidió tomarse su **recreo** para **almorzar**. Avisó a su **jefe** y salió de la Catedral, cruzando el Patio de los Naranjos. Estaban **en flor**. Cada vez que sentía el aroma a azahar de los **naranjos**, Laura agradecía mentalmente a Hércules, fundador mitológico de Sevilla, por traer la "manzana de oro" a España. Y agradecía también al califato almohade, que gobernó la ciudad durante el **medioevo**, porque había plantado naranjos en toda la ciudad.

La Plaza del Triunfo estaba **llena** de turistas. La primavera era siempre la **época** más **concurrida**. Laura caminó hasta **alejarse** de la **multitud**. Era imposible comer alrededor de esa plaza. Todo era muy caro.

Laura caminó hasta un pequeño bar a orillas del Guadalquivir. Le gustaba almorzar mirando el río. Por ese **mismo** río, pensaba, habían entrado todas las riquezas de América durante el siglo XVI. Había sido mucho tiempo atrás, pero su impacto **todavía** era notable. El Real Alcázar, a **apenas** unos metros, era un buen testimonio de eso.

—¿Qué quieres hoy, Laura? —preguntó Gonzalo, el **camarero**. Se conocían bien. Laura había visitado ese bar prácticamente todos los días durante dos años. Sabía que Gonzalo era fanático del Betis y que su madre había nacido en Venezuela.

— Salmorejo y chipirones, por favor —respondió Laura.

Gonzalo fue a la cocina, y Laura miró el río. Todavía le quedaban tres tours para esa tarde, pero eso no le preocupaba. Le gustaba su trabajo. Contar la historia de su ciudad le hacía sentir parte de algo más grande. Grande como el Guadalquivir. Algo que fluía, crecía, avanzaba, y que sin embargo era siempre parte de lo mismo.

## Vocabulary List

| Spanish | English |
|---|---|
| el ladrillo | brick |
| los auriculares | headphones |
| barato, barata | cheap |
| el recreo | break |

| | |
|---|---|
| almorzar | have lunch |
| el jefe, la jefa | boss |
| en flor | in bloom |
| el naranjo | orange tree |
| el medioevo | Middle Ages |
| lleno, llena | full |
| la época | time |
| concurrido, concurrida | crowded |
| mismo, misma | same |
| todavía | yet |
| apenas | barely |
| el camarero, la camarera | waiter, waitress |

## Grammar Section

We have already seen how to talk about the present. But you also need to know how to talk about the past. There are four past tenses in Spanish, and they are precisely the ones we are going to talk about in this chapter:

- *pretérito perfecto simple* (simple past);
- *pretérito perfecto* (perfect past);
- *pretérito imperfecto* (imperfect past); and
- *pretérito pluscuamperfecto*.

Don't let the names of those verb tenses scare you. We will go one by one, explaining the conjugations and giving you many examples. Let's go!

### Pretérito perfecto simple

Let's start with the simplest of all. *Pretérito perfecto simple*, also known as *pasado simple* ("simple past") or *pretérito indefinido,* is used to talk about actions that happened at a specific time and have already been finished. This tense is usually accompanied by a time expression that specifies when that action took place, but it can also be implicit.

*Pretérito perfecto simple* is used to talk about:

1. Specific events that happened at a specific time:
   - *El año pasado,* **cambié** *de trabajo* ("Last year, I changed jobs.")
2. Events that happened during a specific period of time.
   - **Estuve** *más de dos horas esperando que me atendieran* ("I waited for more than two hours to be served.")
3. A new action that interrupts another.
   - *Ayer estaba paseando y* **me encontré** *a mi hermana* ("Yesterday I was taking a walk and I ran into my sister.")
4. A sequence of actions that have already been finished.
   - *Esta mañana,* **me desperté** *temprano,* **desayuné** *ligero y* **salí** *a dar una vuelta* ("This morning, I woke up early, I had a light breakfast and I went for a walk.")

Now that you know in what contexts you have to use the simple past in Spanish, let's see some example sentences.

- *Ayer* **vi** *una comadreja en el patio trasero* ("Yesterday I saw a weasel in the backyard.")
- *¿***Viajaste** *alguna vez al Caribe?* ("Have you ever been to the Caribbean?")
- *Rodrigó* **comió** *pizza, pero Rebeca* **pidió** *una hamburguesa* ("Rodrigo had pizza but Rebeca ordered a hamburger.")

- *Mis amigas y yo **fuimos** a la fiesta anoche* ("My friends and I went to the party last night.")
- *Vosotros **tuvisteis** mucha suerte* ("You were very lucky.")
- *Los gatos **treparon** al techo de la casa* ("The cats climbed to the roof of the house.")

Now let's see a table with the conjugations in *pretérito perfecto simple* of some common verbs in Spanish. Let's start with three regular verbs ending in -AR, -ER and -IR: *amar* ("to love"), *temer* ("to fear") and *partir* ("to leave").

|  | amar | temer | partir |
|---|---|---|---|
| yo | amé | temí | partí |
| tú | amaste | temiste | partiste |
| él/ella | amó | temió | partió |
| nosotros/nosotras | amamos | temimos | partimos |
| vosotros/vosotras | amasteis | temisteis | partisteis |
| ellos/ellas | amaron | temieron | partieron |

Now, let's see the conjugations with four irregular verbs: *hacer* ("to do"), *ser* and *ir* ("to be" and "to go"; in this tense they have the same conjugation), and *andar* ("to walk" or "to be").

|  | hacer | ser/ir | andar |
|---|---|---|---|
| yo | hice | fui | anduve |
| tú | hiciste | fuiste | anduviste |
| él/ella | hizo | fue | anduvo |

| | | | |
|---|---|---|---|
| nosotros/nosotras | hicimos | fuimos | anduvimos |
| vosotros/vosotras | hicisteis | fuisteis | anduvisteis |
| ellos/ellas | hicieron | fueron | anduvieron |

### Pretérito perfecto

*Pretérito perfecto*, also known as *pasado compuesto* ("compound past"), is another verb tense used to talk about actions that took place in the past.

It's formed with the auxiliary verb *haber* ("to have") conjugated in *pretérito perfecto simple* (*he, has, ha, hemos, habéis, han*), followed by the verb that denotes the action conjugated in the *participio* ("participle"). But... what is the *participio*? Here you have some examples:

| Verb | Participle |
|---|---|
| ser | sido |
| tener | tenido |
| saber | sabido |
| hacer | hecho |
| correr | corrido |
| amar | amado |

In sum, the formula to conjugate a verb in *pretérito perfecto* is the following:

**Subject + auxiliary verb *haber* (conjugated in *pretérito perfecto*) + participle of the main verb**

This tense is used to:

1. Talk about past actions that have some link with the present:

- *He pensado* en viajar a Perú a fin de año ("I've been thinking about going to Peru at the end of the year.")

2. Talk about life experiences:

- *Ha visitado* Francia en más de una ocasión ("She's been to France more than once.")

Now, let's see some example sentences with the *pretérito perfecto*.

- *He visto* una película muy buena en el cine ("I've seen a very good movie in the theatre.")
- ¿*Le has dado* de comer a los perros? ("Have you fed the dogs?")
- Creo que tu teléfono *se ha roto* ("I think your phone's broken.")
- *Nos hemos puesto* muy contentos cuando llamasteis ("We were very happy when you called.")
- *Habéis sabido* manejar la situación muy bien ("You managed to handle the situation perfectly.")
- Esos mosquitos **me han molestado** toda la tarde ("Those mosquitoes have been bothering me all afternoon.")

Now, we are going to see a table with common verb conjugations. We are going to use the same verbs ending in -AR, -ER and -IR that we used in the previous section.

|  | amar | temer | partir |
|---|---|---|---|
| yo | he amado | he temido | he partido |
| tú | has amado | has temido | has partido |
| él/ella | ha amado | ha temido | ha partido |
| nosotros/nosotras | hemos amado | hemos temido | hemos partido |
| vosotros/vosotras | habéis amado | habéis temido | habéis partido |

| | | | |
|---|---|---|---|
| ellos/ellas | han amado | han temido | han partido |

Now, let's see three irregular verbs: *hacer* ("to do"), *ser* ("to be"), and *ir* ("to go").

| | hacer | ser | ir |
|---|---|---|---|
| yo | he hecho | he sido | he ido |
| tú | has hecho | has sido | has ido |
| él/ella | ha hecho | ha sido | ha ido |
| nosotros/nosotras | hemos hecho | hemos sido | hemos ido |
| vosotros/vosotras | habéis hecho | habéis sido | habéis ido |
| ellos/ellas | han hecho | han sido | han ido |

### Pretérito imperfecto

P*retérito imperfecto* ("imperfect past") is a past tense used when the beginning or end of an action is not indicated. It is used to:

1. Talk about habitual or repeated actions in the past:

- *Cuando era una niña, **dibujaba** todo el día* ("When I was a little girl, I used to draw all day.")

2. Describe how an action took place in the past:

- *Los caballos **corrían** en el campo* ("The horses **were running** in the field.")

3. Point out an action in the past that is interrupted by a specific new action; the latter, expressed in *pretérito perfecto simple*:

- *Mientras **caminaba** por la playa, se acercó un amistoso perro* ("As he walked along the beach, he was approached by a friendly dog.")

4. Describe the state of a person or an object:

- *Martín **estaba** muy nervioso* ("Martín was very nervous.")

Let's see some example sentences with *pretérito imperfecto*:

- *¡Yo no sabía que me **estabais** organizando una fiesta sorpresa!* ("I didn't know you were organizing a surprise party for me!")
- *Recuerdo que **bailabas** tango muy bien* ("I remember that you danced tango very well.")
- *Teresa **trabajaba** en una inmobiliaria, pero le **pagaban** bastante mal* ("Teresa used to work in a real estate agency, but she was paid quite poorly.")
- *Mi madre y yo **pensábamos** que el vestido era más caro* ("My mother and I thought the dress was more expensive.")
- *¿Vosotros **veíais** esa serie cuando erais pequeños?* ("Did you watch that TV show when you were little?")
- *Mis tíos **vivían** en Sevilla* ("My aunt and uncle used to live in Seville.")

*Pretérito imperfecto* is formed with the stem of the verb followed by the corresponding ending according to each type of verb. Let's take a look at them.

## Verbos terminados en -AR

| | | |
|---|---|---|
| yo | | -aba |
| tú | | -abas |
| él/ella | raíz del verbo | -aba |
| nosotros/nosotras | | -ábamos |
| vosotros/vosotras | | -abais |

| ellos/ellas | | -aban |

Examples:

| | dar ("to give") | bailar ("to dance") | soñar ("to dream") |
|---|---|---|---|
| yo | daba | bailaba | soñaba |
| tú | dabas | bailabas | soñabas |
| él | daba | bailaba | soñaba |
| nosotros/nosotras | dábamos | bailábamos | soñábamos |
| vosotros/vosotras | dabais | bailabais | soñabais |
| ellos/ellas | daban | bailaban | soñaban |

## Verbos terminados en -ER y en -IR

| | | |
|---|---|---|
| yo | | -ía |
| tú | | -ías |
| él/ella | raíz del verbo | -ía |
| nosotros/nosotras | | -íamos |
| vosotros/vosotras | | -íais |
| ellos/ellas | | -ían |

Examples:

|  | **beber** ("to drink") | **comer** ("to eat") | **abrir** ("to open") |
|---|---|---|---|
| yo | bebía | comía | abría |
| tú | bebías | comías | abrías |
| él | bebía | comía | abría |
| nosotros/nosotras | bebíamos | comíamos | abríamos |
| vosotros/vosotras | bebíais | comíais | abríais |
| ellos/ellas | bebían | comían | abrían |

Finally, we have three verbs that follow their own rules: *ser* ("to be"), *ir* ("to go"), and *ver* ("to see").

|  | **ser** | **ir** | **ver** |
|---|---|---|---|
| yo | era | iba | veía |
| tú | eras | ibas | veías |
| él | era | iba | veía |
| nosotros/nosotras | éramos | íbamos | veíamos |
| vosotros/vosotras | erais | ibais | veíais |
| ellos/ellas | eran | iban | veían |

### Pretérito pluscuamperfecto

The final past tense we'll see in this book is *pretérito pluscuamperfecto*. It may sound complicated, but we assure you it's pretty simple: it is used to talk about the past of the past. Thus, you have to use it when talking about a past story and referring to something that happened before.

To conjugate *pretérito pluscuamperfecto*, you must take the auxiliary verb *haber* ("to have") in *pretérito imperfecto* followed by the *participio* of the main verb.

Let's see how to use *pretérito pluscuamperfecto* with some example verbs.

| Subject | Auxiliary Verb (*haber*) | Participle of the Main Verb |
|---|---|---|
| yo | había | andado<br>comido<br>hecho<br>bebido<br>temido<br>soñado |
| tú | habías | |
| él | había | |
| nosotros/nosotras | habíamos | |
| vosotros/vosotras | habíais | |
| ellos/ellas | habían | |

Now, let's see the *pretérito pluscuamperfecto* in action with some example sentences:

- *Nunca antes **había caminado** por ese vecindario* ("I had never walked through this neighborhood.")
- *¿Ya **habías comido** paella alguna vez?* ("Had you had paella before?")
- *La profesora dijo que Rubén **había hecho** trampa en el examen* ("The professor said Rubén had cheated in the exam.")
- ***Habíamos pensado** vacacionar en Brasil, pero finalmente optamos por el sur de Argentina* ("We had thought about going on holiday to Brazil, but we ended up deciding to go to the south of Argentina.")

- *¿Habíais pensado* alguna vez en casaros? ("Had you ever thought about getting married?")
- Cuando le llegó su turno, le dijeron que los boletos *se habían agotado* ("When it was his turn, they told him that the tickets had sold out.")

**Exercises**

1. Below, you'll find a dialogue full of verbs in the past tense. Decide to which tense each one belongs (*pretérito perfecto simple, pretérito perfecto, pretérito imperfecto* or *pretérito pluscuamperfecto*).
   A. Me **ha dicho** (..............) Cristina que eres ingeniero. Yo también **quería** (..............) estudiar esa carrera cuando era joven, pero finalmente me **decidí** (..............) por Medicina.
   B. Sí, **estudié** (..............) Ingeniería, aunque al principio me **había anotado** para estudiar Arquitectura. ¡Pero me **arrepentí** (..............) en el último momento!

2. Decide whether the following statements are true or false. Correct the false ones.
   a. To form *pretérito perfecto* you need the participle of the verb.
   b. *Pretérito imperfecto* is the past tense that indicates the beginning or the end of an action.
   c. *Había hecho* is conjugated in *pretérito imperfecto*.
   d. *Pretérito perfecto simple* is used to talk about actions that occurred at a certain time but have already finished.

3. Complete the sentences with the correct ending of *pretérito imperfecto* (-ABA, -ABAS, -ÁBAMOS, -ABAIS, -ABAN).
   a. Mis amigos bail.......
   b. Juan cant.......
   c. Yo soñ.......
   d. Nosotros estudi.......

4. Go back to the short story at the beginning of the chapter and write down all the verbs conjugated in the *pretérito pluscuamperfecto* that you can find.

5. Complete the story below with the correct conjugated verbs. The verbs can be in any of the four past tenses we saw throughout the chapter.

María .......... *(estar)* abriendo las persianas de su tienda, como todas las mañanas, cuando .......... *(entrar)* un cliente nuevo. .......... *(ser)* un hombre al que nunca .......... .......... *(ver)* antes, aunque algo en su cara le .......... *(resultar)* familiar. .......... *(tener)* un tupido bigote bajo la gran nariz.

—¡Buenos días! ¿En qué lo puedo ayudar? —.......... *(preguntar)* María.

—Quiero un café grande, por favor —.......... *(pedir)* el hombre, mientras .......... *(jugar)* con su bigote.

María se .......... *(dirigir)* hacia la cafetera y .......... *(empezar)* a hacer el café. Mientras lo .......... *(preparar)*, .......... *(notar)* que la voz del hombre también le .......... *(sonar)* conocida.

—Disculpe, ¿nos .......... .......... *(ver)* antes?

Entonces, con una sonrisa, el hombre se .......... *(quitar)* el bigote de la cara. .......... *(ser)* un bigote falso, por supuesto. María .......... *(dejar)* el café sobre el mostrador, incrédula.

—¿Eduardo? —.......... *(preguntar)*—. ¡Qué bonita sorpresa me .......... .......... *(dar)*!

# Chapter 9: The Verb III. Towards the Future

## Short Story: La feria del futuro

Manuel toma la mano de su madre. Tiene miedo de **perderse** entre la **multitud**. Nunca ha visto tanta gente junta en su vida.

Su madre le **señala** el cartel que decora el edificio donde van a entrar.

—Manuel, ¿qué dice allí? —pregunta.

Manuel mira detenidamente. En la escuela está aprendiendo a leer, pero todavía le **cuesta** hacerlo **de corrido**.

—Expo-sición Inter-na-cional —dice Manuel con dificultad— de Barcelona. 1929 —concluye, satisfecho.

Su madre sonríe y lo lleva al interior del edificio. Es uno de los muchos pabellones que construyeron en la ciudad para **albergar** la exposición. Manuel nunca ha estado en un lugar tan grande.

Caminan entre los distintos expositores. Su madre avanza despacio, porque no quiere perderse nada. Manuel escucha fragmentos de distintos **discursos**.

—En el futuro, cada familia tendrá un cine... ¡en su propia casa! —dice un hombre con **bigote**.

—¿Cansada de hacer la **colada**? —pregunta otro hombre a una mujer del público, mientras señala **una especie de** gran caja de metal—. Con esta maravillosa máquina, ¡no lavará una **prenda** más en su vida!

—Nadie tendría que **perder el tiempo** haciendo tediosas cuentas matemáticas —dice un tercer hombre, mientras **teclea** sobre algo que parece una **máquina de escribir**—. ¿Saben lo que Newton habría podido hacer con esta calculadora mecánica? ¡Maravillas!

Manuel piensa que a él también le vendría bien esa calculadora. La tarea de matemáticas sería mucho más sencilla.

Finalmente, su madre se detiene frente a un **puesto** de automóviles. Allí está el padre de Manuel, hablando frente a la multitud.

—Tres cosas son seguras —dice—. En el futuro, no hará falta trabajar. Trabajarán las máquinas. Además, ya no comeremos la porquería que comemos hoy. Habrá **pastillas** científicamente diseñadas para darnos fuerza y vigor. Y finalmente, por supuesto, los coches volarán por los aires. —En ese momento, el padre de Manuel señala al vehículo que tiene detrás—. Este modelo no vuela, pero está muy cerca.

Manuel mira el coche que su padre señala y recuerda todos los avances que vio en su **recorrido**. "El futuro será un lugar maravilloso", piensa. "No puedo esperar".

## Vocabulary List

| Spanish | English |
|---|---|
| perderse | get lost |
| la multitud | crowd |
| señalar | point at |
| costarle algo a alguien | find it hard |

| de corrido | fluently |
|---|---|
| albergar | be home to |
| el discurso | speech |
| el bigote | mustache |
| la colada | laundry |
| una especie de | a kind of |
| la prenda | item of clothing |
| perder el tiempo | waste time |
| teclear | type |
| la máquina de escribir | typewriter |
| el puesto | stand |
| la pastilla | pill |
| el recorrido | tour |

## Grammar Section

We've already talked about the past and the present. Now is the time to talk about the future! In this chapter we'll see the following future tenses:

- *futuro simple*;
- *futuro compuesto*;
- *condicional simple*; and
- *condicional compuesto*.

**Futuro simple**

In Spanish, *futuro simple* ("simple future") is used to:

1. Express the intention of doing an action in the future:
   - *Mañana **viajaré** a Buenos Aires* ("Tomorrow I will travel to Buenos Aires.")
2. Express hypotheses or assumptions:
   - *María se fue a pie; **vivirá** cerca* ("María left on foot; she probably lives nearby.")

Now, it's time to learn how to conjugate verbs in *futuro simple*. For verbs of the first, second, and third conjugation (verbs ending in -AR, -ER, and -IR, respectively), you have to include the stem of the verb followed by the corresponding ending, as we show in the chart below:

| | | |
|---|---|---|
| yo | | -é |
| tú | | -ás |
| él/ella | raíz del verbo | -á |
| nosotros/nosotras | | -emos |
| vosotros/vosotras | | -éis |
| ellos/ellas | | -án |

Let's see the conjugation in action with the verbs *amar*, *temer* and *partir*.

| | **amar** | **temer** | **partir** |
|---|---|---|---|
| yo | amaré | temeré | partiré |
| tú | amarás | temerás | partirás |
| él/ella | amará | temerá | partirá |

| | | | |
|---|---|---|---|
| nosotros/nosotras | amaremos | temeremos | partiremos |
| vosotros/vosotras | amaréis | temeréis | partiréis |
| ellos/ellas | amarán | temerán | partirán |

And now let's check a few examples:

- ***Partiré*** *mañana a las ocho en punto* ("I will leave tomorrow at 8 o'clock.")
- *Carlos me dijo que* ***vivirá*** *en Bogotá un año* ("Carlos told me that he will live in Bogotá for a year.")
- *Te* **amaré** *por siempre* ("I will love you forever.")
- *Lucía* **cenará** *con sus amigas esta noche* ("Lucía will have dinner with her friends tonight.")

As we have seen in chapter 4 of this book, reflexive pronouns are used to indicate that an action falls on the subject. In this tense, the reflexive pronoun (*me, te, se, nos, os, se*) is always placed before the verb:

- ***Me bañaré*** *por la noche* ("I will shower tonight.")
- ***Nos encontraremos*** *a las siete* ("We will meet at 7.")
- ***Te diré*** *lo que pienso* ("I'll tell you what I think.")

When it comes to irregular verbs, the formula changes. We can divide them into three groups; let's look at them below.

**Poner, salir, tener, venir, and valer**

To conjugate these verbs in *futuro simple*, you must replace the E or the I of the infinitive by a D. Then, you have to add the corresponding ending according to the subject. Let's see a table with the conjugation of *poner, salir* and *tener*.

| | **poner** | **salir** | **tener** |
|---|---|---|---|
| yo | pondré | saldré | tendré |
| tú | pondrás | saldrás | tendrás |

| él/ella | pondrá | saldrá | tendrá |
| --- | --- | --- | --- |
| nosotros/nosotras | pondremos | saldremos | tendremos |
| vosotros/vosotras | pondréis | saldréis | tendréis |
| ellos/ellas | pondrán | saldrán | tendrán |

Let's see some examples:

- **Pondré** *el libro de quejas a disposición de los clientes* ("I will make the complaint book available to customers.")
- *Imagino que* **saldrás** *a almorzar pronto* ("I imagine you'll be out for lunch soon.")
- *Esto es una reliquia, ¡***valdrá** *mucho más en el futuro!* ("This is a relic, it will be worth much more in the future!")
- **Tendremos** *una noche magnífica junto a toda la familia* ("We will have a magnificent night with the whole family.")
- **Vendréis** *al pícnic en el parque, ¿verdad?* ("You're coming to the picnic in the park, right?")
- *Roberto y Paco* **saldrán** *a comer algo* ("Roberto and Paco are going out to have something to eat.")

**Saber, querer, haber, poder, and caber**

In this second group, the vowel ending of the infinitive (the E) disappears. For example, with *saber* we have to remove the E and we'll get *sabr-*. Then, we add the corresponding ending to this new stem. Let's see it in more detail:

|  | **saber** | **querer** | **poder** |
| --- | --- | --- | --- |
| yo | sabré | querré | podré |
| tú | sabrás | querrás | podrás |

| | | | |
|---|---|---|---|
| él/ella | sabrá | querrá | podrá |
| nosotros/nosotras | sabremos | querremos | podremos |
| vosotros/vosotras | sabréis | querréis | podréis |
| ellos/ellas | sabrán | querrán | podrán |

For example:

- *No sé si **podré** hacer eso que me pides* ("I don't know if I can do what you're asking me.")
- *Supongo que **querrás** saber las razones de esta decisión* ("I guess you want to know the reasons for this decision.")
- *¿**Cabremos** todos en el mismo coche?* ("Will we all fit in the same car?")
- *Confiad en mí: **sabréis** qué hacer* ("Trust me: you'll know what to do.")
- *Me imagino que mis gatos **querrán** su alimento* ("I imagine my cats want their food.")

**Hacer and decir**

The third group is made up of the verbs *hacer* ("to do") and *decir* ("to say"). These two verbs change their stems and then take the ending of *futuro simple*. Let's see them in the table below.

| | hacer | decir |
|---|---|---|
| yo | haré | diré |
| tú | harás | dirás |
| él/ella | hará | dirá |
| nosotros/nosotras | haremos | diremos |

| vosotros/vosotras | haréis | diréis |
|---|---|---|
| ellos/ellas | harán | dirán |

For example:

- **Haré** las maletas por la tarde ("I'll pack in the afternoon.")
- ¿Le **dirás** a Martín la verdad? ("Will you tell Martín the truth?")
- Cristina **hará** su especialidad: ¡lasagna! ("Cristina will make her speciality: lasagna!")
- **Diremos** todo lo que pensamos al respecto ("We will say everything we think.")
- **Haréis** un gran espectáculo mañana ("You will put on a great show tomorrow.")
- Estoy ansiosa por saber qué **dirán** los críticos ("I'm anxious to know what the critics will say.")

**Futuro compuesto**

*Futuro compuesto* ("compound future", also known as *futuro perfecto*) is used to:

1. Talk about an action that will happen in the future, but will end before another future action:

- Ya **habré finalizado** mis estudios universitarios para el año que viene.

2. Express the assumption that an action happened in the past:

- Juan aún no llega. ¿**Habrá tenido** algún problema?

As you have undoubtedly noticed, the formula for *futuro compuesto* is quite simple: it's made up of the auxiliary verb *haber* in the *futuro simple*, followed by the *participio* of the main verb. Let's see how to form the *futuro compuesto* with some example verbs.

| Subject | Auxiliary Verb (*haber*) | Participle of the Main Verb |
|---|---|---|
| yo | habré | andado comido hecho bebido temido soñado |
| tú | habrás | |
| él/ella | habrá | |
| nosotros/nosotras | habremos | |
| vosotros/vosotras | habréis | |
| ellos/ellas | habrán | |

Now, let's see the *futuro compuesto* in action with some example sentences. Note how, when it expresses an action that will happen in the future, but will end before another future action, it is used together with some time adverb or some expression that refers to time.

- *Ya **habré cenado** para las nueve* ("I'll have had dinner by nine.")
- *¿El lunes **habrás vuelto**?* ("Will you be back by Monday?")
- *¡Está todo mojado! **Habrá llovido*** ("It's all wet! It has probably rained.")
- *Cuando nos demos cuenta, **habremos llegado*** ("When we realize it, we will have arrived.")
- *Mi casa no está por ese barrio. Os **habréis perdido*** ("My house isn't in that neighborhood. You're probably lost.")
- *Para mañana a esta hora, Juan y Teresa se **habrán casado*** ("By this time tomorrow, Juan and Teresa will have gotten married.")

## Condicional simple

*Condicional simple* has many uses:

1. To express a desire:

- *Me **encantaría** adoptar un gatito* ("I would love to adopt a kitten.")

2. To make a polite invitation:

- *¿**Querrías** venir a casa mañana por la tarde?* ("Would you like to come to my house tomorrow afternoon?")

3. To ask for something politely:

- *¿**Podrías** llevarme en tu coche?* ("Could you take me in your car?")

4. To make a suggestion:

- *Lo mejor **sería** salir ahora, o llegaremos tarde* ("The best thing would be to leave now or we will be late.")

5. To express an assumption about the future by placing the starting point of the action in the past:

- *Bárbara dijo que **llegaría** tarde* ("Barbara said she would be late.")

Let's see how to conjugate in *condicional simple* the regular verbs ending in -AR, -ER, and -IR.

| | | |
|---|---|---|
| yo | | -ía |
| tú | | -ías |
| él/ella | verbo en infinitivo | -ía |
| nosotros/nosotras | | -íamos |
| vosotros/vosotras | | -íais |
| ellos/ellas | | -ían |

## Condicional compuesto

*Condicional compuesto* is made up of the verb *haber* as an auxiliary, followed by the participle of the main verb. In this tense, *haber* is conjugated in the conditional. The *condicional compuesto* is used to:

1. Talk about hypothetical possibilities:

    - *Si hubiera llegado más temprano,* **habría conseguido** *sitio* ("If I had arrived earlier, I would have gotten a seat.")

2. Express unfulfilled desires:

    - *Me* **habría encantado** *viajar el año pasado, pero tuve mucho trabajo* ("I would have loved to travel last year, but I had a lot of work.")

3. Talk about imaginary situations:

    - *La fiesta* **habría estado** *más divertida con otro tipo de música* ("The party would have been more fun with another type of music.")

4. Express that we agree, or not, with the past actions of other people:

    - *María renunció al trabajo, y yo* **habría hecho** *lo mismo* ("María quit her job, and I would have done the same.")

To conjugate verbs in *condicional compuesto,* follow this structure:

| | | |
|---|---|---|
| yo | habría | |
| tú | habrías | |
| él/ella | habría | participio del verbo principal |
| nosotros/nosotras | habríamos | |
| vosotros/vosotras | habríais | |
| ellos/ellas | habrían | |

**Exercises**

1. Go back to the short story at the beginning and reread it. Then, answer the following questions in Spanish.
   a. ¿Qué dice el hombre con bigote?
   b. ¿Por qué Manuel piensa que le vendría bien una calculadora?
   c. ¿En qué puesto está el padre de Manuel?
   d. ¿Cuál es la primera cosa de la que está seguro el padre de Manuel?

2. Complete the following short story with the correct conjugations of the verbs in the *futuro simple*.
   *Te ......... (decir) lo que ......... (hacer) en mis vacaciones. ......... (ir) a Europa y a África. Mi primera parada ......... (ser) Madrid. Luego, ......... (bajar) hasta Málaga, en la costa. Finalmente, ......... (tomar) un buque y ......... (viajar) por el Mediterráneo hasta llegar a Marruecos. ¡Seguramente, ......... (ser) las mejores vacaciones de mi vida!*

3. Match each pronoun with the corresponding conjugation of the auxiliary verb *haber* to form the *futuro compuesto* tense.

   | | |
   |---|---|
   | 1. yo | a. habremos |
   | 2. tú | b. habrán |
   | 3. él/ella | c. habré |
   | 4. nosotros/nosotras | d. habrá |
   | 5. vosotros/vosotras | e. habrás |
   | 6. ellos/ellas | f. habréis |

4. Decide whether each sentence is conjugated in *futuro simple* or in *futuro compuesto*.
   a. Para el año que viene ya **me habré graduado**.
   b. Manuel **visitará** Barcelona.
   c. Daniela y Felipe **estudiarán** toda la tarde.
   d. No sé qué **habrán comido** mis gatos.

5. Decide whether the following statements are true or false. Correct the false ones.

a. *Condicional simple* is used to politely ask something.

b. *Condicional simple* is used to talk about an action that is currently taking place.

c. *Condicional compuesto* is used to talk about imaginary situations.

d. *Condicional compuesto* is conjugated with the verb *tener*.

# Chapter 10: Prepositions and Conjunctions

## Short Story: La procesión

José siente un peso inmenso sobre su espalda. A esta altura del recorrido, ya está completamente **agotado**. Pero no puede **darse por vencido**. Toda la cofradía entrenó durante meses para este momento. Sabe que puede hacerlo.

A su izquierda, José ve a Antonio, otro de los portadores. Se conocen desde pequeños, porque vivían a dos casas de distancia en uno de los barrios más humildes de Málaga. Él también parece cansado.

No es para menos. La procesión, que ya está volviendo a la Catedral de la Encarnación, duró ocho horas. Es mucho tiempo para estar cargando una estatua gigante sobre las espaldas. José no está seguro, pero la imagen de Jesús el Rico, con su trono, su cruz y sus velas, debe pesar unos tres mil kilos. No por nada hacen falta doscientos hombres para levantarla. "Es obvio que el **escultor** no era portador", piensa José, mientras acomoda el paso para distribuir mejor su carga.

La lluvia ha sido un tema importante ese día. Un **suelo húmedo** es un suelo **resbaladizo**. Precisamente, eso hace más lenta su marcha, por lo que todos han tenido que resignarse a pasar media hora más con el Cristo **a cuestas**. Sin embargo, José siente que le ha tocado la mejor parte. En su puesto, en el flanco derecho, la lluvia lo ha refrescado durante el recorrido.

De pronto, José nota que ya llegaron a destino. La catedral está justo enfrente: puede ver perfectamente el escenario que han montado. En él, a la derecha de los representantes comunales, hay un hombre vestido íntegramente de negro, con una **capucha** que le cubre el **rostro**. Ese hombre es Pablo, el hermano de José, **preso** desde hace un año por delito de **estafa**. José no se engaña: el Ponzi de Pablo ha tenido muchas víctimas. Él inclusive. Durante mucho tiempo le guardó rencor por eso. Pero sigue siendo su hermano.

José **atestigua** la firma de los decretos. Entonces, prepara la espalda para soportar la puesta en funcionamiento de la **maquinaria**. Jesús el Rico mueve su mano robótica y hace la señal de la cruz. Cuando termine, Pablo será oficialmente un hombre libre. Será otro de los beneficiados por el indulto anual que Jesús el Rico de Málaga ejerce sobre uno de los presos de la ciudad en Semana Santa.

Antonio también conoce a Pablo de toda la vida. Él ha escapado de su estafa, por suerte. José lo mira y nota que está llorando. Justo entonces detecta, en su mirada, un punto nuboso, **fuera de foco**. Sus manos están ocupadas en soportar el peso de la imagen, así que no puede usarlas para limpiarse. Se limita a mirar el suelo. Entonces deja caer una lágrima sobre el suelo húmedo, justo entre sus pies cansados.

## Vocabulary List

| Spanish | English |
| --- | --- |
| agotado, agotada | exhausted |
| darse por vencido | give up |
| el escultor, la escultora | sculptor |
| el suelo | ground |

| | |
|---|---|
| húmedo, húmeda | wet |
| resbaladizo, resbaladiza | slippery |
| a cuestas | on somebody's back |
| la capucha | hood |
| el rostro | face |
| el preso, la presa | prisoner |
| la estafa | scam |
| atestiguar | witness, attest |
| la maquinaria | machinery |
| fuera de foco | out of focus |

## Grammar Section

We've already seen verbs, adverbs, adjectives, nouns, pronouns, determiners... But we are still missing two types of words that are very necessary to have fluid conversations in Spanish. These are the "linking" words–those that are inserted between all the others. In this chapter, we will look at:

- prepositions;
- conjunctions; and
- idioms with prepositions and conjunctions.

**Prepositions**

Prepositions, by themselves, have no meaning. They make up a group of words that link other words, such as nouns, verbs, and pronouns. Prepositions have several senses: they can indicate origin, destination, location, direction, duration, starting point, means, reasons... and much more!

The good thing about these words is that they are invariable, i. e., they don't suffer any alteration of person, gender, or number. In Spanish, there are 23 prepositions, although we currently use only 19. Four (*cabe, so, versus,* and *vía*) are archaic.

Unfortunately, for the most part, prepositions don't have a literal translation into English. Therefore, below we will see a list of the 19 most used prepositions in Spanish with some possible equivalents. Later in this chapter, we'll go into each of the most used prepositions and see example sentences.

| Preposición | Traducción |
|---|---|
| a | at, to |
| ante | before |
| bajo | under |
| con | with |
| contra | against |
| de | from, of |
| desde | from, after, since |
| durante | during, for |
| en | in, within |
| entre | between |
| hacia | towards, to, around |
| hasta | by, until |

| | |
|---|---|
| mediante | through |
| para | for |
| por | by, in, at |
| según | according to |
| sin | without |
| sobre | above, on |
| tras | behind, after |

**Spanish most common prepositions**

Now, let's see in detail the uses of the most common prepositions. In addition, we'll see them within an example sentence.

1. A

    - Direction: *Me voy a la universidad* ("I'm going to college.")
    - Distance: *La tienda está a una calle* ("The store is one block away.")
    - Location of something or someone with respect to something else: *Cristina está a mi izquierda* ("Cristina is to my left.")
    - Time of day: *Ven a las cuatro en punto* ("Come at four o'clock.")
    - Objective: *Estoy dispuesto a hacerlo* ("I'm willing to do it.")

Note: When *a* is followed by the article *el*, they come together to form *al*.

2. Con

    - Company: *Carmen vino **con** su esposo* ("Carmen came with her husband.")

- Means or instruments: *Sebastián escribe **con** un bolígrafo* ("Sebastián writes with a pen.")
3. De
    - Possession: *Este vestido es **de** Paula* ("This dress belongs to Paula.")
    - Material or content: *Es una caja **de** bombones* ("It's a box of chocolates.")
    - Starting point: *Viajé **de** Santiago a Lima* ("I traveled from Santiago to Lima.")
    - Origin or procedence: *Roberto es **de** Argentina* ("Roberto is from Argentina.")

Note: When *de* is followed by the article *el*, they come together to form *del*.

4. En
    - Place: *Estoy **en** España* ("I'm in Spain.")
    - Time: *Mi cumpleaños es **en** mayo* ("My birthday is in May.")
    - Means of transportation: *Viajo **en** tren* ("I travel by train.")
5. Para
    - Recipient: *Esto es **para** ti* ("This is for you.")
    - Destination: *Voy **para** allá* ("I'm going there.")
6. Por
    - Person who did something: *El paciente fue atendido **por** el médico* ("The patient was seen by the doctor.")
    - Duration: *Te esperé **por** tres horas* ("I waited for you for three hours.")
    - Cause: ***Por** tu talento, ganamos el partido* ("Because of your talent, we won the match.")
    - Transit: *Pasaré **por** el supermercado de camino al trabajo* ("I will stop by the grocery store on my way to work.")

7. Sin
- Lack: *El plato del perro está* **sin** *comida* ("The dog's bowl is without food.")

**Conjunctions**

Conjunctions are words that connect other words and sentences. These can be *coordinantes* ("coordinating") or *subordinantes* ("subordinating").

*Conjunciones coordinantes* join elements of the same hierarchy. Let's see them in detail in the table below.

| Conjunciones coordinantes | | |
|---|---|---|
| **Type** | **Use** | **Examples** |
| *Copulativas* (copulative) | To indicate addition | *y* (*e* when the next word begins with I or HI) *como* *tanto* *cuanto* *así* |
| *Adversativas* (adversative) | To oppose ideas | *pero* *sino* |
| *Disyuntivas* (disjunctive) | To indicate alternation | *o* (*u* when the next word begins with O or HO) |

Let's see some example sentences with *conjunciones coordinantes*:
- *Tengo dos hijos, Gabriel* **y** *Simón* ("I have two sons, Gabriel and Simon.")
- *No tengo dos perros,* **sino** *tres* ("I don't have two dogs, but three.")

- *¿Qué prefieres, la carne o el pollo?* ("What do you prefer, beef or chicken?")

Now, it's the turn of *conjunciones subordinantes*. In these cases, one of the elements has a higher hierarchy than the other.

| Conjunciones subordinantes | | |
|---|---|---|
| Type | Use | Examples |
| *Causales* (causal) | To express the reason for the main sentence | *porque* *como* |
| *Comparativas* (comparative) | To compare the subordinated sentence with the main sentence | *que* *como si* |
| *Concesivas* (concessive) | To oppose the main sentence | *aunque* *si bien* |
| *Consecutivas* (consecutive) | To express consequence | *que* |

Let's see some example sentences:
- *Llegué más tarde **porque** se demoró el autobús* ("I arrived late because the bus was delayed.")
- *Lo dulce me gusta más **que** lo salado* ("I like sweet more than salty.")
- *El té me gusta, **aunque** prefiero el café* ("I like tea, although I prefer coffee.")
- *Estoy tan aburrida **que** no sé qué hacer* ("I'm so bored I don't know what to do.")

**Idioms**

Now, let's see some idiomatic expressions, or idioms, that have prepositions and conjunctions.

1. Irse por las ramas

*Irse por las ramas* (literally, "to go through the branches") is an idiom used when someone is avoiding a topic or when someone is not going to the point of what they are saying. The equivalent idiom in English is "to beat around the bush." Let's see an example:

- *Te estás **yendo por las ramas**. Cuéntame exactamente lo que ocurrió* ("You're beating around the bush. Tell me exactly what happened.")

2. Tener que ver con (alguien/algo)

*Tener que ver* is used as a synonym for *estar relacionado*. The English equivalent for this idiom would be "to have to do with." Let's look at an example:

- *Mi gato **no tiene nada que ver** con ese jarrón roto* ("My cat has nothing to do with that broken vase.")

3. Dar gato por liebre

*Dar gato por liebre* (literally, "giving a cat by a hare") refers to cheating someone by giving them something of little value, making them believe that's something better. It's similar to the English idiom "giving a pig in a poke." Let's look at an example:

- *Eres muy ingenuo. ¡Siempre te dan gato por liebre!* ("You are so naive. You always get a pig in a poke!")

4. Tirar la casa por la ventana

This funny expression literally means "to throw the house out the window." It is used when someone makes a large expense, higher than usual. It is often used to talk about big parties:

- *Pienso **tirar la casa por la ventana** cuando me gradúe* ("I plan to throw a big party when I graduate.")

5. Levantarse con el pie izquierdo

This idiom literally means "waking up with the left foot," but the English equivalent is "to get out of the wrong side of the bed." For example:

- *Hoy todo me salió mal. Creo que **me levanté con el pie izquierdo*** ("Today everything went wrong. I think I got off on the wrong foot.")

6. Estar como una cabra

*Estar como una cabra* (literally, "to be like a goat") means to be mad or off your head. For example:

- *Cruzó la calle con el semáforo en rojo. ¡**Está como una cabra**!* ("He crossed the street with a red light. He's completely mad!")

7. No tener ni pies ni cabeza

This is equivalent to "not being able to make heads or tails." If something *no tiene ni pies ni cabeza* (literally, "has neither feet nor head"), it means that it makes no sense.

- *Lo que estás diciendo **no tiene ni pies ni cabeza*** ("What you are saying has neither head nor tail.")

8. Hablar hasta por los codos

*Hablar hasta por los codos* (literally, "to speak even through the elbows") is similar to "to talk somebody's head off" or "to talk somebody's ear off," i.e., to talk a lot. For example:

- *Mi sobrino solo tiene tres años, pero **habla hasta por los codos*** ("My nephew is only three, but he talks his head off.")

9. Ponerse manos a la obra

*Ponerse manos a la obra* means to get to work or get to do what you have to do. For example:

- ***Me pondré manos a la obra** y empezaré a estudiar* ("I'll get to work and start studying.")

10. Sin pelos en la lengua

Someone who speaks *sin pelos en la lengua* ("without hairs in their tongue") is someone who doesn't watch their words, somebody outspoken:

- *Mi abuela, que **no tiene pelos en la lengua,** me dijo que le gustaba más mi antiguo corte de pelo* ("My outspoken grandmother told me she liked my old haircut better.")

What did you think of these funny idioms? Were they helpful in studying the prepositions and conjunctions? Let's see how much you've learned!

**Exercises**

1. Go back to the short story at the beginning and write down all the prepositions you can find in the first three paragraphs.
2. Decide whether the following statements are true or false. Correct the false ones.
    a. Prepositions in Spanish have an exact translation into English.
    b. *Sin* is a conjunction.
    c. Conjunctions can be coordinating or subordinating.
    d. Adversative conjunctions are used to oppose ideas.
    e. Complete the following sentences with the correct preposition, contraction (*al* or *del*), or conjunction.
        a. Almería, ...... sur de España, está ...... el mar ...... las montañas.
        b. Ernesto viaja todos los días ...... su casa ...... el trabajo ...... autobús.
        c. Ya no quedan entradas para el concierto, ...... este sitio web.
        d. Mi comida favorita no es la paella, ...... el gazpacho.
        e. Try to use these four idioms in a sentence:
            i. Tirar la casa por la ventana.
            ii. Hablar hasta por los codos.
            iii. Levantarse con el pie izquierdo.
            iv. No tener ni pies ni cabeza.

f. Find all the idioms in the next dialogue:
A. Voy a la tienda de música de la otra calle a comprar unas cuerdas para mi guitarra. ¿Quieres acompañarme?
B. ¿A la tienda de música de la otra calle? ¡Mejor no! El dependiente es... particular.
A. ¿Qué quieres decir? ¿Te ha intentado vender gato por liebre?
B. No, no tiene que ver con eso. Es solo que habla hasta por los codos. La última vez que fui a comprar a su tienda, me contó que era un músico muy famoso hace algunas décadas, y que tiraba la casa por la ventana cada noche. ¿Te imaginas? ¿Un músico muy famoso?
A. Suena como alguien que está como una cabra. ¿Cómo se llama?
B. Claudio "el Magnífico", dice que lo llamaban. Un apodo sin pies ni cabeza, como verás.
A. ¿Claudio "el Magnífico"? ¿El famosísimo guitarrista retirado?

# Chapter 11: Interrogative, Affirmative, and Negative sentences

## Short Story: La vaca

El oficial García peina su cabello hacia atrás con la mano. Después **suspira**.

—Vamos **de vuelta** —dice García—. ¿Cómo se llama usted?

—Me llamo Segundo Sánchez —responde el **interrogado** con seguridad.

—Muy bien —dice García—. Eso ya ha quedado **asentado** en el registro. ¿A qué se dedica?

—Soy veterinario —contesta Sánchez.

—¿Cuál es su especialidad? —pregunta García.

—**Ganado** vacuno —contesta Sánchez, sin dudar.

García acerca su silla a la mesa para apoyar los **codos**. Siempre odió que las sillas de la sala de interrogatorios no tuvieran **apoyabrazos**. Son demasiado incómodas.

—¿Qué estaba haciendo anoche en el campo del señor Obrador? —pregunta García.

—Estaba atendiendo una de sus vacas —contesta Sánchez—. Estaba **tumbada** desde hacía horas. Creían que estaba enferma.

—¿Y qué averiguó usted? —pregunta García.

—Que sí, que estaba enferma —contesta Sánchez.

—¿Cuál era su **enfermedad**? —continúa García.

—Un problema estomacal, casi **con seguridad** —responde Sánchez—. Se soluciona con un poco de medicación.

—Hasta aquí, **todo en orden** —dice García—. Pero usted no vino a la estación de policía por esto.

—No —contesta Sánchez—. Yo quiero denunciar un caso de robo de ganado.

—¿Por qué quiere denunciar eso? —pregunta García.

—Porque esa vaca desapareció —responde Sánchez.

—Eso lo entiendo —dice García—. Pero... A ver, ¿cómo desapareció esa vaca?

—Bueno, yo le puedo contar lo que vi —contesta Sánchez—. **Averiguar** qué ocurrió depende de ustedes.

—Agradezco que nos deje esa parte a nosotros —responde García, con **un deje de ironía**—. De acuerdo, cuente.

—Era de noche —dice Sánchez—. Yo estaba atendiendo a la vaca. Estaba solo, porque Obrador había vuelto a su casa a buscar una buena **linterna**. Y entonces empecé a ver luces.

—¿Qué tipo de luces? —pregunta García.

—Luces brillantes. Venían desde el cielo, desde una nube negra —responde Sánchez—. Y había también un sonido extraño. Un **pitido**.

—¿Usted estaba solo? —pregunta García.

—Sí, completamente solo —contesta Sánchez—. Y después... Bueno, una especie de reflector iluminó a la vaca. Y la vaca subió hacia el cielo, hasta la nube negra. Cuando llegó a la nube, desapareció.

—¿Qué dice Obrador de todo esto? —contesta García, mientras masajea su hombro derecho.

—No lo sé —responde Sánchez—. No hablé con él. Vine directo hacia aquí.

—Muchas gracias, Sánchez —dice García—. Ha **cumplido con su deber**. Puede retirarse.

## Vocabulary List

| Spanish | English |
| --- | --- |
| de vuelta | back, again |
| interrogado, interrogada | questioned |
| asentado, asentada | settled |
| el ganado | cattle |
| el codo | elbow |
| el apoyabrazos | armrest |
| tumbado, tumbada | lying down |
| la enfermedad | illness |
| con seguridad | safely |
| todo en orden | all good |
| averiguar | figure out |
| un deje de ironía | a hint of irony |
| la linterna | flashlight |
| el pitido | beep |

| cumplir con el deber | fulfill the duty |

## Grammar Section

Questions are everywhere, don't you think? Knowing how to ask questions in Spanish is necessary to have a fluent conversation. Thus, by the end of this next-to-last chapter, you'll master:

- yes/no questions;
- wh- questions;
- rhetorical questions;
- tag questions;
- polite questions; and
- affirmative and negative statements.

Let's get to it!

**Yes/no questions**

There are many types of questions in Spanish. Yes/no questions are (as you have no doubt noticed) the ones that can be answered with *sí* or *no*. Best of all: there's nothing complex here. In English, the structure of a question is not the same as the structure of a statement, but in Spanish, yes/no questions have the same word order as affirmative sentences. To distinguish one another in writing, you have to add the opening question mark (¿). When talking, you just give it a question intonation towards the end of the sentence. Let's look at some examples:

- *Esta casa es grande* (affirmative statement: "This house is big.")
- *¿Esta casa es grande?* (question: "Is this house big?")
- *María tiene treinta años* (affirmative statement: "María is 30 years old.")
- *¿María tiene treinta años?* (question: "Is María 30 years old?")

**Open questions**

Now, it's time to talk about open questions. Formulating them can be a bit more complicated than yes/no questions. In this case, adding an interrogative intonation at the end of the sentence is not enough. Open questions have their own structure. Don't worry, though; with practice, you will master them all!

When you ask an open question, you are not expecting the person to answer *sí* or *no*: you are waiting for the person to answer with another phrase, giving you specific information. In English, these questions are called "wh- questions" because they start with interrogative pronouns whose first letters are WH (except "how," of course). In Spanish, the interrogative pronouns are the following (note how they all have an accent mark):

| Pronombre interrogativo | Traducción |
|---|---|
| qué | what |
| quién | who |
| cuándo | when |
| cómo | how |
| dónde | where |
| por qué | why |

Let's see some example sentences with the interrogative pronouns in Spanish:

- *¿Dónde está Juan?* ("Where is Juan?")
- *¿Quién es ese hombre?* ("Who's that man?")
- *¿Cuándo llegaste?* ("When did you come?")
- *¿Cómo está el clima?* ("How is the weather?")
- *¿Dónde dejé mis llaves?* ("Where did I leave my keys?")
- *¿Por qué no fuiste a trabajar?* ("Why didn't you go to work?")

## Tag questions

Tag questions are those small questions attached to a statement's end. They have the particularity that they say the opposite thing in the main sentence; if a sentence is affirmative, the question will be negative, and vice versa. Tag questions transform a statement into a question, and in English, they are used often. For example, in the sentence "He said he'd come tomorrow, didn't he?", "didn't he?" is a tag question.

Let's see the most common tag questions in Spanish, with an example sentence below each one.

1. ¿*No*?
   - *Tu hijo se llama Fernando, ¿no?* ("Your son's name is Fernando, right?")

2. ¿*O no*?
   - *Ya conoces Colombia, ¿o no?* ("You've been to Colombia, haven't you?")

3. ¿*Verdad*?
   - *Este lugar es muy bonito, ¿verdad?* ("This place is very nice, isn't it?")

4. ¿*Cierto*? / ¿*No es cierto*?
   - *Mañana es lunes, ¿cierto?* ("Tomorrow's Monday, right?")

Another group of tag questions in Spanish is made up by the ones used after an imperative sentence. For example:

1. ¿*Sí*?
   - *Pórtate bien, ¿sí?* "(Be good, okay?")

2. ¿*De acuerdo*?
   - *Limpia tu dormitorio, ¿de acuerdo?* ("Clean your room, okay?")

3. ¿*Vale*?
   - *Te espero a las siete, ¿vale?* ("I'll wait for you at seven, alright?")

4. ¿*Lo harás*?
   - *Llámame mañana, ¿lo harás?* ("Call me tomorrow, will you"?)

**Rhetorical questions**

A rhetorical question is a question in which the speaker is not looking for an answer; instead, they are trying to emphasize what's being said. Usually, the answer is implicit within the question. Many times, they are used in arguments and ironically.

Some examples of rhetorical questions in Spanish are:

- *¿Cuándo terminará esta pesadilla?* ("When will this nightmare end?")
- *¿De dónde sacaste esa idea?* ("Where did you get that idea from?")
- *¿Cuántas veces te lo tengo que decir?* ("How many times do I have to tell you?")
- *¿Por qué siempre tienes razón?* ("Why are you always right?")
- *¿Quién sino tú me iba a ayudar?* ("Who but you was going to help me?")
- *¿Cómo puedes decir eso?* ("How can you say that?")

**Polite questions**

One of the most common ways to ask a question politely is by adding the verb *disculpar* ("to excuse") at the beginning of the interrogation. Of course, you will conjugate the verb depending on the person you are talking to. Let's see some examples:

- *Disculpe, ¿me puede decir qué hora es?* ("Excuse me, can you tell me what time it is?")
- *Disculpad, chicos, ¿sabéis dónde queda la calle Independencia?* ("Excuse me, guys, do you know where Independencia street is?")

Another expression you can use instead of *disculpar* is *perdonar*:

- *Perdona, ¿tú trabajas aquí?* ("Excuse me, do you work here?")

Now, there are a few basic expressions that you can use when you want to ask polite questions. Some of them are:

1. *¿Te importaría...?* ("Would you mind...?")

- *¿Te importaría alcanzarme el azúcar?* ("Would you mind passing me the sugar?")

2. *¿Qué te parece si...?* ("What do you think if...?")

- *¿Qué te parece si vamos a un restaurante el sábado?* ("How about if we go to a restaurant on Saturday?")

3. *¿Te gustaría...?* ("Would you like...?")

- *¿Te gustaría acompañarme a hacer la compra?* ("Would you like to go shopping with me?")

4. *¿Podrías...?* ("Could you...")

- *¿Podrías darme un kilo de bananas, por favor?* ("Could you give me a kilo of bananas, please?")

**Negative statements**

To make a negative sentence, you have to take into account a series of negation adverbs. Adverbs of negation modify verbs, adjectives or other adverbs. They are invariable, i.e, they are always written in the same way. There are four negation adverbs in Spanish:

| Negation Adverb | Translation |
|---|---|
| no | no |
| nunca | never |
| jamás | never |
| tampoco | either |

Let's see some example sentences with these negation adverbs:

- ***No** quiero comer pizza esta noche* ("I don't want to eat pizza tonight.")
- ***Nunca** me fui de vacaciones a las montañas* ("I never went on holidays to the mountains.")
- ***Jamás** he tenido un perro como mascota* ("I've never had a dog as a pet.")

- *A mí **tampoco** me parece que sea una buena idea* ("I don't think it's a good idea either.")

However, negation adverbs are not the only words we can use to form negative sentences in Spanish. There are also some useful pronouns, like *nadie* ("nobody") and *nada* ("nothing"), adjectives like *ningún* or *ninguna* ("none"), conjunctions like *ni* ("nor"), and expressions like *ni siquiera* ("not even"). Normally, these words go together with the adverbs of negation that we just saw, forming double negations.

Let's see some example sentences:

- ***No** fue **ninguno** de los chicos a la fiesta* ("None of the guys went to the party.")
  You could also say ***Ninguno** de los chicos fue a la fiesta*.
- *Este vecindario es aburrido, ¡**nunca** pasa **nada**!* ("This neighborhood is boring, nothing ever happens!")
- *Esta chaqueta **no** es de **nadie** que yo conozca* ("This jacket doesn't belong to anyone that I know.")
- ***No, ni siquiera** se despidió* ("No, he didn't even say goodbye.")
- ***No** me gusta este vestido **ni** tampoco aquel* ("I don't like this dress and I don't like that one either.")

**Affirmative statements**

Just as there are negative sentences, there are affirmative ones. The most important words to keep in mind are the following:

| Affirmative Words | Translation |
|---|---|
| sí | yes |
| siempre | always |
| también | also |
| algo | something |

| | |
|---|---|
| alguien | somebody |
| algún, alguno, alguna | some |
| por supuesto | of course |
| claro | sure |
| obvio | obvious |
| desde luego | for sure |

Let's see some example sentences with these words:

- *Por supuesto que me gusta el rock. ¡Siempre estoy escuchando algún disco!* ("Of course I like rock. I'm always listening to some record!")
- *Juan es alguien que ama la fotografía: siempre va a la playa y toma algunas imágenes* ("Juan is someone who loves photography: he always goes to the beach and takes some pictures.")
- *Desde luego, a Luisa también le gustaría adoptar un perro algún día* ("Of course, Luisa would also like to adopt a dog some day.")

**Exercises**

1. Go back to the short story at the beginning and answer the following questions in Spanish:
    a. ¿Qué hacía el señor Sánchez en el campo del señor Obrador?
    b. ¿Cuál es la profesión del señor Sánchez?
    c. ¿Qué problema afectaba a la vaca y cómo se resolvió?
    d. ¿Por qué el señor Obrador no estaba con el señor Sánchez?

2. Below are four answers to four open (or wh-) questions. Following the examples, write down the corresponding question:
    a. Lucía se siente un poco cansada. *¿Cómo se siente Lucía?*
    b. Es mi esposo.
    c. Los chicos están en el colegio.
    d. La última vez que vi a Tomás fue ayer.

3. Decide whether the following statements are true or false. Correct the false ones.
    a. Interrogative pronouns in Spanish are used to make yes/no questions.
    b. Rhetorical questions are those to which we don't expect an answer.
    c. *Sí, siempre* and *por supuesto* are used to make affirmative statements in Spanish.
    d. Adverbs of negation are written differently depending on the gender of the word they modify.

4. Complete the following dialogue to form a polite conversation between two people. Use the following words: *gustaría, disculpe, por favor, podría*.
   A. ........., ¿usted trabaja en esta tienda?
   B. Sí. Dígame en qué puedo ayudarla.
   A. ¿.......... indicarme dónde están los probadores, .......... ?
   B. Claro. Están al fondo de la tienda. ¿le .......... que la acompañe?

5. In the following text, select the correct negation word in each case.

   *Florencia mira el reloj. (Nunca/No) es tan temprano como pensaba. Si (no/nunca) se apresura, llegará tarde al trabajo. Se sube a su coche y, como hay mucho tráfico, decide tomar una ruta alternativa. (Ni siquiera/Jamás) ha ido por esa zona. No parece haber (ninguno/nada) por allí: es una calle desierta. (Nada/No) hay ningún coche y (tampoco/nunca) hay (nadie/ningún) caminando. ¡(Ni siquiera/Nunca) tiene que esperar, porque (ni/no) hay (ningún/ninguno) semáforo! Llega a su trabajo más temprano que de costumbre. Ahora, ya sabe qué ruta debe tomar cada día.*

# Chapter 12: Reporting Information (Indirect Speech)

## Short Story: La conversación

El oficial García se acerca a la **máquina de café**. Aprieta un botón y coloca un **vaso desechable** debajo del pico vertedor. Después espera.

—¿Qué te dijo Sánchez? —pregunta el sargento Moreno.

—No me vas a creer —responde García, mientras retira el vaso de la máquina. Después bebe un sorbo de café negro. Es el segundo del día.

—**Anda**, dime —dice Moreno—. **No me obligues a leer** el reporte.

—Sánchez dijo que vio una **abducción extraterrestre** —responde García, mientras se encoge de hombros.

—Hombre, no digas tonterías —contesta Moreno.

—Es en serio —dice García—. Dijo que una luz se llevó a la vaca que estaba atendiendo. La vaca enferma de Obrador.

—¿Y Obrador qué opina? —pregunta Moreno.

—No sé, todavía no he hablado con él —contesta García—. Lo fueron a buscar. Dicen que **está en camino**.

Moreno se quita la **gorra** y se limpia el **sudor** de la **frente**. El aire acondicionado de la estación está roto, y el lugar no tiene buena circulación de aire. No es una buena época para hacer **trabajo de escritorio**.

—No lo puedo creer —dice Moreno—. Sánchez parecía un hombre **serio**. Veterinario. ¿Tú qué hiciste?

—Hice lo que pude —responde García—. Le pregunté si estaba solo. Le pregunté cómo eran las luces.

—¿Y él qué hizo? —pregunta Moreno.

—Me dijo que estaba solo, que las luces eran brillantes... —contesta García—. Todo ese **rollo**. No sé, tampoco quería hacerlo sentir mal. Por lo menos, no antes de hablar con Obrador. Quiero tener una **denuncia** concreta antes de interrogarlo.

Moreno apoya la **cadera** contra la pared para descansar los pies. Después coloca ambos **pulgares** en sus bolsillos y suspira.

—¿Qué crees que dirá Obrador? —pregunta Moreno, mirando al frente.

—Me dirá que le falta una vaca —responde García.

## Vocabulary List

| Spanish | English |
|---|---|
| la máquina de café | coffee machine |
| el vaso desechable | disposable cup |
| anda | come on |
| (no) obligar a alguien a hacer algo | (not) make someone do something |
| la abducción extraterrestre | alien abduction |
| estar en camino | be on the way |
| la gorra | cap |

| | |
|---|---|
| el sudor | sweat |
| la frente | forehead |
| el trabajo de escritorio | desk job |
| serio, seria | reliable |
| el rollo | yarn |
| la denuncia | complaint |
| la cadera | hip |
| el pulgar | thumb |

## Grammar Section

Direct and indirect speech are two ways to quote or reproduce a message from someone else – or even yourself! They exist both in English and Spanish, but each language has its own characteristics. Direct speech is the style in which the speaker reproduces word by word what someone else said without modifying it. It is marked graphically with dashes of dialogue (–) or with quotation marks (" "). Indirect speech is the style in which the speaker relates what was said – but in their own words. It requires the interpretation of the message, which is altered in its form, but without changing the meaning.

In this chapter, you will:

- understand what direct speech is and when it is used;
- understand what indirect speech is and when it is used;
- learn the differences between direct and indirect speech;
- learn to transform direct speech into indirect speech; and
- learn what happens with questions in indirect speech.

Let's get to it!
## What is direct speech?
Direct speech is the reproduction of a message in the same way in which it was said, without alterations or interpretations. In other words, it's quoting a sentence of one's own or someone else's, just the way it was said. In Spanish, there are two graphical ways to indicate what is being said in direct speech: quotation marks and em-dashes (or r*ayas de diálogo*).

## Quotation marks
In written text, direct speech can be recognized by quotation marks, which indicate that the words that follow are from another person or have been copied as they were originally written. For example:

- *Ella me dijo: "prefiero cenar fuera"* ("She said, 'I prefer to eat out.'")
- *La ministra declaró: "Me siento satisfecha con mi gestión"* ("The minister declared, 'I am satisfied with my management.'")

Direct speech is widely used in media, especially in journalism, where the use of quotation marks to indicate that someone's words are being used is common. It's also used in academic texts (dissertations, specialized books, research papers, etc.) to point out ideas of other authors. English also uses quotation marks to indicate direct speech. Still, if you pay attention to the examples above, you will see that, in contrast, Spanish uses a colon (:) before the opening quotation mark, while English uses a comma (,).

## Em-dashes
Another way to recognize direct speech is by using dashes, which mark the beginning of a dialogue. The dashes indicate that what follows is an exchange between two or more people, which is reproduced verbatim.

For example:

- *—¿Sabes a qué hora llega la jefa hoy?* ("Do you know at what time the boss is arriving today?")
- *—No lo sé* ("I don't know.")

- *—Tal vez no venga...* ("Maybe she's not coming...")
- *—Sí, ayer se sentía mal, así que es probable que hoy se quede en casa* ("Yea, she was feeling bad yesterday, so she's probably staying home today.")

Dashes are common in written interviews and literary texts such as plays, short stories (like the ones you've read throughout this book!) or novels, which indicate each character's words. This dash doesn't have an extended use in English, where dialogue is also distinguished with quotation marks.

### What is indirect speech?

Indirect speech is how we paraphrase a message. That is, the speaker takes a message from someone else (or a previous message by themselves), interprets it, and incorporates it into their speech in their own words.

We must make some changes to transform direct speech into indirect speech. We adapt the original message to the way we want to convey it. Let's see the changes in an example:

- *Hoy no puedo. Pero si tú quieres, mañana paso a verte* ("Today I can't. But if you want, tomorrow I can go visit you.")

In an indirect form, it would change to:

- *Victoria dijo que ese día no podía, pero que al día siguiente pasaría a verme si yo quería* ("Victoria said that she couldn't that day, but that she would come visit me the next day if I wanted.")

Take a look at the following chart to see the changes that we made to transform direct speech into indirect speech:

| Direct Speech | Indirect Speech |
| --- | --- |
|  | me dijo que |
| hoy | ese día |
| puedo | podía |

| tú | yo |
|---|---|
| quieres | quería |
| mañana | al día siguiente |
| paso | pasaría |
| verte | verme |

As we can see, first of all, in indirect speech we add the verb *decir* ("say") and the conjunction *que* ("that"). Other verbs we use to report speech are *anunciar* ("announce"), *explicar* ("explain"), *narrar* ("narrate"), *declarar* ("claim"), *preguntar* ("ask"), *exponer* ("present"), *asentir* ("affirm"), *informar* ("inform"), *citar* ("quote"), and *señalar* ("point").

We can also see that the first person of the direct speech becomes a third person in the indirect speech because the speaker has changed; Victoria is no longer speaking. This is reflected in the conjugation of the verbs and in the pronouns used. Also, the second person of the direct speech (the addressee) becomes the first person because they are the ones doing the talking in the second sentence.

Then, we notice that place and time adverbs are modified to match the new communication situation. The two sentences weren't uttered on the same day, so *hoy* and *mañana* don't mean the same in both contexts – and need to be changed accordingly.

Finally, verbal tenses are also updated to the new communication situation, and apart from person, the *tense* also changes. Now, we'll look at some tense changes in more detail.

**How to modify verb tenses in indirect speech**

1. Direct speech in *presente*, *futuro* or *pretérito perfecto*: sometime, the tense in indirect speech will not be affected.

- *Me gusta el queso* ("I like cheese," direct speech in the present)

- *Luis dice que le gusta el queso* ("Luis says he likes cheese," indirect speech in the present)

Other times, the tense of the direct speech will change from *presente* to *pretérito imperfecto* in the indirect speech.

- *Llego tarde* ("I'm late," direct speech in the present)
- *Luz dijo que llegaba tarde* ("Luz said she was late," indirect speech in *pretérito imperfecto*)

2. Direct speech in *pretérito indefinido, pretérito perfecto* or *pretérito pluscuamperfecto*: indirect speech in *pretérito pluscuamperfecto*.

- *¿Has visitado a tu abuela el domingo pasado* ("Have you visited your grandma last Sunday?" direct speech in *pretérito perfecto*)
- *Tomás me preguntó si había visitado a mi abuela el domingo pasado* ("Tomás asked me if I had visited my grandma last Sunday," indirect speech in *pretérito pluscuamperfecto*)

3. Direct speech in *pretérito imperfecto*: indirect speech in *pretérito imperfecto*.

- *La comida estaba rica* ("The food was good," direct speech in *pretérito imperfecto*)
- *Juan señaló que la comida estaba rica* ("Juan pointed that the food was good," indirect speech in *pretérito imperfecto*)

4. Direct speech in *futuro simple* or *condicional simple*: indirect speech in *condicional simple*.

- *Lo haré la semana que viene* ("I'll do it next week," direct speech in *futuro simple*)
- *Pablo prometió que lo haría la semana que viene* ("Pablo promised he'd do it next week," indirect speech in *condicional simple*)

5. Direct speech in *futuro compuesto* or *condicional compuesto*, indirect speech in *condicional compuesto*.

- *Mañana a esta hora, habremos terminado la tarea* ("By this time tomorrow, we'll have finished the homework," direct speech in *futuro compuesto*)

- *Clara afirmó que para esa hora del día siguiente, habrían terminado la tarea* ("Clara declared that, by that time tomorrow, they would have finished the homework," indirect speech in *condicional compuesto*)

6. Direct speech in *imperativo, presente del subjuntivo* or *condicional compuesto*: indirect speech in *pretérito imperfecto del subjuntivo*.

- *Vayamos al cine* ("Let's go to the cinema," direct speech in *presente del subjuntivo*)
- *María me dijo que fuéramos al cine* ("María said that we should go to the cinema," indirect speech in *pretérito imperfecto del subjuntivo*)

7. Direct speech in *pretérito perfecto del subjuntivo*: indirect speech in *pretérito pluscuamperfecto del subjuntivo*.

- *Quizás Lucas no haya oído el mensaje* ("Maybe Lucas didn't hear the message," direct speech in *pretérito perfecto del subjuntivo*)
- *Javiera supuso que quizás Lucas no hubiese oído el mensaje* ("Javiera guessed that maybe Lucas hadn't heard the message," indirect speech in *pretérito pluscuamperfecto del subjuntivo*)

**Questions in indirect speech**

To finish the chapter (and this book!), we'll look at what happens with questions in indirect speech. Let's start with an example.

- *¿Cómo estás?* ("How are you doing?")
- *Me preguntó cómo estaba* ("She asked me how I was doing.")

First, as you can see in indirect speech, interrogations lose the question marks. As with other sentences in reported speech, they are introduced by a saying verb, but instead of *que*, they are followed by an interrogation pronoun or adverb, or the conjunction *si*. Let's see some more examples:

- *¿Estás bien?* ("Are you okay?")
- *Le pregunté si estaba bien* ("I asked him if he was okay.")

- *¿Qué te pasó ayer?* ("What happened to you yesterday?")
- *Me preguntó qué me había pasado el día anterior* ("She asked me what had happened to me the day before.")

Note that the *qué* we use when we are reporting questions has an accent, and it's not the same conjunction *que* we use to report statements.

**Exercises**

1. Go back to the short story at the beginning and answer the following questions in Spanish using reported or indirect speech. Follow the example:

    a. ¿Qué es lo primero que le preguntó el sargento Moreno al oficial García? *Moreno le preguntó qué le había dicho Sánchez.*

    b. ¿Qué le respondió García?

    c. ¿Qué le dijo Moreno a García después de que este le hablara de la abducción extraterrestre?

    d. ¿Qué le preguntó Moreno a García sobre Obrador?

2. Decide whether the following statements are true or false. Correct the false ones.

    a. Direct and indirect speech are used only to reproduce someone else's message.

    b. Direct speech quotes the message said word by word.

    c. Em-dashes and quotation marks are used in English and Spanish to indicate indirect speech.

    d. To change a sentence from direct to indirect speech, first, we need to add a speaking verb plus the conjunction *que*.

3. Go back to the short story in the previous chapter and reread the first few lines. Below, we've transformed those lines of dialogue into reported speech. Complete the blanks with the verbs in the correct conjugation.

    a. García le preguntó a Sánchez cómo .........

b. Con seguridad, el interrogado ...... que se llamaba Segundo Sánchez.

c. García dijo que eso ya ...... en el registro.

d. Luego, le preguntó a qué ........

e. Sánchez contestó que ...... veterinario.

f. García le ...... cuál era su especialidad.

4. The following sentences are all in indirect speech. Choose the correct adverb or conjunction so that they make sense:

   a. Le dije a mi padre ...... (que/cuando) me viniera a visitar.

   b. Camila le preguntó a su novia ...... (que/qué) quería comer.

   c. Nos prometieron ...... (si/que) estaría terminado para la semana que viene.

   d. Me preguntó ...... (si/cual) iría al cine al día siguiente.

5. Imagine you had a conversation with a friend. Write it down as if you were telling it to another friend. You can start the following way:

   El lunes pasado le pregunté a María si... Ella me respondió que...

Now that you've finished the last chapter, you can go back and check all the things you've learned from the list at the beginning!

# Final Quiz

Congratulations! You've reached the end of the book. We're sure that, by now, you will have learned a lot of Spanish. Now, all that remains is to put it into practice!

But before letting you go, it's time to do a final quiz. In this quiz, we are going to review the last six chapters, where we have seen the *pasado, presente* and *futuro* tenses of the Spanish verbs, prepositions and conjunctions, how to ask questions, direct and indirect speech, – and more.

Like in the Mid-Book Quiz, each correct answer is worth 2 points.

- If your final result is between 15 and 20 points: Congratulations! You've mastered the grammar, and the vocabulary needed to be an intermediate Spanish student.
- If your final result is between 10 and 15 points: You're doing very well. However, we recommend you to go back to the chapters that explain the topics you've failed and review them.
- If your final result is less than 10 points: Don't worry; there's no rush. Take your time and reread this book. Once you have done it, repeat this quiz. Be patient and practice a lot. You'll do better soon!

Now, let's get started!

1. What is *presente del indicativo* used for? Three of the following answers are true, and one is false; find the false one.
    a. To talk about situations that will happen in the near future.
    b. To talk about something that is happening right now.
    c. To express a hypothesis.
    d. To talk about things that are always true.
2. Complete with *presente progresivo*.
    a. Tú - caminar
    b. Ella - dormir
    c. Nosotros - salir
    d. Vosotros - dibujar
3. Complete the following dialogue with the past tenses in Spanish.
   A. ¿Qué ........... (**hacer** - *pretérito perfecto simple*) el fin de semana?
   B. Nada, no ........... (**tener** - *pretérito imperfecto*) muchas ganas de salir. ¿Y tú?
   A. Yo ........... (**ir** - *pretérito perfecto simple*) a dar un paseo por la costa. La noche ........... (**ser** - *pretérito imperfecto*) perfecta, aunque ........... (**hacer** - *pretérito imperfecto*) un poco de frío. ........... (**llover** - *pretérito pluscuamperfecto*) un rato antes.
   B. Pero ¿........... (**llevar** - *pretérito pluscuamperfecto*) abrigo?
   A. No. ¡Quizá por eso no ........... (**dejar** - *pretérito perfecto*) de estornudar desde entonces!
4. Complete the following short story with the *futuro simple* form of the verbs in brackets. *Juan Pablo ............... (hacer) una fiesta este fin de semana. Sus amigos lo ............... (ayudar) a planearla y ............... (llevar) comida. Juan Pablo ............... (encargarse) de la bebida. Todos los conocidos de Juan Pablo están invitados, pero él cree que muchos ............... (ir).*

5. Decide if the following sentences are in *condicional simple* or *condicional compuesto*.
    a. Disculpe, ¿me diría la hora?
    b. Habría pagado lo que fuera por ver ese concierto.
    c. Me habría encantado estudiar piano cuando era joven.
    d. Me encantaría viajar al Caribe el próximo año.
6. Choose the correct preposition in each of the following sentences.
    a. Quiero una porción de pizza ..... (que/con) mucho queso.
    b. Martín es el hijo ..... (de/por) Pablo y Susana.
    c. Dormí ..... (mediante/durante) todo el viaje.
    d. Me levanté temprano ..... (por/para) ver el amanecer.
7. Underline the conjunctions in the following sentences, and decide whether they are *conjunciones coordinantes* (coordinating conjunctions) or *conjunciones subordinantes* (subordinating conjunctions).
    a. Cenaré pizza porque me encanta.
    b. Matías y Pedro son mis hermanos.
    c. Voy a estudiar, aunque estoy un poco cansado.
    d. Mi hija menor quiere estudiar Medicina u Odontología.
8. Here you have some typical idioms in Spanish. Match them with their explanation or equivalent idiom in English.

| | |
|---|---|
| *irse por las ramas* | to talk somebody's head off |
| *hablar hasta por los codos* | to be completely mad |
| *dar gato por liebre* | to give a pig in a poke |
| *estar como una cabra* | to beat around the bush |

9. Complete with the correct interrogative pronoun.
    a. ¿............ se llama tu perro?
    b. ¿............ está tu hermano?
    c. ¿............ es ese hombre?
    d. ¿............ haces esta noche?
10. Decide whether the following statements are true or false. Correct the false ones.
    a. Direct speech consists of interpreting and rewriting someone else's message.
    b. Direct speech is mostly used in the press.
    c. Direct speech can be written with quotes or em-dashes.
    d. Indirect speech is the reproduction of a message in the same way in which it was said, without alterations or interpretations.

# Answer Key

## Chapter 1

1.
   a. Woman: Mujer: eme-u-jota-e-erre.
   b. Man: Hombre: hace-o-eme-be-erre-e.
   c. Girl: Niña: ene-i-eñe-a.
   d. Dog: Perro: pe-e-doble erre-o.
   e. House: Casa: ce-a-ese-a.

2.
   a. *Cancion*: It should have a tilde in the O because it's an *aguda* word that ends in N: *canción*.
   b. *Papel*: It doesn't need a tilde because it's an *aguda* word that ends in L.
   c. *Tragico*: It should have a tilde in the A because it's an *esdrújula* word: *trágico*.
   d. *Esposa*: It doesn't need a tilde because it's a *grave* word that ends in a vowel.
   e. *Lapiz*: It should have a tilde in the A because it's a *grave* word that ends in Z: *lápiz*.

3. *Tildes* tell us which letter of a word we have to stress when we say it aloud.
4.
   b. They are all graves
5. *Fuerza* is pronounced with a soft R; *rápido* is pronounced with a rolled R; *perro* is also pronounced with a rolled R.
6. We use a softer R for single Rs in the middle of a word; we use the rolled R for Rs at the beginning of words and for double Rs.
7.
   a. *Agua*, because it's the only one in which the U is not silent.
8. All of these sentences are grammatically correct. However, there's one in each pair that is more commonly used. Can you point out which one?
   b. María escribió el libro.
   c. Los alumnos se portan mal.
   e. José preparó la cena.
9.
   a. Mi hermana **juega** muy bien al fútbol.
   b. Tu casa nueva es muy **linda**.
   c. Los niños **tienen** hambre.
   d. Correct.
   e. Siempre desayuno algo **dulce**.
   f. Correct.
   g. Hice las compras, pero me **las** olvidé en el mercado.
   h. Estoy llevando al perro al parque. **Lo** llevo todas las mañanas.
10. True.
11. False. In Spanish, the subject can be left out when it has already been mentioned and it's understood from context.
12. False. In Spanish, the order of a statement doesn't change to turn it into a question. You just need to add the

opening and closing marks.

13. True.

14.
- a. El cielo es celeste/azul.
- b. Las bananas son amarillas.
- c. Las hojas de los árboles son verdes.
- d. La sangre es roja.
- e. Las nubes son grises.
- f. Si mezclas blanco y negro, obtienes gris.
- g. Por fuera, el kiwi es marrón.
- h. Las naranjas son naranjas/anaranjadas.

15.
- a. Cuatro.
- b. Ocho.
- c. Catorce.
- d. Trece.
- e. Diecinueve.
- f. Cincuenta.
- g. Sesenta.
- h. Noventa y cinco.

16.
- a. El esposo de mi abuela es mi abuelo.
- b. El hijo de mi tía es mi primo.
- c. La hija de mi madre y mi padre es mi hermana.
- d. El hermano de mi padre es mi tío.
- e. Mi mamá y mi papá son mis padres.
- f. La pareja de mi padre es mi madrastra.

17.
- a. Árbol, porque no es una parte de la casa.
- b. Banana, porque no es un objeto de la casa.
- c. Cerdo, porque no es una fruta.
- d. Pasto, porque no es comida.

e. Habitación, porque no es un plato.
f. Blanco, porque no es un método de cocción.
g. Estrella, porque no es un edificio de una ciudad.
h. Acera, calle, semáforo, río.
i. Marzo, porque no es un día de la semana.
j. Viernes, porque no es el nombre de un mes.

18.
a. ¿Cómo te llamas?: el nombre.
b. ¿Cuántos años tienes?: la edad.
c. ¿A qué te dedicas?: la profesión.
d. ¿Tienes correo electrónico?: el correo electrónico.
e. ¿Cuál es tu número de teléfono?: el número de teléfono.
f. ¿Cuál es tu nombre?: el nombre.
g. ¿En qué trabajas?: la profesión.
h. ¿De dónde eres?: la nacionalidad/el lugar de origen.
i. ¿Tienes móvil?: el número de teléfono

19. _____

20.
a. El verbo **ser** se utiliza para hablar de estados que duran mucho tiempo o son permanentes.
b. El verbo **estar** se utiliza para hablar de estados temporales.

21.
a. Mi nombre **es** Alejandra.
b. **Soy** de Argentina.
c. En este momento, **estoy** en Venezuela.
d. Mi amiga **es** de aquí.
e. Su nombre **es** María.
f. **Estamos** de vacaciones juntas.

22.

|  | AMAR | TEMER | PARTIR |
|---|---|---|---|
| yo | amo | temo | parto |
| tú | amas | temes | partes |
| él / ella | ama | teme | parte |
| nosotros / nosotras | amamos | tememos | partimos |
| vosotros / vosotras | amáis | teméis | partís |
| ellos / ellas / ustedes | aman | temen | parten |

23.
   a. Alejandro Amenábar nace en 1972.
   b. Cuando su familia se muda a España, tiene un año de edad.
   c. En la universidad estudió Imagen y Sonido. No, no terminó la carrera.
   d. La película que tiene como protagonista a Nicole Kidman es de terror y suspense.
   e. En los últimos años ha hecho películas, video clips de música y series de televisión.

24.

# Chapter 2

1.
   a. Cien más treinta y cinco es ciento treinta y cinco.
   b. Quinientos sesenta menos veinte es quinientos cuarenta.
   c. Diez mil cien más cuatro mil setecientos es catorce mil ochocientos.
   d. Doscientos veinticinco por cinco es mil

trescientos cincuenta.

e. Un millón dividido dos coma cinco es cuatrocientos mil.

2.
   
   a. En el año mil novecientos setenta y cinco, se vendieron quinientos cincuenta y seis camisetas, doscientos dos sombreros y cincuenta y nueve bolsos.
   
   b. En el año mil novecientos ochenta y seis, se vendieron doscientos ochenta y nueve camisetas, doscientos diez sombreros y trescientos cincuenta y nueves bolsos.
   
   c. En el año mil novecientos noventa y tres, se vendieron cincuenta y seis camisetas, ciento noventa y cinco sombreros y quinientos noventa y ocho bolsos.
   
   d. En el año dos mil siete, se vendieron setenta camisetas, doscientos siete sombreros y ochocientos ochenta y dos bolsos.

3.

   a. En el año 1975 se vendieron más bolsos que sombreros. Falso: En el año 1975 se vendieron más sombreros que bolsos.
   
   b. Se vendieron más bolsos en 2007 que en 1993. Verdadero.
   
   c. En 1986 y 2007 se vendió casi la misma cantidad de sombreros. Verdadero.
   
   d. El año en el que más bolsos se vendieron fue 1993. Falso: El año en el que más bolsos se vendieron fue 2007.

4.

   a. Son las nueve y veinticinco.
   
   b. Cinco minutos.
   
   c. Es a las nueve y media.

5. "De lunes a viernes, me levanto a las...".

# Chapter 3

1.
   a. Silvia y Alberto pasean por un barrio comercial de la ciudad.
   b. La historia transcurre durante la noche.
   c. En la historia se mencionan conejos, perros, palomas, ratas y ratones.
   d. La aventura no dura mucho porque una niña recoge a la coneja.

2.
   a. False. Grammatical gender is a property of languages used to divide nominal elements into classes.
   b. True.
   c. False. In Spanish, there are two grammatical genders: masculine and feminine.
   d. True.

3. Complete the sentences with these endings: -TUD; -OR; -SIÓN; -A; -MA; -O. Provide an example of each.
   a. Most nouns ending in -A are feminine, for example *manta*.
   b. Most nouns ending in -O are masculine, for example *lago*.
   c. Other typically feminine endings are -TUD (for example: *gratitud*), and -SIÓN (for example: *pasión*).
   d. Other typically masculine endings are -OR (for example: *dolor*), and -MA (for example: *problema*)

4. *favorito; la; el; muchos; cómoda; la; la; una; clara; pintadas; oscuro; cómoda; ella; preferida; la; un; él; doblada.*

5. _____

# Chapter 4

1. ella, lo, todas, eso, tú, les, los, quiénes, todos, ese, el que, esos, se, cualquiera, le.
2. 
    a. False. Pronouns are the words we use to replace names or nouns in a sentence.
    b. True.
    c. False. Pronouns also serve to refer to elements that function as antecedents of a topic.
3. 
    a. Nosotras.
    b. Lo.
    c. Vosotras/ustedes.
    d. Mí.
4. Choose the correct possessive pronoun:
    a. Suyas.
    b. Nuestro.
    c. Los suyos.
    d. Mía/tuya
5. Write one sentence using each of the following pronouns:
    a. Saludó a cuanta gente se cruzó.
    b. Le ofrecí varios sabores, pero no le gusta ninguno.
    c. No hace falta que traigas azúcar para el pastel. Hay bastante.
    d. De todos los alumnos que dieron el examen, un tercio desaprobó.

# Chapter 5

1. 
    c. Poco. It's replacing an adverb.
    d. Alto. It's replacing a noun.
    e. Bajo. It's replacing an adverb.
    f. Azul. It's replacing a noun

2.
   a. True.
   b. False. In Spanish, the adjective is generally placed after the noun it's modifying.
   c. False. Demonstrative and possessive adjectives come before the noun.
   d. True.

3.
   a. Before.
   b. After.
   c. After.
   d. Before.

4.
   a. Superiority: "más + adjetivo/adverbio + que": Corro más rápido que mis rivales.
   b. Inferiority: "menos + adjetivo/adverbio + que": Es menos peleador que su hermano
   c. Equality: "tan + adjetivo/adverbio + como" or "igual de adjetivo/adverbio que": Mis hijas son igual de inteligentes.
   d. Positive superlative: "el/la/los/las + más + adjetivo": Buenos Aires es la más divertida de todas las ciudades que conozco.
   e. Negative superlative: "el/la/los/las + menos + adjetivo": Aunque el transporte público es el menos organizado.

5.
   a. 2
   b. 4
   c. 1
   d. 3

# Chapter 6

1. <u>El</u> viaje; <u>La</u> maleta; <u>Una</u> vida; <u>una</u> maleta; <u>una</u> vida; <u>las</u> playeras; <u>una</u> bola; <u>los</u> calcetines; <u>los</u> pantalones; <u>Un</u> abrigo; <u>una</u> chaqueta; <u>un</u> sobretodo; <u>un</u> saco; <u>la</u> chaqueta; <u>las</u> demás prendas; <u>la</u> habitación; <u>la</u> persona; <u>la</u> relación; <u>lo</u> necesario; <u>unos</u> zapatos; <u>la</u> ropa; <u>la</u> maleta; <u>la</u> ropa; <u>la</u> maleta; <u>la</u> cama; <u>las</u> playeras; <u>los</u> suéteres; <u>los</u> pantalones; <u>el</u> espacio; <u>las</u> prendas; <u>los</u> calcetines, <u>la</u> ropa interior; <u>la</u> chaqueta; <u>la</u> maleta; <u>los</u> zapatos; <u>el</u> trabajo; <u>una</u> ciudad; <u>los</u> cajones; <u>la</u> habitación; <u>una</u> bufanda; <u>el</u> cuello.
2. 
    a. True.
    b. False. *Lo* is a neuter article, it carries no gender.
    c. True.
    d. False. Definite articles are used to talk about things that are known to the people involved in the conversation.
3. 
    a. Lo bello de la vida es compartirla con los seres queridos.
    b. María se desesperó ante lo difícil del problema.
    c. Debieron cancelar la excursión por lo frío del día.
    d. Lo simple de la vida en el campo resulta muy atractivo.
4. una; un; el; una; un; la; los; la; el; el; los; la; el; el; los; el; el; los; un.

# Mid-Book Quiz

1. 
    a. Mil setecientos treinta y cinco.
    b. Diecinueve mil quinientos ochenta y tres.
    c. Mil setecientas treinta y cinco vacas.
    d. Diecinueve mil quinientas ochenta y tres vacas.

2. ¿Qué hora es?; ¿Tienes hora?; ¿Puedes decirme la hora?
   a. Son las doce menos cuarto de la mañana.
   b. Son las cuatro y diez de la tarde.
3. Are the following nouns masculine or feminine? Decide by choosing the correct article
   a. la solución
   b. el problema
   c. la foto
   d. la tortuga
   e. la lumbre
   f. la mano
   g. el pie
4. It means that all nouns have gender, and that the pronouns, articles and adjectives around them have to reflect that gender. It is the need to change a word to make it match a grammatical feature of another word, to which it's syntactically connected.
5. What is the bolded pronoun replacing in each case?
   a. María.
   b. Tu hermano, un rompecabezas.
   c. Estás enojado.
   d. Mi madre.
6. Complete with the corresponding demonstrative pronoun.
   a. aquella.
   b. ese.
   c. aquel.
   d. Estas.
7. After the noun. Demonstrative and possessive adjectives; limiting adjectives; adjectives that describe an essential quality of the noun; and adjectives that have a change in meaning are placed before the noun.

8.
   Superiority: "más + adjetivo/adverbio + que"
   Inferiority: "menos + adjetivo/adverbio + que"
   Equality: "tan + adjetivo/adverbio + como"
   Positive superlative: "el/la/los/las + más + adjetivo"
9.
   a. indefinido.
   b. definido.
   c. definido.
   d. definido/indefinido.
10. Match the common saying in the left with their meanings in the right:
    a. 4
    b. 3
    c. 1
    d. 2

# Chapter 7

1. es; piensan; está; sitúan; hay; lleva
2. tenemos; estamos; decimos; hacemos; somos
3. está yendo; estás teniendo; están construyendo; está haciendo
4. siendo; comiendo; haciendo; bailando
5.
   a. True.
   b. False. The present indicative can be used to talk about situations that are going to happen in the near future.
   c. True.
   d. True.

# Chapter 8

1. 
   A. pretérito perfecto; pretérito imperfecto; pretérito perfecto simple
   
   B. pretérito perfecto simple; pretérito pluscuamperfecto; pretérito perfecto simple

2. 
   a. True
   
   b. False. *Pretérito imperfecto* is the past tense in which the beginning or end of an action is not indicated.
   
   c. False. *Había hecho* is conjugated in *pretérito pluscuamperfecto*.
   
   d. True

3. 
   a. bailaban
   
   b. cantaba
   
   c. soñaba
   
   d. estudiábamos

4. había perdido; había tenido; había plantado; habían entrado; había sido; había nacido.

5. María <u>estaba</u> abriendo las persianas de su tienda, como todas las mañanas, cuando <u>entró</u> un cliente nuevo. <u>Era</u> un hombre al que nunca <u>había visto</u> antes, aunque algo en su cara le <u>resultaba</u> familiar. <u>Tenía</u> un tupido bigote bajo la gran nariz.

    —¡Buenos días! ¿En qué lo puedo ayudar? —<u>preguntó</u> María.

    —Quiero un café grande, por favor —<u>pidió</u> el hombre, mientras <u>jugaba</u> con su bigote.

    María se <u>dirigió</u> hacia la cafetera y <u>empezó</u> a hacer el café. Mientras lo <u>preparaba</u>, <u>notó</u> que la voz del hombre también le <u>sonaba</u> conocida.

    —Disculpe, ¿nos <u>hemos visto</u> antes?

    Entonces, con una sonrisa, el hombre se <u>quitó</u> el bigote de la cara. <u>Era</u> un bigote falso, por supuesto. María

<u>dejó</u> el café sobre el mostrador, incrédula.

—¿Eduardo? —<u>preguntó</u>—. ¡Qué bonita sorpresa me <u>has dado</u>!

# Chapter 9

1.
   a. Dice que en el futuro cada familia tendrá un cine en su propia casa.
   b. Porque la tarea de matemáticas sería mucho más sencilla.
   c. En el puesto de automóviles.
   d. De que en el futuro no hará falta trabajar.
2. diré; haré; iré; será; bajaré; tomaré; viajaré; serán
3. Match each pronoun with the corresponding conjugation of the auxiliary verb *haber* to form the *futuro compuesto* tense.
   1. yo: habré
   2. tú: habrás
   3. él/ella: habrá
   4. nosotros/nosotras: habremos
   5. vosotros/vosotras: habréis
   6. ellos/ellas: habrán
4.
   a. futuro compuesto.
   b. futuro simple.
   c. futuro simple.
   d. futuro compuesto.
5.
   a. True.
   b. False. *Presente simple* is used to talk about an action that is currently taking place.
   c. True.
   d. False. *Condicional compuesto* is conjugated with the verb *haber*.

# Chapter 10

1. sobre; a; del; por; durante; para; a; a; de; desde; a; de; en; de; de; para; a; de; para; sobre; de; con; por; para.

2. 
   a. False. There are many possible translations for each Spanish preposition.
   b. False. *Sin* is a preposition.
   c. True.
   d. True.

3. 
   a. al; entre; y.
   b. desde; hasta; en.
   c. según.
   d. sino.

4. 
   a.
   b.
   c.
   d.

5. vender gato por liebre; tiene que ver con eso; habla hasta por los codos; tiraba la casa por la ventana; está como una cabra; apodo sin pies ni cabeza.

# Chapter 11

1. 
   a. Estaba atendiendo a una de sus vacas.
   b. Veterinario.
   c. Tenía un problema estomacal. Se soluciona con un poco de medicación.
   d. Porque había vuelto a su casa a buscar una linterna.

2.
- a. ¿Cómo se siente Lucía?
- b. ¿Quién es él?
- c. ¿Dónde están los chicos?
- d. ¿Cuándo fue la última vez que viste a Tomás?

3.
- a. True.
- b. True.
- c. True.
- d. False. They are invariable, i.e., they are always written in the same way.

4. Disculpe; podría; por favor; gustaría.

5. Florencia mira el reloj. <u>No</u> es tan temprano como pensaba. Si <u>no</u> se apresura, llegará tarde al trabajo. Se sube a su coche y, como hay mucho tráfico, decide tomar una ruta alternativa. <u>Jamás</u> ha ido por esa zona. No parece haber <u>nada</u> por allí: es una calle desierta. <u>No</u> hay ningún coche y <u>tampoco</u> hay <u>nadie</u> caminando. ¡<u>Ni siquiera</u> tiene que esperar, porque <u>no</u> hay <u>ningún</u> semáforo! Llega a su trabajo más temprano que de costumbre. Ahora, ya sabe qué ruta debe tomar cada día.

# Chapter 12

1.
- a. Moreno le preguntó qué le había dicho Sánchez.
- b. García le respondió que no le iba a creer.
- c. Le dijo que no dijera tonterías.
- d. Le preguntó qué opinaba Obrador.

2.
- a. False. Direct and indirect speech can also be used to reproduce something you have said.
- b. True.
- c. False. Em-dashes and quotation marks are used in Spanish to indicate direct speech.

d. True.
3.
   a. se llamaba.
   b. respondió.
   c. había quedado asentado.
   d. se dedicaba.
   e. era.
   f. preguntó.
4.
   a. que.
   b. qué.
   c. que.
   d. si.
5. _____

# Final Quiz

1.
   a. True.
   b. True.
   c. False.
   d. True.
2.
   a. Tú estás caminando.
   b. Ella está durmiendo.
   c. Nosotros estamos saliendo.
   d. Vosotros estáis dibujando.
3. hiciste; tenía; fui; era; hacía; había llovido; habías llevado; he dejado
4.
   hará - ayudarán - llevarán - se encargará - irán - _____

5.
   a. Condicional simple.
   b. Condicional compuesto.
   c. Condicional compuesto.
   d. Condicional simple.

6.
   a. con.
   b. de.
   c. durante.
   d. para.

7.
   a. <u>porque</u>: conjunción subordinante.
   b. <u>y</u>: conjunción coordinante.
   c. <u>aunque</u>: conjunción subordinante.
   d. <u>u</u>: conjunción coordinante.

8. irse por las ramas: to beat around the bush
   *hablar hasta por los codos*: to talk somebody's head off
   *dar gato por liebre*: to give a pig in a poke
   *estar como una cabra*: to be completely mad

9.
   a. cómo.
   b. cómo/dónde.
   c. quién.
   d. qué.

10.
   a. False. Indirect speech consists of interpreting and rewriting someone else's or your own message.
   b. True.
   c. True.
   d. False. Direct speech is the reproduction of a message in the same way in which it was said, without alterations or interpretations.

# Part 3: Advanced Spanish

*The Step-By-Step Guide to Perfecting Your Grammar, Speaking, and Comprehension Skills*

# Introduction

Hello, there! Welcome to *Advanced Spanish: The Step-By-Step Guide to Perfecting Your Grammar, Speaking, and Comprehension Skills*. If you are reading this, you have probably been studying Spanish for quite some time. However, there's always room for improvement! And maybe you still have some trouble understanding difficult terms, keeping a conversation going, or reading complex texts.

If that's the case, this book is designed specifically for you, so read on! Through entertaining stories, and thanks to many examples and exercises, by the end of this book, you will have all the tools to speak, read and write like a native Spanish speaker.

To warm up and get down to work, we'll start by reviewing everything you already know. Then, we will delve into the basic tools you need to understand any written text, and we'll teach you how to answer reading comprehension questions. This is important because you'll find these types of questions throughout the book.

In chapters 3 to 8, we will be paying attention to verbs. To study them, we'll divide them according to their conjugation. We'll start with the verbal paradigm of the regular verbs of the first conjugation (verbs ending in *-ar*), then we'll take a look at the second conjugation (verbs ending in *-er*), and finally, we'll study the third conjugation (verbs ending in *-ir*).

Once we finish with the regular verbs, we'll move on to irregular conjugations, reflexive verbs, and the non-conjugated forms of the verb: the gerund, the participle, and the infinitive. Throughout these chapters, you'll find lots of exercises to practice and get to master the verbs and their conjugations.

After this, in chapter 9, we will talk about passive voice: when we use it, and how we form its different types. In this chapter, we will also take a look at the conditional. You'll learn the different types of conditionals, when to use each one, and the mistakes we should avoid.

Chapter 10 is dedicated to different uses of language in everyday speech. We'll talk about how to reproduce people's words – and to do this, we'll see the terms we use to report questions, requests, and statements. Moving forward, in chapter 11, we will delve into Spanish prepositions, which are known to be particularly difficult. But there's no need to worry! We'll study them together with a great variety of idioms – to make it fun!

And finally, in the last chapter, we'll see the features of formal texts. Then, we'll give you the tools to write a formal email and an academic paper. Lastly, we'll explain what aspects to avoid in this type of writing so that you can write a formal text properly.

By the time you finish reading this book and completing all the exercises, you'll have an advanced level of Spanish that will allow you to engage in any oral or written conversation. What are you waiting for? Let's get started!

# Chapter 1: Are You a Master of Main Concepts?

Did you know that Spanish comes from Latin? And that, besides Spain, there are more than 20 countries around the world where it's an official language? And what about the fact that it's the second mother tongue in the world by *number of speakers*, only behind Mandarin Chinese? Spanish is a fascinating language... and so is its history!

We want you to get a little closer to Spanish history and culture in this first chapter. Then, we'll give you a quiz to test your knowledge of the language. Finally, we will present the International Phonetic Alphabet chart, in case you don't know it. It's a very useful system that will help yproperly ou identify the correct sounds to pronounce Spanish. Are you ready? *¡Empecemos!*

## History of the Spanish Language

With 560 million people using it as their native, second, or foreign language, Spanish is one of the world's world's most popular and important languages But how was it born? Just like French or Italian, Spanish comes from Latin. This is beginning 206 B.C., most of the Iberian Peninsula (where Spain is today) was conquered by the Roman Empire

However, from the 5th century onwards, Rome began to lose its influence over those lands. In that context, people stopped using Latin as their main language. In the Castile region, in the center of the peninsula, a new dialect began to take shape: Castilian.

During the Middle Ages, present-day Spain was divided into five Christian kingdoms that began to expand more and more, especially the Castilian one. Because of that, the language spoken in that region took on increasing presence. In 1492, a very important book appeared: *Gramática de la lengua castellana* ("Grammar of the Castilian language"), by Antonio de Nebrija. It was the first treatise to study and try to define the grammar of a European language! The unification of Spain under the Castilian Kingdom made Castilian the territory's official language. However, it should be mentioned that this is not the only language spoken in Spain. There are also other dialects, such as Catalan, Galician and Basque.

As the Middle Ages ended, the Spaniards were reaching the shores of the American continent, where they started to expand their dominance. The Hispanization process made Spanish the main language of almost twenty Latin American countries. The most notable exception is Brazil, which, having been conquered by Portugal, has Portuguese as its official language. In addition, all Latin American countries have speakers of the languages of their native peoples. Some of the most widely spoken indigenous languages are Quechua, Guaraní, Nahuatl, and Aymara.

Although everyone understands each other, there are some important differences between the Spanish spoken in Spain and the different Latin American varieties. For example, the Spanish spoken in the Iberian Peninsula (known as *castellano, español ibérico* or *español de España*) uses *vosotros* as the second personal plural pronoun, instead of *ustedes*, the preferred option in Latin America. There are a lot of other grammatical, lexical and syntactical differences between the Spanish varieties. The good thing is that no matter which one you use or hear, you'll always be able to communicate with people.

# Are You an Advanced Speaker?

Now, it's time for a quiz! We are going to test how much you remember about the basics of intermediate Spanish. The quiz topics are:

- the Spanish alphabet
- accents, hyphenation, capitalization, and punctuation
- word order in sentences
- simple and intermediate vocabulary
- numerical expression
- the singular and the plural
- the verbs and their conjugations
- reading comprehension

After completing the quiz, you can go to the Answer Key section at the end of the book to find out how you did. *¡Buena suerte!*

**1. Translate the following words into Spanish. Then, spell each one out loud. Follow the example of the first word.**

a. Balloon → Globo → ge-ele-o-be-o
b. Dog →
c. Butterfly →
d. City →

**2. Separate the following words into syllables.**

a. Televisor
b. Hombre
c. Ruido
d. Cuchara

**3. Below, there are four misspelled sentences. Correct them by adding accent marks on the words that require it.**

a. Ayer escuche una cancion que me gusto mucho.
b. Mañana ire a visitarte.
c. El español es hablado por muchas personas de America.

d. Soy bueno con los numeros, asi que me gustan las matematicas.

**4. In the following text, add periods and commas where necessary.**

El reino de Castilla fue el primer territorio en el que se habló español Durante los siglos posteriores el idioma se expandió por todo el mundo Hoy en día es hablado en más de 20 territorios aunque cada país tiene su propia variedad

**5. Read the following news article.**

### Arqueólogos hallan 17 objetos prehispánicos en México

Un grupo de diez arqueólogos halló al menos 17 objetos prehispánicos en el pueblo de Xochimilco, al sur de la Ciudad de México, según informó el Instituto Nacional de Antropología e Historia (INAH). El hallazgo se dio en el marco de excavaciones previas a la construcción de un centro comercial en la zona.

Entre los objetos encontrados, hay una pequeña embarcación, dos jarrones y una figura tallada en madera. Todos los hallazgos han sido asociados con la cultura maya y están en buen estado de conservación.

"Las excavaciones en esta zona eran necesarias debido al alto potencial arqueológico del lugar, que forma parte de la Zona de Monumentos Históricos de la alcaldía", explicó María Sánchez, arqueóloga encargada de la expedición.

Los 17 objetos serán estudiados y se espera que su destino sea la colección de arqueología del Museo Nacional de Antropología.

**Now, answer the questions in Spanish.**

a. ¿Cuántos arqueólogos componían la expedición? ¿Quién era la persona a cargo?

b. ¿Cuántos objetos se encontraron? ¿Puedes mencionar algunos?

c. ¿Por qué era importante realizar excavaciones en el área?

d. ¿A dónde llevarán los objetos?

6. **Can you write the following times in Spanish? Follow the example.**

   a. 3:45 pm. Son las *tres y cuarenta y cinco de la tarde* (or *Son las cuatro menos cuarto de la tarde*)

   b. 2:00 pm.

   c. 8:30 pm.

   d. 9:15 am.

7. **The following sentences are not grammatically correct. Can you correct them?**

   a. Mi favorito color es el verde.

   b. David va al universidad en tren.

   c. Miguel y su familia vive en Madrid.

   d. Les llevé el perro mis padres.

8. **Complete the following text with the words *arroz* (rice), *mariscos* (seafood), *vino* (wine) and *sartén* (skillet).**

   La paella es una típica comida española. El alimento más importante de la paella es el _____. Se cocina en una _____ junto a otros ingredientes, a menudo _____. Una buena bebida para acompañar la paella es el _____ blanco.

9. **Below, there are some adverbs. List them under the correct group.**

   - rápidamente, luego, fácilmente, alrededor, arriba, nunca, mucho, aquí, poco, menos, bastante, siempre, mal, ayer, detrás, bien.

   Grupo 1. Adverbios de lugar: _____ _____ _____ _____

   Grupo 2. Adverbios de modo: _____ _____ _____ _____

   Grupo 3. Adverbios de tiempo: _____ _____ _____ _____

   Grupo 4. Adverbios de cantidad: _____ _____ _____ _____

10. **Do you remember where to place the adverb in Spanish? Decide if the following sentences are right or wrong. Correct the wrong ones.**

    a. Había estado en Colombia nunca.

    b. El maratonista corrió rápidamente.

    c. Hace bastante calor.

d. Tengo sueño mucho.

**11. Now, let's see how much you remember about prepositions. In each sentence, choose the correct preposition between the two options to fill in the blanks.**
   a. Viajaré a Málaga _____ mi hermana (con/en).
   b. Ese tren va _____ el sur (hacia/hasta).
   c. Mi cumpleaños es _____ febrero (en/de).
   d. Este regalo es _____ ti (por/para).

**12. Correct the next sentences.**
   a. Valencia está ubicada a el este de la Península Ibérica.
   b. Además de el español, en Barcelona hablan catalán.
   c. En Cuba llaman "guagua" a el autobús.
   d. Santiago de Chile es una de las ciudades más grandes de el sur del continente americano.

**13. Fill in the blanks with the conjunctions *y, aunque, pero,* or *que.***
   a. Me dijo Paula _____ vendría hoy.
   b. Intenté conseguir entradas, _____ fue imposible.
   c. Iré a la fiesta _____ estoy un poco cansada.
   d. Francisco y Marcelo vendrán esta noche _____ cenaremos juntos.

**14. Typically, the present tense is used to talk about something that is happening right now. However, it has other functions. Decide which of the following uses (1 to 4) is present in the sentence below (a to d).**

Uses:
   1. narrating events from the past
   2. talking about frequent actions
   3. talking about the near future
   4. mentioning present desires

Sentences:
   a. Tengo una entrevista de trabajo el jueves.
   b. Quiero casarme en mayo.
   c. Voy a la escuela en autobús.

d. Colón llega a América en 1492.

15. **The following dialogue is a telephone conversation. Complete the blank spaces using the present progressive tense – like in the example.**

A. ¿Qué <u>estás</u> <u>haciendo</u> (hacer)?
B. _____ _____ (leer) un libro. ¿Y tú?
A. Yo _____ _____ (cocinar) ceviche. ¿Quieres venir a cenar?
B. ¡Claro! ¡Ya lo _____ _____ (saborear)!

16. **Below, you'll find a text with verbs in the past tense. Decide whether each verb is conjugated in *pretérito perfecto simple*, *pretérito perfecto*, *pretérito imperfecto*, or *pretérito pluscuamperfecto*.**

Nunca <u>he sido</u> un artista, pero siempre <u>estuve</u> cerca de ellos. Sin duda, mi empleo más curioso <u>fue</u> en un circo. Yo me <u>encargaba</u> de montar los trapecios. El dueño del circo <u>era</u> un tipo muy amargado. Antes de eso, <u>había trabajado</u> como empleado en un banco. ¡No tengo ni idea de cómo <u>llegó</u> al circo!

17. **Complete the following dialogue with the verbs in brackets conjugated in *futuro simple* or *futuro compuesto*.**

A. ¡Hola! Busco a Carla.
B. Lo siento, pero Carla me dijo que no _____ (salir) hoy. Tiene un examen importante mañana, así que _____ (estudiar) toda la tarde.
A. Estoy seguro de que lo _____ (hacer) bien.
B. ¡Yo también lo creo! Para mañana a esta hora, _____ _____ (aprobar) ese examen.

18. **Now you'll read 4 answers to open questions. Following the example, write down the corresponding question.**

a. El restaurante está lleno de gente. *¿Cómo está el restaurante?*

b. Fernando vive en Santiago de Chile.
   _____

c. Marcela festejará su boda en mayo.
   _____

d. Lucas es el hermano de Martín.
   _____

19. Go back and reread the section on the history of the language. Then, answer these questions in Spanish.
   a. ¿En qué siglo comenzó a perder poder el Imperio romano?
   b. ¿Cómo se llama el español que se habla en España?
   c. ¿Cuál era la característica del libro *Gramática de la lengua castellana*?
   d. ¿Puedes mencionar una diferencia entre el español de España y el español de Latinoamérica?

20. It's time to test your ability to describe spaces and objects! Look around you and write a short text in Spanish about what you see. Follow the example below:

Estoy en la sala de mi casa, sentado en una silla. Sobre la mesa, hay bolígrafos y cuadernos. Frente a mí, hay un gran cuadro con un caballo pintado. Detrás de mí, hay una mesa de madera con un jarrón encima. El jarrón tiene flores rojas.

**IPA Phonemic Chart**

We know that you are an intermediate or advanced Spanish learner. Therefore, we are pretty sure that you have some knowledge of Spanish pronunciation. However, we also know that Spanish pronunciation can be a bit difficult. That's why we provide you with our version of the IPA phonemic chart below.

The IPA chart is the summary of a standardized system of phonetic symbols that represent the exact sounds we use to produce words. In our version of it, you'll find a phoneme (that is, a sound that can distinguish a word from another), followed by a Spanish word that contains that sound and, lastly, an English word that has the same or a similar sound (you'll see a couple of Xs in the sounds that have no equivalent in English). You can come back to this section whenever you have a pronunciation doubt.

| | ä<br>s*a*l<br>"dad" | e̞<br>m*e*sa<br>"Ted" | i<br>r*i*sa<br>"lean" | o̞<br>*o*so<br>"pot" | u<br>n*u*be<br>"loom" |
|---|---|---|---|---|---|
| Vocales | | | | | |
| Consonantes | b<br>*f*u*tb*ol<br>"*b*at" | β<br>*b*ata<br>X | d<br>man*d*o<br>"*d*ay" | ð<br>*d*iente<br>"*th*ing" | f<br>*f*eria<br>"*f*ellow" |
| | g<br>*g*orro<br>"*g*ate" | j<br>pla*y*a<br>X | k<br>*c*omer<br>"*c*oem" | l<br>*l*ámpara<br>"*l*ong" | ʎ<br>*ll*avero<br>"*y*outh" |
| | m<br>*m*i*m*o<br>"*m*om" | n<br>la*n*a<br>"*n*ote" | ɲ<br>Espa*ñ*a<br>"*Ka*nye" | ŋ<br>ma*n*ga<br>"doi*ng*" | p<br>*p*erro<br>"*p*ool" |
| | r<br>*r*ana<br>X | ɾ<br>mi*r*ar<br>"later" (in American English) | s<br>*s*alsa<br>"*s*un" | θ<br>*z*anahoria<br>"*th*rew" | t<br>*t*alco<br>"*t*iny" |
| | tʃ<br>*ch*isme<br>"*ch*ocolate" | v<br>A*f*ganistán<br>"*v*ital" | x<br>*h*ija<br>"*h*ome" | ʃ<br>*sh*erpa<br>"*sh*ell" | |

# Chapter 2: Reading Strategies for the Advanced Learner

## Short Text: "Breve historia del teatro"

Los orígenes del teatro se encuentran en antiguos ritos prehistóricos. Ciertas ceremonias religiosas tenían ya desde sus **inicios** un componente de **escenificación** teatral. Por ejemplo, en los **ritos de caza**, el hombre primitivo imitaba a animales y combinaba el movimiento y la comunicación gestual con la música y la danza. También utilizaban **máscaras** que servían para expresar roles o estados de ánimo.

Entre los siglos VI y V **a. C.**, en Grecia, nació el teatro entendido como «arte dramático». Desde un principio estuvo **ligado** tanto a **fiestas religiosas** en honor al dios Dionisio como a la formación de los ciudadanos. Era organizado por el Estado y tenía un componente educativo: la transmisión de valores.

En el siglo IV a. C., el filósofo Aristóteles aportaría un estudio riguroso sobre uno de los géneros dramáticos: la tragedia. Esta se caracterizaba por presentar personajes pertenecientes a la realeza y la aristocracia guerrera, con lenguaje elevado y conflictos con el destino. Tenía como finalidad lograr la purificación de las pasiones. **En contrapartida**, el otro género dramático, la comedia, **era protagonizado** por personajes populares, cotidianos, quienes se enfrentaban a las dificultades de la vida desde sus propias debilidades y picardías.

En la Edad Media (hasta el siglo XV d. C.), el teatro profano se representaba en la calle, era **lúdico** y festivo; mientras que el teatro religioso tenía lugar en los atrios de las iglesias.

Más adelante, en el siglo XVI, el teatro renacentista pasó del teocentrismo al antropocentrismo, es decir, dejó de tener como centro a Dios para hablar del hombre y sus capacidades.

Llegado el siglo XIX, el teatro romántico se destacó por el sentimentalismo, el dramatismo, la predilección por temas oscuros y **escabrosos**, la exaltación de la naturaleza y del folklore popular, surgiendo así un nuevo género: el melodrama.

Más cerca de la actualidad, el teatro del siglo XX puso mayor énfasis en la dirección artística y en la **escenografía**, en el carácter visual del teatro y no solo en el literario. Se avanzó en la técnica interpretativa, con mayor profundización psicológica en los personajes. **Asimismo**, reivindica el gesto, la acción y el movimiento en el intento de enfatizar esa experiencia **plurisensorial** en la que se convierte cada espectáculo teatral. (Source: *Delgado, M., Aprendamos Lengua y Literatura 2, Argentina: Comunicarte, 2014).*

**Vocabulary List**

| Español | Inglés |
|---|---|
| los inicios | beginning |
| la escenificación | staging |
| el rito de caza | hunting ritual |
| la máscara | mask |
| a. C. | B.C. |
| ligado, ligada | tied |

| | |
|---|---|
| la fiesta religiosa | religious festivity |
| en contrapartida | in contrast |
| protagonizar | star in |
| lúdico, lúdica | playful |
| escabroso, escabrosa | thorny |
| la escenografía | scenography |
| asimismo | likewise/furthermore |
| plurisensorial | multisensory |

**Reading Comprehension**

After reading any text, it's a good exercise to try to answer a few questions and check if we have truly understood what we've just read. Let's try it with these four simple questions:

1. ¿Cuándo nació el concepto de arte dramático?
2. ¿Quién fue el primero en hablar de la tragedia?
3. ¿De quiénes hablaba la comedia?
4. ¿Qué cambia en el teatro en el siglo XX?

**Grammar Section**

How did it go with the questions above? Were you able to answer them? If you had a hard time trying, don't worry. In this chapter, we'll give you some tips to comprehend the meaning of any kind of text. When you get to the end, you'll be able to:

- distinguish text types
- use different strategies to understand the meaning of a text
- answer reading comprehension questions

Let's get to it!

## How to Approach a Text

Okay. We are sitting in front of a Spanish text... And now? Where to begin? Well, we have a couple of tips that will come in handy when we are faced with a Spanish text for the first time. Paying attention to a few very important elements will help us to have a global understanding of what we are about to read. The elements are the following:

- **Paratext**: The paratext is material that surrounds the main text. It's made up of images, captions, titles, subtitles. These elements will give us an overall idea of the subject of the text beforehand.
- **Reading assumptions**: Thanks to the paratextual elements, we can make a hypothesis of the main topic of the text. This is our assumption of what we will be reading.
- **Text type**: Finally, it's very helpful to identify the type of text at a glance (below, we'll see the characteristics of each one). If we know which structure to expect, it will be easier to understand the text.

So, before you start reading, pay attention to the elements surrounding the text, identify what type of text you are about to read, and make your reading assumptions.

## Text Types

As we've just said, identifying the type of text before starting to read is very important. Let's take a look at the most common text types, how to identify them and what structure they have.

- **Narrative text**: The function of this type of text is to entertain the reader by telling a story. The classic structure of these texts is orientation, complication or problem, and resolution. After reading a narrative text, you should be able to explain what happened (the plot); where and when the story took place (the setting); who took part in the story (the characters); and if there is a central topic or message (the theme).
- **Expository text**: This text type is used to explain or develop a topic. Its structure involves first, analyzing and then summarizing different complex ideas around the

general theme. A tip to really understand these texts is to write down the central idea developed in each paragraph as you read it.

- **Instructive text**: These texts are easy to recognize. They give instructions on how to complete a task, usually step by step. The clearest example is a cooking recipe or the instructions to assemble a piece of furniture. This last one can be tough!

- **Journalistic text**: Its main function is to report news stories. It tends to be written in short sentences and paragraphs, and it goes straight to the point. A journalistic text should answer the famous 5W questions: what?, who?, where?, when?, and why? To fully understand these texts, it's useful to highlight the answers to those questions.

### First Overall Reading

After paying attention to the paratext, identifying the type of text, and anticipating what we'll find, it's time to start with the first reading. There will probably be words we don't know. If we can't guess their meaning from context, it's best not to stop there. Instead, mark the words to look them up later and continue reading.

In the first reading, we should also identify and underline the main ideas, points of interest, and definitions. By now, we have to be able to say which text type we are dealing with – and roughly – what it is about.

### Second Reading

In our second reading, we can look up the words we don't know in the dictionary—even the ones whose meanings we've guessed from the context, to check if we were right—in order to expand our vocabulary. Some texts offer a vocabulary list, so we can look into it to clear our doubts. If the text doesn't provide any, we recommend you write down your own vocabulary list.

When we read the text for the second time, we should be able to identify the structure of the text. To be sure we've done it correctly, we can give a title to each paragraph. At this point, we can say that we've understood the text in depth and that we will be able to answer questions about it. We'll deal with that next.

# How to Answer Reading Comprehension Questions

In academic contexts, to check if we were able to grasp the meaning of a text, we can be faced with different types of questions. The first thing we have to do is to read and make sure we understand all the questions. Then, we need to identify what information is required to answer each one. Finally, we have to go back to the text and look for that information.

Below, we'll take a look at the most common questions and how to answer them.

### Define, Characterize and Describe

These questions ask about something's meaning, function, or distinguishing features. They could be asking about a fact, an object or a person. In order to answer them, we have to make objective observations about it, describing its properties or identifying aspects. We have to put together complete answers, using all the information provided by the text.

Now, we'll take a look at some examples of these questions and of the answers they require:

- *Según Aristóteles, ¿qué era la tragedia?* ("According to Aristotle, what was tragedy?")

- *Para Aristóteles, la tragedia **era** un género dramático que **se caracterizaba por** presentar personajes pertenecientes a la realeza y la aristocracia guerrera, con lenguaje elevado y conflictos con el destino* ("For Aristotle, tragedy was a dramatic genre characterized by presenting royal and aristocratic characters, who used elevated language and had conflicts with destiny.")

- *¿Cómo era el teatro profano de la Edad Media? ¿Y el teatro religioso?* ("How was the profane theater of the Middle Ages? And the religious theater?")

- *El teatro profano de la Edad Media **se representaba** en la calle, **era** lúdico y festivo. **En cambio**, el teatro religioso **tenía lugar** en los atrios de las iglesias* ("Profane theater of the Middle Ages was represented in the streets; it was playful and festive. On the other hand, religious theater took place in churches' atriums.")

Finally, here's a summary of the constructions we use to answer "define, characterize and describe" questions:

- Sustantivo + verbo "ser" conjugado + definición ("noun + verb to be + definition")
- Sustantivo + se define por/se caracteriza por + características ("noun + is defined by/is characterized by + characteristics")
- Comparaciones: como, más que, igual que, en cambio ("comparisons: as, more than, just as, on the other hand.")

**Exemplify**

As it's clear by their name, to answer these questions, we have to give examples connected to the topic; we have to find particular cases related to the subject of the text and include them in a full answer. Sometimes, the examples are in the text itself, but other times we have to use our knowledge of the word to demonstrate we understood everything.

Let's read an example of this type of question and answer:

- ¿*Qué géneros teatrales se mencionan en el texto? ¿Puedes dar ejemplos de otros géneros teatrales?* ("What theatrical genres are mentioned in the text? Can you give examples of other theatrical genres?")
- *En el texto se mencionan los siguientes géneros teatrales: la tragedia, la comedia, el teatro romántico y el melodrama. Existen otros géneros teatrales,* **como** *el teatro musical, la ópera y la tragicomedia* ("The text mentions the following theatrical genres: tragedy, comedy, romantic theater, and melodrama. There are other theatrical genres, such as musical theater, opera and tragicomedy.")

These are some of the constructions we use to give examples:

- *Como* ("like")
- *Por ejemplo* ("for example")

- *Al igual que* ("as well as")

**Justify**

These questions ask for the reasons to prove an affirmation or a negation. To do so, we have to use the arguments provided by the text. Let's see what we are talking about in an example:

- *¿Por qué en el texto se sostiene que los orígenes del teatro están en los antiguos ritos prehistóricos?* ("Why does the text argue that the origins of theater were in ancient prehistoric rites?")

- *Se sostiene que los orígenes del teatro están en los antiguos ritos prehistóricos* **porque** *ciertas ceremonias religiosas tenían un componente de escenificación teatral* ("It is argued that the origins of theater were in ancient prehistoric rites because certain religious ceremonies had a theatrical staging element.")

To justify a statement, we can use one of the following expressions:

- *Porque* ("because")
- *Dado que* ("given that")
- *Ya que* ("since")

**Classify**

These questions make us group certain elements into sets or classes. That is, we have to order the elements according to some criterion, which may be specified in the text or in the question. Here is an example of how *classify* questions look – and how you can answer them:

- *¿Cuáles eran los elementos del teatro que estaban presentes en los ritos de caza?* ("Which were the elements of theater that were present in hunting rites?")

- *Los elementos del teatro que estaban presentes en los ritos de caza* **comprendían** *la imitación de animales, la combinación de movimiento y comunicación gestual con música y la danza, y la utilización de máscaras* ("The elements of theater that were present in hunting rites included the imitation of animals, the combination of movements and gestural communication with music and dance, and the use of masks.")

Let's take a look at some of the expressions we use to classify elements:

- *Se dividen en* ("are divided into")
- *Se agrupan en* ("are grouped into")
- *Contiene* ("contains")
- *Comprende* ("includes")

**Ponting, Indicating, Marking**

This last type of question doesn't require a full answer. We just need to search the text for that specific word or name and write it down or underline it. Let's check out an example:

- *Marque en el texto quién fue el que aportó un estudio riguroso sobre la tragedia* ("In the text, indicate who was the one who provided a rigurous study of tragedy.")
- *El filósofo Aristóteles* ("Philosopher Aristotle.")

**Exercises**

1. Take a quick look at the short texts below and try to identify which text type they belong to. Then, read them in detail to confirm your assumption:

**El increíble hallazgo de un dinosaurio acorazado en Patagonia Norte**

El pasado 11 de agosto, científicos argentinos y españoles encontraron una nueva especie de dinosaurio acorazado.
El descubrimiento tuvo lugar en el Área Paleontológica de La Buitrera, en la provincia de Río Negro, Argentina.
Los científicos tardaron más de cinco años en dar con los restos fósiles del nuevo dinosaurio, al que llamaron *Jakapil kaniukura*.

   a. Una vez que tengas todos los ingredientes, sigue estos pasos:
      i. verter la harina en una fuente;
      ii. condimentar;

  iii. agregar el aceite;
  iv. mezclar hasta conseguir un arenado;
  v. agregar poco a poco el agua e ir integrando con las manos hasta obtener una masa firme.

 b. **¡Lina al rescate!**
  Kala es un león que vive en un desierto. Un día, se estaba bañando y un grupo de hienas se acercó a él para atacarlo. Si bien el león era fuerte, las hienas eran muchas. Cuando estaban a punto de vencer, llegó Lina, una leona. Lina espantó a las hienas y lamió las heridas que le habían hecho a Kala.

 c. **Los pulpos**
  Los pulpos son un tipo de animal de agua. Tienen ocho tentáculos. Pueden vivir hasta dos años, ya que mueren al reproducirse. Entre sus tácticas defensivas se encuentra la capacidad de expulsar una especie de tinta y la posibilidad de camuflarse con el entorno. Su cuerpo es gelatinoso y blando, por lo que pueden cambiar de forma rápidamente.

2. One of the texts above is a narrative text; do you know which one? Go back to it and identify the three parts of the narrative structure.

3. In 50-100 words, write a recipe in the form of an instructive text.

4. Read the following text, underline the words you don't know, and look them up in the dictionary. Then, write them down in a vocabulary list like the one at the beginning of this chapter. It's a good idea to add the article of nouns (*el* or *la*) to learn the word together with its gender, and to write down both the masculine and the feminine form of adjectives. Besides, we recommend listing the verbs in their infinitive form.

Los organismos necesitan transmitirse información entre ellos por muchas y variadas razones. Por ejemplo, entre animales, la existencia de una comunicación efectiva es vital para reunir a individuos de sexos diferentes para el apareamiento. Las señales realizadas durante el cortejo pueden determinar si dos individuos forman la pareja adecuada. La comunicación también sirve para marcar límites territoriales entre vecinos o para establecer el lugar de un individuo dentro de la jerarquía social.

El tacto solamente se puede utilizar de cerca. En los primates, el desparasitado mutuo refuerza los lazos entre las parejas y los miembros de la misma familia. Las señales vibratorias son eficaces en distancias cortas. Así, en algunas especies de araña, el macho puntea la telaraña de un modo determinado, mostrando a la hembra su disponibilidad.

Los sonidos son percibidos a distancias mayores que las señales visuales, pueden ser utilizados por la noche y llegan a todos los rincones. Los mamíferos grandes (por ejemplo, ballenas y elefantes) emiten sonidos de baja frecuencia que son inaudibles para el oído humano, pero que pueden viajar largas distancias. De modo semejante, las llamadas y los cantos de las aves sirven para delimitar territorios y atraer a la pareja. (Enciclopedia científica Larousse, T. 3. México, DF: Larousse, 1997)

5. Now, highlight the main ideas of the paragraphs individually. Then, write down a title for each paragraph and, finally, one for the whole text.

# Chapter 3: First Conjugation (-*ar*)

## Short Story: La última empanada

Lucía y Natalia van a cenar con su padre, Fabián. Las dos están muy **tentadas** de probar las **empanadas** del lugar. En el restaurante, la **moza** les **pincha el globo**: solo queda una empanada.

—Van a tener que ordenar otra cosa —les avisa el papá.

—Bueno, yo deseo una **milanesa de carne** con papas fritas... y la última empanada —determina Lucía, con mucha rapidez.

—¡No! ¡A mí me toca la última empanada! Y, además, un **pancho**. —Natalia está **indignada**.

Fabián piensa cómo manejar la situación. Le gustaría que se solucionara de una manera divertida. Las invita a jugar a algo: la que gane, se quedará con la empanada. Las chicas están muy **entusiasmadas**. ¡Les encanta cuando su papá les hace preguntas!

—¿En qué año se declaró la Independencia de Argentina? —pregunta Fabián.

—En 1810 —grita Natalia.

—No, en 1816 —Lucía está muy calmada.

—¡Muy bien Lucía! El 9 de julio de 1816 —dice Fabián—. Ahora, otro tema: ¿dónde conocí a su mamá?

—En el bar que quedaba al lado de la **facultad**: ella trabajaba ahí y vos ibas a estudiar —asegura Natalia.

—Excelente —dice Fabián—. ¿Quién fue Gustavo Cerati?

—¡Un músico argentino! —contestan Natalia y Lucía al mismo tiempo.

—¡Bien! Tenemos un **empate**. A ver...

Mientras Fabián piensa otra pregunta, llega la moza con el pedido: una milanesa con papas fritas para Lucía, un pancho para Natalia, unos ravioles para Fabián y... la última empanada. Lucía y Natalia se miran, **desafiantes**. Fabián se quedó sin preguntas. Además, no quiere que se enfríe la comida, y **de pronto** tiene muchas ganas de probar una empanada. Mientras Lucía y Natalia se **fulminan con la mirada**, la agarra rápido y se la traga.

—¡Papá! —grita Lucía.

—¡No puede ser! —exclama Natalia al mismo tiempo.

Fabián lanza una carcajada mientras disfruta de su empanada.

—No estaba tan rica. Es lo mejor para ustedes. La próxima vez, vamos a comer a un **local de empanadas**.

**Vocabulary List**

| Español | Inglés |
|---|---|
| tentada, tentado | tempted to |
| la moza, el mozo (en Argentina), la camarera, el camarero | waitress, waiter |
| pinchar el globo | to burst someone's bubble |
| la milanesa de carne | beef schnitzel |
| el pancho (en Argentina y Uruguay), el perrito caliente | hot dog |

| indignada, indignado | outraged |
|---|---|
| entusiasmada, entusiasmado | excited |
| la facultad (en Argentina), la universidad | university, college |
| el empate | tie |
| desafiante | defiant |
| de pronto | suddenly |
| fulminar con la mirada | to look daggers at someone |

**Reading Comprehension**

Let's put into practice everything we've learned in chapter 2 by answering these questions:

1. ¿Por qué el cuento se llama "La última empanada"?
2. ¿Cómo soluciona Fabián la disputa entre sus hijas?
3. ¿Quién ordena ravioles para cenar?
4. ¿Por qué se enojan Natalia y Lucía con su papá?

**Grammar Section**

Since you are not new to Spanish, we're sure you already know many verbs and their past, present, and future conjugations. But in chapters 3, 4, and 5, we want to take you further: we'll give you the tools to correctly conjugate any Spanish *regular verb*. But first, we are going to recap some basic features of verbs. In this chapter, we'll review:

- number
- person
- voice
- mood
- tense

- the regular verbs of the first conjugation

**Properties of Verbs**

You probably already know that verbs in Spanish are a little bit tricky. The verb itself gives us information not only about tense, mood and voice (like it does in English), but also about the subject of the sentence. If we want to understand verbs and use them correctly, we need to study their properties and their importance in conjugation.

Spanish verbs are divided into three main groups: in the first conjugation, we have the verbs that, in the infinitive, end in *-ar* (like *amar,* "to love"). In the second conjugation, we have the verbs that, in the infinitive, end in *-er* (like *comer,* "to eat"). Finally, in the third conjugation, we have the verbs that, in the infinitive, end in *-ir* (like *salir,* "to go out"). They are grouped like this because the regular verbs of each conjugation behave in the same way.

That being said, we should establish the difference between the stem and the ending of the verb. The stem is the part where the semantic information is, i.e., the part that carries the meaning. With regular verbs, this part of the word doesn't change: it always remains the same. For verbs of the first conjugation, the stem is whatever comes before the *-ar* ending. This ending, on the other hand, changes according to the different "grammatical accidents" (that's how verb properties are called). The good thing is that, in regular verbs, the ending changes following a pattern, which depends on whether the infinitive finishes in *-ar, -er* or *-ir.*

Let's take a look at an example so that we learn to identify the stem and the ending. If we take *cantamos* ("we sing"), the stem is *cant-* (the same as in <u>*cant*</u>*ar,* <u>*cant*</u>*aré or* <u>*cant*</u>*ó*) and the ending is *-amos,* which expresses the first person of the plural in the present simple (the same as in *am*<u>*amos*</u>*, camin*<u>*amos*</u> or *cocin*<u>*amos*</u>).

Now, we'll review the grammatical accidents.

**Number**

The number indicates how many people are carrying out the action of the verb. It can be one (singular) or more than one (plural). For example:

- *Yo como una empanada* ("I eat an *empanada*")
- *Nosotros comemos una empanada* ("We eat an *empanada*")

**Person**

The person indicates who is doing the action. The first person is reflected in the pronouns *yo* ("I") or *nosotros/nosotras* ("we"). The second person is reflected in the pronouns *usted, tú* or *vos* ("you," singular); and *ustedes* or *vosotros* ("you," plural). At this point, you'll find some differences depending on where you are. In Rioplatense Spanish (spoken mainly in Uruguay and Argentina) the second person singular *vos* and plural *ustedes* are used. In the rest of Latin America and Spain, the second person *tú* is used and, almost exclusively in Spain, the plural *vosotros* is used. Finally, we have the third person, reflected in *él, ella, ellos* or *ellas* ("he, she, they"). Let's see some examples.

- *Yo bailé con él* ("I danced with him")
- *Bailemos juntos* ("Let's dance together")
- *Esa chica no baila bien* ("That girl doesn't dance nicely")
- *Tus papás bailan mucho* ("Your parents dance a lot")
- *¿Bailaste con ella?* ("Did you dance with her?")

**Voice**

In Spanish, like in English, we can use the active or the passive voice of verbs. This depends on whether we want to emphasize the subject or the object of the sentence. The passive voice is formed by transforming the verb of the active voice into two parts: the verb *ser* + the participle of the main verb. Let's see a few examples.

- Active voice: *Los residuos de las empresas contaminaron el río* ("The waste the companies made polluted the river.")
- Passive voice: *El río fue contaminado por los residuos de las empresas* ("The river was polluted by waste from the companies.")

- Active voice: *Un arquitecto diseñó esta biblioteca* ("An architect designed this library.")

- Passive voice: *Esta biblioteca fue diseñada por un arquitecto* ("This library was designed by an architect.")

There's much more to know about passive voice, but we'll talk about that in chapter 9.

**Mood**

The mood of the verb indicates the attitude of the speaker or, to put it another way, the *intention* of the sentence. In Spanish, there are three moods:

- Indicative, to talk about things that are certain.

- Subjunctive, to talk about possibilities, wishes, and doubts.

- Imperative, to give orders or commands.

Let's see some examples:

- Indicative mood: *Me compraré una casa* ("I'm going to buy a house.")

- Subjunctive mood: *¡Ojalá pudiera comprarme una casa!* ("I wish I could buy a house!")

- Imperative mood: *Cómprame una casa* ("Buy me a house.")

**Tense**

In each mood, we have past tenses, future tenses, and present tenses. Being an intermediate student of Spanish, you probably know them and use many of them. That's why in this table, we'll simply review the most common verb tenses to refresh your memory.

| Tiempo | ¿Para qué se usa? | Ejemplos |
| --- | --- | --- |
| Presente simple | Actions in the present | *Yo lloro* ("I cry") *Ustedes piensan* ("You think") |

| | | |
|---|---|---|
| Pretérito imperfecto | Durative or reiterative actions in the past | *Me gustaba ir* ("I liked going") *Ella solía jugar conmigo* ("She used to play with me") |
| Pretérito perfecto simple | Actions that have a defined beginning and ending | *Ayer me cuidó mi papá* ("My dad took care of me yesterday") *Te llamé a la tarde* ("I called you in the afternoon") |
| Futuro simple | Actions that will happen in the future | *La doctora llegará más tarde* ("The doctor will arrive later") *Gastarás mucho dinero* ("You'll spend a lot of money") |
| Pretérito pluscuamperfecto | Actions that happened before other action in the past | *Cuando llegó, sus amigos ya se habían ido* ("When he arrived, his friends had already left") *Me dijo que me lo había enviado, pero nunca lo vi* ("She told me that she had sent it, but I never saw it") |

### First Conjugation

Now that we know the characteristics of the verb, we'll take a look at all the possible conjugations. The table below shows the complete Spanish verbal paradigm for the first conjugation. Pay special attention to the bolded endings because all regular verbs ending in *-ar* will be conjugated like this. It's worth noting that compound tenses are built with the auxiliary verb *haber* conjugated plus the participle of the main verb. We'll talk more about the participle and the other nonfinite verb forms in chapter 8.

Cortar

| Modo | Tiempo | Conjugación |
|---|---|---|
| Indicativo | Presente | Yo cort**o** <br> Tú cort**as** <br> Él, ella, usted cort**a** <br> Nosotros/as cort**amos** <br> Vosotros/as cort**áis** <br> Ellos, ellas, ustedes cort**an** |
| | Pretérito perfecto simple | Yo cort**é** <br> Tú cort**aste** <br> Él, ella, usted cort**ó** <br> Nosotros/as cort**amos** <br> Vosotros/as cort**asteis** <br> Ellos, ellas, ustedes cort**aron** |
| | Pretérito imperfecto | Yo cort**aba** <br> Tú cort**abas** <br> Él, ella, usted cort**aba** <br> Nosotros/as cort**ábamos** <br> Vosotros/as cort**abais** <br> Ellos, ellas, ustedes cort**aban** |

| | | |
|---|---|---|
| | Futuro simple | Yo cort**aré**<br>Tú cort**arás**<br>Él, ella, usted cort**ará**<br>Nosotros/as cort**aremos**<br>Vosotros/as cort**aréis**<br>Ellos, ellas, ustedes cort**arán** |
| | Condicional simple | Yo cort**aría**<br>Tú cort**arías**<br>Él, ella, usted cort**aría**<br>Nosotros/as cort**aríamos**<br>Vosotros/as cort**aríais**<br>Ellos, ellas, ustedes cort**arían** |
| | Pretérito perfecto compuesto | Yo **he** cortado<br>Tú **has** cortado<br>Él, ella, usted **ha** cortado<br>Nosotros/as **hemos** cortado<br>Vosotros/as **habéis** cortado<br>Ellos, ellas, ustedes **han** cortado |
| | Pretérito anterior | Yo **hube** cortado<br>Tú **hubiste** cortado<br>Él, ella, usted **hubo** cortado<br>Nosotros/as **hubimos** cortado<br>Vosotros/as **hubisteis** cortado<br>Ellos, ellas, ustedes **hubieron** cortado |

|  |  |  |
|---|---|---|
|  | Pretérito pluscuamperfecto | Yo **había** cortado<br>Tú **habías** cortado<br>Él, ella, usted **había** cortado<br>Nosotros/as **habíamos** cortado<br>Vosotros/as **habíais** cortado<br>Ellos, ellas, ustedes **habían** cortado |
|  | Condicional compuesto | Yo **habría** cortado<br>Tú **habrías** cortado<br>Él, ella, usted **habría** cortado<br>Nosotros/as **habríamos** cortado<br>Vosotros/as **habríais** cortado<br>Ellos, ellas, ustedes **habrían** cortado |
|  | Futuro compuesto | Yo **habré** cortado<br>Tú **habrás** cortado<br>Él, ella, usted **habrá** cortado<br>Nosotros/as **habremos** cortado<br>Vosotros/as **habréis** cortado<br>Ellos, ellas, ustedes **habrán** cortado |
| Subjuntivo | Presente | Yo cort**e**<br>Tú cort**es**<br>Él, ella, usted cort**e**<br>Nosotros/as cort**emos**<br>Vosotros/as cort**éis**<br>Ellos, ellas, ustedes cort**en** |

| | | |
|---|---|---|
| | Pretérito imperfecto | Yo cortara o cortase<br>Tú cortaras o cortases<br>Él, ella, usted cortara o cortase<br>Nosotros/as cortáramos o cortásemos<br>Vosotros/as cortarais o cortaseis<br>Ellos, ellas, ustedes cortaran o cortasen |
| | Futuro simple | Yo cortare<br>Tú cortares<br>Él, ella, usted cortare<br>Nosotros/as cortáremos<br>Vosotros/as cortareis<br>Ellos, ellas, ustedes cortaren |
| | Pretérito perfecto compuesto | Yo **haya** cortado<br>Tú **hayas** cortado<br>Él, ella, usted **haya** cortado<br>Nosotros/as **hayamos** cortado<br>Vosotros/as **hayáis** cortado<br>Ellos, ellas, ustedes **hayan** cortado |

|  |  |  |
|---|---|---|
|  | Pretérito pluscuamperfecto | Yo **hubiera** o **hubiese** cortado<br>Tú **hubieras** o **hubieses** cortado<br>Él, ella, usted **hubiera** o **hubiese** cortado<br>Nosotros/as **hubiéramos** o **hubiésemos** cortado<br>Vosotros/as **hubierais** o **hubieseis** cortado<br>Ellos, ellas, ustedes **hubieran** o **hubiesen** cortado |
|  | Futuro compuesto | Yo **hubiere** cortado<br>Tú **hubieres** cortado<br>Él, ella, usted **hubiere** cortado<br>Nosotros/as **hubiéremos** cortado<br>Vosotros/as **hubiereis** cortado<br>Ellos, ellas, ustedes **hubieren** cortado |
| Imperativo | Presente | Tú cort**a**<br>Vosotros cort**ad** |

Let's look at some example sentences with the verb *cortar* in different conjugations:

- **Condicional simple del modo indicativo**

    *Señor, ¿me **cortaría** un pedazo de torta?* ("Sir, would you cut me a piece of cake?")

- **Pretérito imperfecto del modo indicativo**

    *Los alumnos **cortaban** pedazos de tela* ("Students cut pieces of cloth.")

- **Pretérito perfecto compuesto subjuntivo**

    *Ojalá que los leñadores no **hayan cortado** el árbol* ("Hopefully the loggers didn't cut down the tree.")

- **Futuro compuesto del modo indicativo**

    *No te preocupes, para mañana **habré cortado** todas estas figuras* ("Don't worry, by tomorrow I will have cut all these figures.")

- **Presente simple del modo subjuntivo**

    *Quizás me **corte** el pelo hoy* ("Maybe I'll get a haircut today.")

**Other Verbs of the First Conjugation**

Now we'll take a look at other verbs of this conjugation so that we can see how they work in speech.

1. *Abandonar*

    - *Me parece muy triste que te hayan abandonado así* ("I find it very sad that you have been abandoned like that.")
    - *Marta abandonará los estudios* ("Marta will drop out of school.")
    - *Quizás sea mejor que abandones esa idea* ("Maybe it will be better for you to give up to that idea.")

2. *Cuidar*

    - *Ramón te cuidó mucho* ("Ramón took great care of you.")
    - *Si tan solo me hubieras cuidado* ("If only you had taken care of me.")
    - *Me dijo que se había cuidado en la carretera* ("He told me he'd taken care of himself on the road.")

3. *Llorar*

    - *Él lloraba por ti todas las noches* ("He cried for you every night.")
    - *Ese bebé llora mucho* ("That baby cries a lot.")
    - *No creo que hayan llorado cuando se despidieron* ("I don't think they cried when they said goodbye.")

4. *Necesitar*
    - *Necesitaréis hablar mucho de esto* ("You'll need to talk about this a lot.")
    - *Hubiera necesitado saberlo antes* ("I would have needed to know sooner.")
    - *Los niños han necesitado muchas horas de sueño* ("The kids have needed many hours of sleep.")
5. *Bailar*
    - *Me duele el cuerpo hoy porque bailé mucho ayer* ("My body aches today because I danced a lot yesterday.")
    - *Vamos, ¡bailen!* ("Come on, dance!")
    - *Si hubieras bailado mejor, habrías aprobado* ("If you had danced better, you would have passed.")
6. *Saltar*
    - *Jamás saltaría desde tan alto* ("I would never jump from that height.")
    - *¿Vosotras ya habéis saltado?* ("Have you already jumped?")
- *Mira como saltan las niñas* ("Look at the girls jumping.")
7. *Cantar*
    - *Mañana cantaré en el parque* ("Tomorrow I'll sing in the park.")
    - *Mamá, ¡no cantes ahora!* ("Mom, don't sing now!")
    - *Habéis cantado precioso* ("You sang beautifully.")

**Exercises**
1. Decide whether the following statements are true or false. Correct the false ones.
    a. The number of the verb expresses how many people are involved in the action.
    b. There are four moods in Spanish.
    c. The first conjugation is for verbs ending in *-er*.
    d. Imperfect past (*pretérito imperfecto*) is used for actions that have a defined beginning and ending.

2. Complete the sentences with the correct form of the verb in brackets:
   a. *Ayer mi mamá _____ (visitar) a mi abuela.*
   b. *Mañana Martín _____ (copiar) la tarea de la escuela.*
   c. *Mañana quizás _____ (confirmar) mi asistencia.*
   d. *Cuando llamaste, nosotros ya _____ _____ (comprar) las entradas.*
3. Convert these sentences into active voice:
   a. La fiesta de Navidad será organizada por los estudiantes.
   b. Los libros serán firmados por el autor en la presentación.
4. Convert these sentences into passive voice:
   a. La banda interpretará esta canción.
   b. Los arqueólogos descubrieron estos huesos.
5. Go back to the short story at the beginning of the chapter and write down all the verbs that belong to the first conjugation. Then, determine in which tense they are conjugated.

# Chapter 4:
# Second Conjugation (-*er*)

## Short Story: El mensaje

Álvaro se había puesto muy nervioso. Corría de un lado a otro de su habitación. No podía permanecer **quieto**. Para distraerse, decidió llamar a su amiga Jazmín.

—¿Hola?

—Hola, Jazmín, ¿puedes hablar ahora?

—Sí, claro, ¿qué **sucede**?

—Creo que **cometí un error**. Le reconocí a Matías toda la verdad.

—¡¿Qué?! ¿Cómo? ¿Cuándo?

—**Recién**. Se lo hice saber por un **mensaje de texto**.

—¿Y qué te respondió? —preguntó Jazmín.

—Nada **aún**. Quisiera deshacer el mensaje —dijo Álvaro.

—¡No! No lo hagas —respondió Jazmín—. Tienes este amor por Matías desde hace siglos. Ya es hora de que él lo sepa. Además, ¡es evidente que también le **atraes**!

—¿Y entonces por qué no me ha respondido?

—Tranquilo. Verás cómo mañana todo se resuelve. Pon el móvil en la cocina y no leas más ese mensaje.

Álvaro obedeció a su amiga. Finalmente, lo **venció** el sueño. Al día siguiente, cuando amaneció, la mamá lo estaba **reprendiendo** desde la cocina.

—¡Álvaro, **atiende** tu móvil que me va a **enloquecer**! Y ten tu desayuno, que se va a **enfriar**.

A Álvaro se le detuvo el corazón. ¿Quién era? ¿Sería Matías?

Corrió a la cocina con el pijama puesto y, sin detenerse en su madre, cogió su móvil. Tenía cuatro mensajes (¡qué exagerada su mamá!), pero ninguno era de Matías.

Le habría gustado detener el tiempo y no ver a Matías nunca más. Pero debía ir a la escuela: ¡su madre era **implacable**!

En la puerta del colegio apareció Matías, con una cara muy triste. Álvaro se escondió, pero Matías lo vio y le devolvió una **amplia sonrisa**.

—¡Álvaro! Qué bueno verte. He leído tu mensaje, pero no te he podido responder porque he perdido el móvil. ¡No lo encuentro por ningún sitio!

Álvaro esbozó una sonrisa nerviosa. ¡Había leído su mensaje!

—¿Y entonces? —preguntó.

—No me atrevía a reconocer mis sentimientos, pero ahora que conozco los tuyos, ¡soy feliz!

## Vocabulary List

| Español | Inglés |
| --- | --- |
| quieto, quieta | still |
| suceder | to happen |
| cometer un error | to make a mistake |
| recién | just now |
| el mensaje de texto | text message |

| | |
|---|---|
| aún | yet |
| atraerse | to be attracted to each other |
| vencer | to defeat |
| reprender | to tell off |
| atender (el móvil) | to answer (the phone) |
| enloquecer | to drive crazy |
| enfriar | to get cold |
| implacable | relentless |
| la amplia sonrisa | broad smile |

**Reading Comprehension**

Let's see if you got the gist of what you've just read:
1. ¿Por qué está nervioso Álvaro?
2. ¿Qué le recomienda Jazmín?
3. ¿Qué le pasó a Matías?
4. ¿Por qué Álvaro no pudo faltar al colegio?

# Grammar Section

In the previous chapter, we saw everything there is to know about regular verbs of the first conjugation. Now it's time for the second conjugation, the verbs ending in *-er*. Chapter 4 is dedicated to their complete verbal paradigm so that you learn how to conjugate any regular verb ending in *-er*.

# Second Conjugation

The model for the regular verbs of the second conjugation is the verb *temer* ("to fear"). This means that all regular verbs ending in *-er* will change their ending in the way *temer* does. In order to show you, we'll use the verb *comer* ("to eat").

Comer

| Modo | Tiempo | Conjugación |
|---|---|---|
| Indicativo | Presente | Yo como<br>Tú comes<br>Él, ella, usted come<br>Nosotros/as comemos<br>Vosotros/as coméis<br>Ellos, ellas, ustedes comen |
| | Pretérito perfecto simple | Yo comí<br>Tú comiste<br>Él, ella, usted comió<br>Nosotros/as comimos<br>Vosotros/as comisteis<br>Ellos, ellas, ustedes comieron |
| | Pretérito imperfecto | Yo comía<br>Tú comías<br>Él, ella, usted comía<br>Nosotros/as comíamos<br>Vosotros/as comíais<br>Ellos, ellas, ustedes comían |

| | | |
|---|---|---|
| | Futuro simple | Yo com**eré**<br>Tú com**erás**<br>Él, ella, usted com**erá**<br>Nosotros/as com**eremos**<br>Vosotros/as com**eréis**<br>Ellos, ellas, ustedes com**erán** |
| | Condicional simple | Yo com**ería**<br>Tú com**erías**<br>Él, ella, usted com**ería**<br>Nosotros/as com**eríamos**<br>Vosotros/as com**eríais**<br>Ellos, ellas, ustedes com**erían** |
| | Pretérito perfecto compuesto | Yo **he** comido<br>Tú **has** comido<br>Él, ella, usted **ha** comido<br>Nosotros/as **hemos** comido<br>Vosotros/as **habéis** comido<br>Ellos, ellas, ustedes **han** comido |
| | Pretérito anterior | Yo **hube** comido<br>Tú **hubiste** comido<br>Él, ella, usted **hubo** comido<br>Nosotros/as **hubimos** comido<br>Vosotros/as **hubisteis** comido<br>Ellos, ellas, ustedes **hubieron** comido |

|  |  |  |
|---|---|---|
|  | Pretérito pluscuamperfecto | Yo **había** comido<br>Tú **habías** comido<br>Él, ella, usted **había** comido<br>Nosotros/as **habíamos** comido<br>Vosotros/as **habíais** comido<br>Ellos, ellas, ustedes **habían** comido |
|  | Condicional compuesto | Yo **habría** comido<br>Tú **habrías** comido<br>Él, ella, usted **habría** comido<br>Nosotros/as **habríamos** comido<br>Vosotros/as **habríais** comido<br>Ellos, ellas, ustedes **habrían** comido |
|  | Futuro compuesto | Yo **habré** comido<br>Tú **habrás** comido<br>Él, ella, usted **habrá** comido<br>Nosotros/as **habremos** comido<br>Vosotros/as **habréis** comido<br>Ellos, ellas, ustedes **habrán** comido |
| Subjuntivo | Presente | Yo com**a**<br>Tú com**as**<br>Él, ella, usted com**a**<br>Nosotros/as com**amos**<br>Vosotros/as com**áis**<br>Ellos, ellas, ustedes com**an** |

| | | |
|---|---|---|
| | Pretérito imperfecto | Yo comiera o comiese<br>Tú comieras o comieses<br>Él, ella, usted comiera o comiese<br>Nosotros/as comiéramos o comiésemos<br>Vosotros/as comierais o comieseis<br>Ellos, ellas, ustedes comieran o comiesen |
| | Futuro simple | Yo comiere<br>Tú comieres<br>Él, ella, usted comiere<br>Nosotros/as comiéremos<br>Vosotros/as comiereis<br>Ellos, ellas, ustedes comieren |
| | Pretérito perfecto compuesto | Yo haya comido<br>Tú hayas comido<br>Él, ella, usted haya comido<br>Nosotros/as hayamos comido<br>Vosotros/as hayáis comido<br>Ellos, ellas, ustedes hayan comido |

|  |  |  |
|---|---|---|
|  | Pretérito pluscuamperfecto | Yo **hubiera** o **hubiese** comido<br>Tú **hubieras** o **hubieses** comido<br>Él, ella, usted **hubiera** o **hubiese** comido<br>Nosotros/as **hubiéramos** o **hubiésemos** comido<br>Vosotros/as **hubierais** o **hubieseis** comido<br>Ellos, ellas, ustedes **hubieran** o **hubiesen** comido |
|  | Futuro compuesto | Yo **hubiere** comido<br>Tú **hubieres** comido<br>Él, ella, usted **hubiere** comido<br>Nosotros/as **hubiéremos** comido<br>Vosotros/as **hubiereis** comido<br>Ellos, ellas, ustedes **hubieren** comido |
| Imperativo | Presente | Tú com**e**<br>Vosotros com**ed** |

To really understand the verbal paradigm, let's see some examples of the verb *comer* conjugated:

- **Pretérito perfecto compuesto del modo indicativo**

    *Creo que **hemos comido** mucho, ¿no?* ("I think we've eaten too much, haven't we?")

- **Pretérito pluscuamperfecto del modo indicativo**

    *¿Te **habías comido** toda tu cena?* ("Had you eaten all your dinner?")

- **Pretérito imperfecto del modo subjuntivo**

    *Ojalá **comiéramos** mejor en la escuela.* ("I wish we ate

better at school")

- **Presente simple del subjuntivo**

  *Quiero que **coman** toda su comida antes de levantarse de la mesa.* ("I want you to eat all your food before you leave the table")

- **Imperativo**

  *¡No **comas** eso, se cayó al piso!* ("Don't eat that, it fell on the floor!")

## Other Verbs of the Second Conjugation

Now that we know the verbal paradigm of the second conjugation, let's see some other verbs in action!

1. *Barrer*

   - *Qué bien, ya han barrido todo* ("Good, they've already swept everything.")
   - *Nosotros barreremos mañana* ("We'll sweep tomorrow.")
   - *¿Barristeis el patio?* ("Did you sweep the yard?")

2. *Beber*

   - *No bebéis todo el agua que deberíais* ("You don't drink as much water as you should.")
   - *Volveremos en taxi, porque, para el final de la fiesta, habremos bebido mucho* ("We'll take a cab back, because by the end of the party, we will have drunk too much.")
   - *Los niños beberán chocolatada* ("The children will drink chocolate milk.")

3. *Arder*

   - *¡Arderán en el infierno!* ("They will burn in hell!")
   - *Ojalá no me arda el esófago cuando añadan el alcohol* ("I hope my esophagus doesn't burn when they add the alcohol.")
   - *¿Te ardía mucho la herida?* ("Did your wound burn a lot?")

4. *Coser*

- *Hoy he cosido mis propios botones* ("Today I sewed my own buttons.")
- *Mi abuela cosía cortinas en su trabajo* ("My grandmother sewed curtains at work.")
- *Saldrá cuando le hayan cosido la herida* ("She'll come out when she's had her wound stitched.")

5. *Correr*

- *Mi perro corrió más rápido que el tuyo* ("My dog ran faster than yours.")
- *¡Qué sudado está! Quizás haya corrido hasta aquí* ("How sweaty he is! Maybe he's run all the way up here.")
- *José, te dije que no corras* ("José, I told you not to run.")

6. *Vender*

- *¿Ya habéis vendido todo?* ("Have you sold everything?")
- *Si no vienes a buscarlas antes del martes, venderé todas tus cosas* ("If you don't come to get them by Tuesday, I'll sell all your stuff.")
- *Ojalá me vendan la muñeca, la estoy buscando hace años* ("I hope they sell me the doll, I've spent years looking for it.")

7. *Romper*

- *Fue él quien rompió tu computadora* ("It was him who broke your computer.")
- *Ojalá los perros se porten bien y no rompan nada* ("I hope the dogs behave and don't break anything.")
- *No lo haré, me rompería una pierna* ("I won't do it, I would break a leg.")

You may have noticed that, in the examples, we haven't included all the verb tenses of the paradigm. That's because there are some tenses that we hardly use in current Spanish, such as *pretérito anterior del indicativo, futuro simple del subjuntivo*, or *futuro compuesto del subjuntivo*. However, it's still important to know how to use them and recognize them; that's why we include the complete table of the verbal paradigm.

## Exercises

1. Go back to the short story at the beginning of the chapter and write down all the verbs that belong to the second conjugation.
2. Complete the following table with these five verbs from the story.

| Verbo | Tiempo | Modo | Persona | Número |
|---|---|---|---|---|
| *Sucede* | | | | |
| *Puedes* | | | | |
| *Cometí* | | | | |
| *Apareció* | | | | |
| *He perdido* | | | | |

3. Rewrite the following sentences using one of these verbs properly conjugated, keeping the original meaning: *aprender, esconder, comprender, retroceder.*
    a. El camión fue hacia atrás rápidamente.
    b. Los niños se habían ocultado tras la puerta.
    c. Ojalá no estudiemos geometría en la escuela.
    d. Nunca entenderé los motivos de su renuncia.
4. Complete the following sentences conjugating the verbs in brackets in the specified tense.
    a. Juana le _____ (deber, pretérito imperfecto del indicativo) dinero a su madre.
    b. Mi familia _____ (poseer, presente del indicativo) muchas propiedades.

    c. Te _____ (responder, futuro simple del indicativo) cuando lo sepa.

    d. ¡_____ (correr, imperativo)! ¡Vienen por ti!

5. Think of an alternative ending to the short story and write it using only verbs of the second conjugation.

# Chapter 5: Third Conjugation (-ir)

## Short Story: La escuela de salsa

—Es aquí —dijo Marisol, y se detuvo frente a la puerta de una casa **antiquísima**.

—¿Segura? —preguntó José, sin mucha convicción.

—Sí, por el mensaje que me escribió Sandra —explicó Marisol, sacudiendo el papel **arrugado** que **aferraba** entre sus dedos—. «Una puerta de madera verde, entre la **pescadería** y la **panadería**, justo enfrente del **malecón**».

José respiró hondo. «Es verdad», pensó. «Lo que Sandra describió encaja con este lugar». Dio tres golpes a la puerta. Esperaron un minuto, dos, tres. Nadie los recibió.

—¿De verdad crees que él vive aquí, Marisol? —preguntó José finalmente—. Este lugar está abandonado. ¿Por qué no volvemos al hotel? Seguramente...

—¡Tiene que ser aquí! —interrumpió Marisol, enfadada—. Mi amiga Sandra me lo dijo. Me dijo: «Es la mejor escuela de salsa de todo el Caribe». Me encantaría aprender a bailar salsa, ¿y qué mejor que compartir las clases con mi hermanito? ¡Vamos, cúmpleme este **capricho**!

—¡Pero si aquí no hay nadie! —dijo José—. Sandra debe haberse equivocado. No es posible que haya ninguna escuela de salsa tras esta puerta. ¡Y mucho menos que funcione **a estas horas** de la noche! —añadió.

Marisol resopló. José tenía razón. Aquello era **una pérdida de tiempo. Dieron media vuelta**, dispuestos a marcharse. Entonces, escucharon la puerta crujir al abrirse. Marisol y José **voltearon**. Había un hombrecito de pie. Probablemente, no **medía** más de un metro cincuenta.

—¿Los puedo ayudar? —preguntó, con un marcado acento de Cartagena.

—Buenas noches, señor —dijo José—. Nos queremos unir a la Escuela Nocturna de Salsa... pero creo que nos hemos **confundido**.

—No, no se han confundido —respondió el hombrecito—. Mi nombre es Julio Salinas, y soy uno de los mejores instructores de salsa del Caribe. Bueno, eso es lo que dicen de mí.

—Entonces ¿es verdad? —preguntó Marisol, entusiasmada—. ¿Usted puede enseñarnos a bailar salsa?

Julio Salinas sonrió y respondió:

—La salsa no se aprende ni se enseña: la salsa se vive. Pero ya habrá tiempo para eso. ¡Bienvenidos!

## Vocabulary List

| Español | Inglés |
|---|---|
| antiquísimo, antiquísima | ancient |
| arrugado, arrugada | crumpled |
| aferrar | to cling to |
| la pescadería | fish market |
| la panadería | bakery |

| el malecón | boardwalk |
|---|---|
| el capricho | whim |
| a estas horas | this late |
| una pérdida de tiempo | a waste of time |
| dar media vuelta | to turn around |
| voltear | to turn around |
| crujir | to creak |
| medir | to be (plus height) |

**Reading Comprehension**

Are you ready for some reading comprehension questions? Let's see how much you understood!

1. ¿Cuáles son las referencias para encontrar la escuela de salsa?
2. ¿Quién le habló a Marisol acerca de la escuela de salsa?
3. ¿Por qué José quería regresar al hotel?
4. ¿Qué es lo que dicen acerca de Julio Salinas?

## Grammar Section

We've already seen the regular verbs of the first and second conjugations. So, as you might have guessed, in this chapter, we'll talk about the third conjugation; that is, the verbs ending in *-ir*.

**Third Conjugation**

The model verb of the third conjugation for regular verbs is *partir* ("to leave"). Next, we are going to see a table with all the possible conjugations of that verb. But first, let's review why it's useful to have these verbal paradigms.

As we said before, when we conjugate regular verbs, we follow a pattern, and that pattern is given by the ending of the verb (*-ar, -er, -ir*). Therefore, to conjugate any regular verb of the third conjugation, we have to keep the stem (the part before the *-ir* ending), and only change the ending in the same way as *partir* does.

Regarding the non-personal forms of the verbs of the third conjugation, to create the participle, we just have to add *-ido* to the stem. For example, the participle of the verb *vivir* ("to live") is *vivido*. If, on the other hand, we need the gerund, then we have to add *-iendo* to the stem. For example, *viviendo* is the gerund of *vivir*.

Now . . . yes! We are ready to take a look at the verbal paradigm of the third conjugation.

Partir

| Modo | Tiempo | Conjugación |
| --- | --- | --- |
| Indicativo | Presente | Yo part**o** <br> Tú part**es** <br> Él, ella, usted part**e** <br> Nosotros/as part**imos** <br> Vosotros/as part**ís** <br> Ellos, ellas, ustedes part**en** |
| | Pretérito perfecto simple | Yo part**í** <br> Tú part**iste** <br> Él, ella, usted part**ió** <br> Nosotros/as part**imos** <br> Vosotros/as part**isteis** <br> Ellos, ellas, ustedes part**ieron** |

| | | |
|---|---|---|
| | Pretérito imperfecto | Yo part**ía**<br>Tú part**ías**<br>Él, ella, usted part**ía**<br>Nosotros/as part**íamos**<br>Vosotros/as part**íais**<br>Ellos, ellas, ustedes part**ían** |
| | Futuro simple | Yo part**iré**<br>Tú part**irás**<br>Él, ella, usted part**irá**<br>Nosotros/as part**iremos**<br>Vosotros/as part**iréis**<br>Ellos, ellas, ustedes part**irán** |
| | Condicional simple | Yo part**iría**<br>Tú part**irías**<br>Él, ella, usted part**iría**<br>Nosotros/as part**iríamos**<br>Vosotros/as part**iríais**<br>Ellos, ellas, ustedes part**irían** |
| | Pretérito perfecto compuesto | Yo **he** partido<br>Tú **has** partido<br>Él, ella, usted **ha** partido<br>Nosotros/as **hemos** partido<br>Vosotros/as **habéis** partido<br>Ellos, ellas, ustedes **han** partido |

| | | |
|---|---|---|
| | Pretérito anterior | Yo **hube** partido<br>Tú **hubiste** partido<br>Él, ella, usted **hubo** partido<br>Nosotros/as **hubimos** partido<br>Vosotros/as **hubisteis** partido<br>Ellos, ellas, ustedes **hubieron** partido |
| | Pretérito pluscuamperfecto | Yo **había** partido<br>Tú **habías** partido<br>Él, ella, usted **había** partido<br>Nosotros/as **habíamos** partido<br>Vosotros/as **habíais** partido<br>Ellos, ellas, ustedes **habían** partido |
| | Condicional compuesto | Yo **habría** partido<br>Tú **habrías** partido<br>Él, ella, usted **habría** partido<br>Nosotros/as **habríamos** partido<br>Vosotros/as **habríais** partido<br>Ellos, ellas, ustedes **habrían** partido |
| | Futuro compuesto | Yo **habré** partido<br>Tú **habrás** partido<br>Él, ella, usted **habrá** partido<br>Nosotros/as **habremos** partido<br>Vosotros/as **habréis** partido<br>Ellos, ellas, ustedes **habrán** partido |

| | | |
|---|---|---|
| Subjuntivo | Presente | Yo part**a**<br>Tú part**as**<br>Él, ella, usted part**a**<br>Nosotros/as part**amos**<br>Vosotros/as part**áis**<br>Ellos, ellas, ustedes part**an** |
| | Pretérito imperfecto | Yo part**iera** o part**iese**<br>Tú part**ieras** o part**ieses**<br>Él, ella, usted part**iera** o part**iese**<br>Nosotros/as part**iéramos** o part**iésemos**<br>Vosotros/as part**ieras** o part**ieseis**<br>Ellos, ellas, ustedes part**ieran** o part**iesen** |
| | Futuro simple | Yo part**iere**<br>Tú part**ieres**<br>Él, ella, usted part**iere**<br>Nosotros/as part**iéremos**<br>Vosotros/as part**iereis**<br>Ellos, ellas, ustedes part**ieren** |
| | Pretérito perfecto compuesto | Yo **haya** partido<br>Tú **hayas** partido<br>Él, ella, usted **haya** partido<br>Nosotros/as **hayamos** partido<br>Vosotros/as **hayáis** partido<br>Ellos, ellas, ustedes **hayan** partido |

| | | |
|---|---|---|
| | Pretérito pluscuamperfecto | Yo **hubiera** o **hubiese** partido<br>Tú **hubieras** o **hubieses** partido<br>Él, ella, usted **hubiera** o **hubiese** partido<br>Nosotros/as **hubiéramos** o **hubiésemos** partido<br>Vosotros/as **hubierais** o **hubieseis** partido<br>Ellos, ellas, ustedes **hubieran** o **hubiesen** partido |
| | Futuro compuesto | Yo **hubiere** partido<br>Tú **hubieres** partido<br>Él, ella, usted **hubiere** partido<br>Nosotros/as **hubiéremos** partido<br>Vosotros/as **hubiereis** partido<br>Ellos, ellas, ustedes **hubieren** partido |
| Imperativo | Presente | Tú par**te**<br>Vosotros part**id** |

Now, let's see some example sentences with the verb *partir*.

- **Presente de indicativo:**
  *Martín **parte** a Madrid en tren* ("Martín leaves for Madrid by train.")
- **Futuro simple de indicativo:**
  *Gabriel **partirá** a Perú esta noche* ("Gabriel will leave for Perú tonight.")
- **Pretérito perfecto simple de indicativo:**
  *Ese vuelo **partió** a las once* ("That flight left at eleven o'clock.")
- **Pretérito pluscuamperfecto de subjuntivo:**
  Si ***hubieseis partido*** *más temprano, habríais llegado*

*antes* ("If you had left earlier, you would have arrived sooner.")

- **Imperativo**:
  *¡Partid esta noche y llegaréis a tiempo!* ("Leave tonight and you'll be on time!")

### Other Verbs of the Third Conjugation

Next, we are going to see a list of other regular verbs in Spanish that end in *-ir* (you can use the table above to conjugate them.) We are also going to see some example sentences with each of them.

1. *Abrir*
   - *Gastón abrió su corazón y me contó todo* ("Gastón opened his heart and told me everything.")
   - *El supermercado abre de nueve de la mañana a seis de la tarde* ("The supermarket is open from nine in the morning to six in the evening.")
   - *¡Abre la puerta, por favor!* ("Open the door, please!")

2. *Compartir*
   - *Ulises es un niño que siempre comparte sus juguetes* ("Ulises is a boy who always shares his toys.")
   - *Gracias por haber compartido tu punto de vista* ("Thanks for sharing your point of view.")
   - *Te comparto una canción* ("I'll share a song with you.")

3. *Cumplir*
   - *Fernanda cumplió años en octubre* ("Fernanda had her birthday in October.")
   - *Marcos cumplirá con su palabra* ("Marcos will keep his word.")
   - *Habéis cumplido con vuestro deber* ("You have done your duty.")

4. *Decidir*
   - *Decidí que voy a hacer más ejercicio* ("I decided that I'm going to exercise more.")

- *¿Ya has decidido qué te vas a poner para la fiesta?* ("Have you already decided what you are going to wear to the party?")
- *No sé qué podemos comer. Decide tú* ("I don't know what we can eat. You decide.")

5. *Escribir*

- *Esa autora escribió varios libros románticos* ("That author wrote several romantic books.")
- *¿Habéis escrito vuestros votos matrimoniales?* ("Have you written your wedding vows?")
- *Esta noche le escribiré a mi tío* ("Tonight I will write to my uncle.")

6. *Recibir*

- *Mis primos del norte siempre me reciben muy bien* ("My northern cousins always welcome me very nicely.")
- *He recibido un paquete esta mañana* ("I have received a package this morning.")
- *Recibiréis una sorpresa pronto* ("You will receive a surprise soon.")

7. *Vivir*

- *Sandra vivió muchos años en Caracas, Venezuela* ("Sandra lived for many years in Caracas, Venezuela.")
- *Viviré en Colombia durante el año que viene* ("I will live in Colombia next year.")
- *¿Vivirías en este pueblo?* ("Would you live in this town?")

## Exercises

1. Go back to the short story at the beginning of the chapter and write down all the verbs that belong to the third conjugation.

2. Take a look at the following verbs in the infinitive. Find them in the short story and determine in which mood and tense they are conjugated: *escribir, describir, recibir, vivir, compartir, cumplir, abrir, confundir*.

3. Below, you will find three short texts. Fill in the blanks with the verbs in brackets conjugated in the correct tense.

   a. Venid a mi casa. Os _____ (recibir) sin problema. Tengo algunas camas extra, así que _____ (decidir) vosotros mismos dónde dormiréis.

   b. Yo _____ (vivir) muchos años en Madrid. Al principio vivía con mi novia, pero luego me he separado. Desde entonces, _____ (compartir) piso con compañeros de la universidad.

   b. Si yo _____ (escribir) el guion de una película, sería sobre vaqueros.

4. Match the verbs in the left column with their corresponding tenses.

   a. Viviréis                  1. Pretérito perfecto compuesto de subjuntivo
   b. Recibiera                 2. Futuro simple de indicativo
   c. Hayamos escrito           3. Pretérito perfecto simple
   d. Partisteis de indicativo  4. Pretérito imperfecto de subjuntivo

5. Complete the following table with the correct conjugations of the verb *insistir*.

| Pretérito perfecto simple de indicativo | tú | insististe |
|---|---|---|
| Condicional simple de indicativo | vosotros | |
| Futuro compuesto de indicativo | nosotros | |
| Presente de subjuntivo | ella | |
| Pretérito pluscuamperfecto | ustedes | |

# Chapter 6:
# Irregular Conjugations

### Short Story: Día de los Muertos

—¿De verdad tengo que ir contigo a la fiesta? —quiso saber Paula, mientras le acomodaba la **corbata** a Damián.

—Sí, de verdad —dijo Damián—. Para mí es importante que estés.

—¡Pero no conozco a nadie! —se quejó Paula—. Además, **aborrezco** las **calaveritas** de azúcar, la gente pintada y todo lo vinculado a esta fiesta.

—Vamos un rato y si quieres te vuelves, ¿sí? Me mantendré todo el tiempo a tu lado.

Cuando llegaron a la fiesta, fueron interceptados por una señora que les dio un **chupito** de tequila y quiso pintarles la cara. Cuando la señora terminó, Paula se vio en el **espejo** y su malhumor comenzó a crecer.

Damián le dijo que lo esperara allí y fue a buscar unas cervezas. Paula se dio cuenta de que había dejado sus lentes en la mesa de la señora que le había pintado la cara. Intentó recuperarlos, pero cuando llegó ya no estaban. La señora le **guiñó un ojo**, alegre.

—¡Estoy buscando mis lentes! —gritaba Paula, por encima de la música.

—¡Sí, hay que usar **repelente**! —le respondía la señora, que evidentemente no la oía.

Paula buscó con la mirada a Damián, pero sin sus lentes no podía reconocer nada. Empezó a moverse **a tientas** entre la gente para ver si lo encontraba. Dentro de la casa hacía mucho calor, el piso estaba **pegajoso** y las personas **sudadas**. Todo le **daba asco** y su malhumor era cada vez más grande.

Logró salir al jardín, que estaba tan lleno de gente como de altares. Mientras caminaba buscando a Damián, empezó a sentir un calor en la rodilla. Siguió moviéndose, para poder salir del **amontonamiento** y respirar un poco, hasta que se dio cuenta de dónde venía el calor: ¡su falda se había encendido con la vela de un altar y se estaba prendiendo fuego!

Paula empezó a correr hasta que llegó a la **alberca** y, sin pensarlo dos veces, se tiró dentro. El agua estaba helada, pero eso era justo lo que necesitaba. No solo para apagar el fuego de su falda (que ahora estaba arruinada), sino para calmar su malhumor.

Empezó a reír sola, metida en el agua, cuando apareció Damián, con sus lentes en la mano.

—Veo que no la estás pasando tan mal.

—¡Solo un poco! —gritó Paula, divertida.

—Ya podemos irnos —le dijo Damián, mientras la ayudaba a salir del agua.

—Gracias a Dios —respondió **aliviada** Paula—. ¡Es la última vez que te acompaño a una fiesta!

# Vocabulary List

| Español | Inglés |
|---|---|
| la corbata | tie |
| aborrecer | to detest |
| las calaveritas | little skulls |
| los chupitos | shots |
| el espejo | mirror |
| guiñar un ojo | to wink |
| el repelente | repeller |
| a tientas | blindly |
| pegajoso | sticky |
| sudada, sudado | sweaty |
| dar asco | to disgust |
| amontonamiento | crowding |
| alberca | pool |
| aliviada | relieved |

**Reading Comprehension**

Damián was very confused by the end of the party... How about you? Did you understand what happened to Paula?

1. ¿Por qué no quería ir Paula a la fiesta?
2. ¿Qué beben al llegar?
3. ¿Qué pierde Paula durante la fiesta?
4. ¿Dónde encuentra Damián a Paula?

## Grammar Section

As we've seen in previous chapters, to conjugate regular verbs, we need to follow a pattern that depends on their ending. So, to master them, we only need to study the paradigm of each conjugation. Irregular verbs are a bit trickier: because they present variations. These irregularities can appear in the stem of the verb, in the ending, or in both! However, there's no need to worry. By the end of this chapter, you'll be an expert in irregular verbs, and you'll be able to:

- understand the various irregularities
- conjugate irregular verbs

Are you ready? Let's get to it!

As an intermediate student of Spanish who wants to become an advanced one, you probably know a hing or two about irregular verbs; for example, that English verbs also have irregularities. In English, to express the different variations of tense or person, we add -ing, -s, -es, -d, or -ed to regular verbs. Thus, "talk" becomes "talk**ed**," "talk**ing**," and "talk**s**." Irregular verbs, on the other hand, do not follow these rules, like "teach," that becomes "taught" in the past tense, or "fly" that becomes "flew." Also, you probably know that, just as in English, the only way to know and master Spanish irregularities is by studying them and practicing a lot.

### False Irregularities

There are some verbs that change - but only for phonetic reasons. These verbs look like they are irregular, but, in fact, only some letters change for sound or spelling reasons. For example, the verb *llegar* ("to arrive"):

- *Llegué tarde al teatro y no me dejaron entrar* ("I was late for the theater and they didn't let me in.") In this case, the verb follows the pattern for verbs of the first conjugation. However, we need to add a "u" because in Spanish, there must be a silent "u" between a "g" and an "e" to maintain the soft pronunciation of the "g."

The same happens with the verb *surgir* ("to emerge"):

- *Es una obra de teatro muy extraña, en un momento muero y luego surjo de mis cenizas como un ave fénix* ("The play is quite strange, at some point I die and then I emerge from my ashes like a phoenix.") In this case, we need to change the "g" for a "j" to keep the strong "g" sound we have in "surgir."

Let's see some of the most common orthographic changes with a few examples:

| | | |
|---|---|---|
| Verbs ending in -*gar*: *entregar* | *entregué* | In these three cases, something similar happens. We have to pay attention to the sound of the "g" and the "j" to maintain either the soft or the strong pronunciation of the infinitive in each conjugation. If it's strong, we use -*ja*, -*ge*, -*gi*, -*jo*, and -*ju*. And if it's soft, we use -*ga*, -*gue*, -*gui*, -*go*, and -*gu*. |
| Verbs ending in -*ger* or -*gir*: *elegir, coger* | *elijo, cojo* | |
| Verbs ending in -*guir*: *seguir* | *sigo* | |

| Verbs ending in -car: *pescar* | *pesqué* | With these verbs, we change the "c" for "q + u" to keep the strong sound in front of an "e" or an "i." |
|---|---|---|
| Verbs ending in -cer: *vencer* | *venzo* | Here we need to keep the soft pronunciation of "c." So, we change it to a "z" in front of "o," "a," and "u." |

These are what we call "false irregularities" because we only make orthographic changes for phonetic reasons. Now we'll see the real irregularities.

## Categories of Irregular Verbs

Irregular verbs can be classified into series or groups of tenses. This means that when a verb is irregular in one tense of the group, it will also be irregular in the others. The series or groups are:

- **Irregularity of the present:** these verbs are irregular in the present of the indicative, the subjunctive, and the imperative moods. For example:

| Infinitivo | Presente del indicativo | Presente del subjuntivo | Presente del imperativo |
|---|---|---|---|
| volver | vuelvo | vuelva | vuelve |

- **Irregularity of the past:** these verbs are irregular in the past perfect simple of the indicative mood, in the past imperfect of the subjunctive mood, and in the future imperfect of the subjunctive mood (yes, there's a future tense included in this group and we have to deal with it).

For example:

| Infinitivo | Pretérito perfecto simple del indicativo | Pretérito imperfecto del subjuntivo | Futuro imperfecto del subjuntivo |
|---|---|---|---|
| pedir | pidió | pidiera o pidiese | pidiere |

- **Irregularity of the future:** these verbs are irregular in the future, and in the conditional simple of the indicative. For example:

| Infinitivo | Futuro del indicativo | Condicional simple del indicativo |
|---|---|---|
| saber | sabré | sabría |

Verbs can be irregular in one series or in more than one. This means that there are verbs that are not irregular in all of their conjugations but only in some of them.

## Common Variations

Irregular verbs can change in the stem or in the ending, or they can change completely. We'll start with the verbs that present changes in the stem, which are divided into three types:

- In this group, we have the verbs that go from one vowel to two vowels. This is known as "diphthongization." Let's see a few examples:

| Infinitivo | Primera persona singular del presente del modo indicativo |
|---|---|
| poder | puedo |
| sentir | siento |

- In this second group, we change one vowel for another vowel. The most common changes are replacing an "e" with an "i," or an "o" with a "u." For example:

| Infinitivo | Tercera persona singular del pretérito perfecto simple del modo indicativo |
|---|---|
| pedir | pidió |
| dormir | durmió |

- Finally, we have to add a consonant to some verbs. For example:

| Infinitivo | Primera persona singular del futuro simple del modo indicativo |
|---|---|
| saber | sabré |
| salir | sal**d**ré |

### Particular Cases

Would it make sense to learn every irregular Spanish verb by heart? Not really! And, even if it made sense, it wouldn't be possible. Not even native speakers know them all; but don't worry, we can start by studying the basics. These are the most common irregular verbs in Spanish, together with their conjugations.

**Ser**

| Modo | Tiempo | Conjugación |
|---|---|---|
| Indicativo | Presente | Yo soy<br>Tú eres<br>Él, ella, usted es<br>Nosotros/as somos<br>Vosotros/as sois<br>Ellos, ellas, ustedes son |
| | Pretérito perfecto simple | Yo fui<br>Tú fuiste<br>Él, ella, usted fue<br>Nosotros/as fuimos<br>Vosotros/as fuisteis<br>Ellos, ellas, ustedes fueron |
| | Pretérito imperfecto | Yo era<br>Tú eras<br>Él, ella, usted era<br>Nosotros/as éramos<br>Vosotros/as erais<br>Ellos, ellas, ustedes eran |
| Subjuntivo | Presente | Yo sea<br>Tú seas<br>Él, ella, usted sea<br>Nosotros/as seamos<br>Vosotros/as seáis<br>Ellos, ellas, ustedes sean |

|  |  |  |
|---|---|---|
| | Pretérito imperfecto | Yo fuera o fuese<br>Tú fueras o fueses<br>Él, ella, usted fuera o fuese<br>Nosotros/as fuéramos o fuésemos<br>Vosotros/as fuerais o fueseis<br>Ellos, ellas, ustedes fueran o fuesen |
| | Futuro simple | Yo fuere<br>Tú fueres<br>Él, ella, usted fuere<br>Nosotros/as fuéremos<br>Vosotros/as fuereis<br>Ellos, ellas, ustedes fueren |
| Imperativo | Presente | Tú sé<br>Vosotros sean |

*Estar* (to "be")

| Modo | Tiempo | Conjugación |
|---|---|---|
| Indicativo | Presente | Yo estoy<br>Tú estás<br>Él, ella, usted está<br>Nosotros/as estamos<br>Vosotros/as estáis<br>Ellos, ellas, ustedes están |

|  |  |  |
|---|---|---|
|  | Pretérito perfecto simple | Yo estuve<br>Tú estuviste<br>Él, ella, usted estuvo<br>Nosotros/as estuvimos<br>Vosotros/as estuvisteis<br>Ellos, ellas, ustedes estuvieron |
| Subjuntivo | Presente | Yo esté<br>Tú estés<br>Él, ella, usted esté<br>Nosotros/as estemos<br>Vosotros/as estéis<br>Ellos, ellas, ustedes estén |
| Subjuntivo | Pretérito imperfecto | Yo estuviera o estuviese<br>Tú estuvieras o estuvieses<br>Él, ella, usted estuviera o estuviese<br>Nosotros/as estuviéramos o estuviésemos<br>Vosotros/as estuvierais o estuvieseis<br>Ellos, ellas, ustedes estuvieran o estuviesen |
| Subjuntivo | Futuro simple | Yo estuviere<br>Tú estuvieres<br>Él, ella, usted estuviere<br>Nosotros/as estuviéremos<br>Vosotros/as estuviereis<br>Ellos, ellas, ustedes estuvieren |

| Imperativo | Presente | Tú estés<br>Vosotros estad |

## Ir

| Modo | Tiempo | Conjugación |
|---|---|---|
| Indicativo | Presente | Yo voy<br>Tú vas<br>Él, ella, usted va<br>Nosotros/as vamos<br>Vosotros/as vais<br>Ellos, ellas, ustedes van |
| | Pretérito perfecto simple | Yo fui<br>Tú fuiste<br>Él, ella, usted fue<br>Nosotros/as fuimos<br>Vosotros/as fuisteis<br>Ellos, ellas, ustedes fueron |
| | Pretérito imperfecto | Yo iba<br>Tú ibas<br>Él, ella, usted iba<br>Nosotros/as íbamos<br>Vosotros/as ibais<br>Ellos, ellas, ustedes iban |

| | | |
|---|---|---|
| Subjuntivo | Presente | Yo vaya<br>Tú vayas<br>Él, ella, usted vaya<br>Nosotros/as vayamos<br>Vosotros/as vayáis<br>Ellos, ellas, ustedes vayan |
| | Pretérito imperfecto | Yo fuera o fuese<br>Tú fueras o fueses<br>Él, ella, usted fuera o fuese<br>Nosotros/as fuéramos o fuésemos<br>Vosotros/as fuerais o fueseis<br>Ellos, ellas, ustedes fueran o fuesen |
| | Futuro simple | Yo fuere<br>Tú fueres<br>Él, ella, usted fuere<br>Nosotros/as fuéremos<br>Vosotros/as fuereis<br>Ellos, ellas, ustedes fueren |
| Imperativo | Presente | Tú ve<br>Vosotros id |

**Haber**

| Modo | Tiempo | Conjugación |
|---|---|---|
| Indicativo | Presente | Yo he<br>Tú has<br>Él, ella, usted ha<br>Nosotros/as hemos<br>Vosotros/as habéis<br>Ellos, ellas, ustedes han |
| | Pretérito perfecto simple | Yo hube<br>Tú hubiste<br>Él, ella, usted hubo<br>Nosotros/as hubimos<br>Vosotros/as hubisteis<br>Ellos, ellas, ustedes hubieron |
| | Futuro simple | Yo habré<br>Tú habrás<br>Él, ella, usted habrá<br>Nosotros/as habremos<br>Vosotros/as habréis<br>Ellos, ellas, ustedes habrán |
| | Condicional simple | Yo habría<br>Tú habrías<br>Él, ella, usted habría<br>Nosotros/as habríamos<br>Vosotros/as habríais<br>Ellos, ellas, ustedes habrían |

|  |  |  |
|---|---|---|
| Subjuntivo | Presente | Yo haya<br>Tú hayas<br>Él, ella, usted haya<br>Nosotros/as hayamos<br>Vosotros/as hayáis<br>Ellos, ellas, ustedes hayan |
| | Pretérito imperfecto | Yo hubiera o hubiese<br>Tú hubieras o hubieses<br>Él, ella, usted hubiera o hubiese<br>Nosotros/as hubiéramos o hubiésemos<br>Vosotros/as hubierais o hubieseis<br>Ellos, ellas, ustedes hubieran o hubiesen |
| | Futuro simple | Yo hubiere<br>Tú hubieres<br>Él, ella, usted hubiere<br>Nosotros/as hubiéremos<br>Vosotros/as hubiereis<br>Ellos, ellas, ustedes hubieren |
| Imperativo | Presente | Usted haya |

## Tener

| Modo | Tiempo | Conjugación |
|---|---|---|
| Indicativo | Presente | Yo tengo<br>Tú tienes<br>Él, ella, usted tiene<br>Nosotros/as tenemos<br>Vosotros/as tenéis<br>Ellos, ellas, ustedes tienen |
| | Pretérito perfecto simple | Yo tuve<br>Tú tuviste<br>Él, ella, usted tuvo<br>Nosotros/as tuvimos<br>Vosotros/as tuvisteis<br>Ellos, ellas, ustedes tuvieron |
| | Futuro simple | Yo tendré<br>Tú tendrás<br>Él, ella, usted tendrá<br>Nosotros/as tendremos<br>Vosotros/as tendréis<br>Ellos, ellas, ustedes tendrán |
| | Condicional simple | Yo tendría<br>Tú tendrías<br>Él, ella, usted tendría<br>Nosotros/as tendríamos<br>Vosotros/as tendríais<br>Ellos, ellas, ustedes tendrían |

| | | |
|---|---|---|
| Subjuntivo | Presente | Yo tenga<br>Tú tengas<br>Él, ella, usted tenga<br>Nosotros/as tengamos<br>Vosotros/as tengáis<br>Ellos, ellas, ustedes tengan |
| | Pretérito imperfecto | Yo tuviera o tuviese<br>Tú tuvieras o tuvieses<br>Él, ella, usted tuviera o tuviese<br>Nosotros/as tuviéramos o tuviésemos<br>Vosotros/as tuvierais o tuvieseis<br>Ellos, ellas, ustedes tuvieran o tuviesen |
| | Futuro simple | Yo tuviere<br>Tú tuvieres<br>Él, ella, usted tuviere<br>Nosotros/as tuviéremos<br>Vosotros/as tuviereis<br>Ellos, ellas, ustedes tuvieren |
| Imperativo | Presente | Tú ten |

Saber

| Modo | Tiempo | Conjugación |
|---|---|---|
| Indicativo | Presente | Yo sé<br>Tú sabes<br>Él, ella, usted sabe<br>Nosotros/as sabemos<br>Vosotros/as sabéis<br>Ellos, ellas, ustedes saben |
| | Pretérito perfecto simple | Yo supe<br>Tú supiste<br>Él, ella, usted supo<br>Nosotros/as supimos<br>Vosotros/as supisteis<br>Ellos, ellas, ustedes supieron |
| | Futuro simple | Yo sabré<br>Tú sabrás<br>Él, ella, usted sabrá<br>Nosotros/as sabremos<br>Vosotros/as sabréis<br>Ellos, ellas, ustedes sabrán |
| | Condicional simple | Yo sabría<br>Tú sabrías<br>Él, ella, usted sabría<br>Nosotros/as sabríamos<br>Vosotros/as sabríais<br>Ellos, ellas, ustedes sabrían |

|  |  |  |
|---|---|---|
| Subjuntivo | Presente | Yo sepa<br>Tú sepas<br>Él, ella, usted sepa<br>Nosotros/as sepamos<br>Vosotros/as sepáis<br>Ellos, ellas, ustedes sepan |
| | Pretérito imperfecto | Yo supiera o supiese<br>Tú supieras o supieses<br>Él, ella, usted supiera o supiese<br>Nosotros/as supiéramos o supiésemos<br>Vosotros/as supierais o supieseis<br>Ellos, ellas, ustedes supieran o supiesen |
| | Futuro simple | Yo supiere<br>Tú supieres<br>Él, ella, usted supiere<br>Nosotros/as supiéremos<br>Vosotros/as supiereis<br>Ellos, ellas, ustedes supieren |
| Imperativo | Presente | Usted sepa |

**Dar**

| Modo | Tiempo | Conjugación |
|---|---|---|
| Indicativo | Presente | Yo doy<br>Tú das<br>Él, ella, usted da<br>Nosotros/as damos<br>Vosotros/as dais<br>Ellos, ellas, ustedes dan |
| | Pretérito perfecto simple | Yo di<br>Tú diste<br>Él, ella, usted dio<br>Nosotros/as dimos<br>Vosotros/as disteis<br>Ellos, ellas, ustedes dieron |
| Subjuntivo | Presente | Yo dé<br>Tú des<br>Él, ella, usted dé<br>Nosotros/as demos<br>Vosotros/as deis<br>Ellos, ellas, ustedes den |
| | Pretérito imperfecto | Yo diera o diese<br>Tú dieras o dieses<br>Él, ella, usted diera o diese<br>Nosotros/as diéramos o diésemos<br>Vosotros/as dierais o dieseis<br>Ellos, ellas, ustedes dieran o diesen |

|  | Futuro simple | Yo diere<br>Tú dieres<br>Él, ella, usted diere<br>Nosotros/as diéremos<br>Vosotros/as diereis<br>Ellos, ellas, ustedes dieren |
|---|---|---|
| Imperativo | Presente | Usted dé |

## Hacer

| Modo | Tiempo | Conjugación |
|---|---|---|
| Indicativo | Presente | Yo hago<br>Tú haces<br>Él, ella, usted hace<br>Nosotros/as hacemos<br>Vosotros/as hacéis<br>Ellos, ellas, ustedes hacen |
| | Pretérito perfecto simple | Yo hice<br>Tú hiciste<br>Él, ella, usted hizo<br>Nosotros/as hicimos<br>Vosotros/as hicisteis<br>Ellos, ellas, ustedes hicieron |
| | Futuro simple | Yo haré<br>Tú harás<br>Él, ella, usted hará<br>Nosotros/as haremos<br>Vosotros/as haréis<br>Ellos, ellas, ustedes harán |

| | | |
|---|---|---|
| | Condicional simple | Yo haría<br>Tú harías<br>Él, ella, usted haría<br>Nosotros/as haríamos<br>Vosotros/as haríais<br>Ellos, ellas, ustedes harían |
| | Pretérito perfecto compuesto | Yo he hecho<br>Tú has hecho<br>Él, ella, usted ha hecho<br>Nosotros/as hemos hecho<br>Vosotros/as habéis hecho<br>Ellos, ellas, ustedes han hecho |
| | Pretérito anterior | Yo hube hecho<br>Tú hubiste hecho<br>Él, ella, usted hubo hecho<br>Nosotros/as hubimos hecho<br>Vosotros/as hubisteis hecho<br>Ellos, ellas, ustedes hubieron hecho |
| | Pretérito pluscuamperfecto | Yo había hecho<br>Tú habías hecho<br>Él, ella, usted había hecho<br>Nosotros/as habíamos hecho<br>Vosotros/as habíais hecho<br>Ellos, ellas, ustedes habían hecho |
| | Condicional compuesto | Yo habría hecho<br>Tú habrías hecho |

|  |  |  |
|---|---|---|
|  |  | Él, ella, usted habría hecho<br>Nosotros/as habríamos hecho<br>Vosotros/as habríais hecho<br>Ellos, ellas, ustedes habrían hecho |
|  | Futuro compuesto | Yo habré hecho<br>Tú habrás hecho<br>Él, ella, usted habrá hecho<br>Nosotros/as habremos hecho<br>Vosotros/as habréis hecho<br>Ellos, ellas, ustedes habrán hecho |
| Subjuntivo | Presente | Yo haga<br>Tú hagas<br>Él, ella, usted haga<br>Nosotros/as hagamos<br>Vosotros/as hagáis<br>Ellos, ellas, ustedes hagan |
|  | Pretérito imperfecto | Yo hiciera o hiciese<br>Tú hicieras o hicieses<br>Él, ella, usted hiciera o hiciese<br>Nosotros/as hiciéramos o hiciésemos<br>Vosotros/as hicierais o hicieseis<br>Ellos, ellas, ustedes hicieran o hiciesen |

| | | |
|---|---|---|
| | Futuro simple | Yo hiciere<br>Tú hicieres<br>Él, ella, usted hiciere<br>Nosotros/as hiciéremos<br>Vosotros/as hiciereis<br>Ellos, ellas, ustedes hicieren |
| | Pretérito perfecto compuesto | Yo haya hecho<br>Tú hayas hecho<br>Él, ella, usted haya hecho<br>Nosotros/as hayamos hecho<br>Vosotros/as hayáis hecho<br>Ellos, ellas, ustedes hayan hecho |
| | Pretérito pluscuamperfecto | Yo hubiera o hubiese hecho<br>Tú hubieras o hubieses hecho<br>Él, ella, usted hubiera o hubiese hecho<br>Nosotros/as hubiéramos o hubiésemos hecho<br>Vosotros/as hubierais o hubieseis hecho<br>Ellos, ellas, ustedes hubieran o hubiesen hecho |
| | Futuro compuesto | Yo hubiere hecho<br>Tú hubieres hecho<br>Él, ella, usted hubiere hecho<br>Nosotros/as hubiéremos hecho<br>Vosotros/as hubiereis hecho<br>Ellos, ellas, ustedes hubieren hecho |

| Imperativo | Presente | Tú haz<br>Usted haga |

## Poder

| Modo | Tiempo | Conjugación |
|---|---|---|
| Indicativo | Presente | Yo puedo<br>Tú puedes<br>Él, ella, usted puede<br>Nosotros/as podemos<br>Vosotros/as podéis<br>Ellos, ellas, ustedes pueden |
| | Pretérito perfecto simple | Yo pude<br>Tú pudiste<br>Él, ella, usted pudo<br>Nosotros/as pudimos<br>Vosotros/as pudisteis<br>Ellos, ellas, ustedes pudieron |
| | Futuro simple | Yo podré<br>Tú podrás<br>Él, ella, usted podrá<br>Nosotros/as podremos<br>Vosotros/as podréis<br>Ellos, ellas, ustedes podrán |

|  |  |  |
|---|---|---|
|  | Condicional simple | Yo podría<br>Tú podrías<br>Él, ella, usted podría<br>Nosotros/as podríamos<br>Vosotros/as podríais<br>Ellos, ellas, ustedes podrían |
| Subjuntivo | Presente | Yo pueda<br>Tú puedas<br>Él, ella, usted pueda<br>Nosotros/as podamos<br>Vosotros/as podáis<br>Ellos, ellas, ustedes puedan |
| Subjuntivo | Pretérito imperfecto | Yo pudiera o pudiese<br>Tú pudieras o pudieses<br>Él, ella, usted pudiera o pudiese<br>Nosotros/as pudiéramos o pudiésemos<br>Vosotros/as pudierais o pudieseis<br>Ellos, ellas, ustedes pudieran o pudiesen |
| Subjuntivo | Futuro simple | Yo pudiere<br>Tú pudieres<br>Él, ella, usted pudiere<br>Nosotros/as pudiéremos<br>Vosotros/as pudiereis<br>Ellos, ellas, ustedes pudieren |

| Imperativo | Presente | Tú puede<br>Ustedes puedan |

### Decir

| Modo | Tiempo | Conjugación |
|---|---|---|
| Indicativo | Presente | Yo digo<br>Tú dices<br>Él, ella, usted dice<br>Nosotros/as decimos<br>Vosotros/as decís<br>Ellos, ellas, ustedes dicen |
| | Pretérito perfecto simple | Yo dije<br>Tú dijiste<br>Él, ella, usted dijo<br>Nosotros/as dijimos<br>Vosotros/as dijisteis<br>Ellos, ellas, ustedes dijeron |
| | Futuro simple | Yo diré<br>Tú dirás<br>Él, ella, usted dirá<br>Nosotros/as diremos<br>Vosotros/as diréis<br>Ellos, ellas, ustedes dirán |

| | | |
|---|---|---|
| | Condicional simple | Yo diría<br>Tú dirías<br>Él, ella, usted diría<br>Nosotros/as diríamos<br>Vosotros/as diríais<br>Ellos, ellas, ustedes dirían |
| | Pretérito perfecto compuesto | Yo he dicho<br>Tú has dicho<br>Él, ella, usted ha dicho<br>Nosotros/as hemos dicho<br>Vosotros/as habéis dicho<br>Ellos, ellas, ustedes han dicho |
| | Pretérito anterior | Yo hube dicho<br>Tú hubiste dicho<br>Él, ella, usted hubo dicho<br>Nosotros/as hubimos dicho<br>Vosotros/as hubisteis dicho<br>Ellos, ellas, ustedes hubieron dicho |
| | Pretérito pluscuamperfecto | Yo había dicho<br>Tú habías dicho<br>Él, ella, usted había dicho<br>Nosotros/as habíamos dicho<br>Vosotros/as habíais dicho<br>Ellos, ellas, ustedes habían dicho |

|  |  |  |
|---|---|---|
|  | Condicional compuesto | Yo habría dicho<br>Tú habrías dicho<br>Él, ella, usted habría dicho<br>Nosotros/as habríamos dicho<br>Vosotros/as habríais dicho<br>Ellos, ellas, ustedes habrían dicho |
|  | Futuro compuesto | Yo habré dicho<br>Tú habrás dicho<br>Él, ella, usted habrá dicho<br>Nosotros/as habremos dicho<br>Vosotros/as habréis dicho<br>Ellos, ellas, ustedes habrán dicho |
| Subjuntivo | Presente | Yo diga<br>Tú digas<br>Él, ella, usted diga<br>Nosotros/as digamos<br>Vosotros/as digáis<br>Ellos, ellas, ustedes digan |
|  | Pretérito imperfecto | Yo dijera o dijese<br>Tú dijeras o dijeses<br>Él, ella, usted dijera o dijese<br>Nosotros/as dijéramos o dijésemos<br>Vosotros/as dijerais o dijeseis<br>Ellos, ellas, ustedes dijeran o dijesen |

| | | |
|---|---|---|
| | Futuro simple | Yo dijere<br>Tú dijeres<br>Él, ella, usted dijere<br>Nosotros/as dijéremos<br>Vosotros/as dijereis<br>Ellos, ellas, ustedes dijeren |
| | Pretérito perfecto compuesto | Yo haya dicho<br>Tú hayas dicho<br>Él, ella, usted haya dicho<br>Nosotros/as hayamos dicho<br>Vosotros/as hayáis dicho<br>Ellos, ellas, ustedes hayan dicho |
| | Pretérito pluscuamperfecto | Yo hubiera o hubiese dicho<br>Tú hubieras o hubieses dicho<br>Él, ella, usted hubiera o hubiese dicho<br>Nosotros/as hubiéramos o hubiésemos dicho<br>Vosotros/as hubierais o hubieseis dicho<br>Ellos, ellas, ustedes hubieran o hubiesen dicho |
| | Futuro compuesto | Yo hubiere dicho<br>Tú hubieres dicho<br>Él, ella, usted hubiere dicho<br>Nosotros/as hubiéremos dicho<br>Vosotros/as hubiereis dicho<br>Ellos, ellas, ustedes hubieren dicho |

| Imperativo | Presente | Tú di<br>Usted diga |
|---|---|---|

**Exercises**

1. Complete the sentences with the correct conjugation of the verb in brackets.
    a. Dalma _____ (ser) la más inteligente del grupo.
    b. Hoy a la noche no _____ (poder), _____ (ir) a una fiesta.
    c. Ayer Juan me _____ (dar) una sorpresa, pero yo ya _____ (saber) qué era.
    d. Espero que Patricia _____ (estar) en su casa a la tarde.
    e. ¡No te _____ (acercar)! _____ (haber) una rata ahí.
2. Go back to the short story at the beginning of the chapter and find all the irregular verbs.
3. Determine which of the following verbs are irregular and which ones are not.
    a. tomar
    b. delegar
    c. dormir
    d. pensar
    e. sacar
4. Determine which type of irregularity each of the following verbs has.
    a. despedir
    b. apretar
    c. mentir
    d. vestir
5. Write a short text using the verbs of the previous exercise conjugated.

# Mid-Book Quiz

*¡Muy bien!* You've done it: you're halfway through the book! We are sure that you have improved your grammar, your vocabulary, and your Spanish in general. However, how about doing some exercises to see how much you've learned so far?

Below, there are five exercises on the topics that we've seen in the first six chapters of the book. Once you finish the quiz, go to the "Answer Key" section at the end of the book to see how well you did. Each exercise is worth 2 points. If your score is 8 or higher, *¡felicitaciones!* You're doing great, and you're on your way to becoming an expert in Spanish. If your score is between 4 and 8 points, we recommend that you go back to those chapters that were more challenging. If your score is less than 4 points, don't worry: take your time, reread the book, and take the quiz again. We're sure you'll do better next time!

Now, let's go for it. *¡Buena suerte!*

1. **Decide whether the following sentences are in the passive or active voice. Then, rewrite the passive ones in their active form and the active ones in their passive form.**
    a. Pedro de Mendoza fundó Buenos Aires.
    b. Sevilla fue fundada por Julio César.
    c. El gato fue alimentado por el dueño.
    d. Julián amasó las pizzas caseras.

2. Following the example, write the sentences below with the information provided.

   a. Primera persona del plural / presente de indicativo / verbo *estudiar*.
   *Nosotros estudiamos.*

   b. Tercera persona del singular / pretérito imperfecto de indicativo / verbo *saltar*.
   _____.

   c. Segunda persona del plural / pretérito perfecto / verbo *cocinar*.
   _____.

3. Primera persona del singular / condicional / verbo *comprar*.
   _____.

**Complete the following short text with the verb *correr* conjugated in the corresponding tenses.**

Anoche salí a _____ al parque. Mientras _____, sentí que alguien me seguía. Primero pensé que era otra persona, pero no había nadie _____ allí, aparte de mí. No le di importancia y seguí _____. Sin embargo, volví a sentir que alguien me seguía. Finalmente, dejé de _____ y me di media vuelta. Y entonces lo vi. ¡Un conejo blanco me había estado siguiendo mientras _____!

4. Below, there is a list of verbs. Decide which are from the first conjugation, which are from the second conjugation, and which are from the third conjugation.

mirar, pretender, responder, vender, bajar, cumplir, beber, abrir, comer, caminar, partir, construir, preguntar, revisar, invadir.

First conjugation: _____, _____, _____, _____, _____.

Second conjugation: _____, _____, _____, _____, _____.

Third conjugation: _____, _____, _____, _____, _____.

**5. Now, complete the following story with the verbs from the previous exercise properly conjugated.**

El viernes por la noche, un enorme crucero lleno de turistas llegó al puerto de Santiago de la Ribera, en Murcia. Tras _____ del barco, todos los turistas fueron a los bares del centro para _____ mariscos y _____ cerveza. Luego, muchos se quedaron _____ por la costa mientras _____ la puesta de sol.

Al día siguiente, José _____ su tienda muy temprano. Como todos los comerciantes, estaba entusiasmado: la noticia del grupo de turistas había llegado a cada rincón del pueblo. Sin embargo, durante el transcurso de la mañana, José apenas _____ un par de souvenirs.

—Oye, José, ¿qué te pasa? —le _____ Ramón, el cantinero del bar de enfrente, cuando José salió a almorzar.

—Es que _____ que los turistas fuesen a mi tienda, pero no vendí ni un solo recuerdo.

—¡Oh, eso! Es que el barco _____ anoche. Solo estuvo unas horas —le explicó Ramón—. Santiago de la Ribera era una parada técnica para _____ el motor. _____ el protocolo, eso es todo.

—¡Ah! —_____ José, decepcionado—. Es una lástima. Hace mucho tiempo que no venían tantos turistas al pueblo.

—Ah, ¿no te has enterado todavía? —le dijo Ramón—. Han empezado a _____ un puerto de cruceros aquí cerca. Apuesto a que este barco solo fue el primero de muchos. ¡Ya verás como en poco tiempo nos _____ los turistas!

# Chapter 7: Reflexive Verbs

## Short Story: Un animal en las vías

—**Damas** y **caballeros** —dijo alguien por el **altavoz**—, **han dado aviso** de un animal en el sistema de túneles del metro. Mientras lo buscamos, esperen pacientemente dentro del **vagón**. Muchas gracias.

Los murmullos no se hicieron esperar. Todos los pasajeros comenzaron a **cuchichear**. Mientras tanto, Marisa se sentó en el banco del vagón, preguntándose qué tipo de animal se habría **colado** en los túneles.

"Quizás es un perro", pensó. "A lo mejor se alejó de su dueño y se perdió. Pero ¿cómo terminó aquí abajo? Eso sí que es un misterio".

Marisa resopló. Se sentía cansada. Solo esto le faltaba para completar un día de lo más caótico. Era **la fresa del postre**.

A su lado, una pasajera la miró y le dijo:

—Parece increíble, ¿no?

—¡Ni me lo diga! —contestó Marisa—. He tenido **un día de locos**. Me levanté tarde porque mi despertador se averió. Luego, mientras me bañaba, me quedé sin agua. Más tarde, cuando estaba vistiéndome, rompí accidentalmente mi vestido favorito.

—Parece que no ha sido su día —se lamentó la mujer—. Me llamo Susana, por cierto.

—Marisa —se presentó, y le estrechó la mano.

—Un placer —Susana miró por la ventana—. ¿Qué cree que hay ahí afuera?

—No lo sé —respondió Marisa, y miró por el cristal—. ¿Un gatito?

La oscuridad era casi total; solo había una **luz de emergencia** que iluminaba débilmente unos cuantos cables contra la pared del túnel. Entonces, Susana exclamó:

—¡He visto algo! —Tanto Marisa como otros pasajeros se acercaron a ella, expectantes—. Estaba muy oscuro, pero creo que era un perro. Un perro pequeño, como un pekinés.

—Yo también lo he visto —anunció un pasajero de gafas que estaba en el otro extremo del vagón—. Pero me pareció más un perro labrador.

—Yo creo que era un **perro salchicha** —dijo otra pasajera.

Marisa pegó la nariz a la ventana, esforzándose por ver algo. Y entonces, lo vio: tenía pelo corto y **rojizo**, un **hocico** largo y orejas grandes. No era un pekinés, ni un labrador, ni un perro salchicha. De eso estaba segura.

Llegaría tarde a su casa, sí. Quizá se acostaría más tarde que de costumbre por la **demora**. "Pero, después de todo, ¡una no ve un zorro en las vías del metro todos los días!", pensó.

## Vocabulary List

| Español | Inglés |
|---|---|
| damas y caballeros | ladies and gentlemen |
| el altavoz | speaker |
| dar aviso (a alguien) | to give (somebody) notice |
| el vagón | coach |
| cuchichear | to murmur |

| colarse | to sneak in |
|---|---|
| la fresa del postre | the cherry on the cake, the last thing you need |
| un día de locos | a crazy day |
| la luz de emergencia | emergency light |
| el perro salchicha | dachshund |
| rojizo, rojiza | reddish |
| el hocico | snout |
| la demora | delay |

**Reading Comprehension**

That was an interesting story, wasn't it? Let's see what you remember about it:

1. ¿Qué le pasó a Marisa mientras se bañaba?
2. ¿Qué ve por la ventana Marisa la primera vez que mira hacia afuera?
3. ¿Dónde está el hombre de anteojos?
4. ¿Cuál es la descripción física del zorro?

## Grammar Section

In this chapter, we will focus on reflexive verbs and pronouns. These words are super common in casual conversation because they are normally used to talk about the activities we do every day. Therefore, knowing them is very important! Be ready to learn everything there is to learn about:

- reflexive verbs
- reflexive pronouns

*¡Hora de ponerse a estudiar!*

## Reflexive Verbs

In Spanish, we call them *verbos reflexivos*. A reflexive verb is one that shows that the result of the action performed by the subject falls on the subject itself. In other words, the subject and the direct object (i.e., the recipient of the verb) are the same person.

Luckily, they are easy to spot. As we've stated in previous chapters, in the infinitive, verbs in Spanish end in -*ar*, -*er*, or -*ir*. However, reflexive verbs are special: the infinitive form of a reflexive verb has -*se* attached to the end of it. Let's see this more clearly:

| Verbo en infinitivo | Verbo reflexivo |
|---|---|
| bañar ("to bathe") | bañar<u>se</u> ("to bathe oneself") |
| dormir ("to sleep") | dormir<u>se</u> ("to fall asleep") |
| mirar ("to look") | mirar<u>se</u> ("to look at oneself") |

As you can see in this table, reflexive verbs are the verbs you know with an added -*se* ending. However, keep in mind that it doesn't always make sense to make a verb reflexive in Spanish. In general, reflexive verbs refer to daily life activities, and they indicate that the action is done by – and to –the subject. The question you must ask yourself to know if a reflexive verb makes sense is if you do *that* to *yourself*. For example, if *you* change your clothes (*cambiar*), then *cambiarse* works.

Let's see a list of the most common reflexive verbs, along with their translation to English.

| Verbo reflexivo | Traducción |
|---|---|
| afeitarse | to shave |
| animarse | to bring oneself to do [sth] |

| | |
|---|---|
| atreverse | to dare |
| bañarse | to take a bath, to take a shower |
| cambiarse | to change (clothes) |
| despertarse | to wake up |
| dormirse | to fall asleep |
| levantarse | to get out of bed |
| llamarse | to be called |
| peinarse | to brush one's hair |
| ponerse | to put on (clothes) |
| sacarse | to take off (clothes) |
| sentirse | to feel |
| verse | to look at oneself |
| vestirse | to get dressed |

One thing worth noting is that not all verbs with a *-se* ending are reflexive verbs; some are pronominal verbs, which are not necessarily reflexive. To distinguish a true reflexive verb from other pronominal verbs, you need to be able to add the phrases *a mí misma/o, a ti misma/o, a sí misma/o, a nosotras/os mismas/os, a vosotras/os mismas/os,* or *a ellas/os mismas/os*. With these phrases, we make it clear that the subject is doing the action on itself. If it's possible to add one of them, we can be sure that we are talking of a reflexive verb.

### Reflexive Pronouns

Now that we know what a reflexive verb is, we have to talk about reflexive pronouns to fully understand how these verbs work. Reflexive pronouns are special pronouns that, unlike personal pronouns (*yo, tú, él/ella, nosotros/nosotras, vosotros/vosotras, ellos/ellas*), don't refer to a subject but to an object, and they indicate who is affected by an action. Reflexive pronouns complement reflexive verbs and must agree in person and number with the subject of the sentence.

In the infinitive, the reflexive pronoun is the *-se* ending. When we conjugate the verb, we need to make that pronoun agree with the subject. Let's see a table with the reflexive pronouns in Spanish, according to each personal pronoun.

| Pronombre personal | Pronombre reflexivo | Ejemplo |
| --- | --- | --- |
| yo | me | Yo me baño |
| tú | te | Tú te bañas |
| él/ella/usted | se | Él se baña |
| nosotros/nosotras | nos | Nosotros nos bañamos |
| vosotros/vosotras | os | Vosotros os bañáis |
| ellos/ellas | se | Ellos se bañan |

As you can see in the table above, reflexive pronouns are normally placed before the verb. To form sentences with reflexive pronouns, we have to follow this structure: subject + reflexive pronoun + conjugated verb. Let's see a few examples:

- *Martín se baña todas las mañanas* ("Martín takes a bath every morning.")

- *Yo siempre <u>me visto</u> de negro* ("I always dress in black.")
- *No <u>me atrevo</u> a hablar en público* ("I don't dare to speak in public.")
- *Gerardo <u>se mira</u> en el espejo* ("Gerardo looks at himself in the mirror.")
- *¿Las niñas todavía no <u>se despertaron</u>?* ("The girls haven't woken up yet?")
- *Roberta y Pedro <u>se vieron</u> en el reflejo de la laguna* ("Roberta and Pedro saw themselves in the reflection of the pond.")

Beyond the fact that the most common position is before the verb, there are occasions in which reflexive pronouns can be placed after the verb. For example:

- With imperatives:
  *Ya duérme<u>te</u>* ("Just go to sleep.")
  *Quíte<u>se</u> esos zapatos mojados* ("Take off those wet shoes.")
- With gerunds:
  *¿Por qué estás miránd<u>ome</u>?* ("Why are you looking at me?")
  *Sandra está duchándo<u>se</u>* ("Sandra is taking a shower.")

## Exercises

1. Write down all the reflexive verbs you can find in the short story "Un animal en las vías." Remember to check if you can add the phrases *a mí misma/o, a sí misma/o*, etc. so as not to add pronominal verbs which are not reflexive.

2. Complete the following sentences with the correct reflexive pronoun.
    a. Yo ___ baño por la noche y Juan ___ baña por la mañana.
    b. En nuestra familia, siempre ___ acostamos tarde.
    c. ¿___ sientes bien?
    d. Mis hijos ___ llaman Teodoro y Bárbara.

3. Fill in the blanks:

| Pronombre personal | Pronombre reflexivo | Verbo presente indicativo | Verbo reflexivo |
|---|---|---|---|
| **yo** | **me** | **peino** | **peinarse** |
| tú |  | vistes |  |
|  | se |  | cambiarse |
| nosotras |  |  | maquillarse |
| vosotros |  | despertáis | despertarse |
| ellos |  | afeitan |  |

4. In the short story below, fill in the blanks with one of these reflexive verbs properly conjugated: *ponerse, ducharse, cepillarse, despertarse, levantarse, vestirse, mirarse* and *limpiarse*:

Después de _____, Úrsula entró en el baño, como todas las mañanas, para _____ y _____ sus cremas. Era temprano; ___ _____ _____ con suficiente tiempo como para hacer una limpieza a fondo de su rostro antes de salir para la universidad.

Mientras ___ _____ con su crema facial, sintió un olor algo extraño; algo como la menta. Definitivamente, su crema no olía de esa forma...

Entonces, escuchó la voz de Cristian, su novio, que estaba en el pasillo.

—¿Ya estás lista, cariño? —le preguntó.

—¡No! —respondió Úrsula—. Me estoy poniendo mis cremas. Todavía tengo que _____ y _____ el pelo.

—Vale, te espero abajo, con el desayuno —respondió Cristian—. Por cierto, ¿has visto mi espuma de afeitar? ¡No puedo encontrarla por ningún lado!

Entonces, Úrsula ___ _____ al espejo. Pero ¡cómo podía haber estado tan distraída! ¡Se estaba poniendo la espuma de afeitar de Cristian en lugar de su crema de limpieza facial!

5. Decide whether the following statements are true or false. Correct the false ones.

   a. You have to add the ending *-se* after an infinitive verb to form a reflexive one.

   b. Any verb can be transformed into a reflexive verb.

   c. Reflexive pronouns must agree in person and number with the subject of the sentence.

   d. Normally, reflexive pronouns are placed after the verb.

# Chapter 8: Infinitives, Gerunds, and Participles

## Short Story: El bromista

Tras bajar del taxi, Claudia empezó a caminar rápidamente por la **acera**. No tardó en **apretar el paso**. Sus **tacones** se estaban **clavando** entre los **adoquines**, pero no le importó. Por culpa del tráfico, estaba llegando bastante tarde a su encuentro con Matías.

Matías no era su novio: era "el chico con el que se estaba viendo". **Ambos** se habían conocido trabajando en una cafetería **unos cuantos** meses atrás. A Claudia le gustaba Matías porque era divertido: siempre estaba bromeando para hacerla reír.

Al llegar al restaurante, Claudia se dio cuenta de que era una hamburguesería con juegos de arcade. Es decir: estaba llena de niños corriendo y gritando. "No es un lugar muy romántico para mantener una cita", pensó Claudia, sonriendo. Matías era especial: como a los niños, le encantaban las hamburguesas y los videojuegos.

Tras haber entrado en la hamburguesería, a Claudia no le costó encontrar a Matías. Se acercó a él y, después de saludarlo con un beso en la **mejilla**, no pudo **evitar** notar que parecía algo **consternado**.

—Lamento la **tardanza** —dijo Claudia—. Estaba deseando llegar pronto, pero había mucho tráfico. Parece que todos han salido a la calle al mismo tiempo. ¿Está todo bien?

—¡Sí, todo está bien! —respondió Matías, **frunciendo el ceño**; estaba pensativo—. Es solo que he reflexionado mucho.

—¿Sí? —preguntó Claudia, repentinamente preocupada—. ¿Y se puede saber en qué has estado pensando?

Entonces, Matías sonrió.

—Bueno, no quería decírtelo hasta después de cenar, pero... He elegido este restaurante por una razón en especial.

Claudia se quedó helada. Miró a su alrededor. El lugar no era muy romántico, es verdad, pero **tenía su encanto**. ¿Acaso Matías iba a pedirle, finalmente, que fuera su novia?

—¿Quieres...? —preguntó Matías.

—¿Sí? —preguntó Claudia, emocionada.

—¿Quieres pedir conmigo el menú XXL? ¡No creo que pueda comérmelo todo!

Claudia se quedó decepcionada. ¡No podía creerlo! ¡Había sido tan tonta! Pero entonces, riendo, Matías dijo:

—Te estaba **tomando el pelo**, por supuesto. ¿Quieres ser mi novia?

## Vocabulary List

| Español | Inglés |
|---|---|
| la acera | sidewalk |
| apretar el paso | to go faster |
| el tacón | heel |
| clavar | to stick |
| el adoquín | cobblestone |

| | |
|---|---|
| ambos, ambas | both |
| unos cuantos, unas cuantas | a few |
| la mejilla | cheek |
| evitar | to avoid |
| consternado, consternada | troubled |
| la tardanza | delay |
| fruncir el ceño | to frown |
| tener encanto | to be charming |
| tomar el pelo | to pull someone's leg |

**Reading Comprehension**

Let's put your practice your reading comprehension skills to work:

1. ¿Por qué Claudia llega tarde a su cita con Matías?
2. ¿Qué es lo que le gusta a Claudia de Matías?
3. ¿Dónde cita Matías a Claudia? ¿Cómo es el lugar?
4. ¿Qué opina Claudia acerca del lugar?

# Grammar Section

We've mentioned in passing that, in Spanish, each verb has three special forms that don't admit any conjugation and, therefore, are not defined by the verb's characteristics (tense, mood, number, and person). We're talking about the *verboides*: the infinitive, the gerund, and the participle.

These three non-personal forms of the verbs are necessary to conjugate other verb tenses. Just to give an example: in order to conjugate the compound forms of *dormir*, we need to know its participle: *dormido*.

In this chapter, we'll deal with Spanish nonfinite verb forms:
- infinitives
- gerunds
- participles

By the end of the chapter, you will be an expert in *verboides*!

**Infinitives**

The first of these special verb forms is the *infinitivo* ("infinitive"). As in English, the Spanish infinitive is used to enunciate the verb itself. Besides, they can also function as nouns.

Infinitive verbs will always end in *-ar*, *-er*, or *-ir*, as we saw in chapters 3, 4 and 5 of this book. Also, as we saw in the previous chapter, pronominal verbs in the infinitive end in *-se*. If you don't remember, don't worry: here's a memory refresher.

- Verbs ending in *-ar* belong to the first conjugation. For example: *cantar, bailar, saltar*.
- Verbs ending in *-er* belong to the second conjugation. For example: *beber, comer, saber*.
- Verbs ending in *-ir* belong to the third conjugation. For example: *salir, dormir, vivir*.

Now that we know what an infinitive is (which is pretty easy, right?), it's time to ask ourselves... what do we use them for? Well, they have several functions. Let's see some of them.

1. Acting as a noun, the infinitive can take the place of the **subject of a sentence**. For example:
   - *Estudiar es lo único que tienes que hacer* ("Studying is the only thing you have to do.")

2. Also working as a noun, the infinitive can function as a **direct or indirect object**:
   - *Hoy no puedo salir* ("Today I can't go out.")

3. Sometimes, we use the infinitive **to give instructions**, especially in recipes and in signs on the street or in a building. For example:
   - *No fumar* ("No smoking.")

- *No **pasar*** ("No trespassing.")
- ***Evitar** la zona* ("Avoid this area.")

Now, it's time for some example sentences with verbs in the infinitive.

- *Siempre te voy a **amar*** ("I will always love you.")
- *Me encantaría **trabajar** en esa empresa* ("I would love to work for that company.")
- *Toda mi vida he querido **viajar** al sur de Chile* ("All my life I have wanted to travel to the south of Chile.")
- *¿Vamos al cine a **ver** una película?* ("Shall we go to the cinema to watch a movie?")
- ***Tener** un perro tan grande en un apartamento no es buena idea* ("Having such a large dog in an apartment is not a good idea.")
- *¿Me vas a **decir** la verdad?* ("Are you going to tell me the truth?")
- *Siempre disfruto de **compartir** mi experiencia* ("I always enjoy sharing my experience.")
- *PROHIBIDO **FUMAR*** ("NO SMOKING.")
- ***Derretir** la manteca a baño maría. Luego, **incorporarla** a la mezcla* ("Melt the butter in a double boiler. Then, add it to the mix.")

### Gerunds

In the second group of *verboides* we have the gerund or, in Spanish, *el gerundio*. This nonfinite verb form is used as an adverb. Of course, we also have gerunds in English, and their most notable characteristic is that they all end in "-ing." Well, in Spanish, they also have a distinctive feature, which we've talked about: all of them end in *-ndo*. This is a very easy way to distinguish Spanish gerunds!

However, besides distinguishing them, to be an advanced speaker of Spanish, you need to be able to form the gerund of any verb. Gerund formation is pretty simple, but it varies a bit between regular and irregular verbs, so let's get to it:

With regular verbs, things are quite easy:
- We add *-ando* to the stem of verbs ending in *-ar*. For example:
  *cantar* → *cant**ando***
  *amar* → *am**ando***
- We add *-iendo* to the stem of verbs ending in *-er* and *-ir*. For example:
  *aprender* → *aprend**iendo***
  *beber* → *beb**iendo***
  *escribir* → *escrib**iendo***

When we talk about irregular verbs... Well, as always, things get a bit more complicated. But don't worry, here's all you need to know:
- If the stem ends in a vowel, then the *i* of *-iendo* becomes a *y*:
  *ir* → ***yendo***
  *construir* → *constru**yendo***
  *leer* → *le**yendo***
- If the verb belongs to the third conjugation (i.e., if the infinitive of the verb ends in *-ir*) and, in its present form, there is a vowel change, then the gerund also has changes:
  *sentir* → *siento* → *s**intiendo***
- If the verb belongs to the second or third conjugations (i.e., if the infinitive of the verb ends in *-er* or *-ir*) and in the present form there is a vowel change from *ue* to *u*, the gerund also changes:
  *poder* → *puedo* → *p**udiendo***
  *dormir* → *duermo* → *d**urmiendo***
- Finally, after *ñ* and *ll*, the *i* is removed:
  *gruñir* → *gruñ**endo***
  *bullir* → *bull**endo***

Now that we know how to form it, it's time to talk about the most common uses of the gerund in Spanish. As we said before, they tend to be used as adverbs, and we use them to modify verbs:

1. **Progressive gerund.** It is the gerund that expresses the continuity of action. For example:
   - *Estoy **bailando** cumbia* ("I'm dancing cumbia.")
   - *Estoy **viviendo** en la misma ciudad de siempre* ("I'm living in the same old town.")
2. **Gerund to indicate mode.** This is the gerund that explains how something happens or how it's done:
   - *Pedro siempre va al trabajo **caminando*** ("Pedro always walks to work.")
3. **Temporary gerund.** This type of gerund adds information related to the moment in which the action takes place. For example:
   - ***Estando** de vacaciones, María hizo una llamada* ("While on vacation, María made a phone call.") By the way, note that, in this case, the gerund can often be replaced by the construction *mientras* + the verb conjugated in *pretérito imperfecto*. Thus, you could say: *Mientras estaba de vacaciones, María hizo una llamada.*
4. **Causal gerund.** As you can probably guess, this gerund states a cause. To use it correctly, it's necessary to confirm that it answers the questions "why?" or "how?" For example:
   - *Ellos ganaron el concurso **bailando** estupendamente* ("They won the contest by dancing beautifully.")
5. **Gerund of simultaneity.** This gerund expresses that two actions happened at the same time:
   - *La Navidad está **llegando** y las tiendas están **decorando** sus escaparates* ("Christmas is coming and shops are decorating their windows.")
6. **Conditional gerund.** Finally, we have the gerund that states a condition:
   - ***Trabajando** duro, cumplirás tus objetivos* ("By working hard, you'll meet your goals.") In this case, it's always possible to replace the gerund with the construction *si* + the verb in the present indicative. So you could also say: *Si trabajas mucho,*

*cumplirás tus objetivos.*

Bear in mind that English and Spanish gerunds are not used in exactly the same way. Below, you'll find the three conditions that gerunds in Spanish must comply in order to be considered correct:

- They must act as an adverb or as a verb
- They must express a simultaneous or previous action to that of the main verb
- The subject of the gerund and the subject of the main verb must be the same, or the gerund must have its own subject

### How not to use the gerund in Spanish

We have seen the correct uses of the gerund, but we also think it's important to know when not to use it. There are two very common mistakes when using the gerund that even native speakers make! Next, we will tell you in which two cases you shouldn't use a gerund, even if common sense tells you to use one.

- To express posteriority. Let's see an example sentence: "Marta went down to the basement, discovering that there was a raccoon."
  *Marta bajó al sótano, **descubriendo** que había un mapache.* ✗
  *Marta bajó al sótano **y descubrió** que había un mapache.*

- As an adjective. Except for a limited number of set phrases, the gerund in Spanish is never used to modify a noun. Let's see an example: "Buenos Aires is a cultural city, having one of the opera houses with the best acoustics in the world."
  *Buenos Aires es una ciudad cultural, **contando** con uno de los teatros de ópera con mejor acústica del mundo.*

  *Buenos Aires es una ciudad cultural **y cuenta** con uno de los teatros de ópera con mejor acústica del mundo.*

Now let's take a look at several gerunds in Spanish and their translations into English.

| Verbo | Gerundio | Traducción |
|---|---|---|
| amar | amando | loving |
| bailar | bailando | dancing |
| dormir | durmiendo | sleeping |
| freír | friendo | frying |
| hervir | hirviendo | boiling |
| jugar | jugando | playing |
| llover | lloviendo | raining |
| nadar | nadando | swimming |
| reír | riendo | laughing |
| sonreír | sonriendo | smiling |
| tener | teniendo | having |

### Participles

Finally, we're going to talk about the last of the *verboides*: *el participio* ("participle"). Participles are necessary for many things, but first, let's see how they are formed.

As is often the case with regular verbs, things are easier:
- For verbs of the first conjugation (i.e., those ending in -*ar*), we need to change the ending for -*ado*: *cantar → cant**ado***

- For verbs of the second and third conjugations (those ending in -*er* and -*ir*), replace the ending with -*ido*: *vivir* → *viv**ido***

It could be said that each irregular participle is a world of its own, so here are some of the most common ones:

*decir* → dicho
*morir* → muerto
*abrir* → abierto
*ver* → visto
*volver* → vuelto

Now, let's see some of the most common uses of the participle:

1. To **form compound verb tenses.** We've already seen this use: we need the auxiliary verb *haber* conjugated plus the participle of the verb that carries meaning. For example:
   - *Hemos **decidido** que saldremos a cenar mañana* ("We have decided that tomorrow we'll go out for dinner.")
   - *¿Has **visto** mi teléfono?* ("Have you seen my phone?")

2. As **an adjective.** Participles can modify nouns; in that case, they have to agree in gender and number with the noun they are modifying:
   - *Mi hermana está **emocionada** por su nuevo trabajo* ("My sister is excited about her new job.")
   - *El domingo **pasado** fui al parque* ("Last Sunday I went to the park.")

Let's see a few examples of participles.

| Verbo | Participio |
|---|---|
| andar | andado |
| barrer | barrido |
| crear | creado |

| dar | dado |
|---|---|
| girar | girado |
| ignorar | ignorado |
| leer | leído |
| morder | mordido |
| nacer | nacido |
| traer | traído |

**Exercises**

1. Here is a list of words that appear in the short story "El bromista". Decide which are infinitives, which are gerunds, and which are participles.
   bajar, reflexionado, clavando, viendo, caminar, apretar, conocido, entrado, llegar, elegido, bromeando, mantener, encontrar, corriendo, sonriendo, notar, pedir.

2. In the following dialogue, fill in the blanks with the correct nonfinite form of the verb in brackets.
   A. Mi hijo mayor está _____ (vivir) en Barcelona.
   B. ¿Y qué está _____ (hacer) allí?
   A. Está _____ (estudiar) Arquitectura. Pero me dijo que, últimamente, está _____ (dormir) poco. Dice que solo sacará buenas notas _____ (trabajar) duro.
   B. ¡Estoy de acuerdo! Aunque creo que también es importante que él pueda _____ (disfrutar) de la universidad.

3. Decide whether the following statements are true or false. Correct the false ones.
   a. Infinitives, gerunds and participles change according to the verb's characteristics (tense, mood, number and person).

b. Infinitives work like nouns.

c. Gerunds can be used to express posteriority.

d. Participles are used to form compound verb tenses.

4. Write the infinitive, the gerund and the participle of the following verbs.

| Verbo | Infinitivo | Gerundio | Participio |
|---|---|---|---|
| saliste | salir | saliendo | salido |
| hizo | | | |
| llegó | | | |
| comimos | | | |
| disfrutasteis | | | |
| bailaba | | | |

5. Can you find all the participles in the following news article?

## El Parque del Retiro en Madrid ha cerrado por fuertes vientos

Debido a los intensos vientos que la Agencia Estatal de Meteorología ha pronosticado para este fin de semana, el Ayuntamiento ha decidido cerrar las puertas del Parque del Retiro.

"Se estiman vientos de hasta 60 kilómetros por hora, que pueden provocar caídas de ramas o incluso de árboles en algunas áreas", ha explicado un técnico del organismo meteorológico.

El Ayuntamiento también ha trasladado la información de riesgo a los adjudicatarios de los bares y restaurantes de un kilómetro a la redonda del parque, para evitar que habiliten las terrazas.

# Chapter 9: The Passive and the Conditional

## Short Story: El accidente

Javier entró a la sala de profesores con una **escayola** en el brazo izquierdo. Intentó pasar **desapercibido**, pero no lo logró. Lucía lo vio y, luego de dar un pequeño grito de sorpresa, preguntó:

—Javier, ¿qué te ha pasado?

—Fui chocado por un camión —contestó Javier, con poco **ánimo**.

—¿Cómo? —preguntó Lucía, que siempre tenía muchas ganas de hablar.

—Pues con la **trompa**.

Lucía entendió la **indirecta** y dejó de hablar. Pero no era fácil para Javier evitar la conversación. Cada vez que alguien entraba a la sala, Javier era **atosigado** por el recién llegado para saber lo que había pasado. Javier quería evitar lo que terminó pasando: toda la sala de profesores opinaba sobre su accidente.

—Podrías haber faltado al trabajo —dijo Martina, que nunca quería trabajar.

—Yo me habría **dado un susto de muerte** —murmuró Susana, mientras se tapaba la cara.

—Deberías ir al médico —lo **increpó** Fabián.

—¿Querrías que te ayude a hablar con la **aseguradora**? —le preguntó por lo bajo Mario, su único amigo.

—¿Me dirías en qué carretera fue? Así la evito —le preguntó Susana, que seguía **conmocionada**.

—Si hubieras usado el **cinturón de seguridad**, no habrías tenido ni un **rasguño** —lo **regañó** Angelina, que ni siquiera sabía lo que había sucedido.

—Me gustaría saber cómo ha quedado el camión —dijo Eduardo, divertido.

Con el chiste de Eduardo, Javier perdió la paciencia.

—¡Por favor, ya! ¡Parad todos! No he tenido ningún accidente de auto. Me he caído por las escaleras de mi casa anoche mientras iba al cuarto de baño. Ni seguro, ni médico, ni carretera. Solo es un **esguince**. Ahora, ¿podríais volver todos a vuestras cosas? Muchas gracias.

—Bueno... —dijo Lucía—. ¡Si hubieras empezado por ahí, nos habríamos ahorrado toda esta charla!

## Vocabulary List

| Español | Inglés |
|---|---|
| la escayola | plaster/cast |
| desapercibido, desapercibida | unnoticed |
| los ánimos | spirits |
| la trompa | nose / drunkenness (colloquial) |
| la indirecta | hint |
| atosigado, atosigada | bugged |

| dar un susto de muerte | to be scared to death |
|---|---|
| increpar | to tell off |
| la aseguradora | insurance company |
| conmocionada, conmocionado | shocked |
| el cinturón de seguridad | seat belt |
| el rasguño | scratch |
| regañar | to scold |
| el esguince | sprain |

**Reading Comprehension**

Javier's coworkers are a bit annoying; there's no doubt about that. Let's see if you understood the rest of the short story.

1. ¿Qué le molestó a Javier?
2. ¿Cuál fue realmente el accidente?
3. ¿Quién estaba más asustado de sus compañeros?
4. En tu opinión, ¿cuál fue el peor comentario?

## Grammar Section

We are closer to reaching the end of the book, which means that you are closer to becoming an advanced Spanish student. The last section is dedicated to more complex issues, but don't worry; we'll break them down for you. This chapter begins with a topic that we've already mentioned, and then we'll add a new one. When you reach the end of the chapter, you'll know everything about:

- the passive voice
- the conditional tenses

Let's get started!

**Passive Voice**

As we briefly saw in chapter 3, verbs can be conjugated in active or passive voice. In this part of chapter 9, we'll elaborate on the passive voice.

The change from active to passive voice does not change the meaning of a sentence; rather, it changes where the emphasis is placed. Sentences in the passive voice place the emphasis on the person or thing affected by the action instead of on the one who performs it. That is, the **subject** of a sentence in the passive voice is not the one who performs the action but the one who receives it. That is why it's called "passive": it's a passive subject. The one who performs the action becomes the agent, which is often omitted or unknown.

In Spanish, it's not very common to *hear the passive voice* in spoken language. It's only frequent in formal writing and journalistic language.

**Structure of the Passive Voice**

There are some key modifications that occur when we change a sentence from active to passive voice. Let's take a look at them:

- The person or thing that functions as the direct object in the active voice (the one affected by the action of the verb) becomes the subject. This new subjetc is called *sujeto paciente*:
    - *El policía llevó <u>a la mujer</u> a la comisaría* ("The police officer took the woman to the police station.")
    - *<u>La mujer</u> fue llevada a la comisaría por el policía* ("The woman was taken to the police station by the police officer.")

If you paid attention, you might have noticed that *<u>a la mujer</u>* became *<u>la mujer</u>*, without the first *a*. That's because, in Spanish, when the direct object is a person, we use the preposition *a* to introduce it. When we transform the sentence to the passive voice, the direct object becomes the subject, so we drop the preposition.

- We use the verb *ser* ("to be") conjugated in the same tense as the verb in the active voice, and we add the participle, which has to agree in gender and number with the *sujeto paciente*.
    - *Los científicos <u>encontraron</u> la cura* ("Scientists found the cure.")
    - *La cura <u>fue encontrada</u> por los científicos* ("The cure was found by scientists.")
- The subject of the active sentence, preceded by the preposition *por*, becomes the *complemento agente*. It can be omitted when it's not important or unknown.
    - *<u>Mi agencia</u> realiza las encuestas* ("My agency conducts the surveys.")
    - *Las encuestas son realizadas <u>por mi agencia</u>* ("The surveys are conducted by my agency.")
    - *Las encuestas son realizadas* ("The surveys are conducted.")

Let's take a look at this table showing how the different elements of the sentence are ordered when the change is made to the passive voice.

|  | Sujeto | Verbo | Complemento directo | Complemento agente |
| --- | --- | --- | --- | --- |
| **Voz activa** | El terremoto | destruyó | el edificio |  |
| **Voz pasiva** | El edificio | fue destruido |  | por el terremoto |

Keep in mind that, in Spanish, only the direct object of the active voice can become the subject of the passive voice. In English, both the direct and the indirect objects can become subjects. Let's see an example:

- *Le dieron una carta a Susana* ("They gave Susana a letter.")
- *Una carta le fue dada a Susana* ("A letter was given to Susana.")

- *Susana fue dada una carta* ✗ ("Susana was given a letter" is correct in English, but it is ungrammatical in Spanish.)

### Reflexive Passive Voice

This is a different, shorter form of the passive voice. This structure is more common in oral speech, and it's used when there is no definite subject, or the subject is not a person. It's formed by the pronoun *se* followed by a verb in the third person that agrees in number with the passive subject. For example:

- *Se lograron grandes avances* ("Great progress was made.")
- *Se encontró el camino correcto* ("The right path was found.")

Keep in mind that this kind of passive voice doesn't admit an agent with the preposition *por*:

- *Se encontró el camino correcto por los exploradores.* ✗

### Conditional

The conditional is one of the most complex tenses in Spanish, but don't panic: we'll explain it in detail and with lots of examples. Although it's in the indicative mood—which would indicate certainty for the speaker—its main function is to express probability.

The conditional tense can be simple (the verb conjugated in the conditional) or compound (formed by *haber* in simple conditional + the participle of the main verb). Let's see when to use each.

### Simple Conditional

The simple conditional is used to:

- Make polite invitations
    - *¿**Querrías** venir a mi cumpleaños?* ("Would you like to come to my birthday?")
- Ask for something politely
    - *¿Me **servirías** más café?* ("Could you pour me more coffee?")

- Express wishes
  - *Me **encantaría** ir a la playa* ("I would love to go to the beach.")
- Make suggestions
  - *Creo que **deberías** empezar a estudiar* ("I think you should start studying.")
- Express doubts about the past
  - *No pensé que **sobreviviría*** ("I didn't think I would survive.")
- Make assumptions about the future of past actions
  - *El médico dijo que **saldría** al día siguiente* ("The doctor said he would be out the next day")

**Compound Conditional**

The main difference with the simple conditional is that the compound conditional is used to talk about situations that are already finished. As we have seen, it's formed with the conditional of the verb *haber* plus the participle of the main verb. It's used to:

- Make assumptions about the past
  - *Pensé que no **habrías querido** contarme* ("I thought you wouldn't have wanted to tell me.")
- Talk about situations that didn't happen in the past
  - *El viaje **habría sido** divertido con Rubén y Susana* ("The trip would have been fun with Rubén and Susana.")
- Manifest agreement or disagreement with past situations
  - *Ella rechazó la propuesta, pero yo la **habría aceptado*** ("She rejected the proposal, but I would have accepted it.")

**Conditional Sentences**

A conditional sentence is a construction used to speculate, that is, to state a condition on the one hand and, on the other hand, a consequence of that condition. To put it in other words, they are structures used to state hypotheses tied to conditions, whether in the present, in the past, or in the future.

They consist of two clauses. The conditional clause ("if one thing happens") and the main clause ("another thing happens/will happen"). In Spanish, as in English, there are four types of conditional sentences. Let's see them in detail:

### Type 0

This type of sentence is used to express real situations which will actually occur under certain conditions. The probability is very high. We use the present of the indicative in both clauses.

- *Si el agua llega a 100 ºC, hierve* ("If water reaches 100 ºC, it boils.")
- *Si sales cuando llueve, te mojas* ("If you go out when it rains, you get wet.")

### Type 1

This type of sentence is used to express hypothetical situations that are likely to occur in the future. The degree of probability is high. It's formed with the present of the indicative in the conditional clause and the simple future of the indicative in the main clause.

- *Si te portas mal, no iremos a la fiesta de cumpleaños* ("If you misbehave, we won't go to the birthday party.")
- *Si no se callan, les pondré un examen* ("If you don't shut up, I will take a test.")

### Type 2

This type of sentence is used to talk about more unreal situations. The degree of probability is much lower than in type 1 since we are talking about present situations that are not actually happening. We use the *pretérito imperfecto* of the subjunctive in the conditional clause and the simple conditional of the indicative in the main clause.

- *Si tuviera dinero, me iría de viaje* ("If I had money, I would go on a trip.")
- *Si no trabajara tanto, pasaría más tiempo en casa* ("If I didn't work so much, I would spend more time at home.")

## Type 3

This type of sentence is used to talk about hypothetical situations in the past, that is, things that didn't happen. It's used to state alternatives to past situations. The degree of probability is null. It's formed with the *pretérito pluscuamperfecto* of the subjunctive in the conditional clause and the compound conditional of the indicative in the main clause.

- *Si hubiéramos llegado más temprano, no nos habríamos perdido el recital* ("If we had arrived earlier, we wouldn't have missed the show.")
- *Si me hubieras pedido que me quedara, no te habría dejado solo* ("If you had asked me to stay, I wouldn't have left you alone.")

### Common Mistakes

Many Spanish speakers mix up these last two types of conditional sentences and use the conditional in both clauses, but this is a mistake. For example:

- "If you would visit me more often, you would know more about my life":
  *Si me **visitarías** más seguido, sabrías más de mi vida.* ✗
  *Si me **visitaras** más seguido, sabrías más de mi vida.* ✓
- "If they had a bigger house, they would adopt a dog":
  *Si **tendrían** una casa más grande, adoptarían un perro.* ✗
  *Si **tuvieran** una casa más grande, adoptarían un perro.* ✓

### Exercises

1. Go back to the short story and find:
    a. All conditional verbs
    b. All passive voice sentences
    c. All conditional sentences
2. Decide whether the following statements are true or false. Correct the false ones.
    a. There are four types of conditional sentences.

b. The emphasis in the passive voice is on the person or thing that performs the action.

c. The simple conditional tense can be used to express doubt about a time in the past.

d. The compound conditional tense can be used to express wishes.

3. Complete the following sentences with the correct form of the verb in brackets:

   a. Me _____ (gustar) conocer México algún día.

   b. Si me _____ _____ (conocer) antes, no me _____ _____ (querer).

   c. ¿Me _____ (ayudar) con este ejercicio?

   d. Si _____ (subir) la marea, se _____ (mojar) las toallas de los bañistas.

   e. Si no _____ (dejar) de pelear, nos _____ (quedar) en casa.

   f. Le dijo que sí y la verdad, yo le _____ _____ (contestar) lo mismo.

4. Identify the subject in the following sentences. Then, transform the ones that are in the active voice to the passive voice and vice versa.

   a. María fue arrastrada por la ola.

   b. Juana ama a Lucas.

   c. Las sequías son generadas por la deforestación.

   d. Mi equipo ganó el partido.

   e. El sospechoso fue encontrado muerto en un callejón.

5. These sentences are wrong. Correct them.

   a. Si sería más linda, sería más feliz.

   b. Carla fue dada un anillo.

   c. Ojalá venís a la fiesta.

   d. Santiago, ¿darías me un chocolate?

# Chapter 10: From Direct to Indirect Speech

## Short Story: La plática

Emilia estaba sorprendida de que Nina la llamara a esa hora, **solía** estar en el trabajo. Preparó café y la esperó. Cuando llegó, Nina estaba furiosa. Cerró la puerta de un **portazo** y **sin siquiera** saludar a su madre se sentó a la mesa y empezó a gritar.

—¡No lo puedo creer! ¡Estoy **estupefacta**!

—Calma, calma, respira —intentó calmarla Emilia—. ¿Qué pasó?

—Tuve una **plática** con mi jefe. ¡Una horrible plática con mi jefe!

Emilia se preocupó, hacía un tiempo que a Nina le iba mal en el trabajo. Pensó "Ay, finalmente la han despedido". Se acercó a Nina y le dijo:

—Cuéntame, con calma, ¿qué fue lo que hablaron?

—Bueno, mi jefe me llamó y me dijo: "Nina, ven a mi oficina ya mismo. Quiero hablarte".

—¿Y tú qué hiciste?

—¡Qué voy a hacer, mamá! Fui a su oficina. Cuando llegué, me dijo que yo le parecía una niña muy inteligente, que me veía futuro en la empresa...

Emilia respiró aliviada. Le preocupaba **sobremanera** que su hija perdiera el **empleo**, su primer empleo. Pero entonces Nina siguió hablando:

—Pero dijo que de esa manera no podía seguir trabajando conmigo. Siguió diciendo que yo era muy **descuidada**, que llegaba siempre tarde, que tenía **malos modos**...

—Ay, Nina...

—Yo le confesé que sí, que a veces me quedaba dormida, que a veces odiaba cuando me pedía algo...

—Pero Nina, ¡eres la secretaria!

—Sí, eso me dijo él. Y yo pensé: "Bueno, hasta aquí llegué". Pero no me vas a creer lo que pasó. Mi jefe miró una foto de su familia y me dijo que yo le recordaba a su hija, que sabía que era una buena chica, pero que tenía que hacer un esfuerzo, que no quería **despedirme**, que lo intentara un poco más y me daría otra oportunidad.

—Ay, Nina, qué bien, qué susto me has dado. Pensé que estabas **desempleada**.

—Sí... pero yo le dije que no quería ningún favor, que no era una niña ni una buena chica, que había conseguido ese trabajo por ser competente y que, si él creía que no lo era, que buscara otra secretaria. Y me fui.

## Vocabulary List

| Español | Inglés |
|---|---|
| soler | used to |
| el portazo | slamming of the door |
| sin siquiera | without even |
| estupefacta, estupefacto | astonished |

| la plática | talk |
|---|---|
| sobremanera | greatly |
| el empleo | job |
| descuidada, descuidado | careless |
| los malos modos | bad manners |
| despedir | to fire |
| desempleada, desempleado | unemployed |

**Reading Comprehension**

Emilia is a little bit confused with what happened between Nina and her (former?) boss. Let's see if you understood it.

1. Finalmente, ¿Nina conserva su trabajo?
2. ¿Por qué quiere despedirla el jefe?
3. ¿Por qué no la despide?
4. ¿Qué le preocupa a Emilia?

# Grammar Section

Both English and Spanish have two ways of conveying another person's words: directly or indirectly. In this chapter, we'll see how to form direct and indirect speech, with easy explanations and lots of examples. By the end of this chapter, you will know:

- the difference between direct and indirect speech
- how to form direct speech
- how to form indirect speech

Ready? *¡Aquí vamos!*

**Speech Verbs**

We use these verbs to talk about communication actions. They are especially necessary in oral speech since they indicate that we are reproducing someone else's words (or, sometimes, our own past words). In written speech, we have other resources, such as dashes and quotation marks.

The most common speech verbs are:
- *decir* ("to say")
- *avisar* ("to warn")
- *contar* ("to tell")
- *gritar* ("to shout")
- *expresar* ("to express")
- *consultar* ("to ask")
- *proclamar* ("to proclaim")
- *aclarar* ("to clarify")
- *añadir* ("to include")
- *agregar* ("to add")
- *desarrollar* ("to develop")

This list is going to come in handy throughout the chapter!

### Direct Speech

We use direct speech when we want to reproduce a message literally, without modifying or altering it. We can use it to report our own thoughts and past words or to reproduce other people's words. In writing, we just need to add one of the speech verbs we saw in the previous section, followed by a colon and quotation marks or dashes of dialogue. We put the words we are reporting between quotation marks, and we don't modify them at all.

Now, let's see the difference between using quotation marks and dashes.

### Quotation Marks

Quotation marks are generally used by media journalists in TV or newspapers. Besides, they are also used in academic writing to quote other authors' words. Although it's not mandatory, it's very common to use a colon between the speech verb and the opening quotation mark. This colon is equivalent to the pause we make in speech before reproducing verbatim the words of another person. When the speech verb is after the quote, we use a comma.

Let's see a few examples of this:

- *José **dijo**: "Me voy a llevar este perro"* ("José said: 'I'm taking this dog.'")
- *"Me voy a llevar este perro", **dijo** José* ("'I'm taking this dog,' José said.")
- *Paula les **avisó**: "Me voy de casa en octubre"* ("Paula informed them: 'I'm leaving home in October.'")
- *"Me voy de casa en octubre", **avisó** Paula* ("'I'm leaving home in October,'" Paula informed them.")

As we can see in these examples, it doesn't matter if we put the speech verb before or after the quote. The meaning is the same, and the only thing we change is the word order. If we want to add more information to the sentence, we have to make sure that the speech verb is always next to the quotation mark, no matter if it's before or after. For example:

- *En ese momento, Laura **gritó**: "¡Cuidado!"* ("At that moment, Laura shouted: 'Be careful!'")
- *"¡Cuidado!", **gritó** Laura en ese momento* ("'Careful!' shouted Laura at that moment.")
- *Justo antes de llegar, Mónica **preguntó**: "¿Qué vamos a comer?"* ("Just before arriving, Mónica asked: 'What are we going to eat?'")
- *"¿Qué vamos a comer?", **preguntó** Mónica justo antes de llegar* ("'What are we going to eat?' asked Mónica just before arriving.")

Now, we'll see another typographic resource that Spanish has to indicate direct speech: the em dashes, or *rayas de diálogo*.

### Dashes of Dialogue

This punctuation mark is especially used when dealing with longer exchanges. It's usually used in short stories or novels to reproduce the dialogues between characters. When we use dashes, we can sometimes omit the speech verb. Let's see an example:

- *—¡Hola!* ("Hi!")
  *—Ahí estás, te estaba buscando* ("There you are, I was looking for you.")

—¿*Por qué?* ("Why?")
—*Quiero que terminemos nuestra charla de ayer* ("I want us to finish the talk we were having yesterday.")
—*Vale...* ("Okay...")

When we use a speech verb, we have to use a closing dash, and we place the verb right after it. Another option is to omit the speech verb, and continue describing the actions or feelings of the character. Let's look at some examples:

- —*Qué bien se ve la casa —dijo Pablo.* ("'How nice the house looks,' said Pablo.")

- —*Llegarán en cualquier momento. —Josefina caminó hacia la ventana y abrió las cortinas* ("'They will be here any minute.' Josefina walked to the window and opened the curtains.")

- —*Muchas gracias por todo esto. —Fernando sentía como si su pecho fuera a estallar* ("'Thank you so much for all this.' Fernando felt as if his chest was going to burst.")

As it's clear from the examples above, English doesn't use the dashes in the same way, so it can be a bit confusing at first. But don't worry, it's only a matter of practice!

**Indirect Speech**

In indirect speech, the quote we want to report is interpreted and reproduced in a different way. We no longer use the exact same words: we modify the form of the speech without altering its meaning. Below, there are two examples of the same quote reported in direct and indirect speech so that you can see the difference:

- **Direct speech:** *Matías dijo: "La carne está muy rica"* ("Matías said: 'The meat is very tasty.'")

- **Indirect speech:** *Matías me dijo que la carne estaba muy rica* ("Matías told me that the meat was very tasty.")

- **Direct speech:** *Juana prosiguió: "Por eso mismo, debemos hacer algo inmediatamente"* ("Juana continued: 'That's why we must do something immediately.'")

- **Indirect speech:** *Juana prosiguió diciendo que, por eso mismo, debíamos hacer algo inmediatamente* ("Juana went on saying that, for that very reason, we had to do something immediately.")

Did you see what happened there? We modified the original quote to report the same message in our own words, i.e., we transformed direct into indirect speech. Below, we will see the changes we have to apply to do this. While it may seem like a lengthy process, with practice, you'll do it without even noticing it.

### Adding a Linking Word

Just like the colon or the speech verb, when we report words indirectly, we need something to introduce it. So, we add a linking word to the speech verb. This link can be:

- *Que* ("that")
  *Luis dijo: "No puedo trabajar más así"* ("Luis said: 'I can't work like this anymore.'")
  *Luis dijo que no podía trabajar más así* ("Luis said that he couldn't work like that anymore.")

- *Si* ("if")
  *Marta le preguntó: "¿Tienes más de un trabajo?"* ("Marta asked him: 'Do you have more than one job?'")
  *Marta le preguntó si tenía más de un trabajo* ("Marta asked him if he had more than one job.")

### Changing Time Adverbs

When we report speech, we are usually in a different communicative situation than the one the speaker was originally in. So, the deictic words and expressions (the ones that refer to time, place, or situation) they used are no longer applicable, and we need to change them. We are talking about adverbs, pronouns, and determiners. Let's start looking at the changes in adverbs of time:

- *"Ayer fui a la plaza"* ("Yesterday I went to the park.")
  *Dijo que el día anterior había ido a la plaza* ("He said he had gone to the park the day before.")

- *"Te lo entregaré mañana"* ("I will deliver it to you tomorrow.")

- *Me aseguró que me lo entregaría <u>al día siguiente</u>* ("He assured me he would deliver it to me the next day.")
- *"¿Vendrás <u>este</u> fin de semana?"* ("Are you coming this weekend?")
*Le pregunté si vendría <u>ese</u> fin de semana* ("I asked him if would come that weekend.")

When we report speech in the same communicative situation, time deixis doesn't change, but we have to alter other references. For example:

- *"<u>Ya</u> no quiero ir a la plaza"* ("I no longer want to go to the park.")
*Dice Luana que <u>ya</u> no quiere ir a la plaza* ("Luana says she no longer wants to go to the park.")

### Changing Place References

Just as we change time adverbs, we must change any spatial references. In addition to modifying adverbs, here we have to pay attention to verbs such as *llevar/traer* ("to take/to bring") or *ir/venir* ("to go/to come"). For example:

- *"Siga por <u>esta</u> calle"* ("Keep going down this street.")
*Me dijo que siguiera por <u>esa</u> calle* ("He told me to keep going down that street.")
- *"Me encanta estar <u>aquí</u>"* ("I love it here.")
*Comentó que le encantaba estar <u>allí</u>* ("He mentioned that he loved it there.")
- *"Siempre <u>vengo</u> a <u>este</u> bar"* ("I always come to this bar.")
*Asegura que siempre <u>va</u> a <u>ese</u> bar* ("She claims she always goes to that bar.")

### Changing Participants

This is a very important issue to keep in mind when reporting speech. We have to change all the cues that indicate who the speaker is, i.e., all the pronouns and the person and number of the verbs. Let's look at some examples:

- *"<u>Yo puedo</u> hacerlo"* ("I can do it.")
*Afirmó que <u>él podía</u> hacerlo* ("He claimed that he could do it.")
- *"¿Esta es <u>tu</u> habitación?"* ("Is this your room?")

*Me preguntó si esa era mi habitación* ("He asked me if that was my room.")

- *"No quiero verlo"* ("I don't want to see him.")
  *Dice que no quiere verte* ("She says that she doesn't want to see you.")

### Changing the Verb Tense

Perhaps this is the most difficult change to learn. We will see here all the options with all the necessary examples. Keep your verb paradigm table handy, and remember that, with practice, this will come to you without having to think about it.

From *modo imperativo* to *pretérito imperfecto del subjuntivo*

- *"¡Ven rápido!"* ("Come quickly!")
  *Me dijo que fuera rápido* ("She asked me to go quickly.")

- *"Come toda la comida"* ("Eat all your food.")
  *Le pidió que comiera toda la comida* ("He asked her to eat all her food.")

From *presente del indicativo* to *pretérito imperfecto del indicativo*

- *"¿Quieres más pizza?"* ("Do you want some more pizza?")
  *Me preguntó si quería más pizza* ("She ask me if I wanted some more pizza.")

- *"Tengo solo este billete"* ("I only have this ticket.")
  *Afirmó que tenía solo ese billete* ("He claimed that he only had that ticket.")

From *futuro simple del indicativo* to *condicional compuesto del indicativo*

- *"¿Pasarás mañana?"* ("Will you stop by tomorrow?")
  *Le pregunté si pasaría al día siguiente* ("I asked him if he would stop by the next day.")

- *"Caeré encima de la red"* ("I will fall on the net.")
  *Me aseguró que caería encima de la red* ("She assured me that she would fall on the net.")

From *futuro compuesto del indicativo* to *condicional compuesto del indicativo*

- *"No habrá llegado a tiempo"* ("He will not have arrived on time.")
  *Creyó que no habría llegado a tiempo* ("She thought he would not have arrived on time.")

- *"¿Habrá comido en su casa?"* ("Would he have eaten at home?")
  *Me preguntó si habría comido en su casa* ("He asked me if he would have eaten at home.")

From *pretérito perfecto simple del indicativo* to *pretérito pluscuamperfecto del indicativo*

- *"Me compré una camisa"* ("I bought a shirt.")
  *Me contó que se había comprado una camisa* ("He told me that he had bought a shirt.")

- *"¿Fueron a la fábrica?"* ("Did you go to the factory?")
  *Nos preguntaron si habíamos ido a la fábrica* ("They asked us if we had gone to the factory.")

From *pretérito perfecto compuesto del indicativo* to *pretérito pluscuamperfecto del indicativo*

- *"La misión ha salido bien"* ("The mission was successful.")
  *Nos confirmó que la misión había salido bien* ("He confirmed us the mission had been successful.")

- *"¿Has ido a ver a tu abuela?"* ("Have you been to see your grandma?")
  *Me preguntó si había ido a ver a mi abuela* ("He asked me if I had been to see my grandma.")

From *presente del subjuntivo* to *pretérito imperfecto del subjuntivo*

- *"Ojalá llueva mañana"* ("I wish it rains tomorrow.")
  *Pensó que ojalá lloviera al día siguiente* ("He thought that he wished it would rain the next day.")

- *"Quizás me vaya a la tarde"* ("Maybe I'll leave in the afternoon.")
  *Dijo que quizás se fuera a la tarde* ("He said he might

leave in the afternoon.")

From *pretérito perfecto del subjuntivo* to *pretérito pluscuamperfecto del subjuntivo*

- *"Espero que te hayas divertido en el cumpleaños"* ("I hope you had fun at the birthday party.")
  *Me dijo que esperaba que me hubiera divertido en el cumpleaños* ("She said she hoped I had had fun at the birthday party.")

- *"Ojalá no me haya visto"* ("I hope he didn't see me.")
  *Me contó que deseó que no la hubiera visto* ("She told me she hoped he didn't see her.")

Well done! We have seen all the possible changes in verb tenses. Now, it's time to take a look at the cases in which the tense stays the same.

*Pretérito perfecto del indicativo*

- *"Antes bailaba más"* ("I used to dance more.")
  *Me dijo que antes bailaba más* ("He told me that he used to dance more.")

*Condicional simple del indicativo*

- *"Me gustaría saber cantar"* ("I would like to know how to sing.")
  *Le confesó que le gustaría saber cantar* ("She confessed she would like to know how to sing.")

*Pretérito pluscuamperfecto del indicativo*

- *"¿Ya se habían visto?"* ("Had you seen each other before?")
  *Me preguntó si ya nos habíamos visto* ("She asked me if we had seen each other before.")

*Pretérito pluscuamperfecto del subjuntivo* and *condicional perfecto del indicativo*

- *"Si lo hubieses pensado bien, no lo habrías hecho"* ("If you would have given it more though, you wouldn't have done it.")
  *Su amiga concluyó que si lo hubiese pensado mejor, no lo habría hecho* ("Her friend concluded that if she would have given it more though, she wouldn't have

done it.")

*Preterito imperfecto del subjuntivo* and *condicional simple*

- *"Si pudiera, te mataría"* ("If I could, I would kill you.") *Le confesó que si pudiera, lo mataría* ("He confessed that if he could, he would kill him.")

## Exercises

1. Decide whether the following statements are true or false. Correct the false ones.

    a. We use quotation marks or dashes of dialogue to indicate indirect speech.

    b. In indirect speech, we have to change spatial references.

    c. Speech verbs always come before the quote in direct speech.

    d. You can use *que* or *si* as a linking word in indirect speech.

2. Go back to the short story and rewrite - in direct speech - the conversation between Nina and her boss from the moment she arrives in his office until he looks at the family picture.

3. Transform the following sentences to direct or indirect speech:

    a. Nos dijo: "Tengo algo muy importante para contarles".

    b. Me preguntó si ya había salido del trabajo.

    c. Ella confesó que ya lo sabía todo.

    d. Cuando llegó, Luis gritó: "¡Nació mi primer hijo!".

4. Complete these sentences with a linking word, a dash or a quotation mark:

    a. Nos preguntó _____ queríamos irnos.

    b. ___Quiero verlo__ dijo María.

    c. Entonces pensé: ___ Qué bien se ve___.

    d. Le aseguró _____ estaría bien.

5. You are going to read a dialogue between two friends talking about a date one of them had. Fill in the blanks with one of the following speech verbs conjugated in the proper tense: decir (x3), responder (x2), preguntar (x2), pedir, contar.

—¡____ todo! —le ____ Julia.
—Bueno, ha ido genial. Me ____ que se divirtió mucho y que le ha encantado nuestra salida.
—¿Y qué le ____? —____ Julia, muy entusiasmada.
—¡Que yo también la había pasado bien! Le ____ que me había parecido una gran idea ir a la feria y le ____ si quería salir conmigo otro día.
—¿Y? ¿____ que sí?
—¡Sí! Me ____ que sí, que le encantaría.

# Chapter 11: Phrasal Verbs and Useful Idioms

## Short story: El collar perdido

—¡Te he dicho que he dejado mi collar aquí, justo **encima** de la **mesita de noche**! —exclamó Marta. Tenía los pelos de punta.

—Y yo te he dicho que no lo he tocado, ¿**te enteras**? —respondió Florencia. Ella también estaba roja como un tomate. Siempre se ponía así cuando discutía.

Las hermanas oyeron unos pasos provenientes del **rellano**. Un instante después, la puerta de la habitación se abrió **de par en par**. Era Susana, la madre de ambas.

—¿Queréis dejar de discutir? —preguntó—. No me obliguéis a **castigaros**. ¿Qué sucede?

—Que Florencia la ha liado de nuevo. He dejado mi collar favorito esta mañana aquí —dijo Marta, **señalando** la mesita de noche que había junto a su cama— y resulta que he vuelto del **instituto** y ya no está.

—Marta se ha levantado con el pie izquierdo —intervino Florencia— y ha decidido acusarme. Pero lo que dice no tiene ni pies ni cabeza.

La madre miró a las dos y luego le preguntó a Marta:

—¿Por qué crees que tu hermana **ha tenido algo que ver**?

—Porque ella siempre lo pierde todo.

—¡**Menudo morro** tienes! ¿Quieres sacar los trapos sucios a relucir? —preguntó Florencia—. Pues a mí me ha dicho un pajarito que eres bastante despistada.

—En eso tiene razón tu hermana, Marta —dijo su madre, con una sonrisa—. **Apuesto** a que lo has llevado al instituto y te lo has dejado allí. Mañana puedes recuperarlo. Te estás **ahogando** en un vaso de agua.

En ese momento, alguien apareció por la puerta. Era el padre de las chicas, Nicolás. Pero no estaba solo: alzaba a Bigotes, el gato negro de la familia. Y alrededor del **peludo** cuello de Bigotes estaba... ¡el collar de Marta!

—¡Parece que he atrapado al **ladronzuelo**! —dijo el padre con una **sonrisa de oreja a oreja**.

## Vocabulary List

| Español | Inglés |
| --- | --- |
| encima | on, on top |
| la mesita de noche | nightstand |
| (in Spain) ¿Te enteras? | Didn't you hear? |
| el rellano | landing |
| de par en par | wide-open |
| (in Spain) el instituto | high school |
| tener que ver con | to have something to do with |
| (in Spain) Menudo morro | you've got some nerve |
| apostar | to bet |

| | |
|---|---|
| ahogar | to drown |
| peludo, peluda | hairy |
| el ladronzuelo, la ladronzuela | petty thief |
| una sonrisa de oreja a oreja | smile from ear to ear |

### Reading Comprehension

As always, now it's time for some questions about the short story you've just read!

1. ¿Cómo se llaman los cuatro miembros de la familia?
2. ¿Cómo se pone Florencia cada vez que discute?
3. ¿Por qué Marta cree que Florencia ha tenido algo que ver?
4. ¿Quién era el culpable de la desaparición del collar?

## Grammar Section

There's nothing like feeling that you're learning real Spanish. The one that is spoken by real people, not in books! When you are done with this chapter, you will master:

- phrasal verbs in Spanish
- prepositions
- uses of *queísmo* and *dequeísmo*
- useful idioms in Spanish

### Phrasal Verbs in Spanish

In Spanish, there are some verbs that only make sense if they are used accompanied by certain prepositions. They are known as *verbos preposicionales* ("prepositional verbs" or "phrasal verbs").

Just in case, we remind you what prepositions are: they are those invariable words used to establish a dependency relationship between two or more words. There are 23 prepositions in Spanish, although only 19 are usually used.

## List of prepositions in Spanish

Spanish and English prepositions are not 100% equivalent; that's why you'll see that many have more than one translation. Let's take a look at the list of the most common Spanish prepositions.

| Preposición | Traducción |
|---|---|
| a | at, to |
| ante | before |
| bajo | under |
| con | with |
| contra | against |
| de | from, of |
| desde | from, after, since |
| durante | during, for |
| en | in, within |
| entre | between |
| hacia | towards, to, around |
| hasta | by, until |
| mediante | through |
| para | for |

| por | by, in, at |
|---|---|
| según | according to |
| sin | without |
| sobre | above, on |
| tras | behind, after |

Now, we are going to check out some of the most common prepositional verbs in Spanish.

### Verbs that Collocate with *a*

- Obligar a ("to make somebody do something")
    - *El resfrío me **obligó a** cancelar los planes* ("The cold forced me to cancel the plans.")
- Acostumbrarse a ("to get used to")
    - *Desde que vivo en España, me **acostumbré a** cenar más tarde* ("Since I've been living in Spain, I got used to having dinner later.")
- Renunciar a ("to resign, to give up")
    - ***Renuncié a** mi trabajo porque me mudé a Montevideo* ("I quit my job because I moved to Montevideo.")
- Recurrir a ("to ask for help")
    - *Matías **recurrió a** un especialista para solucionar su problema* ("Matías went to a specialist to solve his problem.")

### Verbs that Collocate with *en*

- Insistir en ("to insist")
    - *Claudia **insistió en** que fuéramos temprano* ("Claudia insisted that we went early.")

- Apoyarse en ("to lean")
    - *Me **apoyé en** mi hermano cuando estuve triste* ("I leaned on my brother when I was sad.")
- Intervenir en ("to take part")
    - *Tuve que **intervenir en** la pelea* ("I had to take part in the fight.")
- Consistir en ("to consist")
    - *¿**En** qué **consiste** el examen?* ("What does the exam consist of?")

**Verbs that Collocate with *de***
- Enterarse de ("to find out")
    - *Rosa se **enteró de** que le vamos a hacer una fiesta sorpresa* ("Rosa found out that we are going to throw her a surprise party.")
- Despedirse de ("to say goodbye")
    - *No me quiero **despedir de** ti* ("I don't want to say goodbye to you.")
- Encargarse de ("to take care of")
    - *Yo me **encargaré de** los preparativos para el viaje* ("I will take care of the travel arrangements.")
- Carecer de ("to lack")
    - *Pablo **carece de** argumentos para debatir* ("Pablo lacks the arguments to debate.")

*Queísmo* and *dequeísmo*

Here's a tip for you: the examples above can help you avoid two recurring mistakes in Spanish: *dequeísmo* and *queísmo*. *Dequeísmo* is the erroneous addition of the conjunction *que* after the preposition *de*. Meanwhile, *queísmo* is the opposite: the erroneous omission of the preposition *de* before *que*.

To find out if a sentence needs *que* or *de que*, we just need to analyze it and ask ourselves a question. Let's see some examples:

   - *Yo me encargaré de los preparativos para el viaje.*
     - *¿**De qué** me encargaré?* ✓
     - *¿**Qué** me encargaré?* ✗

- *Me alegra que estés bien.*
  - *¿**Qué** me alegra?* ✓
  - *¿**De qué** me alegra?* ✗

## Useful Idioms in Spanish

Idioms or *expresiones idiomáticas* are typical phrases of the Spanish language. Generally, they only make sense in certain contexts, and it's not possible to deduce their meaning by looking at each word separately.

There are a lot of idioms in Spanish. Some are very old, like *hablar hasta por los codos* ("to talk too much;" it dates back to 1739!). Others belong to youth slang, like *estar colado por alguien* ("to have a crush on someone.")

Below, you'll find a short story full of idioms. As you read, try to guess what they mean. You can check if you guessed correctly with the list of idioms + definition that's after the short story!

### Short Story: El gran premio

—No hay ninguna posibilidad de que haya ganado el gran premio —dijo Mariana—. Hay talentos mucho mejores que yo en esta academia.

—No pienses en eso —respondió Miguel—. Eres una gran artista. Estoy seguro de que ganarás. Y si no ganas... Bueno, **no hay mal que por bien no venga.** Ya habrá otra oportunidad.

—¡El señor Corso va a anunciar quién es el ganador del premio! —exclamó Mariana, nerviosa. Se aferró al apoyabrazos de la butaca mientras el anciano director de la academia se ubicaba en el centro del escenario.

—Y el Gran Premio de Dibujo es para... ¡Felipe Báez!

Todo el anfiteatro aplaudió al tiempo que Felipe se levantaba de su asiento y se dirigía al escenario con una gran sonrisa. Miguel miró a Mariana. A pesar de que aplaudía, tenía el ceño fruncido. Parecía desconcertada con la decisión del jurado.

—**Aquí hay gato encerrado** —dijo Mariana—. ¿Cómo es posible que Felipe haya ganado? Faltó a casi todas las clases este semestre.

—Felipe es un tipo talentoso —dijo Miguel—. ¿Has visto su blog? Tiene un montón de ilustraciones impresionantes.

—No sé, no sé... —dijo Mariana—. ¿Cómo dicen por ahí? **El hábito no hace al monje.**

Mientras tanto, en el escenario, Felipe estaba estrechando la mano del señor Corso. Este le otorgó un pequeño trofeo plateado que representaba a una persona dibujando en un lienzo. El director de la academia tomó el micrófono y se dirigió a la audiencia:

—Felipe Báez ha presentado una impresionante ilustración expresionista que representa un caballo corriendo por una pradera. La obra de arte se llama «La libertad», y tiene un gran sentido de la estética. ¿Algunas palabras, señor Báez?

—Sí, señor Corso —dijo Felipe, sonriente, y le quitó el micrófono de las manos al director—. Quiero decir que he estado trabajando en este dibujo durante mucho tiempo. **No he pegado ojo** por noches enteras. Por suerte, finalmente, ¡tanto esfuerzo ha valido la pena! Después de todo, **al que madruga, Dios le ayuda.**

—Muy inspirador, señor Báez, muy inspirador —dijo el señor Corso, y volvió a tomar el micrófono—. Sin embargo, déjeme decirle que **más sabe el diablo por viejo que por diablo.**

Felipe palideció. En el anfiteatro **no volaba una mosca.** El señor Corso continuó:

—Soy una persona anciana y conozco a muchos dibujantes. Algunos son muy famosos y otros son menos conocidos, pero no por eso menos talentosos. La obra que ha presentado el señor Báez pertenece a una artista local llamada Laura Fuentes. ¿Algo que decir, señor Báez? ¿**O le han comido la lengua los ratones**? —Felipe Báez balbuceó algo, pero no dijo nada. Estaba pálido. —Ya veo. Bueno, **el que calla otorga.**

Finalmente, Felipe habló:

—Está bien. Lo confieso: he plagiado la obra. Vi la ilustración en un sitio web y no pude resistirme. Pensé: **cocodrilo que se duerme es cartera.** Cualquiera de ustedes habría hecho lo mismo.

—Ah, **¡piensa el ladrón que todos son de su condición!** —dijo el señor Corso—. Sin embargo, señor Báez, estoy seguro de que ninguno de mis alumnos habría hecho eso. Excepto la suya, todas las obras presentadas en este concurso son originales. Y la más impresionante de todas ha sido... ¡la de Mariana Sánchez! Mariana, tú eres la verdadera ganadora del Gran Premio de Dibujo. Por favor, sube al escenario.

—No puedo creerlo —dijo Mariana, sonriendo.

—Créelo —le dijo Miguel—. ¡Eres una gran artista!

**List of Idioms**

Could you guess what the idioms mean? Let's take a look at their definition:

- **No hay mal que por bien no venga.** It literally means "No evil comes without good," and it's the Spanish equivalent to "Every cloud has a silver lining."

- **Aquí hay gato encerrado.** It means "There's a cat locked up in there", but this saying has nothing to do with an actual cat. It's similar to "Something's fishy": it sounds strange, it looks like a trap.

- **El hábito no hace al monje.** The literal translation is "The robe doesn't make the monk," and it's something like "Don't judge a book by its cover;" that is, appearances are deceiving!

- **No pegar ojo.** It means "Not to strike an eye." We use it to say that someone hasn't slept for a whole night.

- **Al que madruga, Dios le ayuda.** The literal translation of this idiom would be "God helps those who get up early," similar to the English saying, "The early bird catches the worm."

- **Más sabe el diablo por viejo que por diablo.** Its literal translation is "The devil knows more for being old than for being the devil." It's a phrase from *Martín Fierro*, the most important Argentine literary work. It's used to say that old people are wise.

- **No volar una mosca.** "Not even a fly is flying": it means that the room is completely silent.

- **Te han comido la lengua los ratones.** It is used to refer to someone who was left speechless. Literally, it means "Mice ate your tongue."

- **El que calla otorga.** "Those who keep quiet, concede." It means that if you don't say anything, you are agreeing with what was said.
- **Cocodrilo que se duerme es cartera.** "A crocodile who falls asleep becomes a bag." This is a funny way to warn people to watch their back... otherwise, they could be turned into a handbag!
- **Piensa el ladrón que son todos de su condición.** "The thief believes that everyone is just like him." It denotes the ease with which we tend to think that others act as we do, especially when it comes to dishonest actions.

## Exercises

1. Fill in the blanks with one of the following prepositions: *de, en* or *a.*
   a. Desde que vivo en España, me acostumbré ___ cenar tarde.
   b. Juan insistió ___ pagar la cena.
   c. Paula se fue muy temprano y no pude despedirme ___ ella.
   d. La lluvia torrencial me obligó ___ volver a casa para buscar un paraguas.

2. Only one of the following four sentences is correct. Identify it, and fix the wrong ones.
   a. Mi primo me dijo de que el fin de semana iremos a la playa.
   b. Mi profesor me aconsejó que hiciera resúmenes para estudiar.
   c. Mi jefa me avisó de que tendremos un nuevo compañero en la oficina.
   c. Marcela se encargó que estuviera todo listo para partir.

3. The story at the beginning of this chapter is full of idioms! Can you identify them?

4. In the left column, there are some idioms from the story. Match each one with its meaning or equivalent idiom in English.

ahogarse en un vaso de agua        to make no sense

sacar los trapos sucios a relucir   to get out of bed on the wrong side

levantare con el pie izquierdo      to worry too much

no tener pies ni cabeza             to throw something in someone's face

5. Decide whether the following statements are true or false. Correct the false ones.
a. There are 23 prepositions in Spanish, although only 19 are commonly used.
b. *Verbos preposicionales* are verbs that are accompanied by a preposition.
c. *Dequeísmo* is the incorrect addition of *de* after *que*.
d. *Queísmo* is the incorrect omission of the conjunction *que*.

# Chapter 12: Formal Writing

## Formal Request

De: jp.salgado@holamail.com

Para: profesor.guitierrez@universidadnueva.com

**Asunto**: Solicitud de **prórroga**

**Estimado** profesor Gutiérrez:

Espero que este correo lo encuentre bien. Mi nombre es Juan Pablo Salgado. Estuve **matriculado** en su asignatura durante el primer **trimestre** del año 2020. Le escribo este correo para desarrollar las razones por las que todavía no he presentado mi trabajo final y solicitar una prórroga en la fecha de entrega.

En el **transcurso** de su asignatura, como usted sabe, comenzó la pandemia por el covid-19. Como consecuencia de esto, todas las actividades se vieron suspendidas, y mis dos hijas en **edad escolar**, de 5 y 8 años, tuvieron que quedarse en casa.

Mi esposa es médica, y su tarea fue esencial durante los primeros meses de la pandemia, por lo que nos vimos obligados a **reestructurar** el **cronograma** de cuidados en el hogar. De esta manera, desde marzo de 2020 hasta el momento, he quedado a cargo del cuidado y la educación de nuestras dos hijas.

Es por esta razón que no he podido realizar el trabajo final de su asignatura, cuyo cursado, por cierto, fue muy **gratificante**. Desearía poder realizar el trabajo final **a conciencia** y con una investigación **exhaustiva**, como creo que es necesario en todo trabajo académico.

Por ese motivo solicito a usted, de ser posible, una prórroga en la fecha de entrega. **En caso contrario**, asistiré nuevamente a sus clases el año próximo con mucho gusto.

Quedo **a su disposición** y aguardo una respuesta.

**Saludos cordiales,**

Juan Pablo Salgado

## Vocabulary List

| Español | Inglés |
|---|---|
| asunto | subject |
| la prórroga | extension |
| estimado, estimada | dear |
| matriculado, matriculada | enrolled |
| el trimestre | term |
| el transcurso | course |
| edad escolar | school age |
| reestructurar | to reorganize |
| el cronograma | schedule |
| gratificante | rewarding |
| a conciencia | conscientiously |

| | |
|---|---|
| exhaustiva, exhaustivo | thorough |
| en caso contrario | otherwise |
| a su disposición | at your disposal |
| saludos cordiales | best regards |

**Reading Comprehension**

1. ¿Qué necesita Juan Pablo?
2. ¿Por qué Juan Pablo no pudo entregar su trabajo final?
3. ¿Quién se hizo cargo del cuidado de las hijas de la pareja?
4. Si fueras el profesor Gutiérrez, ¿qué le responderías?

# Grammar Section

*¡Felicitaciones!* You've reached the last chapter of this step-by-step guide to perfecting your Spanish skills! During this journey, you've learned how to read and understand complex texts, you've studied all the verb tenses, you've read about direct and indirect speech, and so much more! Now, it's time to put all that knowledge together and learn how to write a formal text. By the end of this chapter, you'll be able to:

- write a formal email
- write an academic paper
- communicate properly in formal language

*Quedan formalmente invitados a continuar leyendo.*

**Formal Writing**

Knowing the keys to writing formal text is important: we need this type of writing for a variety of activities:

- submitting an academic paper
- applying for a job
- communicating in the workspace
- addressing a bank or other institutions

- communicating with professors

From how to address the recipient to the words we chose to close the text, there are several things to keep in mind when writing a formal text. Let's take a look at some of them.

**Spelling**

When we are writing a text to a friend or an informal email to a family member, we don't pay much attention to the spelling of words. However, when we are writing a formal text, it's important to avoid spelling mistakes.

Although most computers correct mistakes automatically (or at least highlight them), when we are done with our text, we have to check that all the words are spelled correctly. One thing you can do is look up confusing words in a dictionary, just to be sure. These are the things that you should pay attention to:

- Accent marks
  - *perdida* ("lost") is not the same as *pérdida* ("loss")
- When to use "b" and when to use "v"
  - *vota* ("votes") is not the same as *bota* ("boot")
- When to use "c," when to use "s," and when to use "z"
  - *casa* ("home") is not the same as *caza* ("hunting"); *cierra* ("close") is not the same as *sierra* ("saw")
- When to use "g" and when to use "j"
  - *agito* ("shake") is not the same as *ajito* ("little garlic")

Our writing leaves an impression on the people who read it. Correct spelling will help create a positive one!

**Wording**

When speaking or writing informally, we don't pay so much attention to word order. We may use incomplete phrases or short answers. But, in formal writing, we have to be careful because we need our interlocutor to understand what we are saying, and we don't have the chance to clarify any misunderstanding at the moment. Spanish word order is especially tricky because it's different from English, and it can be confusing. Here are some tips to improve your formal writing:

- All sentences should be complete and have a subject and a conjugated verb
    - *Solicitarle una prórroga de la fecha de entrega* ("Requesting an extension on the deadline.") ✗
    - *Le escribo para solicitarle una prórroga de la fecha de entrega* ("I'm writing to you to request an extension on the deadline.") ✓
- We should use short and concrete sentences
    - *El consumo principal de la planta es de dióxido de carbono, gracias al cual le es posible liberar oxígeno al ambiente en el que se encuentra dicha planta* ("The main consumption of the plant is carbon dioxide, thanks to which it is possible to release oxygen to the environment in which the plant is located.") ✗
    - *La planta consume principalmente dióxido de carbono y libera oxígeno al ambiente* ("The plant consumes mainly carbon dioxide and releases oxygen into the environment.") ✓
- We must pay attention to punctuation marks
    - Remember, it's not the same saying *No quiero* ("I don't want to") as saying *No, quiero* ("No, I do want to").

**Vocabulary**

**In informal writing**, we use simpler and more direct language. We can use idioms, slang, or repeated words; *it doesn't matter*. But in formal writing, we must strike a delicate balance. Our vocabulary has to be formal and meticulous, but we shouldn't overdo it and use too many fancy or complex words just to make the text look more formal. Remember that sentences should be short and concise, and adding too many pompous words can hinder understanding.

Below, there's a table showing the differences in vocabulary between formal and informal language:

| Escritura informal | Escritura formal |
|---|---|
| Abreviaturas: bici, profe, cole | Palabras completas: bicicleta, profesor/a, colegio |
| Apodos: Pauli, J. P. | Nombres completos: Paula, Juan Pablo |
| Palabras vacías: esto, esa, la cosa | Palabras específicas: el motivo, la conclusión, la tarea asignada |
| Pronombre de segunda persona del singular: tú/vos | Pronombre de segunda persona del singular: usted |

**Text Formatting**

Beyond the words we use, the text should be neat. Formatting is especially important in academic papers. We must unify:

- fonts
- format of titles (if we will use them, and we should)
- line spacing
- indentation
- page numbers

Although they don't have anything to do with the content of the text itself, these elements are really helpful to have a good reading predisposition.

**Keys to Writing Formal Emails**

There are several things to keep in mind before starting to write a formal email, either to a professor or to an employer. In addition to everything we've mentioned above, emails have some specific features. Let's take a look at them.

**Subject**

The subject line should be short and specific. We have to summarize the content of the email in less than ten words so that the recipient has an idea of what they'll find before opening it. Let's see some do's and don'ts:

| No | Sí |
|---|---|
| *Pregunta* ("Question") | *Consulta acerca de la reunión del jueves* ("Query about Thursday meeting") |
| *Reunión* ("Meeting") | *Solicitud de reunión para la semana próxima* ("Meeting request for next week") |
| *Revisión del tema que tratamos en la última reunión de equipos, no creo que sea conveniente que tomemos ese camino en el área de ventas* ("Review of the topic discussed at the last team meeting, I don't think it is advisable to go down that road in the sales area") | *Revisión de la última reunión* ("Review of last meeting") |
| *Profesor, no recuerdo cuándo es el examen* ("Professor, I don't remember when the exam is") | *Consulta sobre fecha de examen* ("Exam date query") |

### Content

We've already said that our writing has to be specific and clear. Now, let's take a look at some common words and expressions we can include in formal emails.

Greetings:
- *A quien corresponda:* ("To whom it may concern")
- *Estimado/a:* ("Dear")
- *De mi mayor consideración:* ("Of my highest consideration")
- *Señor/Señora:* ("Sir"/"Madam")

Email body:
- *Por medio de la presente* ("Through this email")
- *El motivo de este correo es* ("The purpose of this email is")
- *Le escribo para consultarle acerca de* ("I am writing to inquire about")

Email closing line:
- *Atentamente,* ("Sincerely")
- *Quedo a su disposición,* ("I remain at your service")
- *Saludos cordiales,* ("Kind regards")

**Keys to Writing an Academic Paper**

Academic language can be challenging, even for native Spanish speakers. A good way to get used to academic language is to read many papers in Spanish to become familiar with the wording, the vocabulary, the tone, etc. Also, if you read papers on the topic you have to write about, you'll have a broader knowledge of the specific terminology and of the subject itself. Keep in mind that it's better to plan and write the essay directly in Spanish rather than doing it in English and then translating it.

Let's look at some words and expressions that can be useful in academic writing:

- *Por lo tanto* ("Therefore")
- *Sin embargo* ("However")
- *De este modo* ("Thus")
- *Con respecto a* ("Regarding")
- *A pesar de* ("Despite")
- *Por añadidura* ("In addition")
- *Por un lado* ("On the one hand")
- *Asimismo* ("Likewise, furthermore")

Now that we have some vocabulary, let's review the typical structure of an academic text.

### Introduction

In the introduction, we have to state what our paper will be about. We must be clear and include all the necessary information so that the reader has a general overview of what they will find in it. We have to mention the topics we'll develop, state our hypothesis and indicate why the paper is relevant.

### Body

This is the most important part of the paper. Here we develop our hypothesis, analyze the authors, and answer the questions. We also write down all the results of our research, and what we have studied, learned, or investigated.

### Conclusion

The conclusion is the section at the end of the paper that summarizes the most important points of the text. There, we can state our personal opinion on the results. We can also give an answer to the questions that triggered the research, or we can leave possible queries for further research.

### Exercises

1. Indicate whether these sentences are using formal or informal language:
   a. ¿Me podría recordar la hora de la reunión, por favor?
   b. Manolo, ¡te veo a las 5 ahí!
   c. Papá, recoge eso y luego nos vemos en casa.
   d. Desde ya muchas gracias por su respuesta y que tenga un excelente día.

2. Taking into account the characteristics of a formal email we have seen, write a resignation email.

3. For each of the topics below, write an appropriate email subject:
   a. Un supervisor quiere concretar una reunión con un empleado para despedirlo.
   b. Un alumno quiere discutir su nota con un profesor.
   c. Un hombre quiere pedirle los resultados de sus estudios a su médica.

d. Una gerente quiere avisarle a un candidato que quedó seleccionado para el trabajo.

4. Decide whether the following statements are true or false. Correct the false ones:
   a. It's better to use whole words rather than abbreviations in a formal text.
   b. It's okay to use nicknames in a formal email.
   c. You should use as many formal words as possible in a formal text.
   d. It's better to write an essay in English and then translate into Spanish.

5. Correct this email and change or add the necessary words to make it more formal:

   Hola:

   Quiero pedir un préstamo al vanco. Tengo que hacer una reforma en mi casa, pero no tengo todo el dinero gunto para hacerlo.

   Puedo acreditar mis ingresos para devolver el dinero en un plaso de dos años.

   Espero que me digan que sí.

   Chau

   Juli

# Final Quiz

And with that, you've reached the end of *Advanced Spanish: The Step-By-Step Guide to Perfecting Your Grammar, Speaking, and Comprehension Skills*! Congratulations! You are just one quiz away from becoming a master in Spanish. In this final quiz, we'll check everything we've seen in chapters 6 through 12. Following the format of the quiz you took halfway through the book, there are 5 exercises, each worth 2 points:

- If you score between 8 and 10 points, *¡felicitaciones!* You are an advanced Spanish student!
- If your final result is between 4 and 8 points, you are almost there! You just need to go back to the most challenging chapters for a quick review.
- If your score is 3 or lower, there's no need to worry. You can go back to chapter 6 and reread the second part of the book. Then, take the quiz again. We are sure you'll do better!

Now, let's get started!

1. **Complete the following sentences with the correct reflexive pronoun.**

    a. Ya deja de mirar___ al espejo, Pedro, vamos a llegar tarde.

    b. No le hables a Juan. Hoy no ___ pudo duchar porque no había agua en su edificio y está de mal humor.

   c. Mira, ___ lastimé la pierna. Venía caminando por la calle, pisé algo patinoso y ___ resbalé.

   d. Yo ___ llamo Claudia. Mi esposa ___ llama Marcela. ¿Tú cómo ___ llamas?

2. **Complete the following sentences about the usage of the *verboides* with *participio, gerundio,* or *infinitivo*.**

   a. Usamos el _____ para formar los tiempos verbales compuestos.

   b. Tanto en inglés como en español, usamos el _____ para enunciar el verbo.

   c. El _____ cumple funciones de adverbio. El _____ puede ser usado como un sustantivo. El _____ tiene funciones adjetivales.

   d. A pesar de que en ambos idiomas tiene un uso adverbial, el _____ no se usa exactamente igual en inglés y en español.

3. **These sentences are wrong. Correct them.**

   a. Si llegaras más temprano, habrías conseguido lugar para sentarte.

   b. El robo del banco llevó a cabo por un grupo de cuatro delincuentes.

   c. Se realizó una encuesta por una empresa privada.

   d. La habitación está amoblada con buen gusto, contando con dos camas, una heladera y un baño.

4. **Complete these sentences with a linking word, a dash, or a quotation mark.**

   a. ___ No estoy lista para irme ___ dijo, mientras abrazaba a sus padres___. Voy a extrañaros demasiado.

   b. Mi jefa me dijo ___ estaba trabajando muy bien y me preguntó ___ estaba interesada en un ascenso.

   c. Llevábamos largo rato discutiendo sin ponernos de acuerdo, hasta que me dijo: ___¿Sabes qué? Tienes razón. Tu propuesta es mejor___.

d. Primero quiso saber ___ había visto a su hermana y luego me dijo: ___Llevo días sin poder comunicarme con ella___.

5. **Fill in the blanks with *de, en* or *a*, or leave them empty.**

    a. Lo que plantean desde la dirigencia no tiene ni pies ni cabeza, carece completamente ___ sentido.

    b. Si quería ahorrar el dinero para irse de vacaciones, Pablo sabía que tenía que renunciar ___ muchos de los gustos que se daba.

    c. Es un buen muchacho, pero se apoya demasiado ___ sus padres.

    d. El acto consiste ___ un brindis y, luego, una entrega de premios.

    e. Me confirmaron ___ que había ganado a través de un correo electrónico.

# Answer Key

## Chapter 1

**1.**
a. Balloon → Globo → ge-ele-o-be-o
b. Dog → Perro → pe-e-ere-ere-o
c. Butterfly → Mariposa → eme-a-ere-i-pe-o-ese-a
d. City → Ciudad → ce-i-u-de-a-de

**2.**
a. Te-le-vi-sor
b. Hom-bre
c. Rui-do
d. Cu-cha-ra

**3.**
a. Ayer escuch_é_ una canci_ó_n que me gust_ó_ mucho.
b. Mañana ir_é_ a visitarte.
c. El español es hablado por muchas personas de Am_é_rica.
d. Soy bueno con los n_ú_meros, as_í_ que me gustan las matem_á_ticas.

**4.**

El reino de Castilla fue el primer territorio en el que se habló español. Durante los siglos posteriores, el idioma se expandió por todo el mundo. Hoy en día es hablado en más de 20 territorios, aunque cada país tiene su propia variedad.

**5.**

a. Diez arqueólogos componían la expedición. La persona a cargo era María Sánchez.

b. Se encontraron 17 objetos, entre los que se encuentran una pequeña embarcación, dos jarrones y una figura tallada en madera.

c. Por el alto potencial arqueológico del lugar, que forma parte de la Zona de Monumentos Históricos de la alcaldía.

d. Al Museo Nacional de Antropología, donde formarán parte de la colección de arqueología.

**6.**

a. Son las tres y cuarenta y cinco de la tarde
b. Son las dos en punto de la tarde
c. Son las ocho y media de la noche
d. Son las nueve y cuarto de la mañana

**7.**

a. Mi <u>color favorito</u> es el verde.
Normally (except in very specific cases), the adjective goes after the noun.

b. David va a <u>la</u> universidad en tren.
*Universidad* is a feminine noun, so the article that precedes it must be feminine as well.

c. Miguel y su familia <u>viven</u> en Madrid.
Miguel and his family are *ellos* (they), so the correct conjugation of *vivir* in this case is *viven*, in the plural.

d. Les llevé el perro <u>a</u> mis padres.
Indirect objects are introduced by the preposition *a*.

**8.**

La paella es una típica comida española. El alimento más importante de la paella es el <u>arroz</u>. Se cocina en una <u>sartén</u> junto a otros ingredientes, a menudo <u>mariscos</u>. Una buena bebida para acompañar la paella es el <u>vino</u> blanco.

**9.**

Grupo 1. Adverbios de lugar: arriba, aquí, alrededor, detrás

Grupo 2. Adverbios de modo: rápidamente, fácilmente, mal, bien

Grupo 3. Adverbios de tiempo: luego, nunca, siempre, ayer

Grupo 4. Adverbios de cantidad: mucho, poco, bastante, menos

**10.**
a. Incorrect. Nunca había estado en Colombia.
If the adverb refers to the whole sentence, then it can be placed between the subject and the verb.
b. Correct.
c. Correct.
d. Incorrect. Tengo mucho sueño.
Adverbs of quantity are usually placed after the verb they modify.

**11.**
a. Viajaré a Málaga con mi hermana.
b. Ese tren va hacia el sur.
c. Mi cumpleaños es en febrero.
d. Este regalo es para ti.

**12.**
a. Valencia está ubicada al este de la Península Ibérica.
b. Además del español, en Barcelona hablan catalán.
c. En Cuba llaman "guagua" al autobús.
d. Santiago de Chile es una de las ciudades más grandes del sur del continente americano.

**13.**
a. Me dijo Paula que vendría hoy.
b. Intenté conseguir entradas, pero fue imposible.
c. Iré a la fiesta aunque estoy un poco cansada.
d. Francisco y Marcelo vendrán esta noche y cenaremos juntos.

**14.**
1. narrating events from the past: d. Colón llega a América en 1492.
2. talking about frequent actions: c. Voy a la escuela en autobús.
3. talking about the near future: a. Tengo una entrevista de trabajo el jueves.
4. mentioning present desires: b. Quiero casarme en mayo.

**15.**

A. ¿Qué <u>estás haciendo</u>?
B. <u>Estoy leyendo</u> un libro. ¿Y tú?
A. Yo estoy <u>cocinando ceviche</u>. ¿Quieres venir a cenar?
B. ¡Claro! ¡Ya lo <u>estoy saboreando</u>!

**16.**

he sido: pretérito perfecto (verb: ser)
estuve: pretérito perfecto simple (verb: estar)
fue: pretérito perfecto simple (verb: ser)
encargaba: pretérito imperfecto (verb: encargar)
era: pretérito imperfecto (verb: ser)
había trabajado: pretérito pluscuamperfecto (verb: trabajar)
llegó: pretérito perfecto simple (verb: llegar)

**17.**

A. ¡Hola! Busco a Carla.
B. Lo siento, pero Carla me dijo que no <u>saldrá</u> hoy. Tiene un examen importante mañana, así que <u>estudiará</u> toda la tarde.
A. Estoy seguro de que lo <u>hará</u> bien.
B. ¡Yo también lo creo! Para mañana a esta hora, <u>habrá aprobado</u> ese examen.

**18.**

a. ¿Cómo está el restaurante?
b. ¿Dónde vive Fernando?
c. ¿Cuándo festejará su boda Marcela?
d. ¿Quién es Lucas?

**19.**

a. En el siglo V.
b. Catellano, español ibérico o español de España.
c. Fue el primer intento de definir la gramática de una lengua europea.
d. En el español de España, el pronombre de segunda persona del plural es "vosotros", mientras que en el español de Latinoamérica se usa "ustedes".

# Chapter 2

**Reading Comprehension**

1. Entre los siglos VI y V a. C.
2. Aristóteles.
3. De personajes populares y cotidianos.
4. Se pone más énfasis en la escenografía y en el carácter visual del teatro. No se enfoca solo en lo literario, sino en la interpretación de los personajes, la acción, los movimientos.

**Exercises**

**1.**

a. Journalistic text
b. Instructive text
c. Narrative text
d. Expository text

**2.**

Orientation: "Kala es un león que vive en un desierto".
Complication: "Un día, se estaba bañando y un grupo de hienas se acercó a él para atacarlo. Si bien el león era fuerte, las hienas eran muchas. Cuando estaban a punto de vencer, llegó Lina, una leona".
Resolution: "Lina espantó a las hienas y lamió las heridas que le habían hecho a Kala".

**3.**

This is a possible structure for a recipe, with some of the verbs typically used:

Para esta receta utilizaremos..... El primer paso es mezclar.... Luego tomamos la masa y amasamos...... Finalmente, integramos todo..... Llevamos al horno durante....

**4.**

This a possible vocabulary list for the text:

| Español | English |
|---------|---------|
| entre   | between |

| | |
|---|---|
| reunir | gather |
| el apareamiento | mating |
| el cortejo | courtship |
| adecuada, adecuado | suitable |
| marcar | set |
| el vecino, la vecina | neighbour |
| la jerarquía | hierarchy |
| el tacto | touch |
| el desparasitado | removing parasites |
| puntear | pluck |
| la disponibilidad | availability |
| el rincón | corner |
| semejante | similar |

**5.**

These are possible answers:

Primer párrafo
Idea principal: Para qué sirve la comunicación entre organismos.
Título: Comunicación entre organismos

Segundo párrafo
Idea principal: Para qué sirve el tacto en primates y arañas.
Título: El tacto

Tercer párrafo

Idea principal: Cómo funciona la comunicación a través del sonido en distintos animales.
Título: El sonido

Título del texto: Los sentidos en la comunicación entre seres vivos

# Chapter 3

### Reading Comprehension

1. Porque solo queda una empanada en el restaurante.
2. Propone un juego y, la que gane, podrá comer la empanada.
3. Fabián.
4. Porque él se come la última empanada.

**1.**

a. True
b. False. There are three: indicative, subjunctive and imperative.
c. False. The first conjugation is for verbs ending in *-ar*.
d. False. Imperfect past (*pretérito imperfecto*) is used for durative or reiterative actions in the past.

**2.**

a. Ayer mi mamá <u>visitó</u> a mi abuela.
b. Mañana Martín <u>copiará</u> la tarea de la escuela.
c. Mañana quizás <u>confirme</u> mi asistencia.
d. Cuando llamaste, nosotros ya <u>habíamos comprado</u> las entradas.

**3.**

a. Los estudiantes organizarán la fiesta de Navidad.
b. El autor firmará los libros en la presentación.

**4.**

a. Esta canción será interpretada por la banda.
b. Estos huesos fueron descubiertos por los arqueólogos.

5.

| Verbo | Conjugación |
|---|---|
| están | presente del indicativo |
| probar | infinitivo |
| pincha | presente del indicativo |
| queda | presente del indicativo |
| ordenar | infinitivo |
| avisa | presente del indicativo |
| deseo | presente del indicativo |
| determina | presente del indicativo |
| toca | presente del indicativo |
| piensa | presente del indicativo |
| manejar | infinitivo |
| gustaría | condicional simple del indicativo |
| solucionara | pretérito imperfecto del subjuntivo |
| invita | presente del indicativo |
| jugar | infinitivo |

| | |
|---|---|
| gane | presente del subjuntivo |
| quedará | futuro simple del indicativo |
| encanta | presente del indicativo |
| declaró | pretérito perfecto simple del indicativo |
| pregunta | presente del indicativo |
| grita | presente del indicativo |
| quedaba | pretérito imperfecto simple del indicativo |
| trabajaba | pretérito imperfecto simple del indicativo |
| estudiar | infinitivo |
| contestan | presente del indicativo |
| piensa | presente del indicativo |
| llega | presente del indicativo |
| miran | presente del indicativo |
| fulminan | presente del indicativo |
| agarra | presente del indicativo |
| traga | presente del indicativo |

| grita | presente del indicativo |
|---|---|
| exclama | presente del indicativo |
| lanza | presente del indicativo |
| disfruta | presente del indicativo |
| estaba | pretérito imperfecto simple del indicativo |

# Chapter 4

**Reading Comprehension**

1. Porque le declaró su amor a Matías.
2. Que deje el móvil en la cocina y no lo lea más.
3. Perdió el móvil.
4. Porque su mamá es implacable.

**Exercises**

**1.**

poner, correr, poder, permanecer, distraer, poder, suceder, cometer, reconocer, saber, responder, deshacer, tener, atraer, perder, resolver, ver, poner, leer, obedecer, vencer, amanecer, reprender, atender, enloquecer, ser, detener, coger, querer, deber, aparecer, esconder, devolver, extraer, atrever, conocer.

**2.**

| Verbo | Tiempo | Modo | Persona | Número |
|---|---|---|---|---|
| Sucede | Presente | Indicativo | Tercera | Singular |
| Puedes | Presente | Indicativo | Segunda | Singular |
| Cometí | Pretérito simple | Indicativo | Primera | Singular |

| Apareció | Pretérito simple | Indicativo | Tercera | Singular |
| --- | --- | --- | --- | --- |
| He perdido | Pretérito perfecto compuesto | Indicativo | Primera | Singular |

**3.**

a. El camión <u>retrocedió</u> rápidamente
b. Los niños se habían <u>escondido</u> tras la puerta
c. Ojalá no <u>aprendamos</u> geometría en la escuela
d. Nunca <u>comprenderé</u> los motivos de su renuncia

**4.**

a. Juana le <u>debía</u> dinero a su madre
b. Mi familia <u>posee</u> muchas propiedades
c. Te <u>responderé</u> cuando lo sepa
d. ¡<u>Corre</u>! ¡Vienen por ti!

**5.**

This is a possible alternative ending, using only verbs of the second conjugation:

Al aparecer en la escuela, Álvaro corrió hacia Matías. Matías lo vio y se escondió.

—No debo hacer esto. —Matías retrocedió.

—Vale, pero quiero saber por qué. —Álvaro había perdido toda la vergüenza.

—No lo entenderías. Adiós, Álvaro.

# Chapter 5

### Reading Comprehension

1. Una puerta de madera verde, entre la pescadería y la panadería, justo enfrente del malecón.
2. Su amiga Sandra.
3. Porque pensaba que el lugar estaba abandonado.
4. Dicen que es uno de los mejores instructores de salsa del Caribe.

## Exercises

**1.**

escribir, sacudir, describir, recibir, vivir, interrumpir, compartir, cumplir, añadir, crujir, abrir, unir, confundir.

**2.**

escribir: *había escrito*. Pretérito pluscuamperfecto del modo indicativo.
describir: *describió*. Pretérito perfecto simple del modo indicativo.
recibir: *recibió*. Pretérito perfecto simple del modo indicativo.
vivir: *vive*. Presente del modo indicativo.
compartir: *compartir*. Infinitivo.
cumplir: *cumples*. Presente del modo indicativo.
abrir: *abría*. Pretérito imperfecto del modo indicativo.
confundir: *hemos confundido* y *han confundido*. Pretérito perfecto de indicativo.

**3.**

a. Venid a mi casa. Os <u>recibiré</u> sin problema. Tengo algunas camas extra, así que <u>decidiréis</u> vosotros mismos dónde dormiréis.
b. Yo <u>he vivido</u> muchos años en Madrid. Al principio vivía con mi novia, pero luego me he separado. Desde entonces, <u>he compartido</u> piso con compañeros de la universidad.
c. Si yo <u>escribiera</u> el guion de una película, sería sobre vaqueros.

**4.**

a. Viviréis. 2. Futuro simple de indicativo.
b. Recibiera. 4. Pretérito imperfecto de subjuntivo.
c. Hayamos escrito. 1. Pretérito perfecto compuesto de subjuntivo.
d. Partisteis. 3. Pretérito perfecto simple de indicativo.

**5.**

| Pretérito perfecto simple de indicativo | tú | insististe |
|---|---|---|
| Condicional simple de indicativo | vosotros | insistiríais |

| Futuro compuesto de indicativo | nosotros | habremos insistido |
| Presente de subjuntivo | ella | insista |
| Pretérito pluscuamperfecto de subjuntivo | ustedes | hubieran o hubiesen insistido |

# Chapter 6

### Reading Comprehension

1. Porque no conocía a nadie allí y porque odiaba las calaveritas de azúcar, la gente pintada y todo lo vinculado al Día de Muertos.
2. Chupitos de tequila.
3. Sus lentes.
4. En la alberca.

### Exercises

**1.**

a. Dalma <u>es</u> la más inteligente del grupo.
b. Hoy a la noche no <u>puedo</u>, <u>iré</u> a una fiesta.
c. Ayer Juan me <u>dio</u> una sorpresa, pero yo ya <u>sabía</u> qué era.
d. Espero que Patricia <u>esté</u> en su casa a la tarde.
e. ¡No te <u>acerques</u>! <u>Hay</u> una rata ahí.

**2.**

querer, crecer, buscar, oír, mover, sentir, tener, ir, encender, prender, ser, estar, reír, decir, reír, llegar, dar, ver.

**3.**

a. Regular
b. Regular
c. Irregular
d. Irregular
e. Regular

**4.**
 a. Change one vowel for another
b. From one vowel to two vowels (diphthongization)
c. From one vowel to two vowels (diphthongization)
d. Change one vowel for another

**5.**

This is a possible short story using the four verbs

Un anillo salió despedido por la ventana. José no podía creer que sucediera eso justo en esa situación. Pablo le gritaba y caminaba furioso por la habitación. José intentó identificar si Pablo había visto el anillo, pero no lo logró. Apretó los dientes y volvió a la discusión. Estaba furioso con Pablo, porque le había mentido y porque le había robado dinero. Entonces se acordó del anillo, que había visto caer. Se vistió rápidamente sin pensar, ante la mirada atónita de Pablo. Si encontraba el anillo podía venderlo, seguro ganaría mucho dinero con él. Pero cuando llegó abajo, el anillo ya había desaparecido. Pablo lo miraba desde arriba, decepcionado.

# Mid-Book Quiz

**1.**
 a. It's in the active voice. The passive version would be: Buenos Aires fue fundada por Pedro de Mendoza.
b. It's in the passive voice. The active version would be: Julio César fundó Sevilla.
c. It's in the passive voice. The active version would be: El dueño alimentó al gato.
d. Active voice. The passive version would be: Las pizzas caseras fueron amasadas por Julián.

**2.**
 a. Nosotros estudiamos.
b. Ellos/as saltaban.
c. Vosotros/as habéis cocinado.
d. Yo compraría.

**3.**

Anoche salí a <u>correr</u> al parque. Mientras <u>corría</u>, sentí que alguien me seguía. Primero pensé que era otra persona, pero no había nadie <u>corriendo</u> allí, aparte de mí. No le di importancia y seguí <u>corriendo</u>. Sin embargo, volví a sentir que alguien me seguía. Finalmente, dejé de <u>correr</u> y me di media vuelta. Y entonces lo vi. ¡Un conejo blanco me había estado siguiendo mientras <u>corría</u>!

**4.**

First conjugation: mirar, bajar, caminar, preguntar, revisar.
Second conjugation: pretender, responder, vender, beber, comer.
Third conjugation: cumplir, abrir, partir, construir, invadir.

**5.**

In order: bajar, comer, beber, caminando, miraban, abrió, vendió, preguntó, pretendía, partió, revisar, cumplían, respondió, construir, invaden.

# Chapter 7

### Reading Comprehension

1. Se quedó sin agua.
2. Una luz de emergencia que iluminaba débilmente unos cuantos cables contra la pared del túnel.
3. En el otro extremo del vagón.
4. Tiene el pelo corto y rojizo, un hocico largo y orejas grandes.

### Exercises

**1.**

se hicieron, se sentó, preguntándose, se había colado, se perdió, se sentía, me bañaba, vistiéndome, me llamo, se presentó, se acostaría.

**2.**

a. Yo <u>me</u> baño por la noche y Juan <u>se</u> baña por la mañana.
b. En nuestra familia, siempre <u>nos</u> acostamos tarde.
c. ¿<u>Te</u> sientes bien?
d. Mis hijos <u>se</u> llaman Teodoro y Bárbara.

3.

| Pronombre personal | Pronombre reflexivo | Verbo infinitivo | Verbo reflexivo |
|---|---|---|---|
| yo | me | peino | peinarse |
| tú | te | vistes | vestirse |
| él | se | cambia | cambiarse |
| nosotras | nos | maquillamos | maquillarse |
| vosotros | os | despertáis | despertarse |
| ellos | se | afeitan | afeitarse |

4.

In order: levantarse, ducharse, ponerse, se había despertado, se limpiaba, vestirme, cepillarme, se miró.

5.

a. True.
b. False. Only those verbs that represent an action that the subject can do to itself can be reflexive.
c. True.
d. False. Reflexive pronouns are normally placed before the verb.

# Chapter 8

**Reading Comprehension**

1. Porque había mucho tráfico.
2. Le gusta que sea divertido. Siempre está haciendo bromas para hacerla reír.
3. Es una hamburguesería con juegos de arcade. Está llena de niños corriendo y gritando.
4. Que no es un lugar muy romántico para mantener una cita, pero que tiene su encanto.

**Exercises**

**1.**
Infinitives: bajar, caminar, apretar, llegar, mantener, encontrar, notar, pedir
Gerunds: clavando, viendo, bromeando, corriendo, sonriendo
Participles: reflexionado, conocido, entrado, elegido

**2.**
A. viviendo
B. haciendo
A. estudiando, durmiendo, trabajando
B. disfrutar

**3.**
a. False. Infinitives, gerunds and participles are invariable to tense, mood, number and person.
b. True.
c. False. They must express a simultaneous or previous action to that of the main verb.
d. True.

**4.**

| Verbo | Infinitivo | Gerundio | Participio |
|---|---|---|---|
| saliste | salir | saliendo | salido |
| hizo | hacer | haciendo | hecho |
| llegó | llegar | llegando | llegado |
| comimos | comer | comiendo | comido |
| disfrutasteis | disfrutar | disfrutando | disfrutado |
| bailaba | bailar | bailando | bailado |

**5.**

cerrado, pronosticado, decidido, explicado, trasladado.

# Chapter 9

## Reading Comprehension

1. Que todos opinen sobre su accidente.
2. Se cayó por las escaleras yendo al cuarto de baño.
3. Susana.
4. El de Angelina.

## Exercises

**1.**

a. podrías, habría dado, deberías, querrías, dirías, gustaría, podríais

b. "Fui chocado por un camión"; "Javier era atosigado por el recién llegado para saber lo que había pasado"

c. "Si hubieras usado el cinturón de seguridad, no habrías tenido ni un rasguño"; "Si hubieras empezado por ahí, nos habríamos ahorrado toda esta charla"

**2.**

a. True.
b. False. The emphasis is in the person or thing affected by the action.
c. True.
d. False. It can be used to make assumptions about the past, to talk about situations that didn't happen in the past, or to manifest agreement or disagreement with past situations.

**3.**

a. Me <u>gustaría</u> conocer México algún día.
b. Si me <u>hubieras conocido</u> antes, no me <u>habrías querido</u>.
c. ¿Me <u>ayudarías</u> con este ejercicio?
d. Si <u>sube</u> la marea, se <u>mojan</u> las toallas de los bañistas.
e. Si no <u>dejan</u> de pelear, nos <u>quedaremos</u> en casa.
f. Le dijo que sí y, la verdad, yo le <u>habría contestado</u> lo mismo.

**4.**

a. Subject: María. La ola arrastró a María.
b. Subject: Juana. Lucas es amado por Juana.

c. Subject: Las sequías. La deforestación genera las sequías.

d. Subject: Mi equipo. El partido fue ganado por mi equipo.

e. Subject: El sospechoso. Encontraron al sospechoso muerto en un callejón/Se encontró al sospechoso muerto en un callejón.

**5.**

a. Si fuera más linda, sería más feliz.

b. A Carla le dieron un anillo.

c. Ojalá vengas a la fiesta.

d. Santiago, ¿me darías un chocolate?

# Chapter 10

### Reading Comprehension

1. No, finalmente Nina renuncia.
2. Porque era descuidada, tenía malos modos y llegaba tarde.
3. Porque le recordaba a su hija y era una buena chica.
4. Que despidieran a Nina y se quedara desempleada.

### Exercises

**1.**

a. False. We use them to indicate direct speech.

b. True.

c. False. They can come before or after the quote.

d. True.

**2.**

This is a possible answer:

—Me pareces una niña muy inteligente, te veo futuro en la empresa. Pero de esta manera no puedo seguir trabajando contigo. Eres muy descuidada, llegas siempre tarde, tienes malos modos.

—Sí, es cierto, a veces me quedo dormida y a veces odio cuando me pides algo.

—Pero, Nina, eres mi secretaria...

**3.**

a. Nos dijo que tenía algo muy importante para contarnos.

b. "¿Ya saliste del trabajo?".

c. Ella confesó: "Ya lo sé todo".

d. Cuando llegó, Luis gritó que había nacido su primer hijo.

**4.**

a. Nos preguntó si queríamos irnos.
b. —Quiero verlo —dijo María.
c. Entonces pensé: "Qué bien se ve".
d. Le aseguró que estaría bien.

**5.**

In order: cuéntame, pidió, ha dicho, respondiste, preguntó, dije, pregunté, dijo, respondió.

# Chapter 11

### Reading Comprehension

1. Los padres son Susana y Nicolás. Las hijas son Marta y Florencia.
2. Se pone roja como un tomate.
3. Porque Florencia siempre lo pierde todo.
4. Bigotes, el gato negro de la familia.

### Exercises

**1.**

a. Desde que vivo en España, me acostumbré <u>a</u> cenar tarde.
b. Juan insistió <u>en</u> pagar la cena.
c. Paula se fue muy temprano y no pude despedirme <u>de</u> ella.
d. La lluvia torrencial me obligó <u>a</u> volver a casa para buscar un paraguas.

**2.**

a. Incorrect. Mi primo me dijo <u>que</u> el fin de semana iremos a la playa.
b. Correct.
c. Incorrect. Mi jefa me avisó <u>que</u> tendremos un nuevo compañero en la oficina.
d. Incorrect. Marcela se encargó <u>de que</u> estuviera todo listo para partir.

**3.**

tener los pelos de punta
estar rojo como un tomate
liarla

levantarse con el pie izquierdo
no tener ni pies ni cabeza
tener algo que ver
sacar los trapos sucios a relucir
decir un pajarito (algo)
ahogarse en un vaso de agua

**4.**

ahogarse en un vaso de agua: to worry too much
sacar los trapos sucios a relucir: to throw something in someone's face
levantare con el pie izquierdo: to get out of bed on the wrong side
no tener pies ni cabeza: to make no sense

**5.**

a. True.
b. True.
c. False. *Dequeísmo* is the incorrect addition of *de* before *que*.
d. False. *Queísmo* is the incorrect omission of the preposition *de* before *que*.

## Chapter 12

### Reading Comprehension

1. Una prórroga en la fecha de entrega de su trabajo final.
2. Porque tuvo que hacerse cargo de la educación y el cuidado de sus hijas.
3. Juan Pablo.
4. Le daría un mes más para entregar el trabajo final.

### Exercises

**1.**

a. Formal
b. Informal
c. Informal
d. Formal

**2.**

The following structure could be used:

Estimado...:
Por el presente correo le informo que a partir de... ya no formaré

parte de...
Muchas gracias por todas las oportunidades...
Saluda cordialmente
Firma

**3.**

Here are some possible email subjects:

a. Solicitud de reunión con Recursos Humanos
b. Consulta sobre calificación
c. Consulta sobre resultados
d. ¡Enhorabuena!

**4.**

a. True.
b. False. It's better to avoid nicknames in a formal text.
c. False. You shouldn't use too many formal words.
d. False. It's better to write it directly in Spanish.

**5.**

A quien corresponda:

Escribo este correo para solicitar un préstamo al banco. Debo hacer una reforma en mi casa, pero actualmente no cuento con el dinero suficiente.

Puedo acreditar mis ingresos para devolver el dinero en un plazo de dos años.

Aguardo su respuesta.

Saludos cordiales,

Julia Ledesma

**Final Quiz**

**1.**

a. Ya deja de mirar<u>te</u> al espejo, Pedro, vamos a llegar tarde.
b. No le hables a Juan. Hoy no <u>se</u> pudo duchar porque no había agua en su edificio y está de mal humor.
c. Mira, <u>me</u> lastimé la pierna. Venía caminando por la calle, pisé algo patinoso y <u>me</u> resbalé.
d. Yo <u>me</u> llamo Claudia. Mi esposa <u>se</u> llama Marcela. ¿Tú cómo <u>te</u> llamas?

**2.**
 a. participio
b. infinitivo
c. gerundio; infinitivo; participio
d. gerundio

**3.**
 a. Si <u>hubieras llegado</u> más temprano, habrías conseguido lugar para sentarte/Si llegas más temprano, <u>conseguirías</u> lugar para sentarte.
b. El robo del banco <u>fue llevado</u> a cabo por un grupo de cuatro delincuentes/Un grupo de cuatro delincuentes <u>llevó</u> a cabo el robo del banco.
c. <u>Se realizó</u> una encuesta/Una empresa privada <u>realizó</u> una encuesta/Una encuesta <u>fue realizada</u> por una empresa privada.
d. La habitación está amoblada con buen gusto <u>y cuenta</u> con dos camas, una heladera y un baño.

**4.**
 a. <u>—</u>No estoy lista para irme <u>—</u>dijo, mientras abrazaba a sus padres<u>—</u>. Voy a extrañaros demasiado.
b. Mi jefa me dijo <u>que</u> estaba trabajando muy bien y me preguntó <u>si</u> estaba interesada en un ascenso.
c. Llevábamos largo rato discutiendo sin ponernos de acuerdo, hasta que me dijo: "<u>¿</u>Sabes qué? Tienes razón. Tu propuesta es mejor<u>"</u>.
d. Primero quiso saber <u>si</u> había visto a su hermana y luego me dijo: "<u>L</u>levo días sin poder comunicarme con ella<u>"</u>.

**5.**
 a. de
b. a
c. en
d. en
e. empty

# Free Bonuses from Cecilia Melero

Hi Spanish Learners!

My name is Cecilia Melero, and first off, I want to THANK YOU for reading my book.

Now you have a chance to join my exclusive Spanish language learning email list so you can get the ebooks below for free as well as the potential to get more Spanish books for free! Simply click the link below to join.

P.S. Remember that it's 100% free to join the list.

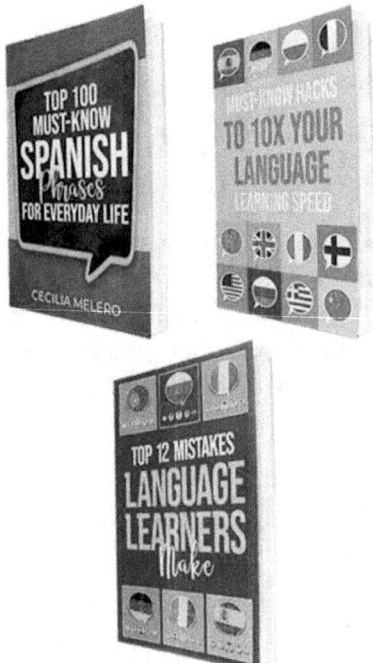

Access your free bonuses here:
*https://livetolearn.lpages.co/learn-spanish-paperback/*